MARTIN LUTHER KING, JR. AND THE CIVIL RIGHTS MOVEMENT

Edited by David J. Garrow

A CARLSON PUBLISHING SERIES

Birmingham, Alabama, 1956-1963

1956-1963

THE BLACK STRUGGLE
FOR CIVIL RIGHTS

Edited with a Preface by David J. Garrow

INTRODUCTION BY
WILLIAM D. BARNARD

CARLSON
Publishing Inc

BROOKLYN, NEW YORK, 1989

Library of Congress Cataloging-in Publication Data

Birmingham, Alabama, 1956-1963.

    (Martin Luther King, Jr., and the Civil Rights
Movement ; 8)
    Includes bibliographical references.
    1. Civil rights movements—Alabama—Birmingham—
History—20th century. 2. Afro-Americans—Civil rights
—Alabama—Birmingham—History—20th century.
3. Birmingham (Ala.)—Race relations. I. Garrow,
David J., 1953-   . II. Series.
F334.B69N417   1989   305.8'960730761781   89-22266
ISBN 0-926019-04-X

Typographic design: Julian Waters

Typeface: Bitstream ITC Galliard

The index to this book was created using NL Cindex, a scholarly indexing program
from the Newberry Library.

For a complete listing of the volumes in this series, please see the back of this book.

Printed on acid-free, 250-year-life paper.

Manufactured in the United States of America.

Contents

Series Editor's Preface

Among place names that are regularly and easily associated with the peak successes and accomplishments of the southern black freedom struggle, no city is more often cited and remembered than Birmingham, Alabama. Perhaps Birmingham public safety commissioner Eugene "Bull" Connor, who deployed both snarling police dogs and high-pressure fire hoses against black demonstrators in 1963, deserves much of the credit for Birmingham's civil rights fame, for no visual images of the southern struggle are more dramatic or memorable than the film and photos of Birmingham's dogs and hoses.

Birmingham's importance in civil rights history significantly pre-dates those memorable 1963 demonstrations, however. Along with Montgomery, Birmingham in the 1956-1960 period generated one of the two most notable local-level civil rights organizations in the South, the Alabama Christian Movement for Human Rights (ACMHR). Founded in June of 1956 in response to the state of Alabama's successful effort to banish the National Association for the Advancement of Colored People (NAACP) from the state, ACMHR and its principal leader, Reverend Fred L. Shuttlesworth, kept up a courageous struggle against municipal segregation year after year, achieving some successes while sustaining an intense onslaught of threats, assaults, and bombings.

Glenn Eskew's excellent 1987 master's thesis represents far and away the best and most complete historical account of ACMHR's activism in the pre-1963 years yet available. One of the most incongruous ironies of civil rights historiography is that Birmingham's importance in the southern black freedom struggle is not yet fully reflected in the published studies on the movement. Greensboro, Selma and St. Augustine, as well as Little Rock, Tuskegee, and Memphis, all have been the subject of at least one significant book-length study, but the local aspects of Birmingham's civil rights experience have not yet received extensive published attention. The national importance and implications of Birmingham's 1963 demonstrations are significantly canvassed in larger studies such as my own *Bearing the Cross* (1986) and Taylor Branch's *Parting the Waters* (1988), but with the partial exception of Robert G. Corley's unpublished 1979 Ph.D. dissertation on interracial relations in Birmingham between 1947 and 1963, no thorough and dependable local level study other than Eskew's carefully traces the important pre-1963 activism of the ACMHR.

William Barnard's valuable introduction to this volume astutely highlights the analytical importance of distinguishing between the local and national significance of long-term municipal protest movements such as the ACMHR. While Mills Thornton's forthcoming comparative study of Montgomery, Birmingham, and Selma ought to richly expand upon this theme, much of the uniqueness and success of the ACMHR's efforts can be traced quite directly to the remarkable and unusual personality of Fred Shuttlesworth, who, both in 1963 and since, has received less journalistic and scholarly attention than should have been the case. Although Andrew Manis is now preparing what will be the first full-length biography of Shuttlesworth, no adequate understanding of either Shuttlesworth or his catalytic role in Birmingham is possible without a careful reading of the late Lewis W. Jones's impressively astute 1961 study of Shuttlesworth, an analysis that is both perceptively critical and warmly sympathetic at the same time.

In time, the local aspects of the dramatically penultimate demonstrations in April and May, 1963, will quite certainly receive extensive and careful treatment from Thornton and other scholars, but as of now, Lee Bains's 1977 Harvard undergraduate thesis is the best-informed academic account yet written. Based upon extensive oral history interviews carried out in 1976, Bains's work will remain a significant contribution to the historiography of the 1963 Birmingham campaign even after professional historians have treated those events in the thoughtful detail they much deserve.

I am very pleased that Carlson Publishing's series of volumes on *Martin Luther King, Jr., and the Civil Rights Movement* is able to bring all three of these significant and previously-unpublished works to a wider scholarly audience, and I hope that their availability will substantively contribute to the increased scholarly study that Birmingham, ACMHR, and Fred Shuttlesworth all deserve.

David J. Garrow

Introduction

WILLIAM D. BARNARD

Birmingham became a symbol of Southern resistance to the civil rights movement. Yet in many ways, it was an atypical Southern city. With an economy based upon heavy industry and with an unusually high percentage of its population (for a Southern city) drawn from recent immigrant stock, Birmingham bore as much resemblance to a middle-western or northeastern industrial city as it did to Savannah, Charleston, Montgomery, or Memphis.

Indeed, Birmingham was a product of a post-Civil War invasion of northern capital. Founded in 1871, it had no antebellum past. The rapid growth of the steel industry in Birmingham attracted the recently freed blacks from the agricultural Black Belt, whose unskilled labor could find productive use in the mines and mills of Jefferson County. Economic opportunity also attracted the impoverished whites from the hill country of Alabama, subsistence farmers caught in the economic depression that characterized the agricultural South throughout the late nineteenth century. The blacks and whites from the rural South were joined by immigrants from Britain, Ireland, Italy, and Greece.

The turbulent social order that gradually took form was rough at the edges, with an undertone of the dark disquiet of rural peoples not yet accustomed either to the regimen of modern industrial life or to the ethnic, racial, and religious diversity among their neighbors.

The city grew so rapidly that, at least among local boosters, it was called "the Magic City." In the twentieth century, middle-class suburbs sprang up "over the mountain," south of town and well removed from the sprawling, bustling—and often troubled—central city. The physical beauty of these suburbs, the tranquil and measured way of life that spread across the foothills of the Appalachians belied the personal violence that often characterized life in Birmingham. More than once the city claimed the unenviable title of "murder capital of the USA."

In the aftermath of the Civil War, local capital was exceedingly scarce in Alabama and in the rest of the South. What capital was available was simply inadequate to develop the rich mineral resources of a region blessed with all three ingredients for the making of iron and steel—iron ore, coal, and limestone. "Outside" corporations soon owned the major industries of Birmingham. The city became an overgrown company town—and the company was U. S. Steel. With absentee ownership and with short-term managers sent in from the outside, the quality of civic leadership suffered. That leadership was further fragmented and crippled by the development of separately incorporated suburbs that drained much of the natural civic leadership out of the city's boundaries. Thus by the 1960s, much of Birmingham's natural civic leadership among its white population had other interests or, if they tried to play an active role in the city's affairs, were themselves subject to being branded "outsiders."

In short, except for the heat of its summers and the accents of its people, there was little in Birmingham that was reminiscent of the South of Margaret Mitchell. An industrial city hampered by absentee ownership of its major industries and by the lack of an effective civic ethos, Birmingham had neither the legacy of patrician white leadership that characterized many older Southern cities nor, given the rawness of industrial life in Birmingham, the ingrained tradition of civility that existed in other Southern towns.

As J. Mills Thornton has pointed out,[1] each of the major episodes of the civil rights movement needs to be viewed in a dual light—both as one in a series of events that together comprise a national effort by black Americans to destroy the system of legally required racial segregation and to achieve the equal rights of American citizenship and as the efforts of black citizens in a specific locality to achieve certain local aims, aims shaped by the particular history of black-white relations in that county or town. That national movement culminated in the Civil Rights Act of 1964 and the Voting Rights Act of 1965, acts that finally lent substance to the promise of equality before the law that had been written into the Constitution in the years just after the Civil War. That national movement is now a matter for the history books. But the local movements, as Thornton argues, continued past the demise of the civil rights movement as a great national force—and, indeed, those local movements continue today in cities and states throughout the nation.

Both perspectives—the national and the local—have much to teach us. We enrich our understanding of the significance and subtlety of the movement by studying both. Given the demands of textbook publishers as well as the ability of any people to know and understand only the general outlines of their history, it is perforce the local perspective, the local context, that is most often overlooked and soon forgotten.

By examining each of the major episodes of the civil rights movement in its local context, however, we gain insight unavailable when the movement is viewed solely as part of a great national crusade. We can, for example, gain a clearer sense of the indeterminacy of it all. In retrospect, we impose more of a pattern upon the past than is warranted—certainly more of a pattern than was apparent to the participants, who (after all) did not have the benefit of knowing (as we do) how it all turned out. Today, looking back, the "civil rights movement" appears all of a piece, each episode building upon another and leading (perhaps inevitably) to a foreordained outcome. We lose the sense of uncertainty that often haunted the participants. After all, they could anticipate neither the next event nor the ultimate outcome. What if Martin Luther King, Jr., had—as both his father and many local black leaders advised—followed his preferred course of action and obeyed the state court injunction against demonstrations in Birmingham, thus delaying or perhaps averting the clash with white Birmingham until Bull Connor was no longer a part of Birmingham's city government? Would the 1964 Civil Rights Act have been possible without the images of police dogs and fire hoses that shocked the nations's conscience and ultimately mobilized the nation's political will to address America's single most difficult and obdurate social ill? What if Bull Connor had accepted the verdict of Birmingham's voters and quietly left office, leaving city affairs to a new and more moderate government, thus denying King and the movement both a critical and decisive moment when the city was paralyzed by having two rival governments, each claiming authority, and more important, denying King an essential ingredient in turning a local effort into a matter of national concern: an opponent who could play to perfection the role of villain, who could personify the rigidity and evil inherent in the system of segregation, who would demonstrate to blacks the intransigence of the system and thereby overcome the preference of many local black leaders for quietly controlling local controversy through traditional channels, while demonstrating to the nation as a whole the depth of the injustice and repression inherent in the system of segregation? By their actions, those opponents—Bull Connor, Jim

Clark of Selma, George Wallace, and others—forced the nation and a sometimes reluctant national administration, to confront the dichotomy between the American ideal of equality before the law and the reality of American practice.

Another important point becomes apparent when we look at each episode in its local context: the critical role of local black leaders. In an effort to grasp the essential elements of the past, to make sense of it as a whole, to make it intelligible without succumbing to information overload, we of necessity simplify, discard detail. That paring down is both necessary and understandable, but it comes at a cost. As a consequence, we often deny ourselves the lessons that can be regained by a look at individual cases in all their subtle richness.

"Case studies," the intense scrutiny of one event that is in some ways a microcosm of the larger whole, are one way of adding flesh and blood to the story, of returning some sense of context and of human drama to the increasingly abstract story of national movements. In many textbooks, the civil rights movement is already portrayed largely a one man crusade. It does not demean the critical role of Dr. King to recognize the equally essential role of local leaders both before and after the brief moments when their communities became the center of national attention. It was they, those local leaders, who had shaped the struggle in their own communities, bearing the wrath of outraged segregationists at a time when there was neither the national media nor the interest of a friendly national administration to provide a modicum of protection from the violence that was the ultimate answer to direct challenges of segregation. Nowhere was the role of local leaders more apparent than in Birmingham, where King worked both with the Reverend Fred Shuttlesworth and with a number of more established (and more cautious) local leaders of the black community.

The Reverend Fred Shuttlesworth had kept alive a flicker of black protest in Birmingham throughout the late 1950s and early 1960s. His was not one of the more established black churches. The emotionalism of his sermons and his highly personalistic style of leadership made him a bit suspect among the pastors of middle class black churches. Yet, as the works contained in this volume make clear, he played a vital role in attracting Dr. King to Birmingham and in shaping the course of events there.

Shuttlesworth's role and his particular position within the black community of Birmingham highlights another seldom recognized aspect of the black community and of the civil rights movement. The brief discussions of the movement that appear in history texts treat the black community as if it were all of a piece, wholly united. Occasionally, brief comment will be made on the differences between King and, perhaps, the leaders of SNCC or the Black Muslims. But the role of the black middle class and the differences in style and manner between organizations and individuals that reflected middle class sensibilities and the great mass of blacks upon whom the movement in Birmingham rested are largely unnoticed. As the works here make clear, however, these differences cannot be obscured when events in Birmingham are studied closely. Indeed, these differences and how King bridged the gap between Shuttlesworth and the established black leadership is central to the story of Birmingham.

Fred Shuttlesworth's personal bravery in confronting segregation in Birmingham in the late 1950s and 1960s (before the national movement came to town) was, in a sense, both a challenge and a reproach to the middle class black leaders. His raw emotionalism and his need to be at the center of any effort he was involved in made middle class blacks reluctant to accept Shuttlesworth's largely self-proclaimed but increasingly real role as leader of civil rights protest in the city.

When King accepted Shuttlesworth's invitation to enter the struggle in Birmingham, he knew that he and the movement needed both Shuttlesworth and his dedicated followers as well as the middle class black leadership. King's ability to harness the energies of both groups was enhanced by his own growing prestige as a national leader. That ability, the good fortune to find in Bull Connor the perfect adversary, and the sheer fortuitousness of the unforseen and unplanned in Birmingham resulted both in the negotiations that broke the back of segregation in Birmingham and, after President John F. Kennedy's assassination in Dallas, the 1964 Civil Rights Act.

Each of the three works included here are important to an understanding of events in Birmingham. None have been readily accessible to researchers in the past. *The Alabama Christian Movement for Human Rights and the Birmingham Struggle for Civil Rights, 1956-1963*, by Glenn T. Eskew, was a 1987 M.A. thesis at the University of Georgia. Eskew's work is particularly useful in understanding the role of the Reverend Fred L. Shuttlesworth in the years prior to 1963. Sympathetic with Shuttlesworth, Eskew nonetheless makes clear the tensions and divisions within the black community over Shuttlesworth's personality and tactics. Eskew makes good use of a source generally unavailable to historians: the intelligence files of the Birmingham

Police Department that, through a rare stroke of good fortune, came to be deposited in the Birmingham Public Library. These reports of police agents who attended the mass meetings held, at times, nightly in Birmingham's black churches, are an exceedingly useful account of the day to day developments in the movement, though they must be viewed with caution.

Lewis W. Jones' unpublished paper, *Fred L. Shuttlesworth: Indigenous Leader*, written in 1961, also provides insight into Shuttlesworth's unusual role in Birmingham. Jones' sympathetic treatment of Shuttlesworth is also sensitive to the diversity and divisions within Birmingham's black community. Based in part upon extensive interviews with Shuttlesworth, Jones' work contains material on Shuttlesworth's early life that does not appear elsewhere.

Lee E. Bains' *Birmingham 1963: Confrontation Over Civil Rights* was a B.A. Honors Essay at Harvard University in 1977. Bains' lengthy treatment of events in Birmingham serves as a useful reminder that each of the great crises of the civil rights movement was shaped not only by the character and calibre of local black leadership but by the nature of the white leadership as well. Central to the unfolding of events in Birmingham was the role of local white leaders like David Vann and Sidney Smyer. Bains' work is a remarkably mature treatment of events written by one who knows the city well.

Together these three works can provide that local context that makes possible a more complete—and thus more accurate—understanding of the major social movement of our time.

1. See his Introduction to *The Walking City: The Montgomery Bus Boycott, 1955-1956*, edited by David J. Garrow, Carlson Publishing, Inc., 1989.

William D. Barnard
Wadham College
Oxford, England
July, 1989

Birmingham, Alabama

1956-1963

The Alabama Christian Movement for Human Rights

and

the Birmingham Struggle for Civil Rights, 1956-1963

GLENN T. ESKEW

Contents

"The mystery of the whole situation is how can these simple home folks be talked into going to jail by a bunch of rabble-rousers?"

— Bull Connor
April, 1963

Preface 1989

The climax of the civil rights movement occurred in Birmingham. The issues of the early civil rights movement culminated in the streets of the industrial town. Under the leadership of the Reverend Fred L. Shuttlesworth, a fanatical group of militant Christians—the Alabama Christian Movement for Human Rights—challenged segregation in the city. The national victory won in Birmingham ultimately changed race relations in the South. Yet the riots of the city's black underclass—when followed by the decade's long, hot summers—belies Birmingham's uniqueness. The clash of black and white in Birmingham underscored the nation's chronic problem of racial prejudice.

As a result of the spring 1963 demonstrations, John F. Kennedy proposed and Congress later passed the 1964 Civil Rights Act. Outwardly the movement emphasized a conflict between black and white, yet within the local movement itself a struggle took place. While the events in Birmingham signaled a national victory for Dr. Martin Luther King, Jr., and the Southern Christian Leadership Conference, a local victory remained in question. Through an analysis of the Birmingham movement from its inception in 1956 to its height in 1963, I have proposed explanations for why the local movement failed to complete its goals. By implication, the struggle in Birmingham offers suggestions as to why the national movement only achieved limited success. It is my hope that this work will make a modest contribution towards a greater understanding of the civil rights movement as a whole.

My advisor, teacher, and friend, Numan V. Bartley, encouraged me to undertake this study, and he guided it to completion in 1987 as an M.A. thesis in history at the University of Georgia. I remain indebted to his assistance and advice. My reading committee of William F. Holmes and Emory Thomas provided valuable insights that strengthened the thesis. William S. McFeely, for whom I worked as a research assistant during the writing of the thesis, permitted me to neglect his work so that I could finish in time for graduation. It is with great appreciation that I remember his kindness. Although I have received assistance from members of my committee, they are in no way responsible for any errors in the thesis. All fault lies with me. In addition I would like to thank Marvin Y. Whiting and his staff in the Department of Archives and Manuscripts of the Birmingham Public Library for all of their help and especially his advice.

Finally, I am forever grateful to my parents, Robert L. and Martha Bonner Eskew, for their unending encouragement and support. To them, I owe the greatest debt.

Introduction

The climax of the civil rights struggle occurred during the Birmingham demonstrations in the spring of 1963. The Negro fight for equal rights had been gaining momentum since the *Brown* decision of 1954, which awoke a new activism within the black community, but by 1963 the movement had yet to score a decisive victory over segregation in the South. The Montgomery bus boycott of 1956, which demonstrated to blacks that they could organize and fight Jim Crow, propelled the Reverend Dr. Martin Luther King, Jr., to national leadership of the civil rights movement. King, suffering from a failure in Albany, recognized Birmingham as the ideal battleground for striking a blow against segregation and in the process salvaging his reputation.

In April 1963, King and the Southern Christian Leadership Conference joined forces with Reverend Fred L. Shuttlesworth and the Alabama Christian Movement for Human Rights in a direct action campaign against racial discrimination in Birmingham. After a month of marches and sit-ins with an accompanying black boycott of white merchants, city business leaders struck a truce with King and the SCLC. The negotiated accord, which ended the demonstrations and started the process of desegregation, was hailed as a victory by King—an interpretation accepted by the American public. Not only did black and white America respond to the violence of Birmingham by supporting the movement, but the President of the United States proposed a civil rights bill that addressed many of the demands made by the black activists. Indeed, the decade long fight for freedom culminated in Birmingham in 1963. But Birmingham also exhibited signs of the direction the movement would take in the years ahead.

To comprehend the demonstrations of 1963, one must first understand race relations in Birmingham. *Harper's Magazine* sent George R. Leighton to Birmingham in 1937 to write an article on the city. In the best tradition of the debunkers, Leighton described a "City of Perpetual Promise" where the unfulfilled promise of wealth and security derived from Birmingham's vast mineral deposits which, in the nineteenth-century, were capable of producing the "gold" of a fledgling world power: steel. The promise remained elusive as northern corporations bought Birmingham's industry in order to prevent southern competition. As a result, labor practices suffered under an absentee ownership that never hesitated to raise the specter of race to avoid the unionization of the working class. In 1937, Leighton saw hope for Birmingham through the strengthening labor movement that had made inroads into the city's industry. Throughout the 1930s and 1940s, unions grew stronger in Birmingham. Once again, people harkened to the "perpetual promise." Thousands of rural laborers, black and white, fled the dying cotton culture and came to Birmingham to find wealth and security. Again the promise proved elusive. While blacks helped whites fight for unions, whites developed a system of job discrimination which prevented blacks from enjoying the benefits of organized labor. With the entrenchment of institutional racism in the work place came an economic advantage for whites to maintain segregation.[1] Newly urbanized blacks in Birmingham found a social structure that segregated Negroes from employment opportunities. In addition, the substandard housing available to Negroes and the unsanitary living conditions of the black residential areas convinced many in-migrants to seek the promise of other cities such as Detroit and Chicago. Despite this out-migration, blacks comprised approximately forty percent of Birmingham's population throughout the first half of the twentieth century—the highest proportion of any city its size in the nation. From 1940 to 1960, the city's black population increased by eighty-four percent, but overall it remained roughly forty percent of Birmingham's total population which reached 340,000 by 1960. A decline in Birmingham's industry during the 1950s hurt blacks more than whites and contributed to the substantial number of unemployed and semi-employed black laborers. Finding little economic security in Birmingham, many blacks turned to the familiar surroundings of the Negro church.[2]

The church had been the most important institution in the Negro community. Blacks could escape white domination within the confines of the sanctuary, for blacks alone dominated this institution. Just as blacks owned the church buildings, so they also controlled the ministers, who wielded an economic independence from whites—an independence uncommon for most blacks. But with the relative freedom granted to ministers came an increased responsibility to the community. Since the antebellum period, ministers had filled the leadership role in black society and the tradition remained strong one hundred years later. With an increase in black demands after World War II came a simultaneous growth in the influence of the social gospel among black ministers. Heretofore, the church had largely concerned itself with the soul of man and the after life, but the idea that the church should also improve man's condition on earth revolutionized the seminaries. These young activist clergymen drew upon the latent protest tradition in the black church to put their beliefs into practice. Many Negro ministers, recognizing the changing attitudes of blacks following the war as well as the deplorable conditions under which they lived, embraced the social gospel.[3]

One such minister was Fred L. Shuttlesworth. On March 18, 1922, Shuttlesworth was born on a farm in Mt. Meigs, Alabama, a village in the northern end of the Black Belt between Montgomery and Tuskegee. While a child, Shuttlesworth's family joined the great migration and moved to Birmingham in search of the "perpetual promise." In 1940, Shuttlesworth, the oldest of nine children, graduated from the community high school in Rosedale, a small black enclave bordering the affluent white suburb of Homewood, located south of the city of Birmingham. A richly dark man, Shuttlesworth had grown to be a trim five-foot-nine, weighing around 150 pounds and boasting a mustache. He married a native of Birmingham, Ruby L. Keeler, and was looking around for a career when the United States entered World War II. Shuttlesworth moved to Mobile and by 1943 worked at Brookley Field Air Force Base. While employed by the military, Shuttlesworth felt a calling to preach the gospel of Christ and began taking courses at a nearby seminary. Two years later, Shuttlesworth accepted the "challenge," quit his job and moved his family to Selma. While both adults worked, Shuttlesworth in his off hours attended classes at Selma University and began to preach in two rural churches. By 1949, Shuttlesworth had started preaching at First Baptist Church in Selma and had begun work toward a teacher's certificate at Alabama State College for Negroes in Montgomery. Shuttlesworth completed an A.B. degree from Selma University in 1951 and a B.S. degree from Alabama State in 1952. While still preaching, the young minister taught in the Dallas County schools. In March 1953, Shuttlesworth accepted a position with Bethel Baptist Church in Birmingham; and, with his wife and three children, he returned to Jefferson county. After a rousing address at the January 1, 1956, Emancipation Day rally in Birmingham, Shuttlesworth was elected membership chairman of the local chapter of the National Association for the Advancement of Colored People.[4] Birmingham's black community had recognized the leadership potential of Shuttlesworth.

As an officer in the NAACP, Shuttlesworth soon realized the inability of the organization to address the needs of the black community. Successful black businessmen controlled the Birmingham chapter of the NAACP, and local blacks considered it elitist. In a blistering critique published in 1957, E. Franklin Frazier coined the term "black bourgeoisie" for members of the Negro business elite who exploited the black masses as "ruthlessly" as did whites. The black bourgeoisie existed as a result of and profited from the system of segregation which had produced a captive black clientele. Indeed, Frazier noted, the black business leaders' obsessions with gaining the acceptance of a white society that continually rejected them, prevented the black bourgeoisie from playing a responsible role of leadership within the Negro community.[5] Shuttlesworth found Birmingham's black leadership inadequate to meet the demands of the black community.

In the years following World War II, the NAACP in Birmingham had become the target of white intimidation in response to the rising expectations of blacks. Membership in the chapter had fallen dramatically. As membership chairman, Shuttlesworth attempted to activate the local NAACP chapter, but white massive resistance precluded his efforts. Alabama's Attorney General John Patterson labeled the NAACP a foreign corporation and charged it with encouraging the Montgomery bus boycott and the Autherine Lucy desegregation attempt at the University of Alabama. Patterson sought a temporary injunction against the NAACP and a circuit judge granted the restraining order on June 1, 1956. The NAACP challenged the injunction in state and federal court but the order remained effective until 1965. As a result of Patterson's actions, the NAACP was forced to close its offices across the state for nine years.[6]

Shuttlesworth described a feeling of "helplessness and hopelessness" among the local black leaders following the injunction. After discussing the state's action with several ministers, Shuttlesworth decided that Birmingham's blacks "could not afford to be without a voice or an organization through which they could secure legal assistance." He joined with four other ministers in issuing a call for a mass meeting on June 5, 1956, "to see if Negroes wanted to organize a fight for their own rights." In addition to the outlawing of the NAACP, several precipitating factors contributed to the need for a new organization. The chronic lack of leadership in the black community necessitated the formation of a group in touch with the changing attitudes of blacks. The *Brown* decision of May 17, 1954, signalled the new direction civil rights would take, but Shuttlesworth noted that Birmingham blacks failed "to grasp the significance of this decision." Local black ministers, including Shuttlesworth, had petitioned the city commission for more than a year to hire Negro policemen, but the officials refused to act on the request. Thus, the frustration felt by Birmingham's blacks had been building over several years, and the outlawing of the NAACP only served to provoke some local black leaders into action.[7]

On the day before the June 5 mass meeting, a group of ministers and other black community leaders gathered at the Smith and Gaston Funeral Home to plan the events of the following night. Several dissenters present attempted to discourage the idea of a new organization. These elderly members called Shuttlesworth and the other activists "hotheaded" and tried to convince them to call off the meeting. Shuttlesworth and the others persisted, and they formulated the goals and strategy of the Alabama Christian Movement for Human Rights (ACMHR). Ministers apparently controlled the meeting, for their influence can be seen in the recommendations drafted by the group. They decided theirs would be a "Christian movement" because, as Shuttlesworth explained, "all our actions, thoughts and deeds would be first, foremost and always Christian." The group selected the name "movement" rather than organization on the grounds that "you can outlaw an organization, but not a movement, and this would be a moving force forward." The leaders cited as their goals, "freedom and democracy and the removal from our society of any form of second-class citizenship." They added: "We will not become rabble-rousers; but will be sober, firm, peaceful, and resolute, within the framework of goodwill." From the onset, the group promoted Christian morals and middle class values.[8]

On Tuesday evening, June 5, 1956, more than 1,000 people overflowed the Sardis Baptist Church to hear Shuttlesworth, Pastor R. L. Alford, and Reverend N. H. Smith, Jr., among other speakers. The mass meeting began with singing and prayer because, according to Shuttlesworth, "the religion of Jesus Christ encompasses . . . freedom, both of body and soul." Indeed, the tenor of the meeting resembled a tent revival. The audience filled the 850-seat church to capacity and spilled outside on the lawn. After seeing the turnout, Shuttlesworth said he knew then that blacks in Birmingham wanted to fight segregation.[9] "The action of the Attorney General makes it more necessary that Negroes come together in their own interests and plan together for the furtherance of their cause," Shuttlesworth said, adding: "The Citizens Councils won't like this, but then, I don't like a lot of things they do." His voice raised to a shout as he addressed the crowd, which responded with cries of "yes, yes," and "that's right." "Our citizens are restive under the dismal yoke of segregation," he declared, mopping his forehead with a handkerchief in the near ninety degree temperature. "The Negro citizens of Birmingham are crying for leadership to better their condition . . . The only thing we are interested in is uniting our people in seeing that the laws of our land are upheld according to the Constitution of the United States." After Shuttlesworth stepped down, Reverend Smith read the report of the planning committee and, because of the dangers ahead, the audience voted three times on the recommendations. Again a dissenting voice was heard, that of Reverend G. W. McMurry: "We should think sanely of what we are doing," he implored, "Birmingham is too over-organized now." The congregation ignored the admonishment and adopted the proposals with a standing ovation. The crowd elected Shuttlesworth president, Alford first vice president, and Smith secretary. The gathering also selected the undertaker, Dr. W. E. Shortridge, as treasurer. Emphasizing the seriousness of the moment, Shuttlesworth stressed the need for money to finance court challenges to segregation. "This is not the time for Uncle Toms," he declared, "We must pledge all we have . . . including our moral support and loyalty." Reflecting back to a greater "perpetual promise," the meeting concluded with the ringing acclamation, "We want a beginning NOW! WE HAVE ALREADY WAITED 100 YEARS.!"[10]

During the mass meeting Shuttlesworth stressed the differences between the NAACP and the ACMHR. He explained the new group did not intend "to carry on the NAACP's work." Indeed, the NAACP in Birmingham had not proved effective in altering race relations in the city. Instead of taking a conservative approach to reform as had been used by the NAACP, the ACMHR selected a more activist strategy to achieve integration. Direct ties did exist between the two organizations, for among the leaders of the ACMHR, three of the ministers, the treasurer and the assistant secretary had all been members of the NAACP. Apparently, the activist members of the now defunct NAACP joined the ACMHR. In fact, the activists structured the ACMHR along the familiar lines of organization used by the local NAACP chapter, but they added the decision-making process popular in the black church. Thus, the president of the ACMHR, like the pastor of a Baptist congregation, held authoritative power, only being answerable to a board of directors. The ACMHR's executive board, comprised of the organization's officers, granted Shuttlesworth extensive freedom in his capacity as the leader of the movement; yet Shuttlesworth sought the approval of the board for any campaign undertaken by the ACMHR.[11]

On the morning of the mass meeting, Emory Jackson, the editor of Birmingham's black newspaper, the *World*, editorialized on the banning of the NAACP: "The fight for freedom in Alabama . . . will continue either with or without the NAACP." Addressing the need for more aggressive action by blacks in Birmingham, Jackson added that he hoped the attack on the NAACP would "awaken more of the leadership" in the black community. Jackson merely echoed the complaints of several blacks in the city. Shuttlesworth and the leaders who joined him in forming the ACMHR did so as a result of the need for a new organization that would actively pursue desegregation on the local level. One scholar has recently argued that blacks created organizations such as the Montgomery Improvement Association because they found the NAACP "too radical." Shuttlesworth and the other Birmingham black activists apparently felt otherwise. The NAACP moved too slowly for these "hotheads" who wanted to challenge segregation in Birmingham immediately.[12]

Not everyone in the Negro community shared Shuttlesworth's views. In addition to McMurry and other conservative ministers, the black bourgeoisie opposed the formation of the ACMHR. Shuttlesworth remarked that "Many of the upper-class persons who worked in the NAACP are professional people who seem to feel that it is almost taboo to align actively with us." Indeed, the president of the defunct NAACP chapter in Birmingham never supported the ACMHR. Other formidable opposition came from the Reverend J. L. Ware, the local president of the Baptist Minsters Conference. Ware disagreed with Shuttlesworth's use of direct action, as did Birmingham's black attorneys, Arthur D. Shores and Orzell Billingsley, Jr., who preferred the legal methods of the NAACP. The religious aspects of the new movement also turned some blacks away from the ACMHR.[13]

Shuttlesworth and the other minsters in the ACMHR preached the social gospel, but most black ministers in Birmingham did not accept this new theology. Describing ministers such as Ware and McMurry, Shuttlesworth said they refused to support the ACMHR because of "their own old priestly philosophy of letting the Lord do it." The young civil rights activists also saw professional jealousy and a fear of potential violence as preventing these old-school ministers from supporting the movement. For the most part, only young ministers answered the community's call for new leadership. The support of a minister in the movement usually implied the support of a congregation as well, so when Shuttlesworth and four other ministers announced a mass meeting, they anticipated the support of their congregations.[14]

The traditional role of the Negro church combined with the influence of the social gospel created a new leadership in the black community. When Shuttlesworth addressed the May 1957 Prayer Pilgrimage in Washington, D. C., he spoke of the new Negro church. "But a new voice is arising all over now—the voice of the church of a living and ruling God, unafraid, uncompromising, and unceasing. Led by her ministers, she cries out that all men are brothers, and that justice and mercy must flow as the waters." For Shuttlesworth, the church represented the congregation—the people; and the ministers merely spoke for them. Characteristics of such an activist minister usually included his youth and his recent arrival to the area. Montgomery leaders selected Martin Luther King, Jr., to lead the boycott because of his lack of ties to special interests in the city. Similarly, Shuttlesworth had been in Birmingham for less than three years before the formation of the ACMHR; but unlike his more famous friend, he had helped organize the movement which he led. Familiar with the bus boycotts in Montgomery and Tallahassee, Shuttlesworth structured the ACMHR after the movements which sponsored these campaigns. Indeed, Shuttlesworth attended the organizational meeting of the Montgomery Improvement Association, and he occasionally preached at the early MIA mass meetings. The unification of the black communities behind the boycotts in these cities showed Shuttlesworth that blacks could organize to fight segregation. He took these lessons of mobilized nonviolent resistance to heart and later applied them in Birmingham.[15]

While dramatic events led to the creation of the Montgomery and Tallahassee boycotts, no such single incident occurred in Birmingham to unify the black community. The ACMHR developed more out of a chronic need for leadership in the black community than from the outlawing of the NAACP. Indeed, a new civil rights organization would have probably formed in Birmingham in spite of the attack on the NAACP just to fill the void in local leadership. Unlike Montgomery and Tallahassee, where veteran civil rights activists petitioned pastors to lead the protests, Birmingham ministers initiated the new movement. For these very reasons the ACMHR faced several initial obstacles. The lack of a unified black community limited the mass-based support of the organization, and disagreements within that community hurt its chances of success. Furthermore, the ACMHR faced a more impressive foe in the opposition of white society. Birmingham's power structure, from the economic elite and the city hall down to the Citizens Council and the Ku Klux Klan, fought every attempt at desegregation. Shuttlesworth recognized this threat and told the crowd at the mass meeting of the dangers in fighting segregation: "We gonna wipe it out, or it's gonna wipe us out. Somebody may have to die."[16]

Willing to take that chance, Shuttlesworth began challenging the sanctity of segregation. He later confessed, "I tried to get killed in Birmingham. I literally believe that he that lose his life shall find it. He who lose it for my sake (meaning Christ) shall find it." Interpreting the conflict in Birmingham as a fight between good and evil, Shuttlesworth saw the ACMHR as a righteous crusade and himself as being "led and impelled by the Divine force to take an active part." King also believed himself to be on a similar mission. During the Montgomery bus boycott, King debated whether to continue in his role as leader of the Montgomery Improvement Association. Late one night after receiving another in a series of threatening phone calls, he prayed to God for guidance. As he silently sat with his head bowed over a cup of coffee, King heard the "voice of Jesus" telling him to fight for righteousness. After this famous "kitchen experience," King took comfort in his deep religious faith by believing that God would never abandon him. The appearance of Shuttlesworth's and King's direct access to the Divine strengthened the support of their followers. More importantly, both Shuttlesworth and King exhibited characteristics of the charismatic leader. Their ability to "personify, symbolize and articulate the goals, aspirations and strivings" of the black community contributed to their success as civil rights leaders. Charisma relied more on performance and experience than religious beliefs. Every white attempt to suppress the charismatic leaders' actions strengthened the ties between them and their followers. In Birmingham, Shuttlesworth's charisma and dedication led him to the leadership of the ACMHR. "I always believed that the minister is God's first line soldier," Shuttlesworth said. He added, "I always believe that a preacher ought to be able to speak out and say what thus say the Lord and then he ought to be acting out thus said the Lord." One of the first members of the ACMHR, Mrs. Rosa Walker, said of Shuttlesworth and the formation of the new organization, "I was frightened, but I figured we needed help to get us more jobs and better education. And we had the man here to help us."[17]

ONE

"God Saved the Reverend to Lead the Movement"

The formation of the Alabama Christian Movement for Human Rights in June, 1956, launched the direct action phase of the struggle for racial desegregation in Birmingham. Led by the Reverend Fred L. Shuttlesworth, the ACMHR challenged Birmingham's segregation laws throughout the late 1950s by focusing its attack on the legal separation of the races in public transportation, schools and parks. The ACMHR effectively combined a direct action approach to desegregation with the traditional legal methods used by the National Association for the Advancement of Colored People. Through confrontation, Shuttlesworth and the ACMHR defied local laws and customs, forcing white officials to arrest the protesters for violating city ordinances. Shuttlesworth would call off the direct action challenge after several blacks had been charged in the desegregation attempt. The ACMHR then used the subsequent convictions to test the validity of local segregation laws. Cases filed by the ACMHR often lasted years before Federal courts handed down final decisions. As president and spokesman, Shuttlesworth personified the aspirations of ACMHR members. Through his actions, the charismatic leader placed himself in danger in order to challenge segregation in Birmingham. In response to such strivings, the minister received the brunt of Birmingham's white resistance to desegregation. Each repressive act by whites strengthened Shuttlesworth's support from blacks; and every attempt at desegregation which resulted in a court case renewed the spirit and energy of the ACMHR. Thus, for the rest of the decade Shuttlesworth led the ACMHR in its efforts to force Birmingham to desegregate through legal methods stemming from direct action challenges to the city's segregation ordinances.

The ACMHR's second mass meeting, held on June 11, 1956, began a tradition in Birmingham's black community. Throughout the civil rights struggle in Birmingham, the ACMHR held mass meetings on Monday nights to organize and strengthen the local black effort. A regular crowd attended most meetings, but in times of confrontation or hardship, the audience grew in numbers. Shuttlesworth used the mass meetings to inform the ACMHR of his planned challenges to segregation, and he gathered volunteers for such attempts at these meetings. Various black ministers and other community leaders often spoke at the ACMHR mass meetings. They used the opportunity to denounce the southern system of segregation and to encourage blacks to join the movement in Birmingham. For example, at the second meeting, Reverend R. L. Alford announced: "The South is dealing with a new Negro. It's too free for some, not free enough for others." The minister urged the audience to seek municipal jobs. Shuttlesworth informed the approximately 800 people gathered in New Pilgrim Baptist Church that the ACMHR's executive officers had appointed a transportation committee that would try to meet with the Birmingham Transit Company in order to discuss desegregation of the city's buses.[1]

The humiliating practice of separating the races on public transportation by forcing blacks to sit in the back of the bus became the first target of the ACMHR. On July 10, 1956, Shuttlesworth sent registered letters to the Birmingham City Commission and the Birmingham Transit Company requesting an end to segregated seating on city buses. The ACMHR asked the transit company to "institute a first come, first-seated policy on all its buses and to begin hiring Negro drivers." Aware of the bus boycotts in Montgomery and Tallahassee, Shuttlesworth did not call for one in Birmingham. Instead, he preferred negotiations. Although the ACMHR received no public acknowledgement of the letters, it claimed that officials from the transit company had decided to consider the request and to meet with the ACMHR transportation committee. City officials refused direct comment on the letter, but Birmingham Mayor James W. "Jimmy" Morgan did dismiss the possibility of a boycott with the observation that "I do not think our colored people here are going to unite in anything of that type." On July 26, 1956, the ACMHR sent a follow-up letter to the city commission asking its views of the federal injunction against bus segregation in Montgomery, which had been appealed to the United States Supreme Court. In the second letter, Shuttlesworth expressed the black community's desire for "a more just and equitable share of this city's economy both in better jobs and better opportunities." Again, the city ignored the letter and the ACMHR took no further action on the issue for five months.[2]

Apparently waiting for the Supreme Court to act on the Montgomery bus boycott appeal, Shuttlesworth turned the ACMHR's attention to the long-standing complaint of Negro representation on Birmingham's police force. For more than two years, Birmingham blacks had petitioned the city to hire Negro policemen to patrol black neighborhoods. An ineffective interracial committee in Birmingham had suggested the hiring of black officers in the early 1950s. The committee, which lost what little influence it had with the rise of massive resistance following the *Brown* decision of 1954, had observed Nashville's and Atlanta's integrated police forces and supported the practice for Birmingham. Petitions signed by approximately 4,500 residents, including 119 whites, requested the hiring of black officers. Even segregationist Mayor "Jimmy" Morgan endorsed the idea, but the city commission continued to ignore the requests. As a result of the Birmingham Police Department's reputation for brutality toward blacks, the issue remained popular in the Negro community. For these reasons, Shuttlesworth probably believed the ACMHR could win a quick victory by fighting to integrate the city's police force.[3]

For the first time in Birmingham's history, two black men, George Johnson and Clyde Jones, attempted to take the city's civil service examination. Shuttlesworth accompanied the two men on August 20, 1956, to the fifth floor, City Hall office of Ray Mullins, the director of personnel. Mullins refused to give Johnson and Jones the test because the application form stipulated "whites only." Shuttlesworth called the action discriminatory and said: "We feel that if our people have the qualifications then this office should recognize them as applicants for the job." Mullins claimed to have no authority over the matter and referred the minister to the city commission, which had set the job requirements. Two days later, the Englander Company fired Jones for his "extracurricular activity." Johnson and Jones again attempted to take the examination the next Monday, August 27, 1956. Mullins again denied the request. After the ACMHR filed suit against the personnel board for failing to accept Negro applications, the officials held a secret meeting and deleted the "whites only" qualification.[4]

In December, 1956, the year-long boycott to desegregate the city buses in Montgomery drew to a close. On December 17, the United States Supreme Court rejected the last attempt by Montgomery City officials to maintain segregated seating. White officials received the court's final decision on December 20, 1956. The action prompted Shuttlesworth and the Reverend N. H. Smith, Jr., to write letters to the Birmingham Transit Company requesting the desegregation of buses. Shuttlesworth warned that if the city did not repeal the segregation ordinance by December 26, then the ACMHR "would ride the buses in a desegregated fashion anyway." He set the deadline to coincide with the next city commission meeting. True to the ACMHR's original intent to challenge discriminatory local laws, Shuttlesworth wrote the officials: "the clear alternative to litigation then, can only be . . . the relinquishing by officials . . . of the laws and proscriptions which have made and would forever make and keep Negroes in an inferior and subservient status." The minister noted that "an emergency meeting" of the ACMHR would follow the commission meeting to plan a challenge to the segregation ordinance if the city failed to act on the request. Shuttlesworth sent a similar letter to the Birmingham Transit Company, which ended with a reminder that company officials had promised an ACMHR committee that they would hire black bus drivers when desegregation occurred.[5]

While remaining optimistic about the bus company, Shuttlesworth recognized the city commission would ignore the ACMHR request, and he decided to use their silence as a "signal for bus riders to seat themselves in accordance with the nonsegregation decision of the United States Supreme Court." Two days after the Montgomery decree, the Birmingham *News*, the white establishment newspaper, editorialized: "It would be helpful, in our view, if action were not pressed at this time to end bus segregation at once here in Birmingham. But apparently action to that end is going to be pressed." The newspaper recognized the ACMHR's challenge and encouraged city officials to maintain segregated seating for as long as possible. That same day, police arrested two prominent Birmingham blacks for refusing to move to the Jim Crow section of the Terminal Station. Carl Baldwin, a local furniture salesman, and his wife, Alexinia, a school teacher, had purchased tickets on the fashionable "City of Miami" passenger train for a Christmas trip to Milwaukee. While the couple waited in the early morning hours of December 22 for their 6 a.m. departure, five patrolmen entered the marble lobby of the train station. Lieutenant J. R. Davis accosted the pair, giving them twenty seconds to move to the colored waiting room. When the Baldwins refused, Davis placed them under arrest. After paying two $100 bonds, the Baldwins left the city jail—an hour and a half after their train departed for Milwaukee.[6]

While most people in Birmingham settled down to celebrate Christmas, the black and white leadership of the city prepared for confrontation. The battle lines seemed drawn, for the ACMHR had received no response to its letters and had continued plans for the desegregation attempt. On Christmas Eve, Shuttlesworth addressed a mass meeting at New Hope Baptist Church attended by approximately 1,500 blacks. He gave the audience instructions on how to integrate the buses peacefully, urging the volunteers "to be courteous and not to strike back" if attacked. The ACMHR distributed leaflets similar to those used in Tallahassee and Montgomery. Earlier in the month Shuttlesworth had attended the Montgomery Improvement Association's week-long Institute on Nonviolence and Social Change. The meeting afforded Shuttlesworth the opportunity to discuss ideas with other civil rights activists such as Reverends Theodore J. Jemison of Baton Rouge, Joseph E. Lowery of Mobile, and C. K. Steele of Tallahassee, as well as with King and the MIA staff. These meetings in Montgomery preceded the Southern Christian Leadership Conference and helped to bring the black activists together. The Institute's program concerned the nonviolent integration of Montgomery's transit system, so Shuttlesworth had just attended a workshop on bus desegregation when he planned the ACMHR's challenge in Birmingham. At the Christmas Eve meeting on Monday, Shuttlesworth explained the ACMHR's executive board would meet following the city commission on Wednesday and that mass meetings would be held that night "to plan specifically what we will do." Already in Montgomery, blacks rode desegregated buses and in Tallahassee Negroes ignored segregation signs and sat where they pleased. "We hope we won't have to do anything but ride," Shuttlesworth told an Associated Press reporter. He specified, "We are pledging ourselves here and now to non-violence."[7]

Instead of preaching "Peace On Earth" in his Christmas sermon, Shuttlesworth said: "If it takes being killed to get integration, I'll do just that thing, for God is with me all the way." At 9:40 Christmas night, someone lobbed six sticks of dynamite at the minister's northside home. Apparently, the missile grazed a chain-link fence which separated the frame parsonage from the church. This chance deflection prevented the bomb from rolling underneath the center of the one-story, five-room house. The dynamite stopped squarely beneath the side room where Shuttlesworth sat on a bed talking with a church deacon. The force from the explosion threw Shuttlesworth into the air and destroyed the frame and box springs, but the mattress apparently protected the minister from the blast. The deacon did not fare so well, for he received injuries, as did two of the Shuttlesworth children.[8]

The strength of the single explosion tore kitchen appliances from the walls of a back room. The blast knocked the foundations out from under the front porch, which collapsed as the roof caved in. Violent shock waves shattered the windows of Bethel Baptist Church next door and carried debris over three houses to a vacant lot down the street. The blast blew a hole through the basement of the brick church. After the explosion, Mrs. Shuttlesworth found herself in the middle of the destroyed home surrounded by "smoke and dust." Yet, she saw the light on the family Christmas tree sparkling beneath the clutter. Neighbors poured out of their shotgun houses upon hearing the familiar, frightening sound. A crowd of more than 500 had gathered around the shell of the structure by the time emergency crews arrived. The fire department set up spotlights to assist officers in sifting through the rubble, for the extensive damage hindered officials in their search for survivors. Several men attempted to hold back the police, but Shuttlesworth's appearance restrained their actions. The minister lifted his hand and the crowd immediately calmed down. "The Lord has protected me," Shuttlesworth said, "I'm not injured." "He's all right," a black woman cried from the gathering, "and he's going to be all right." Someone else shouted, "God saved the Reverend to lead the movement."[9]

Stone-faced White Citizens Council members sat silently through the meeting of the Birmingham City Commission the next morning. The only business discussed during the tense, seven-minute session concerned a school bond issue. Twice, Mayor "Jimmy" Morgan asked the crowd assembled in the City Hall chambers: "Do we have anything else to come before the commission this morning?" After receiving no response, he adjourned the meeting. Of the 150 people present, members of the Citizens Council, a pro-segregationist organization, comprised the majority. Several of the segregationists explained to the press that they anticipated the ACMHR to present a request for bus desegregation. The only two blacks in the audience stood by the doors of the auditorium and observed the meeting.[10]

Across town, more than 175 blacks gathered in the Smith and Gaston Funeral Home to await the outcome of the city commission meeting. Upon entering the room, Shuttlesworth received a standing ovation. "The fight is on," he told the crowd, adding, "We had announced before that we would ride the buses." Noting that "violence will not have any effect," the minister said: "One reason I was sure that God wanted them unsegregated is because I came through this alive. That bomb had my name on it, but God erased it off." One ACMHR member recalled, "When I went to the meeting . . . Reverend Shuttlesworth was the first thing I saw. And I knowed as how their house was blowed up, and I couldn't figure out how he was there. And I said then, that I'm going into it. And I went into it on that day." By that afternoon, Birmingham police had arrested the speaker, Mrs. Rosa Walker, for sitting in the white section of a city bus.[11]

Extensive planning had gone into the ACMHR's challenge to Birmingham's segregated seating laws. Shuttlesworth wanted to show the community that blacks could ride the buses desegregated. He also needed several arrests to file a test case against the ordinance. Recognizing the need to get blacks on the buses and seated in the white section before Birmingham police intervened, Shuttlesworth mapped out an elaborate strategy. For several weeks he had implied the ACMHR would hold a mass meeting Wednesday night after the commissioners failed to act and then on Thursday attempt to integrate the buses. The plan worked beautifully, for not only did it catch Birmingham off guard by taking place on Wednesday, but an hour passed before police began making arrests.[12]

The press waited outside the funeral home for ninety minutes before the closed meeting of the ACMHR ended. At approximately 1:30 p.m. Shuttlesworth emerged at the head of more than fifty activists who walked through Birmingham's black business section and into the heart of the downtown shopping district. Along the way, Shuttlesworth cautioned the volunteers, who had all signed pledges of nonviolence. A few blacks stopped at each bus stand between Second and Third Avenues and Nineteenth and Twentieth Streets. Once on the buses, the protesters rode off in every direction of the city. Shuttlesworth boarded a bus with two other blacks, Elizabeth Anderson and Joe C. Lester, and he took a seat near the front. Lester sat down beside a white woman behind Shuttlesworth. In front of the minister sat two white girls who exited the bus at the next stop, unaware of the desegregation attempt. A police car slowly escorted Shuttlesworth's bus, but the officers made no attempt to arrest the minister. After several blocks, Shuttlesworth disembarked at the University Medical Center. He described white reaction to the effort as "friendly" and "perhaps inquisitive." One journalist reported that "white persons on the buses showed curiosity, but scarcely reacted at all."[13]

The bus drivers did nothing to stop the desegregation endeavor. One operator explained that the drivers had been instructed to complete their scheduled run. After an hour of integrated seating, police boarded the buses and ordered the protesters to move to the Jim Crow section of the vehicle. When the blacks refused, the patrolmen placed them under arrest for violating sections of the city's segregated seating ordinance. Many blacks, apparently unaware of the desegregation attempt, continued to sit in the colored section. By the end of the day, twenty-one blacks had been arrested in connection with the challenge. The ages of the twelve men and nine women charged ranged from sixteen to seventy-five. Ironically, police arrested Shuttlesworth later in the afternoon for driving without a license and having an improper car tag.[14]

Emory Jackson of the Birmingham *World* editorialized on the day of the attempt that Birmingham should recognize "the old law is dead and move immediately into the new reality." In Mobile that morning, the city council announced the desegregation of its city buses; but in Birmingham, Public Safety Commissioner Robert Lindbergh said the Supreme Court's ruling against segregation on city buses only applied to Montgomery and no other Alabama city. The obvious tie between the bombing of Shuttlesworth's home and the desegregation attempt prompted Jackson to write: "Violence is no valid defense for segregation." He elaborated: "Legal segregation is doomed and racial bombings of the sort which happened here are no more than the toll bells ringing it out." Recognizing the inherent dangers in desegregation, Jackson noted three days later: "It is beyond calculation what price there is yet to be paid for the privilege of open seating on Birmingham buses. Yet those twenty-one arrested bus-riders symbolize the fact that there are those willing to pay the price."[15]

The ACMHR convened two mass meetings on the north and south sides of town following the bus desegregation attempt. At the first rally held in the Saint Paul African Methodist Episcopal Church, emotions ran high as Shuttlesworth addressed the overflowing crowd. Temporarily calling off the challenge to bus segregation, Shuttlesworth said. "We've got enough test cases. We're going to win our fight for integration. There's no sense in filling up the jails." In addition to describing the successful bus desegregation attempt, Shuttlesworth also told of the bombing of his home.[16]

At the second mass meeting held later that night in the Metropolitan Baptist Church on Birmingham's south side, Shuttlesworth almost renewed the desegregation attempt. Singing hymns such as "We Ain't Gonna Hate

Nobody," the congregation tried to convince the minister to keep up the fight. Shuttlesworth explained that the ACMHR executive committee "had decided to await the outcome of the test rides before going further with the ride-where-you-please program." When he read a lengthy telegram from Martin Luther King, Jr., which praised the efforts of the activists and encouraged the continuation of the desegregation attempt, the audience endorsed the idea and responded with a standing ovation. Shuttlesworth then warned that only those who signed a pledge of nonviolence could come to the ACMHR for assistance. The city had released from jail several of the people involved in the attempt and the crowd in the church cheered these protesters wildly as they related the day's events. The enthusiasm of the crowd at the mass meeting encouraged Shuttlesworth to implement other challenges to Birmingham's segregation laws. After the conviction of the twenty-one blacks by Recorder's Court Judge Ralph E. Parker on January 3, 1957, the ACMHR filed an appeal. The case wound through the courts until October 1958, when the ACMHR again staged a challenge to Birmingham's segregated seating laws.[17]

Before the December attempt, Shuttlesworth had received advice from other civil rights leaders. After the outlawing of the NAACP, informal contact had continued to exist among Alabama's black activists, especially Reverends Martin Luther King, Jr., of Montgomery, Joseph Lowery of Mobile, and Shuttlesworth. During 1956, these three leaders had discussed formalizing their meetings in order to coordinate their efforts on a state-wide basis. The idea blossomed into a southern effort with the creation of the Southern Christian Leadership Conference in February, 1957. The SCLC differed from the NAACP in its use of direct action, and Alabama received the brunt of the organization's efforts because of the SCLC's strength in the state. Thus, the ACMHR had direct ties with the SCLC from the latter's inception, for not only had Shuttlesworth helped issue the organizational call with King and C. K. Steele of Tallahassee, but he also played a prominent role in the SCLC's formation.[18]

Throughout 1957, the ACMHR continued its attack against Birmingham's segregation laws. By March, a case stemming from the Baldwins' arrest in the Terminal Station had reached federal court. Although Birmingham had dropped its disorderly conduct charges filed against the couple in December, 1956, the Baldwins still sued the city claiming segregation in the train station's waiting rooms violated their constitutional rights. On March 5, 1957, United States Judge Seybourn H. Lynne dismissed the suit, holding that denial of usage of the main waiting room did not mean that blacks were "compelled" to use another one: "There is no ordinance of the city of Birmingham or statue of the State of Alabama which purports to compel interstate Negro passengers to occupy waiting rooms designated 'colored.'" The infuriating ruling prompted Shuttlesworth to challenge the customary segregation of the Terminal Station.[19]

Early on March 6, 1957, Shuttlesworth announced he would test the federal court's ruling to see if blacks could use the train station in a desegregated fashion. Local radio stations began broadcasting the minister's challenge. By the time he arrived at the station with his wife, Ruby, a crowd of more than fifty men, including members of the Citizens Council, milled around the domed structure. Shuttlesworth tried to enter the front door but a young white man told the minister to leave, and Birmingham Klansman R. E. Chamblis, with two other men, pushed him away from the entrance. Shuttlesworth then entered through another door where, once inside, a local white lay minister, Lamar Weaver, shook his hand and warmly greeted him. Shuttlesworth bought tickets for Atlanta, sat on a bench next to Weaver and talked with him. After five minutes, Birmingham patrolmen approached the minister and his wife and asked to see their tickets. Shuttlesworth complied. The police turned to Weaver, and after discovering he had no ticket, asked him to leave the building.[20]

Weaver faced an angry mob as he exited the Terminal Station. Hollering "nigger lover," the crowd followed Weaver as he headed toward his automobile. A newspaper photographer helped him into the convertible, but then someone in the crowd threw a rock at the vehicle and others joined in, breaking several windows. A few men in the mob tried to turn the car over before the lay minister drove away. The police had done nothing to protect Weaver, who subsequently left Birmingham, but they did guard Shuttlesworth. After the minister arrived safely in Atlanta, he praised Commissioner Lindbergh as a "man of high morals." Shuttlesworth noted that "since they [Birmingham policemen] didn't arrest us for traveling unsegregated it would look bad if they would arrest anybody in the future. They should take the segregated signs down."[21] Again the minister had successfully opposed segregation in Birmingham. While the city did not arrest Shuttlesworth, the policy of separate waiting rooms remained in effect. The minister had survived a racial attack, but Birmingham remained committed to segregation.

A week after the train station incident, the city commission reaffirmed Birmingham's bus segregation ordinances. The commission declared "segregated seating on buses for whites and Negroes is necessary for the avoidance of friction, enmity and violence between the races." The action came in preparation for the trial of the twenty-one blacks arrested during the December, 1956, bus desegregation attempt. On the morning of March 18, 1957, Recorder's Court Judge Ralph Parker heard testimony in the trial. The city attorney stated, "the threat of desegregation" caused violence, such as at the Terminal Station, and if blacks continued to violate the law, the white community would "explode into anonymous and unpreventable acts of violent resentment." Arthur Shores represented the ACMHR and argued that segregation on buses violated the Fourteenth Amendment.[22]

On March 21, 1957, Parker upheld the constitutionality of Birmingham's segregation ordinances and found the twenty-one protestors guilty, ordering them each to pay a $50 fine plus court costs. Modestly, Parker also declared the Fourteenth Amendment "null and void." The judge ruled that Congress "pulled a fast one" by not ratifying the amendment in a "valid, constitutional process"—referring , inaccurately, to the absence of southern whites who supported the Confederacy during the Civil War from the ratification process. The ACMHR had asked a United States District Court to declare the segregation ordinances unconstitutional and it also requested the federal court to restrain Birmingham from enforcing the separate seating law. More than a year passed before the courts took any action.[23]

By June, the ACMHR had celebrated its first anniversary with Reverend C. K. Steele, the leader of Tallahassee's successful bus boycott, preaching on the program's theme, "Christian Emphasis on Freedom and Race Relations." During the past year, the ACMHR had incorporated on August 17, 1956, and attracted increased support from Birmingham's black community. The group had test cases in the court system stemming from direct action confrontations over segregation. Despite a bombing attack and mob action, no one had been killed in these endeavors, and the ACMHR looked forward to achieving new goals. The organization had much to be thankful for after a year of existence, yet the June 4 election of T. Eugene "Bull" Connor over Robert Lindbergh as the new Birmingham commissioner of public safety tarnished the week-long celebration. Connor had served in this post before, until a scandal broke in 1951 that forced the commissioner out of office. The press caught Connor in adultery with his secretary, and after an unfavorable report concerning his activity in office, Connor chose not to run for re-election in 1953. During his four-year hiatus, Connor worked closely with the Citizens Council in Birmingham. By 1957, "Bull," so nicknamed because of an earlier career calling baseball games for radio, had regained support among many of the city's voters, resulting in his defeat of Lindbergh by a margin of only 103 votes.[24] For the next six years, Connor and Shuttlesworth represented opposite poles of the race question in Birmingham.

By summer's end, Shuttlesworth had addressed another goal of the ACMHR: the integration of Birmingham's public schools. On August 22, 1957, the minister and eight other black families petitioned the Birmingham Board of Education to admit their children to three of the city's white schools. Shuttlesworth sent a registered letter to superintendent Dr. Frazier Banks, asking the board to act on the petition before the new school year began on September 4. Banks replied on August 29 that the matter would be discussed at the September 6 board meeting. While Shuttlesworth patiently awaited the board's decision, white extremists responded to his request. On Labor Day, September 2, four members of the Klansmen of the Confederacy wantonly emasculated a black man, Judge Aaron, and ordered him to tell Shuttlesworth "to stop sending colored children and white children to school together." The Klansmen had arbitrarily attacked Aaron near the Birmingham suburb of Tarrant City. Before castrating the helpless man, they warned him that if Shuttlesworth did not stop the integration attempt, he would face the same fate.[25]

The act of mayhem did not deter Shuttlesworth. The board of education responded to his request at its September 6, 1957, meeting by authorizing Banks to handle the case according to Alabama's Pupil Placement Act. Passed by the state legislature in 1955, the order gave school superintendents broad powers in determining where students would go to school. Legislators had passed the act to maintain segregation in Alabama's school system, and the United States Supreme Court later upheld the law when ruling on a case filed by Shuttlesworth. After the board meeting, Banks told the press he would investigate the matter before making a decision. The board's stalling tactics proved too much for Shuttlesworth. The minister decided to confront the issue of integration by attempting to enroll four black children in Birmingham's largest all-white high school on the following Monday.[26]

Driving up Birmingham's Seventh Avenue North shortly before 10:30 a.m., September 9, 1957, Shuttlesworth stopped in front of Phillips High School. Approximately 1,850 white students attended classes in this block-long, limestone-trimmed brick building in downtown Birmingham. The

Reverend J. S. Phifer accompanied Shuttlesworth and his wife, along with the four students to be registered: Ruby Fredricka, twelve, and Patricia Ann Shuttlesworth, fourteen, two of the minister's children, as well as seventeen-year-old Nathaniel Lee and twelve-year-old Walter Wilson. As Shuttlesworth got out of the car, Mrs. Shuttlesworth noticed three groups of white men numbering from eight to ten, coming towards her husband from either side of the school and from across the street. In order to protect her children, Mrs. Shuttlesworth hurriedly climbed in the back seat of the car. A patrolman, who had watched the arrival of Shuttlesworth at Phillips, radioed headquarters for assistance, but a false report that someone had stolen the car of Bull Connor interfered with the plea for help.[27]

When Shuttlesworth saw the cluster of whites rapidly heading toward him, he turned and ran in another direction, only to encounter a different group of men wielding clubs and chains. The mob charged, shouting "Let's kill him!" and attacked the minister, forcing him to the ground with repeated blows from brass knuckles and bicycle chains. Shuttlesworth struggled to his feet and ran toward the police but the crowd knocked him down again. Each time Shuttlesworth regained his footing he headed in a different direction, but inevitably someone was be waiting there. By this point, several officers had arrived at the scene and hurried to the melee. After the police entered the crowd, Shuttlesworth broke free and forced his way into his automobile. Before the car drove off, members of the mob smashed the windows and bashed the body of the vehicle. One man, clutching a chain, reached into the back seat and attempted to pull out a passenger. Another man stabbed Mrs. Shuttlesworth in the hip. As Reverend Phifer began to drive away, the car door slammed shut on Ruby Fredricka's foot, almost fracturing her ankle. The integration attempt had ended in disaster.[28]

Earlier in the morning, Shuttlesworth had notified the local television stations of his plans. He had also sent telegrams to the police department and board of education informing them of the attempt. Yet, the minister had not anticipated the response he received. Just the week before, nine children had attempted to integrate Central High School in Little Rock, Arkansas; and although the students faced jeers from angry whites, violence had not erupted. Shuttlesworth expected the refusal of school officials to register the children, but he believed police would protect him during the attempt. While officers did come to the minister's aid, not enough patrolmen had been dispatched to prevent the mob's action. Birmingham police arrested three of the men involved in the beating, but a grand jury later dropped the charges after the officers failed to identify the suspects.[29]

Following the attack, Shuttlesworth refused to be admitted to University Hospital, although he did receive emergency-room treatment. The minister wanted to be present at the ACMHR mass meeting that night. With his arm in a sling and bandages on his head, Shuttlesworth begged the crowd not to seek revenge against "any white person for what has happened to me." The activist continued: "God is showing the world that there are some Negroes in Birmingham who are not afraid." Members of the ACMHR patrolled the grounds of New Hope Baptist Church during the meeting. A single patrol car quickly drove by the church and past the black guards, who had been posted down the unpaved streets in several directions. One reporter noted that "Negroes, while speaking calmly, seemed prepared to meet any effort of whites to create any disturbance." Several blocks away, policemen kept Phillips High School under surveillance. Indeed, tension remained high in Birmingham throughout the night.[30]

On Tuesday morning, September 10, 1957, white students responded to the integration attempt by boycotting classes. Shuttlesworth had warned that an attempt to integrate Woodlawn High School in the eastern section of town would take place on Tuesday, although he had since called off the challenge. Nevertheless, a large number of students lined the street opposite the school. The crowd chanted: "We want a boycott" and "We want Shuttlesworth." Some time passed before a few students entered the building. One teacher singlehandedly collected ten of the teenagers and returned them to class. The remaining protesters grew nasty and began to throw rocks at passing buses and cars that contained blacks. Ironically, the police threatened to turn firehoses on the white mob of mostly boys if they failed to disperse. The crowd then withdrew to the Woodlawn business district.[31] By the day's end, Birmingham's whites had shown that they would not accept integration peacefully. The violent response to the integration attempt warned Shuttlesworth of what to expect in the future.

Birmingham experienced an unusual calm in race relations during the winter and early spring of 1958. One local observer described the feeling as a "suspicious quiet." The unnatural silence proved short-lived, for Birmingham justified its epithet of "Bombingham" when explosions occurred across the city throughout the summer. Every Saturday night since the Christmas bombing of Bethel Baptist and Shuttlesworth's home in 1956, guards had patrolled the church grounds. Shortly before 1:30 a.m. on June

29, 1958, a young waitress returning home from work spotted a fire by the side of the one-story brick building. She hollered to the guard, sixty-two-year-old Will Hall, and he ran over to investigate. Instead of a fire, Hall found a paint can stuffed with fifteen to twenty sticks of dynamite. The retired coal miner picked up the bomb with its six-inch fuse and ran from the church. When he reached the street, some thirty feet from the structure, Hall set the can on the curb and then raced down the road. One minute later, the bomb exploded just as the guard hit the pavement some twenty-five feet away. The blast shattered the stained glass in Bethel Baptist—windows that had replaced the ones destroyed in 1956—and cracked the plaster in the church's ceiling. The dynamite dug a hole two feet deep in the street. No injuries occurred as a result of the explosion, although several homes in the neighborhood received damage. Despite the blast, Shuttlesworth held Sunday services in the marred sanctuary the next morning. The minister praised Hall for his "heroic deed" and then told the press: "Dastardly as this crime is, nobody here is angry. It's shown us the depth and seriousness of the job at hand. We're going to have to suffer on longer, but we'll hold up our heads."[32] For the second time, Shuttlesworth and the ACMHR had become targets of night riders and survived the attacks with renewed determination.

The Ku Klux Klan remained unchecked in Birmingham as police investigations into bombings failed to result in arrests. After the December, 1956, explosion, the ACMHR had petitioned the city commissioners to place stricter guidelines on the sale and use of high explosives. The request remained ignored. A few weeks before the 1958 Bethel bombing, Bull Connor had harassed Shuttlesworth, asking the police department to give the minister a lie detector test to clear up "rumors" about the Christmas bombing of the church. Shuttlesworth said he would be glad to submit to the test if Connor would do the same. The police commissioner refused.[33]

In April, segregationists had tried to destroy Birmingham's Jewish Temple Beth-el. Outrage followed the attempted bombing of the synagogue. Birmingham's leaders, ministers and newspapers condemned the act. A similar outcry did not follow the bombing of Bethel Baptist, and a few local ministers wrote the Birmingham *News* demanding the attack be equally denounced. They received no reply.[34]

In mid-summer, bombers struck again, this time targeting an integrated neighborhood known as "dynamite hill." Since the late 1940s, blacks had begun moving into the Fountain Heights subdivision of Birmingham, and numerous bombings and arson of homes purchased by blacks had occurred.

On July 17, 1958, a black homeowner discovered three white men attempting to bomb his house. After Earnest Coppin yelled at the trio, the men ran from the scene, dropping six sticks of dynamite on the ground. Two explosions then occurred, one 500 feet up the street at the house of William Blackwell, and the other in the yard of Coppin—the only two black residents on the block. For the first time in the city's history, police arrested the three men suspected of the bombings; and although they were later associated with the Klan, the arrests did not deter the number of dynamite attacks in the city.[35]

The Ku Klux Klan increased its intimidation at the beginning of the new school year. Shuttlesworth had announced there would be no enrollment attempt, but the Klan used the anniversary of the Phillips High School debacle to organize white supremacist demonstrations. On Sunday night, August 31, 1958, Kluxers lit a total of eighteen crosses in Jefferson county, setting them all ablaze at 8 p.m. The segregationists had stationed fourteen of the symbols on or near white schools. The practice continued over the next few years, with the implicit message that integration would not occur peacefully in Birmingham.[36]

The city commission remained as determined as the Klan to prevent change in Birmingham's segregated social structure. The case of the twenty-one blacks arrested in 1956 for attempting to desegregate Birmingham's buses had reached federal court by late 1958. In a surprise move, the commission repealed Birmingham's segregated seating ordinances on October 14. The commissioners acted before the outcome of the case because they feared the federal court would declare the laws "invalid in view of past federal court decisions." Keeping the laws would only "be hurtful to the cause of segregation," the officials deemed. In place of the ordinances, the commission passed a new law allowing the Birmingham Transit company to determine the seating of bus passengers. The transit company president, John S. Jemison, Jr., announced the new bus policy of having blacks sit from the rear and whites from the front of the vehicle. In response to the commission, Shuttlesworth sent a telegram to the Birmingham Transit Company requesting the abandonment of any attempt to maintain segregated seating. The company failed to reply, forcing Shuttlesworth to act.[37]

Wasting no time in responding to the city's provocation, Shuttlesworth issued a call for the ACMHR to gather on Thursday night, October 16, 1958. During the special meeting held at Bethel Baptist Church, the crowd readily endorsed a resolution stating that Birmingham's blacks would "henceforth ride in any seat available with the dignity which becomes American citizens." The next morning, Bull Connor urged blacks to ignore Shuttlesworth's leadership. The ACMHR answered the police commissioner by supporting Shuttlesworth in a second attempt to desegregate Birmingham's buses.[38]

On the morning of October 20, a group of approximately thirty blacks met with Shuttlesworth in a Negro loan office to plan a second confrontation over segregated seating. The minister briefed the volunteers on how to nonviolently integrate the city's buses. After the meeting, the protesters walked downtown, split into two groups and lined up to board the Ensley and Pratt City buses at Second Avenue North and Nineteenth Street. After taking seats in the front of the vehicle, some of the black riders began reading devotional books. A crowd had formed near the stops. Upon noticing the blacks sitting in the white section, the bus driver quit accepting fares. Several other protesters had succeeded in boarding another bus before its driver did likewise. Twenty minutes after an operator notified the Birmingham Transit Company of the attempt, police arrived at the scene. The drivers and the officers asked the black activists to move to the rear of the bus. A few apparently complied, but nine remained seated in the white section of one bus and four on the other. As no white passengers rode on these vehicles, the drivers marked the buses "Special" and followed patrol cars back to the transit company's car barn. After arriving in the compound, officers placed the now hymn-singing thirteen activists under arrest and loaded them into police wagons for the trip to the city jail.[39] For a second time in Birmingham's history, blacks had opposed segregation on city buses through a direct action challenge of the law.

Later in the day Shuttlesworth, who did not ride the buses in the attempt, announced the end of the integration effort. The goal of the ACMHR had been to generate enough arrests to prove segregation still existed on the city buses. The next morning, October 21, 1958, Bull Connor ordered the arrest of Shuttlesworth on charges of inciting to violate the city passenger placement ordinance. Upon hearing of his pending arrest, Shuttlesworth sat on the front porch of his house and awaited the police. After three hours, he went to city hall and surrendered. "Mr. Connor has long expressed his desire that I should be in jail," the minister explained to a reporter. "I don't suppose I could do anything to make Mr. Connor happy except to commit suicide," Shuttlesworth added. Police then locked the thirty-four-year-old activist in a patrol wagon and hauled him off to jail.[40]

Shuttlesworth increased his attack while behind bars in Birmingham jail. The minister sent a telegram to the city commission on Tuesday morning, October 21, 1958, demanding the desegregation of the city's parks. Shuttlesworth warned the commissioners that if they failed to act favorably, he would seek the integration of the city's swimming pools, playgrounds, golf courses and amusement centers in federal court. Several weeks before, the ACMHR had presented a petition signed by 200 blacks requesting the desegregation of the parks to the Birmingham Park and Recreation Board. The board met on Wednesday, October 22, and decided to "study" the ACMHR's petition before acting on the request. The ACMHR filed suit, and two years later United States District Judge H. H. Grooms ruled in favor of desegregation. The city commission declared the parks would never be integrated and when the federal court order went into effect on January 15, 1962, the city closed the recreational facilities. Thus, Shuttlesworth had opened a new front in the ACMHR's campaign to desegregate Birmingham. After sending the telegram, the minister returned his immediate concerns to the arrests and pending convictions of the thirteen protesters.[41]

During the next few days, the city of Birmingham demonstrated its determination to fight desegregation, but the Negro community responded by showing its support for Shuttlesworth and the other black activists. Officers released the minister from the city jail late Tuesday morning after he posted a $1,200 bond for the misdemeanor charges. The city set the trial of Shuttlesworth and the thirteen protesters for Thursday evening. Black and white spectators packed the courtroom of Recorder's Court Judge William Conway by 7:30 p.m., October 23, 1958. A crowd of more than 1,000 blacks knelt outside the city hall in silent prayer throughout the trial. Shortly after midnight, Conway convicted the fourteen defendants and ordered them held in the city jail until sentencing on Monday night. For the next five days, Shuttlesworth and the thirteen activists remained incommunicado. Birmingham had responded to the ACMHR's challenge, but the city's use of force only prompted mass-based support for the movement.[42]

After the judge ordered the fourteen protesters incarcerated over the weekend, lawyers for the ACMHR filed a writ of habeas corpus in an attempt to get them out of jail. City officials gave the Negro attorneys a difficult time on Friday, but did set a hearing for Saturday morning. The attorneys had cited Police Chief Jamie Moore as a witness, but by Saturday, Moore had allegedly left town, so the judge postponed the hearing until Tuesday morning. The court's actions prompted one ACMHR attorney,

Orzell Billingsley, to announce: "The arbitrary, unconstitutional and high-handed methods of the city of Birmingham in confining respectable Negro citizens in the City Jail certainly will not stop or deter their efforts to secure first-class citizenship."[43] While the city blatantly abused the law, Birmingham's police force prepared other forms of intimidation.

While the holding of the fourteen protesters prompted many blacks to demonstrate their support for the bus desegregation attempt, the illegal arrests of three Montgomery ministers on October 27, 1958, rallied Birmingham's black leadership in opposition of city hall. On Monday, more than twenty people had gathered in the Shuttlesworths' home, a brick structure which replaced the house bombed in 1956, and prepared to eat dinner when four plain-clothes officers drove up in an unmarked car and entered the house without search or arrest warrants. One of the detectives told Mrs. Shuttlesworth: "I understand there are a lot of out-of-town visitors here and we would like to meet them." The officers then questioned the people assembled and arrested the three visiting ministers on vagrancy charges because of their failure to show "proper identification." The three men arrested, Reverends A. W. Wilson, H. H. Hubbard and S. S. Seay, all belonged to the Montgomery Improvement Association and Seay held the post of executive secretary in that organization. The ministers explained to the officers that they had come to Birmingham to offer their assistance to Mrs. Shuttlesworth while her husband remained in jail. Nevertheless, the police hauled the Montgomery residents to headquarters and interrogated them for five hours before dropping the charges and releasing them from jail. Bull Connor responded to the incident by threatening that all "outside agitators coming to our city and dabbling in our affairs," faced arrest. Connor received some protest against the action from the white community, but Birmingham's blacks nearly exploded over the issue.[44]

Responding to Birmingham's strong-arm tactics, members of the black community demonstrated their most effective weapon—a show of force in numbers. Several thousand blacks overflowed the mass meeting Monday night and another large crowd of blacks gathered simultaneously on the city hall lawn during the sentencing of the fourteen protesters. City Judge Conway gave twelve of the activists a 180-day suspended sentence and warned them to "stay out of trouble." Shuttlesworth and Reverend J. S. Phifer received stiffer penalties. The court sentenced Shuttlesworth to ninety days in jail and Phifer to sixty with both men ordered to pay $100 fines. Conway then remanded the fourteen back to jail for the habeas corpus proceedings on Tuesday in order to be "certain" the activists would appear. Black spectators again crowded into the courtroom on Tuesday morning, October 28, for the hearing. The judge ruled the habeas corpus writ "moot" because of Monday night's convictions and then released the fourteen protesters on bond pending their appeal. Through illegal detention, Birmingham had prevented Shuttlesworth from exploiting the crisis situation, yet upon release from jail the minister found the black community in a state of rebellion. One observer described the sentiment among Birmingham's blacks as similar to that felt before the launching of the Montgomery bus boycott.[45]

The unwarranted jailing of the fourteen protesters and the illegal arrests of the three Montgomery ministers provoked other blacks in Birmingham to support the ACMHR's endeavors. Under the auspices of the Jefferson County Betterment Association, a group of 110 ministers gathered late Tuesday morning to discuss plans for a bus boycott. Headed by the Reverend J. L. Ware, the JCBA consisted of black ministers who disagreed with Shuttlesworth's direct action tactics but had done little themselves over the past two years. The organization set aside differences with the ACMHR in order to coordinate a volunteer bus boycott. The JCBA posted a letter to the transit company on Wednesday that threatened a boycott unless immediate changes in bus seating policies occurred. The bus company failed to act, and the JCBA endorsed a voluntary boycott. Meanwhile, Shuttlesworth held a mass meeting on Friday October 31, 1958, where 1,000 blacks unanimously voted to boycott the buses. Thus, police repression had forced members of Birmingham's black leadership together in a unified effort to oppose segregated seating.[46]

The time appeared right for the launching of a boycott in Birmingham. Blacks comprised approximately seventy-five percent of the bus passengers in the city, and since the December, 1956, desegregation attempt, the transit company had not shown a profit. In addition, the locally owned company had just purchased $1 million worth of new buses. A successful boycott in Birmingham, such as the MIA's in Montgomery, would have either bankrupted the company or forced a change in seating policies. Yet the bus company held an advantage over Birmingham's blacks because of their dependence on the transit system. Many blacks lived more than ten miles from their places of employment, which prevented them from walking to work. In addition, less than fifty percent of Birmingham's black population owned automobiles, and the size of the city hindered the organization of effective car pools.[47] In essence, despite the financial vulnerability of the bus company, blacks remained dependent on Birmingham's transit system.

Acting in support of the transit company, Birmingham's officials and press moved swiftly to prevent the boycott through intimidation and a news blackout. Policemen monitored street intersections and recorded the license plate numbers of people giving rides to walking blacks. Officers tried to force black school children to ride buses to class, and they even arrested some blacks for transporting their children to school. As the boycott struggled on through November, police arrested two blacks for violating Alabama's anti-boycott law. Officers charged John Harvey Kelly with distributing boycott literature and a week later arrested Reverend Calvin W. Woods for preaching a sermon on the theme of walking in dignity rather than riding in humility. Reports of the boycott surfaced in newspapers outside of Birmingham, but the local press ignored the efforts of the black community. The city's white public remained virtually unaware of the attempt.[48] The opposition of Birmingham's newspapers and city officials proved detrimental to the boycott's success.

Frustrated over the news blackout and police intimidation, the boycott leadership began to falter. Although the ACMHR had held mass meetings nightly since the boycott's beginning and thousands of blacks attended the rallies, many Negroes still rode the buses in Birmingham. Despite the efforts of Ware and Shuttlesworth, the majority of Birmingham's black ministers refused to endorse the boycott. The arrest of Reverend Woods served to silence many of the boycott's supporters. While two of the largest organizations in the black community had joined together in the protest, a unified effort from Birmingham's black population had failed to emerge. The ministers had succeeded in building support for the boycott among their followers, but there remained a large segment of the black community that either failed to organize or had no leadership to represent them in the effort. By the end of the year, the boycott had ended.[49] Although the attempt did not force the desegregation of Birmingham's buses, it did demonstrate support from elements of the black community for civil rights.

Therefore, from June of 1956 until the end of 1958, the ACMHR confronted Birmingham's system of segregation in public transportation, schools and parks. Through direct action, volunteers violated the city's segregation ordinances in order to be arrested. The ACMHR used the subsequent convictions to test the validity of the local laws in federal court. Since Shuttlesworth led the black effort to achieve desegregation, he became the target of Birmingham's white resistance. When city officials over-stepped their bounds and unjustly arrested three ministers from Montgomery, a group of black church leaders opposed to Shuttlesworth's tactics joined the ACMHR in declaring a bus boycott. Although the boycott failed to organize the black community, it did demonstrate growing support for civil rights among some blacks in Birmingham.

TWO

"My Life is
on the Altar"

The Alabama Christian Movement for Human Rights celebrated its third anniversary on June 5, 1959. In the president's annual report, Shuttlesworth outlined the test cases resulting from direct action challenges to segregation made by the ACMHR. Although the organization had lost the December, 1956, bus desegregation case because of the city's repeal of the segregated seating ordinance, a second test case filed in October, 1958, after an additional challenge to segregated seating, had made its way to the Alabama State court of Appeals. As a result of the ACMHR's drive to open civil service examinations to blacks, the city's personnel board had met secretly and deleted the "whites only" qualification. While the city had not begun hiring Negro policemen, the action had allowed for blacks to apply and thus attempt to prove discriminatory hiring practices. Although Shuttlesworth had endeavored to integrate Phillips High School in September, 1957—and nearly lost his life in the process—the ACMHR subsequently pulled back from direct action challenges to school integration and instead relied on petitions presented to the school board. Alabama officialdom had won the first round in school integration when the United States Supreme Court upheld the state's Pupil Placement Law. While the ACMHR no longer confronted school integration, it did hope the petitions and requests for student transfers would prove the discriminatory application of the Pupil Placement Law. Finally, while in jail following the 1958 bus desegregation attempt, Shuttlesworth announced a challenge to park segregation, but the issue stalled over a conflict between the ACMHR and its attorneys.[1] Nevertheless, the organization had made great progress since June, 1956, and vowed to continue the fight.

By June, 1959, Shuttlesworth and the ACMHR had raised over the past three years approximately $53,000 and spent $40,419.65 on court costs and legal fees, with $24,000 of that going to local black attorneys. The executive board of the ACMHR found the legal fees excessive, and the method of payment to lawyers—one-half down and one-half after the initial arguments—objectionable. In an attempt to curtail legal expenses, the ACMHR hired a lawyer from Florida to argue the park desegregation case. Birmingham's black attorneys had wanted $6,000 for the litigation, but the Florida attorney accepted the job for $4,500. Incensed that Shuttlesworth side-stepped them, the black attorneys asked Federal Judge Seybourn Lynne to grant a court order forcing any out-of-town attorneys to associate with a Birmingham law firm. The ruling resulted in the ACMHR paying an additional $1,500 for local counsel. The underhanded action further strained the relationship between the ACMHR and the local Negro attorneys and convinced Shuttlesworth that the attorneys only supported the movement for their own personal gain. He even referred to Birmingham's leading black lawyer, and legal representative of the NAACP in Alabama, Arthur Shores, as Calhoun, the shyster in "Amos and Andy."[2] Probably as a result of this conflict and the expensive cost of cases, the ACMHR slowed down its direct action challenges in order to concentrate on the litigation already in court.

Although Negro leaders had succeeded in organizing a large segment of Birmingham's black community behind the boycott, the ACMHR remained committed to a legal strategy. Shuttlesworth referred to this in May of 1959 when writing a brief history of the ACMHR: "The major problem facing us if we are to be frank is that the City and other white public officials are totally unwilling to negotiate on any aspect, and therefore we must operate on a strictly legal level—a costly level." Shuttlesworth wrote the revealing account of the ACMHR to assist a doctoral student, Jacquelyne Johnson Clarke, in her research. Clarke, a graduate student in sociology at Ohio State University, had undertaken a comparative study of the ACMHR, the Montgomery Improvement Association and the Tuskegee Civic Association, in order to analyze the goals and techniques used by the three civil rights organizations. At an ACMHR mass meeting held in the spring of 1959, Clarke distributed questionnaires to the people present and collected 180 completed forms from which she drew data to analyze the local movement.[3]

In her study, Clarke found the ACMHR overwhelmingly preferred a legalistic approach as the method to secure civil rights. Direct action campaigns placed third behind boycotts in the order of popularity listed by the members.[4] In other words, the ACMHR relied on charismatic leaders to direct the protest of volunteers willing to be test cases in order to achieve litigation, and then through mass meetings the membership morally and financially supported the cause. The violent history of race relations in

Birmingham influenced the average member's hesitation to embark on a direct action campaign. Nevertheless the members of the ACMHR took great risks by associating with an organization that espoused integration.

By 1959, the ACMHR claimed from 900 to 1,200 regular members. Clarke's study contains statistics that drew a composite picture of the ACMHR's membership. Approximately forty percent were male and sixty percent female, with almost ninety percent being married or widowed. Of the members, approximately one-third each were either childless, had one or two children, or three or four children. More than seventy percent of the ACMHR members were between the ages of thirty and sixty, with almost twenty percent younger than thirty and ten percent older than sixty. Financially, members of the ACMHR fared little better than the black community as a whole. One-third of Birmingham's black population as well as approximately one-third of the ACMHR membership earned less than $2,000 a year. While more than eighty percent of the city's blacks earned less than $4,000, approximately sixty percent of the ACMHR members earned that much or less. So forty percent of the ACMHR's membership earned more than $4,000 a year compared to only twenty percent of Birmingham's entire black population. In addition, while less than fifty percent of the city's blacks owned their own homes, approximately fifty-five percent of the ACMHR members could make that claim, although thirty-five percent of the membership owned no property.[5] The statistics on income seemed to indicate a cross-section of the black community belonged to the ACMHR.

The blurring of class lines continued with the statistics on education. While almost forty percent of the ACMHR membership had graduated from high school—with many of these attending college—approximately twenty-five percent had not completed the seventh grade. In employment, around thirty-five percent held unskilled and fifteen percent semi-skilled jobs. On the other end of the spectrum, more than five percent held skilled jobs and ten percent professional jobs.[6]
According to Clarke's study, it appeared that the membership of the ACMHR crossed class lines, with members from the upper, middle and lower strata of the black community in Birmingham belonging to the organization.

Several characteristics of the ACMHR membership differed sharply with the black community in Birmingham as a whole. Almost all of the members were employed and nearly seventy percent were registered to vote. Practically every member of the ACMHR attended church services regularly, with almost ninety percent belonging to a Baptist congregation. While approximately ninety percent were born in Alabama, less than half of these came from Birmingham. Of those born outside of the city, the majority, probably from rural areas, moved to Birmingham during the Great Depression.[7]

Therefore, Clarke's statistics suggested that the ACMHR attracted a cross-section of the black community with members from all levels of employment, income and education. But the members held characteristics in common as well, including middle-age, marriage, small families and intense religious beliefs. While not all of the members of the ACMHR could be characterized as middle class, they all appeared to accept middle class values. But more importantly, one common thread united all of these diverse individuals: a deep faith and belief that God would help them destroy segregation.

Shuttlesworth appealed to this religious faith in his June, 1959, president's report: "We only pray that *Our* methods will always be Christian, that no hate will ever be found nor practiced in our hearts and actions, and that out of the intensity of this struggle we Negroes will become more religious, more consecrated, better Americans." As for his own beliefs, Shuttlesworth wrote in 1959: "I feel that I was destined to play this role and that events (two bombings, mob beatings, etc.) have and even now place me in the possibility of being attacked or killed any day, but I believe that I was saved especially to do this job." The other leaders of the ACMHR exhibited a similar faith in God and dedication to the movement. When Shuttlesworth founded the ACMHR, he formed the organization with the assistance of several ministers and black businessmen. A few years later, five clergymen held all of the key offices in the organization with the exception of treasurer. The group had taken the name "Christian" because of its determination to be first and foremost "Christian." When the Southern Christian Leadership Conference organized, its leaders added the name "Christian" to avoid "the inevitable charges of radicalism and communism."[8] While the leaders of the SCLC were more calculating in their use of religion, the officers of the ACMHR appeared to be sincere in their faith.

Observers of the ACMHR in 1959 described a legitimacy to the Christianity practiced by the organization's members. Clarke wrote that the mass meetings in Birmingham, as opposed to those in Montgomery and Tuskegee, resembled "typical religious prayer meetings" and attracted "regular worshippers." Another contemporary described the ACMHR members as "followers who believe that the cause of the Negro can be advanced through the concerted efforts of Christian people." A reporter for the Pittsburgh *Courier* wrote that "when one sits in their mass meetings and hears them sing and pray and lift their voices to their God, you get the feeling that here is a boundless and ever growing faith in God that will not let these people lose their hope and their faith."[9]

While the militant Christianity practiced by the ACMHR helped unify and strengthen the local membership, it also limited the appeal of the organization to other Birmingham blacks.

There remained some blacks in Birmingham in 1959 who continued to oppose the ACMHR's use of the social gospel. In a letter to the Birmingham *News* published June 15, 1959, the Southern Negro Improvement Association, a pro-segregation group, condemned black ministers, such as Shuttlesworth, who abandoned traditional biblical interpretations for "integration and other social doctrines as a basis of their sermons." While few blacks in Birmingham belonged to this organization, its existence demonstrated the divisiveness in the community. In Clarke's analysis, she observed that the religious nature of the mass meetings in Birmingham attracted a "lower class" element, and she emphasized the need to garner support for the ACHR among upper class blacks. In his essay, Shuttlesworth noted that few upper class blacks supported the movement but he believed the ACMHR had the "sympathy of the majority of Birmingham's Negroes."[10] While the intensely religious nature of the ACMHR might have turned away some blacks who would have otherwise supported the movement, this same deep faith sustained the organization's members and enabled them to face white resistance and challenge segregation in Birmingham.

Throughout the summer of 1959, the Ku Klux Klan in Alabama periodically demonstrated in order to intimidate the black community. In a show of strength, caravans of Klansmen drove through black neighborhoods on several occasions. On July 27, 1959, Klansmen burned a cross in the yard of Robert Hughes, the white director of the Alabama Council on Human Relations (ACHR). An affiliate of the Southern Regional Council, the ACHR served as a pro-integration group that attempted to foster communication between the races. In an August letter to Harold Fleming of the SRC, Hughes quoted an SRC survey which found Alabama leading the South in racial violence. In addition, Hughes noted that the state had yet to actually confront court-ordered school integration. That fall, Shuttlesworth again announced there would be no attempt to integrate Phillips High

School. Nevertheless, the Klan gathered on registration day to "guard" the school. Kluxers burned crosses at eleven schools on August 31 to remind blacks of the dangers of supporting desegregation.[11]

Opposition to school integration extended to the state capital. Alabama's newly elected governor, John Patterson—who had run on the platform of having killed the NAACP and subsequently "out-niggered" George C. Wallace—warned blacks to ignore the leadership of Martin Luther King, Jr., or face the closing of the public schools. In response to the governor's attack on King, Shuttlesworth replied: "Negroes follow . . . King because he is a shining symbol of the hopes of a people tired of oppression, disfranchisement, abuse and economic exploitation." Although publicly supportive, for the past six months, Shuttlesworth had criticized King's leadership. Pushing for a more active SCLC, Shuttlesworth had written King in April: "When the flowery speeches have been made, we still have the hard job of getting down and helping people." In June, Shuttlesworth again wrote the leader: "The times are far too critical for us to get good solid ideas on what should be done in certain situations and then take too long a time to put these ideas into action." By late September, Shuttlesworth's persistence paid off with the creation of a committee to plan the SCLC's program for 1960. King appointed Shuttlesworth to this committee and the leader from Birmingham also replaced T. J. Jemison as the SCLC's secretary.[12] Thus, the ties between the ACMHR and the SCLC drew tighter.

In late October, 1959, the ACMHR, apparently solving its conflict with Birmingham's black attorneys, filed a suit in United States District Court seeking the integration of Birmingham's parks. Following the example of Patterson, Bull Connor appealed to the "decent, thoughtful and good Negroes" of Birmingham to ignore Shuttlesworth's leadership, or face the closing of the city's parks. Shuttlesworth retorted that Connor's comments "gave many people the picture of a once mighty lion, now impotent because of an immoveable thorn in its foot." In a letter to the commissioner, Shuttlesworth replied that the closing of the parks would hurt whites more than blacks. Describing Connor's only contacts with blacks as being "through crooks and racketeers," Shuttlesworth asked for the formation of a biracial committee. The minister stressed: "The days of frank discussions around the conference table are upon us. Negroes want to talk and be brothers."[13] The commissioner ignored Shuttlesworth's request for an interracial meeting and continued his threat to close the city's parks.

While the park integration case got underway, the bus desegregation case drew to a close. State courts had rejected the ACMHR's appeals, and on November 23, 1959, United States District Judge Hobart H. Grooms also dismissed the 1958 suit. Grooms ruled that the Birmingham Transit Company, as a private enterprise, did not fall under the prohibitions of the Fourteenth Amendment, but he reserved judgment on the legality of the new city ordinance. One month later, the ACMHR received the news it had been fighting for since 1956. On December 14, 1959, Grooms ruled that "a willful refusal to obey a request to move from the front to the rear of a bus when unaccompanied by other acts tending to disorder, *does not* constitute a breach of the peace." As a result, Birmingham police could no longer arrest blacks for refusing to ride in the Jim Crow section of the bus. At a mass meeting held that night in the Metropolitan Baptist Church, the ACMHR adopted a resolution which stated: "We are free NOW . . . to ride in ANY seat available on ANY BUS." The ACMHR printed and distributed fliers that announced the end of segregated seating and instructed blacks on how to act on the buses. Connor denounced the leaflets as "dangerous," but Birmingham blacks ignored the commissioner and rode the buses in a desegregated fashion.[14]

Hardly had the ACMHR savored victory when white officials opened a new front against blacks in Birmingham. In an attempt to purge Birmingham's voter lists of blacks, the Jefferson County Commission approved a probe of Recorder's Court records to enable the board of registrars to disenfranchise people convicted of vagrancy, prostitution, gambling and drunkenness. The state legislature had recently approved a provision that limited the ballot to only individuals "who are of good character and who embrace the duties and obligations of citizenship." In Jefferson county, the registrars interpreted the ruling to disenfranchise parents of illegitimate children. Surprisingly, the Birmingham *News* denounced the action as an overt attack against the black community. County statistics showed that an illegitimate birth accounted for one out of every four blacks born in 1959; but few of these people had registered to vote. Throughout the 1950s, blacks comprised less than six percent of the registered voters in Jefferson County.[15] Therefore, while the attack proved insulting to Birmingham's black population, application of the measure failed to purge the voting lists as intended by whites.

The board's action did threaten black voter registration efforts in Jefferson County because it extended the "good citizen" qualification to everyone seeking the franchise. Earlier in the month, the SCLC had met in Birmingham and planned a voter registration campaign for 1960. The civil rights leaders wanted to increase black registration in the South from 1.4 million to 2.5 million by the end of the year. Up to this point, the ACMHR had done little to promote voter registration among blacks in Birmingham. Shuttlesworth had encouraged his church members to get the vote and nearly seventy percent of the ACMHR's membership had registered, but the members considered voter registration a lower priority than dismantling segregation and achieving equality in education.[16] The issue of voter registration took a back seat in Birmingham with the advent of the black student movement during the first months of 1960.

Ten days after black students led a sit-in at the Greensboro, North Carolina Woolworth's on February 1, 1960, a similar demonstration occurred in nearby High Point; and Shuttlesworth, who had been scheduled to preach there, consequently observed the student sit-ins first-hand. Upon his return to Birmingham, Shuttlesworth met with students from the city's black colleges and discussed the new movement rapidly spreading across the South. While a few students from Miles College wanted to stage sit-ins at Birmingham lunch counters, the president of the student body and leader of the young activists, Frank Dukes, opposed the idea out of a fear of possible violence. On the advice of Robert Hughes of the Alabama Council on Human Relations, the Miles students opted for a "round-the-clock prayer vigil in behalf of democracy, fair play and voting rights." At that time, southern congressmen were filibustering a civil rights bill—which later became the weak Civil Rights Act of 1960. The students intended the vigil to last as long as the debate continued in Washington. While Shuttlesworth had advised the Miles students, the ACMHR did not actively support the effort other than to take up a collection for bond money.[17] Shuttlesworth had anticipated the outcome of the students' actions.

The "Prayer Vigil for Freedom" began on March 1, 1960, when a group of students gathered in block-long Kelly Ingram Park, a "colored" facility which separated the Negro community from the downtown business district on the north side of Birmingham. The protestors, all from Miles or Daniel Payne Colleges, carried signs that read "The Law of God Will Be Fulfilled" and passed out leaflets which proclaimed: "We will remain in this public place night and day, regardless of weather, as many weeks as our prayers are needed." Birmingham police had other ideas and picked up twelve of the demonstrators. After fingerprinting and photographing the dozen students, city officials released them without filing charges and that night the evening newspaper published their names and addresses. Two weeks later, a group of white men broke into the home of Robert Jones—a sophomore at Miles College involved in the demonstration—and beat the young black man, his mother and sister with iron pipes, clubs and leather black-jacks. Police arrived forty-five minutes after the attack, but the assailants had fled. The next morning, two sheriff's deputies visited the mother, Mattie Mae Jones, in Bessemer General Hospital. Horrified, she immediately recognized the two officers as having beaten her the night before.[18] The first attempt at protest by the students had failed and the beatings warned of reprisals for further demonstrations.

Ignoring the threat of violence, ten black students, in groups of two, entered five department stores in downtown Birmingham on March 31. After making small purchases, they attempted sit-ins at the stores' lunch counters. Police arrested the students, charged them with trespassing and held them for eighteen hours before releasing them on bond. At 5 p.m., three detectives entered Shuttlesworth's home and charged him with vagrancy. The day before the sit-in attempt, the ACMHR had issued a press release in support of the student movement. Connor apparently suspected Shuttlesworth's involvement in the protest; and after a few of the arrested students admitted that Shuttlesworth had discussed the sit-in movement with them, the commissioner ordered Shuttlesworth's arrest on a conspiracy to violate a city ordinance charge. While the sit-in failed to develop into a sustained challenge to Birmingham's segregated eating ordinances it strengthened the local movement and increased the bond between the students and the ACMHR.[19]

The week after the sit-ins, the New York *Times* sent veteran journalist Harrison Salisbury to report on the situation in Birmingham. In his story, published on April 12, 1960, under the headline "Fear And Hatred Grip Birmingham," Salisbury described a city "fragmented by the emotional dynamite of racism." The reporter's critical analysis outraged the local white population. The city commissioners demanded a retraction and later followed through with a threat to sue for libel. John Temple Graves, a columnist for the Birmingham *Post-Herald* and the South's leading newspaper apologist for segregation, wrote that "Salisbury came here with only half an attention, his story subconsciously already written." Representatives from the Chamber of Commerce and the Committee of 100 Leading Industries wrote a rebuttal to Salisbury's article, disclaiming the acts of violence as extraordinary and supporting the policies of Bull Connor. In a *Times* statement published with the reply by Birmingham's economic elite, Turner Catledge, the managing editor of the newspaper and a native of Mississippi, defended Salisbury's interpretation of the city but added that the article "did not stress the obvious fact that an overwhelming percentage of the citizens of Birmingham lead happy and peaceful lives in a growing and prosperous community."[20] Catledge failed to identify these citizens—many of whom supported segregation—as being middle class whites who depended on the city for their livelihood yet lived in the suburbs and thus "abandoned" Birmingham to Bull Connor.

The *Times* article rekindled fears of negative publicity in the minds of Birmingham's white establishment. The city had received unfavorable publicity after the attempted bus boycott in late 1958. *Time* magazine published an article entitled "Birmingham: Integration's Hottest Crucible," on December 15, 1958, in which the writer warned that "the death of leadership, the silence of fear, the bomb blasts of hatred," all contributed to Birmingham's being "the toughest city in the South, and likely to get tougher." The populace, according to the magazine, viewed "desegregation less as an abstract threat to be fended off by lawyers than as a specific bread-and-butter threat to jobs, promotions, family security." *Time* had suggested a plausible reason for the racial violence and repression which flared from time to time and had occurred again before Salisbury's visit. Such negative publicity hurt the industrial recruitment sponsored by the white elite. While they ran to the defense of Birmingham and denounced Salisbury, some business leaders began to recognize that problems existed in the city. Of course, Shuttlesworth understood the situation in Birmingham and he delighted in the publicity generated by Salisbury's article. But the minister expressed more succinctly than the reporter the issue facing Birmingham: "Evidently Mr. Salisbury became sick of soul as he saw a great city and state being strangled and cut in its jugular vein by men in public office who are so obsessed with the failure of 1865 that their words and acts serve as a deterrent to racial progress so badly needed in 1960."[21] Shuttlesworth blamed many of Birmingham's troubles on the race-baiting policies of Bull Connor.

In mid-April, 1960, Connor addressed a crowd of several hundred people at a meeting of the Selma Citizens Council. In his speech, the commissioner excelled in the demagoguery that made him infamous throughout the nation. Approaching the podium in Baker Elementary School, Connor pushed the microphone away and announced, "I don't need this thing because I feel so strongly about what I'm going to say they can hear me all over the state." A small-statured man, Theophilus—meaning loved of God—Eugene "Bull" Connor warmed the crowd up with a scathing tirade about Russian-influenced northern liberals. His tight lips twitched as he reminded the Dallas County residents of black Republican rule during Reconstruction. Connor, himself a native of Selma, warned the Black Belt audience that a black sheriff and judge had held office in Dallas County before and would again unless the South united to "fight this plague." Beads of sweat formed on his sloping forehead as his small eyes pierced from under bushy black brows. Describing the activities of the ACMHR, Connor's deep voice reverberated as he declared, "they don't want racial equality at all. The Negroes want black supremacy!" He labeled Shuttlesworth and King "fanatical leaders who will not stop at bloodshed in their fight to mix the races." In his conclusion, Connor returned to a metaphor he knew best and one the crowd understood well. "We are on the one-yard line. Our backs are to the wall. Do we let them go over for a touchdown, or do we raise the Confederate flag as did our forefathers and tell them . . . 'You shall not pass!'"[22] The extremist beliefs of Bull Connor promoted violence in Birmingham but also contributed to the determination of the movement.

The vituperative speeches of Bull Connor served to draw the members of the ACMHR closer in their resolution to overthrow segregation in Birmingham. Out of this intimacy grew the Alabama Christian Movement Choir, an interdenominational group organized in July 1960 by ACMHR Treasurer W. E. Shortridge and Mrs. Georgia Price. The choir gave stability to the music of the mass meetings. The combination of gospel music and traditional hymns was a characteristic of the urban black church and Birmingham had a strong gospel music tradition. The movement choir's use of gospel music emphasized the ACMHR's cultural ties to the black community and the indigenous characteristics of the Birmingham movement. Gospel music presented a more personal relationship between the singer and his Savior than freedom songs allowed. In the ACMHR mass meetings, soloists often let emotionalism carry their gospel songs, and many times ushers had to restrain the singers. One choir member remarked that "the choir sings with faith in God, knowing that His power works through their songs and gives them courage to keep singing while struggling for freedom." Carlton Reese, a young gospel music composer, directed the movement choir; and one of his songs, "Ninety-Nine and a Half Won't Do," related the need for total commitment to the cause. The lyrics outlined an undaunted drive to complete a task step by step. The song presented an unstated comparison to dismantling segregation. While the existence of an organized choir diminished the musical input of the regular ACMHR members—something other movements emphasized in order to rally mass based support behind their efforts—the gospel music in Birmingham united the choir and audience on a higher, spiritual level.[23] Thus, the movement choir fostered the religious intensity of the ACMHR.

Toward the end of the summer, three of Shuttlesworth's children surprised their father by following his methods of direct action confrontation. After a trip to the Highlander Folk School in Monteagle, Tennessee, Patricia Ann, 17, Ruby Fredricka, 15, and Fred Lee, 13, refused to sit in the Jim Crow section of an interstate bus on the ride home. When the Greyhound reached Gadsden, Alabama, on August 16, 1960, police arrested the children and charged them with disturbing the peace. Upon hearing of the arrests, Shuttlesworth, who explained that the challenge was "not a planned incident," rushed to Gadsden. Despite Shuttlesworth's arrival to post bond, Gadsden officials kept the children in jail over night. Ruby Fredricka described the experience: "I could hear my brother in his cell singing 'Because All Men Are Brothers.' Just hearing his voice gave my sister and me courage not to be afraid." The next morning officers released the children to Shuttlesworth and they returned to Birmingham.[24] The teenagers had not only participated in a Highlander workshop but also put into practice the lessons taught by the folk school and their father.

By 1960, Highlander Folk School served as a halfway house for civil rights activists. Established by Myles Horton in 1932 to assist the economically oppressed people of Appalachia, the school developed into a staging ground for union organizers and then a workshop for integration leaders. One of the school's directors, Jim Dombrowski, left Highlander in 1942 to serve with the Southern Conference for Human Welfare and in 1947 became head of the Southern Conference Education Fund. By 1960, Shuttlesworth served on the board of the SCEF and he used his influence to invite speakers from the organization to Birmingham. Carl Braden, a field secretary of the SCEF, often addressed the ACMHR mass meetings. As a white man speaking on integration and articulating the goals of the ACMHR, Braden's speeches encouraged the local movement. Therefore, the minister's association with Highlander also extended to friendships with leading white integrationists. As a result, the ACMHR, which occasionally sponsored work trips to

Highlander, had developed contacts through Shuttlesworth with national leaders of the integration effort.[25]

A court case filed by Shuttlesworth in September 1960 shed light on the inner-workings of the ACMHR. After Bull Connor resumed office as police commissioner in November 1958, detectives attended every ACMHR mass meeting. Shuttlesworth and Reverend Charles Billups, an usher in the ACMHR, filed suit in federal court against Connor and Police Chief Jamie Moore in an attempt to get an injunction prohibiting the officers from attending the meetings. Shuttlesworth, himself, represented the ACMHR in court on November 22, 1960, before United States District Judge Seybourn H. Lynne. The minister urged that police attendance at the meetings denied the blacks of their Constitutional rights of freedom of speech and assembly. Justifying his actions, Connor explained: "The police have to keep up with what is going on. If they didn't we would wake up one morning and find ourselves in a hell of a fix." Testimony at the hearing revealed that one of the two white detectives attending the weekly meetings wore a microphone that transmitted to a short wave radio in a nearby patrol car. Officers then wrote comprehensive reports of the meetings and submitted them to Connor. Although Shuttlesworth proved that police attendance hindered the efforts of the ACMHR, Judge Lynne denied the injunction.[26] The hearing not only portrayed police intimidation but also described the organizational structure of the ACMHR and the mass meeting.

Through the mass meeting, Shuttlesworth organized the local black population behind the ACMHR's fight for civil rights. While he appeared to be running a one-man show, Shuttlesworth actually headed an organized movement that could function in his absence. Definite positions of authority existed in the ACMHR, and as a result of the streamlined structure of the organization, it remained fluid and appeared spontaneous. A typical mass meeting began with the pastor of the host church reading scripture, followed by another minister leading the ACMHR in prayer. After a song or two by the church choir, Reverend Edward Gardner, first vice president of the ACMHR, usually made announcements and gave a short sermon. Occasionally a special guest spoke to the crowd. When not out of town as a visiting speaker or in jail, Shuttlesworth gave the main address for the evening. As the charismatic leader of the movement, the membership greeted his sermons with much fanfare. The movement choir often sang at the conclusion of Shuttlesworth's speech and many times members of the congregation became overwhelmed with emotion. Reverend Charles Billups directed the ACMHR's ushers and they restrained the people overcome with the religious intensity of the meeting. W. E. Shortridge, the treasurer of the ACMHR, conducted the collection which financed the projects of the ACMHR. After approximately two hours, the mass meeting concluded. Two other ministers assisted in the operations of the ACMHR. Reverend N. H. Smith, Jr., the secretary of the organization, cosigned the ACMHR press releases with Shuttlesworth, and Reverend J. S. Phifer, second vice president of the ACMHR, often accompanied Shuttlesworth on direct action challenges to segregation. These five men assisted Shuttlesworth in the operations of the ACMHR and, although Shuttlesworth remained the undisputed leader of the movement, Gardner, Billups, Shortridge, Smith and Phifer provided much of the secondary leadership. With the power centered in the office of president, Shuttlesworth controlled the organization with the approval of the ACMHR executive board. Therefore, members of the ACMHR, outside of the handful of officers who loyally supported Shuttlesworth, wielded little influence in the decision-making process, yet more than ninety percent of the members approved of this arrangement. Shuttlesworth's immense power within the ACMHR, and his certainty that only his methods worked, prevented several black leaders in Birmingham from supporting the local movement.[27] But the people who did join the ACMHR were of a more determined and almost fanatical nature.

The mass meetings provided a forum in which a relationship of shared goals and experiences developed between the leaders and the followers of the movement. In an effort to encourage solidarity in the community, the leaders rotated the mass meetings from church to church. In addition to the congregations of the ministers who served as officers in the ACMHR, about 15 other churches regularly supported the movement and hosted mass meetings. Ministers who shared Shuttlesworth's beliefs recruited for the ACMHR during their Sunday services. To join, individuals paid an annual fee of one dollar and received a membership card. The ACMHR kept its financial and membership records secret, but every June in his president's address, Shuttlesworth announced the amount of money collected and spent on the movement. The ACMHR depended on indigenous resources to keep it afloat. The organization raised between $200-$300 at each weekly mass meeting and received very little outside financial support. During the collection, members rose by pew and joined a procession to the altar at the front of the church, often holding money in the air to demonstrate their commitment to the movement. Shortridge, or another ACMHR official, occasionally told the congregation that if some of the members failed to contribute to the collection, then they should get up and give their seat to a "paying customer." Several collections often took place in one night to finance different projects of the organization.[28] Thus, the ability of the ACMHR to collect enough money—dollar by dollar from the local membership—to sustain a fight against segregation in Birmingham demonstrated the dedication, determination and willingness to sacrifice of the blacks in the movement. Not only did they give of themselves, but they also faced white repression in the process.

The presence of the two detectives at the mass meeting prevented many people from joining the ACMHR. In an attempt to prevent the officers from attending the meetings, the ACMHR passed a resolution in November 1958 requiring everyone at the meetings to have a membership card. When the ushers asked the detectives to leave because they had not joined the movement, the officers refused and announced that if anyone tried to force them out of the meeting, they would arrest the "whole house." At this point, several ACMHR members slipped out the side door. Shuttlesworth took the podium and explained that leaving would not solve Birmingham's problems. The ACMHR then resolved to continue the fight. The next week, the city parked four police patrol wagons outside of the church. Officers ticketed cars parked near the mass meeting and randomly stopped and searched members leaving the services. On a December night in 1959, the fire department, accompanied by eight policemen, interrupted a mass meeting held at Saint James Baptist Church. Although no one had reported a fire, the firemen marched around the building carrying axes and fire extinguishers, made a thorough search of the balcony, and then suddenly left.[29] Thus, not only had Shuttlesworth and the volunteers of the direct action confrontations faced police intimidation first-hand but so had the regular ACMHR membership.

Subjects discussed in the mass meetings ranged from comments on political leaders and white resistance to discourses on the evils of segregation and the equality of the races. The content of the ACMHR programs often became more emotional than rational, but this appealed to the militant faith of the organization's membership. Members interpreted the goals of the ACMHR as an acquisition of "human rights" for all individuals. Shuttlesworth expressed the goals of the movement within the confines of the Consensus: "Is the great American ideal of fair play, equality and justice which even now holds communism at bay in the four quarters of the earth to fall from view when challenging the internal enemy of Segregation?" Shuttlesworth believed that blacks had to accept certain responsibilities in order to achieve civil rights. The minister understood only too well that whites pointed to the actions of a minority of blacks as justification for withholding rights to all blacks. Therefore, with progressive zeal, Shuttlesworth launched into attacks against gambling, drinking, stealing, illegitimacy and adultery. One such sermon occurred at a mass meeting attended by approximately 250 people at Saint James Baptist on January 23, 1961. Shuttlesworth read from a local newspaper clipping which reported the ratio of blacks to whites arrested and jailed for certain crimes over the past year. After describing a certain "hell" for blacks who failed to lead responsible lives, he turned the service over to a visiting preacher. The minister, Reverend Oscar Herron, reiterated Shuttlesworth's lecture by admonishing blacks "not to steal, fight and go with other men's wives." He then advanced into a trenchant sermon on integration. A police detective observing the meeting noticed that "during this time at least a dozen or fifteen women had to be carried out. They get to waving their arms and hollering and screaming so it took from four to six men to carry each woman out. They finally placed an overcoat and a scarf around the man that was speaking and got him to sit down." Despite the efforts of several ACMHR officers to restore order to the meeting, emotions continued to run high until the service concluded.[30] While the mass meeting proved an effective way to articulate and define the goals of the ACMHR, it also served as a release for emotions trapped under the repressive rule of segregation.

The mass meeting also functioned as a method of communication. After the Congress of Racial Equality initiated the Freedom Ride in May 1961, Shuttlesworth announced in a mass meeting that "next Sunday, our bus riders will be here." He described them as "a mixed group of whites and Negroes riding together." In addition, he told the detectives to make a special note of the event and tell Bull Connor. Ironically, an April field report of the United States Commission on Civil Rights warned that "racial prejudices are incredibly tense in Birmingham. Until leaders make a concerted effort to control those feelings, the slightest provocation can be expected to unleash acts of violence as ugly and as frightening as any that Birmingham has seen in its . . . history."[31] The provocation occurred the next month with the arrival of the freedom riders.

After whites fire-bombed the first bus of freedom riders outside Anniston, Alabama, on May 14, 1961, Shuttlesworth sent cars to rescue the stranded integrationists. He also notified Bull Connor by telegram that a second bus would arrive in Birmingham later that Mother's Day afternoon and that police should protect the riders in accordance with a 1948 ruling on the desegregation of interstate travel. When the bus pulled into the Trailways station three blocks from police headquarters, a crowd of casually dressed men attacked the bus, dragged the freedom riders off the vehicle and hauled them into the corridors of the building, beating them with lead pipes. Ten minutes later, the mob had dispersed and the police arrived, finding the bloody demonstrators scattered about the station. Bull Connor later denied knowing of the planned protest. He explained that most policemen had the day off to visit their mothers and therefore reached the scene too late to end the violence. Later that Sunday night, the freedom riders boarded an airplane and flew to New Orleans as the bus drivers had refused to drive any further. At a mass meeting on Monday, Shuttlesworth decried: "This is a Democracy? I saw one man with his head laid open. It took fifty stitches to sew his head up. That same man [James Peck, the leader of the Freedom Ride] sat in my house before the TV cameras, in my bed." Shuttlesworth had functioned as CORE's contact in Birmingham, and when that organization called off the protest, John Lewis, Henry Thomas, and Diane Nash of the Student Nonviolent Coordinating Committee resumed the Freedom Ride.[32]

An interracial group of ten students including Lewis and Thomas left Nashville for Birmingham on Wednesday, May 17, 1961. Police arrested the protesters after the bus pulled into Birmingham. On Thursday night, Connor escorted the group to Tennessee and dumped them across the state line. After walking several miles, the students found a phone and called Nash, who sent a car to collect the abandoned activists. On Friday, they returned to Birmingham by car in order to catch a bus to Montgomery and continue the ride. Later in the morning, Birmingham police arrested Shuttlesworth on charges of having "conspired with unknown persons to cause a mob to gather at the Trailways Station," in connection with the beatings of Mother's Day. Shocked by the violence, United States Attorney General Robert Kennedy ordered the FBI to investigate the incident. Although Governor Patterson had refused to discuss the Freedom Ride with Kennedy, claiming the state could not "guarantee the safety of fools," he met with Kennedy's assistant, John Seigenthaler, on Friday and promised that state officers "would uphold their responsibilities." The next morning, Saturday, May 20, a bus escorted by state troopers left Birmingham for Montgomery.[33]

Shuttlesworth followed the bus to Montgomery and the reception awaiting the freedom riders surprised the minister. The escort disappeared outside of the state capital, leaving the bus to enter Montgomery unprotected. Again a mob attacked the integrationists, including Seigenthaler. After the rout, police arrested Shuttlesworth, who had observed the melee, and several other civil rights activists. The MIA held a mass meeting on Sunday night after the release of the black leaders. During the meeting, several hundred riotous whites surrounded the church and threatened the safety of the people inside. Federal marshals and Alabama guardsmen tried to disperse the mob, but it dissolved independently by dawn. Shuttlesworth, who had been in the besieged church all night, left Montgomery on Monday and returned to Birmingham. He later called the event "glorious" and elaborated that "here, Negroes and whites are being beaten together, are riding and suffering together, are praying and working together." In a mass meeting back in Birmingham on May 22, Shuttlesworth described the concerted effort of the black and white protesters and the beatings they sustained for integration.[34] The Freedom Ride had finally focused the nation's attention on the violence of the civil rights struggle in Birmingham and the South and forced the Kennedy Administration to respond to the movement.

Coincidental to the Freedom Rides, CBS Reports broadcast a program entitled "Who Speaks For Birmingham?" on May 18, 1961. Narrated by Howard K. Smith, the program featured interviews with various Birmingham residents, including several ACMHR members. David Lowe of CBS had attended a mass meeting on March 13 and at that time requested the blacks "tell their own story in their own words." A white detective observed the meeting and described Lowe's interviews in a report to Bull Connor: "His first question was, 'What is it like in Birmingham?' No one rose to answer. Next question, 'Do churches have function of leadership?' Again unanswered. 'What are cultural opportunities?'" After several unanswered questions, a few members rose to speak. The officer noted that "Lowe could not get the people to answer his questions as he (Lowe) wished. Instead they . . . began telling of a personal experience wherein they had been arrested or mistreated by the police." Flabbergasted, Lowe told the crowd that he "could not and would not use the film where the people made speeches." Nevertheless, CBS selected for broadcast a few of the approximately twenty testimonials given that night.[35]

The comments suggested the character of the ACMHR membership. A mother of eight children faced the cameras and told the country of her commitment to the ACMHR. "My life is on the altar, and I will die for those eight children, if it takes death to show them that I mean that, I mean that. I'm not afraid . . . For I trust in God and I know God. I walks with God." A veteran who survived a shipwreck in World War II and went on to fight in Korea, suffering substantial injuries in that war, explained he joined the ACMHR to try to "bring about a community of brotherly love" in Birmingham. As a result of his actions, night riders beat him with chains; yet the man remained dedicated to the movement: "I believe that through our fight here that we're going to bring both races close together. There's a lot of peoples here who is afraid—black and white—to speak out, because they're afraid they may lose something. But I have nothing to lose but my life. And I think, now, that the Lord have given me enough and I'm living on borrowed time now."[36] The fatalistic confessions of these two ACMHR members spoke to the seriousness of the movement in Birmingham and to their fanatical faith in God.

Shuttlesworth's dedication to the ACMHR reinforced the faith of his followers, but in June 1961, he jeopardized the local movement by taking a job in Ohio. Despite attempts by the ACMHR leadership to bolster Shuttlesworth's already large ego, the minister accepted the pastorate of Revelation Baptist Church in Cincinnati. He selected Revelation Baptist over other offers because of the direct flight service between Birmingham and Cincinnati. Shuttlesworth planned to continue his leadership of the ACMHR by maintaining his residence in Birmingham and commuting to Ohio every other week. The minister, whose salary tripled with the new job, explained his decision as necessary to finance the college education of his children. Before the new position began on August 1, Shuttlesworth contributed an important facet to the Birmingham movement. At a mass meeting held in his church on June 26, 1961, the minister started a special program for the children of the ACMHR's members. He explained to the crowd: "We will keep them in order and teach them to be non-violent." As a result of this development, the children received special training in direct action techniques while the adults and the detectives remained in the mass meeting.[37] Thus, the movement extended to the children.

Therefore, a maturing period occurred for the ACMHR during the years 1959-1961. Although the organization slowed down its direct action challenges to segregation, it consolidated its forces behind the litigation in process. The militant Christianity practiced by Shuttlesworth and the ACMHR prevented some blacks from joining the movement, but it also unified and strengthened the organization's membership. Shuttlesworth's ties to SCLC, SCEF, CORE and Highlander brought Birmingham's indigenous movement into contact with the leaders of the national civil rights struggle. The advent of the black student movement contributed a new dimension to the Birmingham campaign. Harrison Salisbury's critical article in the New York *Times* following the sit-ins in the city outraged officials but awoke the white community to the situation in Birmingham. The Freedom Rides further demonstrated the need for reforms. During the next year and a half, the ACMHR would draw upon its successful past, which the members attributed to Divine sanction, in order to strengthen the continuing struggle.

THREE

"Boy, if That's Religion, I Don't Want Any"

Beginning in the fall of 1961, a series of events in Birmingham culminated in the spring, 1963, demonstrations which forced the city's white elite to negotiate the dismantling of segregation. Although Reverend Fred L. Shuttlesworth, the leader of the Alabama Christian Movement For Human Rights, had accepted a pastorate in Ohio, the veteran civil rights activist minimized his new responsibilities and continued to lead the Birmingham campaign. The inauguration of a new city commission had occurred in November, 1961, with Arthur Hanes replacing long-time Mayor James "Jimmy" Morgan, who chose not to run because of the increased racial tension in the city. Hanes, who defeated liberal candidate Thomas King with charges that King's election would bring "the fall of Birmingham as the biggest segregation stronghold in the nation," joined former commissioner J. T. "Jabo" Waggoner on a city commission dominated by T. Eugene "Bull" Connor.[1] With the conflict over park desegregation and a resurgence of black student activism in 1962, came an attempt by the black bourgeoisie to negotiate with white businessmen who disagreed with the extremist attitudes of the city commission. Nevertheless, the lines had hardened in Birmingham between an uncompromising Bull Connor and a determined Fred Shuttlesworth.

In December 1961, a suit filed by the ACMHR following the bus desegregation attempt of 1958 forced the city commission to either close Birmingham's recreational and amusement parks or desegregate the facilities. A ruling by federal judge Frank W. Johnson influenced the commission's December 28, 1961, decision to close Birmingham's parks. In September, 1959, Johnson had declared unconstitutional Montgomery's segregation ordinance on city parks. The capital city faced the choice of either closing the parks and thus not enforcing the ordinance, or integrating the facilities. Montgomery selected the former. The ACMHR's case, once it reached federal court in Birmingham, placed the commissioners in the same situation and they followed Montgomery's lead. The action prompted an immediate outcry from Birmingham's white establishment that developed into opposition to Bull Connor.[2]

By late December 1961, white spokesmen from the Birmingham Chamber of Commerce, Jefferson County Board of Mental Health, Birmingham Ministerial Association and the Young Men's Business Club—a group of influential young business leaders—as well as the city's two newspapers opposed the closing of the parks. Despite attempts by white and black elite to negotiate a settlement to keep the parks open, the commissioners posted "no trespassing" signs, dismissed 140 park employees and terminated most of the funding for the facilities. The court had set a January 15 deadline for desegregation, so the commission effectively closed the parks by New Year's Day, 1962. On January 9, the commissioners rejected a petition signed by 1,200 prominent whites that requested the reopening of the parks. The closings had created an outburst of moderation in the heretofore silent white establishment; but most of these new moderates lived outside the city limits of Birmingham in affluent suburbs such as Mountain Brook, the wealthiest city in the South, which ranked eighth in the nation in per capita income. Whenever a delegation of moderates visited the commission, Connor or Hanes angrily asked, "How many of you live in Birmingham?" The question proved fatal to discussions, for the commissioners knew that the Ku Klux Klan, the Citizens Council, and more than fifty percent of the city's electorate supported the closing of the parks.[3]

Despite the obstinate stand of the commissioners, negotiations had begun between black and white elite. A biracial committee established to prevent the closing of the parks petitioned the court for a sixty-day stay of the desegregation order. Throughout the negotiations, Shuttlesworth and the ACMHR remained publicly silent. Earlier at a mass meeting, Reverend Edward Gardner, first vice president of the ACMHR, told the gathering that "these open discussions could keep right on," but that Birmingham blacks were "tired of the same old talk." Growing adamant in his speech, Gardner stressed the position of the ACMHR: "We the Negroes of the movement will tell you how we feel. We are right, our heart is right, and we have come a long way. We will not compromise. We want all the privileges that the white folks have. We will not take less."[4] A discordant note had been struck in the black community. The ACMHR, equally as stubborn as the city commission, had refused to negotiate, leaving the black bourgeoisie without any influence in the local movement.

While the Chamber of Commerce and city commission fought over park desegregation, the local black student movement grasped the occasion to publicize the plight of the Negro in Birmingham. Under the leadership of Frank Dukes, a thirty-one-year-old combat veteran of Korea and president of the student government association at Miles College, the students had conducted a voter registration drive in Birmingham during the summer of 1961; but by the fall of the year, they had grown impatient with the situation in the city and sought to revive the activism of the year before when they had staged sit-ins at downtown department stores. Despite attempts by the Congress of Racial Equality and the Student Nonviolent Coordinating Committee to affiliate with the Miles activists, the students remained independent of all national organizations. On December 29, 1961, 700 students adopted a manifesto entitled "This We Believe." Signed by eight student leaders and distributed throughout Birmingham, the five-page pamphlet denounced segregation as "not in keeping with the ideals of democracy and Christianity." In addition to an end to segregation, the statement demanded equal rights for blacks in such areas as voting, housing and employment and concluded with the warning; "We do not intend to wait complacently for those rights."[5]

By early January, the students, who had grown more militant, formed the Anti-Injustice Committee to plan a strategy of action. AIC members met with Shuttlesworth early in the month to discuss a boycott. The president of Miles College, Dr. Lucius H. Pitts, heard about the possible protest and immediately contacted white leaders to inform them of the boycott plans and to ask for a biracial committee to discuss the situation. A newcomer to Birmingham, Pitts had moved from Atlanta where he had served on the Georgia affiliate of the Southern Regional Council. In 1958, the Southern Christian Leadership Conference attempted to hire Pitts as its executive director, but the educator refused the post. Once installed as president of Miles College in June 1961, Pitts joined the SRC's Alabama Council on Human Relations. As with other members of the interracial ACHR, Pitts, out of a fear of violence, urged negotiations as the method of achieving civil rights. He therefore informed white merchants of the planned boycott and convinced them to meet with student activists in order to discuss the students' demands. Pitts also persuaded the AIC to postpone the boycott and attempt the negotiations.[6] In effect Pitts' actions, and those of the ACHR, while undertaken to gain civil rights without violence, ultimately inhibited the black movement in Birmingham by convincing black activists to negotiate with whites who continually refused to concede any ground.

Members of Birmingham's black bourgeoisie began meeting with representatives of the white establishment during the park desegregation crisis and expanded the negotiations to consider the demands of the Miles students. The black negotiators included Pitts, millionaire A. G. Gaston, attorney Arthur Shores, and businessman John Drew. Reputedly one of the wealthiest black men in America, Gaston had made his money selling burial insurance to blacks and then extended his holdings into real estate and other investments. Shores, the first practicing black attorney in Birmingham, had helped represent the National Association for the Advancement of Colored People in the Autherine Lucy case. He also had represented the defendants during the Montgomery bus boycott. Drew, a close friend of Coretta and Reverend Dr. Martin Luther King, Jr., worked as an executive in A. G. Gaston's insurance firm and he refused to associate with the ACMHR. Probably believing money equaled power, white business leaders preferred negotiating with the black bourgeoisie; but ironically, the wealthy blacks had as much influence over Shuttlesworth and the ACMHR as the white establishment had over Bull Connor and the city commission.[7] Nevertheless, discussions had begun between the races.

The negotiations met immediate rejection by the black community as a whole. Gaston called a mass meeting for January 5, 1962, so that the black negotiators could report on the discussions "and find out what the Negro community wanted them to do in the future." Emory Jackson, the editor of the Birmingham *World* and a Shuttlesworth sympathizer, noted that many blacks went to the meeting to see if they could trust the black bourgeoisie. Resentment against the prominent business leaders "who have been unwilling to go to jail and who have never shown any interest in improving the lot of the Negro," had developed in the black community, according to Jackson. Many blacks opposed negotiations and believed that they had been "sold down the river" because the black mediators had "offered to meet with white people." Gaston's close ties to the white establishment, his aloofness in the black community and his past record of carefully avoiding any confrontations with the white power structure, contributed to his impotence among the movement's membership. The attitude of Birmingham's black activists had hardened. Benjamin Muse, a field worker for the SRC, observed in January that "the park episode is only one of many grievances which they [blacks] are now airing. The outrages of the May riots [Freedom Ride] are not mentioned publicly but are probably uppermost in their hearts."[8] Therefore, blacks in the movement distrusted negotiations despite the efforts of the black bourgeoisie.

Since 1956, the black bourgeoisie had opposed Shuttlesworth and his use of direct action confrontation, and the activist minister had disdain for these self-proclaimed leaders of Birmingham's black community. On January 22, 1962, Pitts, who had respect in black society but little influence in the movement, addressed an ACMHR mass meeting at Saint John's African Methodist Episcopal Church. After confessing his hesitation in coming to speak before the ACMHR, Pitts attempted to convert the members to his method of activism. "I want to ask how Christian is the Christian Movement?" Pitts questioned, adding that if the membership "truly had faith" they would emphasize voter registration. He continued that the ACMHR should use its money wisely by patronizing Negro businesses "instead of spending it on fines and doctor bills and court costs." He concluded that the ACMHR should trust whites and support negotiations. Needless to say, Shuttlesworth disagreed with Pitts and showed his displeasure after the educator finished speaking.[9]

The ACMHR had reason to be skeptical of negotiations. For the past six years the organization had attempted to meet with officials but had always faced rejection. By 1962, negotiations had failed to achieve any progress in race relations in Birmingham, but the ACMHR's method of direct action confrontation had proved successful. The United States Supreme Court heard the case of the ACMHR's 1958 bus desegregation attempt on January 8, 1962, and refused to overturn the convictions of Shuttlesworth and Reverend J. S. Phifer because of a technicality in the case. The ruling forced both men to serve their original jail sentences: Shuttlesworth to serve ninety days and Phifer to serve sixty days. The two men surrendered to city officials on January 25, 1962. Once in jail, they continued the fight by sending the commissioners a petition demanding the desegregation of city hall. The action prompted Mayor Hanes to retort: "I don't correspond with jail birds." Subsequent appeals by ACMHR lawyers on the grounds of the same technicality resulted in the release on bail of the two men—one week after the Supreme Court's decision outlawing segregation on public transportation. Shores had brilliantly defended Shuttlesworth and Phifer and the two men left jail pending appeal on March 2, 1962; yet nearly two years passed before the courts finally overturned the convictions.[10]

With Shuttlesworth in jail, Pitts succeeded in convincing the Miles students to call off the planned boycott and meet with Birmingham's white merchants. On January 31, 1962, members of the Anti-Injustice Committee conferred with members of the white establishment. Discussions continued throughout February, 1962, but by the end of the month no settlement had been reached on the desegregation of the stores. The students had grown frustrated and the black community remained divided. Negotiations collapsed when the merchants refused to desegregate store facilities, citing a possible white backlash. Furthermore, the merchants refused to grant any concessions unless the city commission repealed the segregation ordinances. The students resumed boycott plans and the black bourgeoisie scrambled to salvage the negotiations.[11]

As momentum for a boycott increased, the black bourgeoisie called a summit meeting in an attempt to unify the black community. Gaston, Shores and Drew had recently criticized Shuttlesworth. The black bourgeoisie emphasized that Shuttlesworth was "not the leader of the Negro community" and that less than fifty percent of Birmingham's blacks loyally supported the ACMHR. Gaston stressed the need for "conservative leadership," and the summit meeting on March 2, 1962, would have probably underscored his beliefs had Shuttlesworth not been released from jail in time to unify the black activists at a mass meeting the same night.[12]

Shortly thereafter, Miles students met with Shuttlesworth and other leaders in the ACMHR and decided to initiate a "Selective Buying Campaign." On March 6, 1962, Frank Dukes gave the white merchants a final chance to grant the students' demands. He sent them letters requesting the desegregation of the stores and the hiring of black sales clerks. The merchants refused to concede any points and Dukes called a meeting of the AIC on March 15. At the meeting, the Miles students approved the boycott and adopted as their demands three goals: "1) desegregation of lunch counters, rest rooms and drinking fountains; 2) hiring of Negroes as clerks and sales personnel; and 3) a general upgrading of Negro employees from solely menial jobs." Students from Daniel Payne College and Booker T. Washington Business School as well as the ACMHR endorsed the Selective Buying Campaign. The students distributed leaflets encouraging blacks to support the boycott by "spending money wisely." Some students patrolled the downtown shopping district in order to catch blacks violating the boycott and convince them to return their purchases. Since the boycott fell during the Easter shopping season, the students selected as a slogan "Wear

Your Old Clothes For Freedom." By the end of March, one white merchant admitted that the boycott had been eighty to eighty-five percent effective in curtailing Negro trade.[13]

The initial success of the boycott resulted in retaliation by the city commission. At the commissioners' weekly meeting on April 3, 1962, Bull Connor announced: "Last night, I am reliably informed, the Shuttlesworth crowd met and there was a lot of bragging about the boycott of our downtown stores." The commissioner continued: "I move that we cut off our appropriations to the county for our surplus food program. A boycott can work both ways. I don't intend to sit here and take it with a smile." Mayor Hanes added: "If the Negroes are going to heed the irresponsible and militant advice of the NAACP and CORE leaders, then I say let these leaders feed them." The commission's action meant the withdrawal of $45,000 from a city and county total of $100,000 used to provide distribution and storage of free food donated by the federal government. Blacks comprised approximately ninety-five percent of the 20,000 families in Jefferson County that benefitted from the program.[14] The commission's response to the boycott brought immediate national condemnation and strengthened the local movement.

News of the commission's action prompted offers of assistance from people across the country. The NAACP immediately took advantage of Hanes' challenge by announcing that it would support the surplus food program if the city attorneys would help lift the 1956 injunction, which outlawed the NAACP in Alabama. In another attempt to inhibit the boycott, Birmingham police arrested Shuttlesworth and Phifer on April 4, 1962, charging them with obstructing a sidewalk and refusing to obey an officer. The next day, Recorder's Court found both men guilty, sentenced them to 180 days in prison and released them on bond pending an appeal. That afternoon, the Birmingham *News* editorialized on the need for negotiations. The newspaper's publisher had served on the biracial committee two months before and probably regretted the failure of the discussion. Expressing concern over "unfavorable headlines throughout the nation," the paper admitted: "It is time for Birmingham citizens to sit down and talk together. . . . Pleasant or not, the sitting down must be done."[15] The time for negotiations had passed, and the white establishment recognized its error.

The termination of the city's contribution to the surplus food program actually strengthened black support for the boycott. The firing of black employees from W. W. Woolworth and J. S. Newberry probably helped as well. In an attempt to intimidate the black community, Bull Connor announced he would "sic the dogs" on blacks who entered downtown unless black leaders ended the boycott. Such attempts at white resistance and police repression in Birmingham only fostered solidarity among blacks in the movement.[16]

While the boycott continued, Shuttlesworth attended a board meeting of the Southern Christian Leadership Conference held in mid-May, 1962, in Chattanooga, Tennessee. At that time, the SCLC discussed joining Shuttlesworth and the ACMHR in a direct action campaign against segregation in Birmingham. Shuttlesworth apparently recognized the need for dramatic direct action in addition to the boycott as the best way to challenge the white establishment in Birmingham. He therefore asked King to come to Birmingham; but the highly recognized civil rights leader had his hands full with Albany, Georgia, and apparently refused, for the time being. The SCLC had selected Birmingham as the site of its September convention and shortly after the May meeting, rumors began to spread that King would lead demonstrations in Birmingham during the SCLC's fall convention. After his return to Birmingham, Shuttlesworth found the boycott had been effective. Easter sales had dropped twelve percent below 1961's record and the boycott claimed ninety percent of some stores' black trade. The organization of the Selective Buying Campaign contributed to its success. Before announcing the boycott, Miles students prepared a list of businesses that did not discriminate against blacks. Once the boycott began, the students encouraged the black community to patronize these select stores.[17] The shift in Negro business helped break the black community's dependence on downtown merchants.

Nevertheless, by June the boycott had begun to falter. Birmingham police arrested three students on June 14, 1962, for parading without a permit after they walked down the street carrying signs in support of the Selective Buying Campaign. On June 20, the day of the three students' trial in Recorder's Court, police arrested an additional four students for the same offense. Despite an attempt to generate support for the campaign immediately following the arrests, many blacks had already lost interest in the boycott. At an ACMHR mass meeting held on June 11, 1962, Frank Dukes announced that the merchants had almost surrendered in May when "the Negro started slipping back in and buying stuff." Other student leaders apparently complained about the black bourgeoisie's limited support for the boycott.[18] Therefore, the Selective Buying Campaign ended, not as a result of the city commission's actions but out of a failure by the activists to keep Birmingham's black community interested in the boycott.

As an apparent result of the boycott, Birmingham's white establishment organized a biracial committee comprised of the city's leading merchants and the chief executive officers of Birmingham's major industries. The Chamber of Commerce created the Senior Citizens Committee on August 27, 1962, and selected former Chamber president and real estate executive Sidney W. Smyer to head the eighty-nine member committee. Smyer had been a staunch segregationist but had converted to moderation on the race issue after seeing Birmingham's image tarnished by negative publicity. Approximately ten to fifteen blacks served on the committee, including Gaston and Pitts. The interracial group of black and white elite met in secret and discussed Birmingham's racial problems. The first challenge to the Senior Citizens Committee occurred in September, 1962, when the unsubstantiated rumor of a planned SCLC demonstration escalated into a threat by Shuttlesworth. Despite a lack of mass based support, a limited boycott by the Miles students and the ACMHR had continued over the summer and into the fall. Shuttlesworth had urged King to hold the SCLC convention in Birmingham with the hopes that the merchants would thus desegregate under a threat of demonstrations.[19] The white establishment recognized the threat and used the Senior Citizens Committee to start negotiations with black leaders.

In an attempt to prevent the demonstrations, Dr. Lucius H. Pitts traveled to Washington, D. C. to meet with Attorney General Robert Kennedy and his assistant, Burke Marshall. The negotiator then returned to Birmingham and consulted the black bourgeoisie and the Alabama Council on Human Relations. On September 16, 1962, Pitts met with Sidney Smyer and explained that demonstrations could be avoided if the downtown merchants showed signs of desegregating their stores in advance of the SCLC convention. The white establishment feared King because of his ability to arouse the black masses with his powerful oratory. Furthermore, King's stature as a leader of the civil rights movement assured national press coverage of the demonstrations. Fearing racial protest would affect the outcome of an upcoming election and determined to prevent more negative publicity for Birmingham, Smyer decided to support Pitts' efforts. Shortly before the September 25-28 convention, Smyer and several white merchants met with Pitts, Shuttlesworth, A. G. Gaston, Arthur Shores and John Drew. The white leadership agreed to begin the desegregation of stores and to continue biracial discussions. In return Shuttlesworth held a press conference

71

and announced a moratorium on boycotts and demonstrations, but he warned that if the merchants failed to live up to the agreement, the SCLC would return and lead protest marches. Apparently King was seriously considering Shuttlesworth's offer. Immediately following the meeting, some merchants painted over the "colored" and "white" signs in their stores.[20] As a result of Shuttlesworth's threat, negotiations had achieved limited desegregation.

The SCLC arrived in Birmingham and found desegregated department stores. The convention progressed without any difficulties until the last day of the meeting. On September 28, a young white man climbed up on the stage from which King addressed the crowd and punched the civil rights activist in the face. King refused to press charges against the assailant, but Birmingham police arrested the man—later identified as Roy James, a member of the Nazi party in Maryland—charged him with assault and took him before a city judge who convicted him that afternoon. In addition, Mayor Hanes banished the white supremacist from Birmingham. The swift work of the police to prevent a disturbance and the action of Hanes suggested that the white establishment had pressured the city commission to prevent any disruptions during the convention. Nevertheless, as soon as the SCLC left town, Bull Connor began harassing the merchants who had desegregated their facilities. City building inspectors visited several desegregated stores, cited the owners for code infractions and threatened to close the businesses down. Some merchants claimed that as a result of desegregation, hundreds of whites had cancelled their charge accounts. Needless to say, the "colored" signs quickly went back up.[21] Despite the September agreement, merchants buckled under the pressure of Bull Connor.

The failure of the merchants to maintain desegregated businesses convinced Shuttlesworth and the students to revitalize the Selective Buying Campaign. The students began organizing another mass based boycott to take place during the Christmas shopping season. The Senior Citizens Committee interpreted the students' actions as proof that blacks could not be trusted in negotiations. Shuttlesworth asked King in December to return to Birmingham and lead the local movement in demonstrations, but the leader of the SCLC declined. Birmingham's black bourgeoisie had advised King to postpone any direct action campaign until after the mayoral elections slated for March 5, 1963. In November 1961, Birmingham had voted on a change of government, electing a mayor-council form over a city commission. Efforts to change the government had begun in 1957. Mayor-council advocates cited a need for a more representative government with the accompanying possibility of luring the affluent white suburbs into Birmingham proper as a reason for the change. By 1961, opponents of the mayor-council form had raised the race issue in an attempt to keep the city commission. On November 6, the public elected a more representative mayor-council form of government and mayoral elections were set for March 5. King accepted the advice of the black bourgeoisie and convinced Shuttlesworth to delay the demonstrations. King promised the Birmingham leader that the SCLC would discuss the issue of a direct action campaign in Birmingham at a meeting in January.[22] Thus, the SCLC convinced Shuttlesworth to call off plans for demonstrations in Birmingham and as a result the Christmas Selective Buying Campaign never materialized.

The SCLC held a strategy meeting January 10 and 11, 1963, at Dorchester, Georgia, to determine if the organization would join Shuttlesworth in a direct action campaign in Birmingham. Shuttlesworth had asked King for the SCLC's support on several occasions, beginning in the spring of 1962 during the Selective Buying Campaign; then before the SCLC's fall convention; then after the convention when the merchants resegregated their stores and finally after the November election to change the form of city government. Each time King refused to throw the SCLC's support behind the tentative demonstrations. By January 1963, King's reputation as the leader of the civil rights struggle had been compromised by the dismal defeat of the Albany campaign. King saw in Birmingham an opportunity not only to help the local movement, but in the process to salvage his credibility.

At the Dorchester session, the SCLC discussed the failure of Albany in order to determine the best strategy for Birmingham. The civil rights leaders recognized several factors as contributing to the collapse of demonstrations in Albany. The inability of the campaign to focus on one or two targets instead of segregation as a whole doomed the Albany movement from the start. As a result, King recognized the need to boycott the business sector and therefore put indirect pressure on the white power structure. King believed the merchants, suffering under a loss of black revenues, would force the politicians to negotiate the blacks' demands for desegregation. In addition, King determined that his inability to generate "creative tension," when black nonviolence meets white violence, contributed to the failure of Albany. Throughout the campaign, Police Chief Laurie Pritchett had treated the demonstrators with a synthetic politeness and he also had prevented white

73

extremists from operating in Albany. Pritchett projected a positive image of segregation, which proved detrimental to a direct action campaign that depended on confrontation to achieve its goals. Birmingham had Bull Connor, and King knew that if pressed hard enough, Connor would respond violently, thus shattering the image of Pritchett and revealing the evils of segregation to a watching world.[23]

Secondary reasons for the failure of Albany, the activists resolved, included the divisiveness among civil rights workers, King's obedience of a federal injunction against demonstrations and the apathy of the Kennedy administration. In Albany, the infighting among SCLC, SNCC and NAACP members prohibited a unified effort. Shuttlesworth alone controlled the movement in Birmingham, thus eliminating a threat of disunity. The movement stopped in Albany when King ended the marches in accordance with a federal injunction. As a result, King determined to continue the marches in Birmingham if faced with a similar court order. King obeyed the federal injunction in Albany out of a respect for the Kennedy administration, but that respect changed to frustration when the federal government failed to act on behalf of the movement. King saw the key to Birmingham as "federal commitment." Aware that the national press would follow him to Birmingham, King determined that all he needed to do was generate enough "creative tension" to swing national opinion behind the movement and thus force the federal government to intervene on behalf of the SCLC. King reasoned that if he could get the Kennedy administration to recognize the legitimacy of the movement, the Birmingham campaign would be a success.[24]

King and the SCLC staff viewed Birmingham from a national perspective. King believed that a victory in Birmingham "might well set forces in motion to change the entire course of the drive for freedom and justice." Shuttlesworth recognized the SCLC's goal as a "wholehearted battle against segregation which would set the pace for the nation."[25] In other words, Shuttlesworth interpreted the SCLC's strategy as a local campaign, one that would destroy segregation in Birmingham first and then have national ramifications. King placed the local success second, behind the achievement of his national goals. To be sure, King wanted to win the local movement's demands, but his intent in going to Birmingham remained a desire to achieve federal commitment to the movement. Thus, a complete victory in Birmingham did not matter to King, as long as the movement appeared successful nationally and forced the Kennedys to act. Therefore, from the beginning, a conflict existed between Shuttlesworth's and the SCLC's goals, although the Birmingham leader failed to recognize the inconsistency.

The Dorchester conference concluded with King's warning the staff workers: "I have to tell you that in my judgment, some of the people sitting here today will not come back alive from this campaign. And I want you to think about it." The young organizers recognized the seriousness of the moment but immediately endorsed the project. Two weeks later, Reverend Wyatt T. Walker, a veteran of the movement from Virginia and the executive director of the SCLC, accompanied King to Birmingham to plan the demonstrations, which had been scheduled to begin on March 14—ten days after Birmingham's mayoral elections.[26]

On election day, March 5, 1963, Birmingham voters failed to give a majority to the mayoral candidates, so a run-off between Albert Boutwell and Bull Connor was slated for April 2, 1963. Moderates saw Boutwell as a rational segregationist as opposed to the emotionally racist Connor. A former lieutenant governor, Boutwell had written the Pupil Placement Law and blacks called him "just a dignified Bull Connor," but they preferred Boutwell to the notorious commissioner. The fear of a white backlash of support for Connor convinced King to postpone the demonstrations until after the April runoff. During the interim, Walker completed the SCLC strategy of staging sit-ins at Birmingham department stores to emphasize the boycott. Mapping out the floor plans of the buildings, Walker organized the protest in great detail. Shortly after the March election, Shuttlesworth joined King in a secret meeting with Harry Belafonte in New York. Belafonte had gathered northern friends of the SCLC together to offer their support of King. After describing the Birmingham project, King requested that the group raise bail money. Shuttlesworth impressed the celebrities when he said: "You have to be prepared to die before you can begin to live." The meeting ended with the building of a war chest for the campaign.[27]

Birmingham voters elected Boutwell over Bull Connor as the mayor of the city on April 2, 1963. After the inauguration of the city council, the old city commission refused to vacate their offices, citing a 1959 state act that allowed the commissioners to complete their terms, which expired in 1965. Boutwell and the newly elected council members filed suit in court, citing a 1955 state act that allowed them to take office two weeks after the election. Thus, Birmingham had two municipal governments running the city during the SCLC's spring campaign. Although both governments remained in office until the state Supreme Court ruled in favor of Boutwell on May 23, 1963,

Bull Connor maintained his control over the police and fire departments as public safety commissioner.[28] The situation contributed to the instability of Birmingham's political structure throughout the demonstrations.

The day after the election, April 3, 1963, the SCLC joined the ACMHR and the Miles students in a protest against segregation in Birmingham. The movement listed six demands as the reasons for the demonstrations and they stemmed from the long struggle waged in Birmingham by the students, the ACMHR and Shuttlesworth. The movement wanted the desegregation of lunch counters, rest rooms and drinking fountains and the hiring of black clerks and sales personnel in the city's stores. In addition the activists demanded the city reopen and integrate the parks and implement fair hiring practices for city jobs. The creation of an on-going interracial committee and the stipulation that all charges from previous arrests of protesters be dropped, completed the six demands of the movement. That Wednesday morning, twenty-four Miles students began sit-ins at four local lunch counters. By the end of the day, twenty students had been arrested. The next day, students returned to the stores and again faced arrest.[29] The sit-ins would continue throughout the demonstrations.

While the press interpreted the sit-ins without accompanying marches to mean the Birmingham campaign had gotten off to a slow start, the limited demonstrations had actually been Walker's strategy. King explained to the press that the sit-ins were to emphasize the Easter boycott, and he hinted of new developments. On Saturday, April 6, 1963, the movement increased its attack by adding mass marches to its arsenal. Shuttlesworth led a group of protesters to city hall and they walked several blocks before Birmingham police moved in and arrested the marchers. On Sunday, April 7, Reverend A. D. King, Martin Luther King, Jr.'s younger brother, led a second march on city hall. Fulfilling his promise to "sic the dogs" on demonstrators, Connor ordered the German shepherds out to intimidate the two dozen marchers. A crowd of black bystanders lined the parade route watching the confrontation. As police approached the marchers, a young black bystander apparently poked at a police dog with a piece of pipe. Immediately, the dog attacked the boy, pinning him to the ground. A nearby observer pulled a knife out as the dogs, police and crowd rushed to surround the boy. Officers began dispersing the onlookers with swipes of their billy clubs as other policemen used the dogs to force back the bystanders. Fifteen minutes later, the crowd had broken up and the police had arrested the marchers. Walker who had observed the event, called King to announce: "We've got a movement!" Disappointed by the small number of volunteers for the marches, the SCLC had feared that the press would report a lack of community involvement in the demonstrations.[30] But Sunday's march provided two vital elements necessary for the SCLC's success in Birmingham: violence at the hands of Bull Connor and the appearance of mass based support by the presence of the bystanders.

The small number of blacks willing to march in the demonstrations caused problems for the SCLC. King had anticipated large numbers of volunteers—something necessary for the success of the movement—but few blacks in Birmingham supported protests that resulted in arrests. The black community as a whole endorsed boycotts, but only approximately two percent participated in marches that resulted in jailings.[31] The repressive climate of Birmingham and the tyranny of Bull Connor certainly convinced many blacks to avoid confrontations with police. Yet there existed a few blacks in Birmingham willing to face arrest in support of the movement. The membership of the ACMHR, which had started the fight in 1956, and the young students from the city's black colleges, who joined the struggle in 1960, provided the army King and the SCLC used to protest segregation in Birmingham throughout the month of April.

King addressed the lack of community support for the movement at a meeting attended by 100 of Birmingham's black ministers on Monday, April 8, 1963. Preaching the social gospel, King attempted to convert the group of uninvolved pastors by arguing that "a 'dry as dust' religion prompts a minister to extol the glories of Heaven while ignoring the social conditions that cause man an earthly hell." Frustrated by the ministers' apathy, King scolded the audience: "I'm tired of preachers riding around in big cars, living in fine homes, but not willing to take their part in the fight . . . If you can't stand up with your own people, you are not fit to be a leader!" Most of Birmingham's 250 black ministers supported the movement by wearing blue jeans in the pulpit to emphasize the Easter boycott; but despite King's pleading, only about twenty minsters actually participated in the demonstrations, and the overwhelming majority of these pastors belonged to the ACMHR.[32]

King attempted to recruit the black bourgeoisie to the movement at a meeting held on Tuesday, April 9, 1963. Many Negro businessmen and professionals opposed the demonstrations out of a belief that the new Boutwell administration would address the complaints of blacks in Birmingham. A. G. Gaston and others called the campaign "untimely," but

King argued that Boutwell would "never desegregate Birmingham voluntarily." King failed to convince many members of the black middle class to join the movement, but he succeeded in neutralizing the opposition to the movement within the Negro community. By late Tuesday afternoon, Gaston had thrown his support behind the SCLC, as had the Baptist Ministers conference, headed by Reverend J. L. Ware. Although Ware opposed Shuttlesworth's direct action tactics, he had joined forces with the ACMHR during the bus boycott of 1958. In an apparent attempt to organize the middle class blacks of Birmingham who found the ACMHR too radical or emotional, Ware had created the Inter Citizens Committee. While a more "respectable" organization than the ACMHR, the ICC rarely initiated any protests, although it occasionally supported the ACMHR and the student movement.[33] Thus, Ware probably used his influence to convince the Baptist Ministers Conference to unanimously approve of the campaign.

King solicited the help of two black middle-class churches, and he received their support. The Reverend Andrew Young, King's aide in Birmingham, later recalled that King garnered the assistance of Reverends John Cross, A. D. King, Nelson H. Smith and John Thomas Porter, to supplement Shuttlesworth and the ACMHR. Of the four ministers listed by Young, two had already been active members of the ACMHR. Smith had served as secretary of the ACMHR since its founding in 1956 and he loyally signed every press release of the organization with Shuttlesworth. A. D. King had become a driving force behind the ACMHR after his move to Birmingham in February 1962; and his church, First Baptist Church of Ensley, held numerous mass meetings of the ACMHR. Only Cross and Porter joined the movement because of King. Cross pastored Birmingham's largest, oldest and richest Negro church, Sixteenth Street Baptist Church—Birmingham's equivalent to Atlanta's Ebenezer Baptist Church, King's home church. Because of its size and proximity to Kelly Ingram Park and the downtown business district, Sixteenth Street Baptist became the staging ground for many of the demonstrations. Porter, who had served as King's ministerial assistant at Dexter Avenue Baptist Church in Montgomery, pastored Sixth Avenue Baptist Church, which boasted one of Birmingham's largest black congregations. Neither of the churches had apparently supported the ACMHR in its struggle before King's arrival.[34] Therefore, King's appeal, while bolstering the morale of the movement's activists, achieved tacit approval from the black community's business leaders and professionals, moral support for the boycott from the overwhelming majority of the city's black ministers and the assistance of at least two middle class churches. As a whole, Birmingham's black community recognized King as the leader of the civil rights movement, and they revered him as a charismatic minister, but few people volunteered to support the campaign because of King. Yet, white Birmingham feared King and the negative publicity which followed the demonstrations.

Most members of Birmingham's black middle class disapproved of Shuttlesworth's autocratic style and the religious fanaticism of the ACMHR. While many members of the black bourgeoisie admired Shuttlesworth's courage, they feared that the demonstrations would thrust Shuttlesworth forward as the leader of the black community. Pitts and Gaston especially opposed Shuttlesworth because of this threat. The religious beliefs of Shuttlesworth limited his influence in the middle class. A friend of Shuttlesworth's explained that the minister "sees himself as taking orders only from God who speaks through him." Such an attitude contributed to his dictatorial leadership. In agreement with other members of the black elite, Reverend John Porter believed that Shuttlesworth "could not work with people." Porter later described a confrontation with Shuttlesworth: "He told me once, 'Porter, this is *my* movement. You get in line or get out.'" Perhaps Porter, who had only lived in Birmingham since December 1962—four months before the demonstrations began—and who had been a close friend and assistant of King's, challenged Shuttlesworth's leadership of the ACMHR.[35] Nevertheless, the majority of Birmingham's black middle class opposed Shuttlesworth, thus creating a problem for King to solve in order for the black community to appear unified behind the demonstrations.

After arriving in Birmingham, King created an advisory committee and granted it the power to discuss the movement's demands. King appointed members of the black bourgeoisie, such as Pitts, Gaston, Shores and Drew, to the committee and it organized to negotiate with Birmingham's white establishment. An attempt by the Advisory Committee to determine and direct the movement's strategy failed when the SCLC's staff workers, imported to control the demonstrations, rejected the committee's advice. Understandably, tensions developed between the committee members and the local activists.[36] The black bourgeoisie had never supported the ACMHR in its efforts to overthrow segregation in Birmingham. Shuttlesworth and other local activists disagreed with the black elite's propensity to negotiate through compromise. The black bourgeoisie, on the other hand, viewed Shuttlesworth's recalcitrance as detrimental to negotiations. King stood in the middle of these two forces and skillfully used them to the advantage of the SCLC.

The campaign struggled along as the boycott grew effective with the continuing sit-ins. Yet few people volunteered for the marches, and the SCLC's war chest had begun to run out. On Wednesday, April 10, 1963, two city attorneys applied for a temporary injunction against the movement leaders. State Circuit Court Judge William A. Jenkins granted the request which barred King, Shuttlesworth and Reverend Ralph Abernathy, SCLC's treasurer and King's trusted friend since Montgomery, from leading any further demonstrations. At a mass meeting that night, King announced that he and Abernathy would violate the state injunction. "I can't think of a better day than Good Friday for a move for freedom," he told the 350 people gathered in Saint James Baptist Church. King repeated his plans at a press conference held Thursday morning. That night, word reached King that the movement had depleted Belafonte's bail money, and the civil rights leader began to have second thoughts about violating the court order.[37]

Late Thursday evening, King discussed the situation with his staff and, after spending a fretful night, resumed the discussions Friday morning. King cited as his concern the protesters already behind bars who faced the possibility of not being bonded out until the SCLC generated new funds. He believed he could raise the money but that would entail a trip to New York and the press would accuse him of avoiding arrest and abandoning the movement. Albany weighed heavily on his mind. And he probably compared the failure of Albany with the movement in Birmingham. The campaign had not been going well. Only a handful of people had volunteered to demonstrate and Bull Connor continued to treat the activists with the same politeness used by Laurie Pritchett. King needed to generate "creative tension." After a brief hesitation Friday morning, King decided to march. His pending arrest showed his commitment to violate unjust laws.[38]

Dressed in a new pair of dungarees to emphasize the Easter boycott's slogan of wearing old clothes for freedom, King joined Abernathy at Sixth Avenue Zion Hill Baptist Church. Only about fifty protesters had gathered to march with King and Abernathy. The demonstrators paired off and lined up for the march to city hall. A few bystanders watched the column move down Seventeenth Street. After walking four blocks, the marchers stopped when accosted by police. Officers arrested King, Abernathy and the other activists, including Al Hibler, the blind black singer whom Bull Connor had refused to arrest for the same offense two days before. Although arrested on Good Friday, King experienced no resurrection on Easter morning because Connor kept him in solitary confinement throughout the weekend. By Monday morning, SCLC officials had still not breached King's seclusion. The national press focused its attention on Birmingham and the jailed civil rights leader. By Monday afternoon, a change in events occurred. President John F. Kennedy called Coretta Scott King, expressed his concern and informed her that her husband would be calling. The White House had put pressure on Bull Connor. Thirty minutes later, King called his wife in Atlanta and, upon hearing that the people in Birmingham did not know of the President's involvement, told her to call Wyatt Walker. When Walker heard the news, he rejoiced, for King's arrest had triggered federal recognition of the movement.[39]

Assisted by the momentum of King's arrest, Belafonte raised $50,000 over the weekend, putting the campaign back on its feet. While behind bars, King composed a letter in response to the criticism of eight Birmingham clergymen who had called the demonstrations "unwise and untimely" in a statement made Good Friday. King's subsequent "Letter from Birmingham Jail" legitimized the civil rights movement by justifying direct action. On Thursday, April 18, 1963, the SCLC issued King's response to his critics and "Letter from Birmingham Jail" soon circulated across the country. On Saturday, the SCLC bailed King and Abernathy out of jail and the two ministers left for Atlanta. Both men returned to Birmingham late Sunday to prepare for Monday's court date. Proceedings began in the injunction trial Monday morning in Judge Jenkins' court and continued through Wednesday. On Friday, April 26, 1963, Jenkins found King guilty of violating the state injunction. King appealed the decision and remained out on bond. The movement struggled along during the two weeks King spent in jail and court, with only a few dedicated activists demonstrating.[40]

King called a staff meeting of the SCLC organizers on Monday, April 29, 1963, to decide how to generate "creative tension" and thus keep the press in Birmingham. King told the assembled staff workers: "We've got to pick up everything, because the press is leaving." James Bevel and Isaac "Ike" Reynolds suggested using school children in the protest marches. Wyatt Walker immediately supported the idea, citing the limited number of volunteers as a reason to fill the ranks of marchers with school children. Reynolds, a staff worker from CORE, had been helping Bevel and his wife Diane Nash in organizing the black youth of Birmingham. The SCLC had hired Bevel away from SNCC in order to utilize his skills of communication with young people. The Bevels and Reynolds, with Dorothy Cotton and Bernard Lee of the SCLC, had visited Birmingham's black schools and talked with students. Since 1961, the ACMHR had been training area youth in nonviolence, so contact with some children had existed for almost two years. King initially rejected the idea, but Bevel persuaded him to meet with the students on the following Thursday. The staff workers wasted no time in preparing for the meeting. On Tuesday, April 30, 1963, SCLC workers blanketed area schools with leaflets announcing the noon meeting.[41]

Hundreds of school children answered the call, filling Sixteenth Street Baptist Church by noon on Thursday, May 2, 1963. When twelve o'clock passed and King had still not arrived to talk to the youth, Bevel and Walker decided to let the children march without King's approval. Wave after wave of young protesters filed out of the church and headed toward downtown Birmingham. The cheerful youngsters happily submitted to arrest and by the end of the day more than 500 crowded into Birmingham jail. The need for demonstrators had been filled by the children and the activists viewed this resource as unlimited. At Thursday night's mass meeting, Shuttlesworth described a conversation he had with policemen during the demonstrations. An officer asked, "Hey, Fred, how many more have you got?" to which the minister answered, "At least 1,000 more." "God Amighty," replied the policeman. The young people provided the soldiers the SCLC had been looking for since the beginning of the demonstrations.[42]

Recognizing the success of the children's demonstration, King held a press conference on Friday morning, May 3, 1963, and announced that Thursday was "just the beginning." He promised bigger marches that afternoon and emphasized the protests would continue until the merchants met the demands of the movement. Determined to meet King's threat, Bull Connor ordered his officers out in force. The commissioner stationed firemen around Kelly Ingram Park and sealed off the black district from downtown Birmingham in an attempt to contain the demonstrators. A youthful crowd gathered in the park across the road from Sixteenth Street Baptist Church. The ever-present onlookers stood on the outskirts of the arena and watched the events unfold. Some students jeered and taunted the officers, who responded by pushing the crowd back, using the growling police dogs. As the attack dogs strained on their leashes, snarling at the students and snapping their fangs, a shower of bricks and bottles thrown by the bystanders began to fall on the firemen and policemen. Connor hollered, "Let 'em have it," and the singing of Thursday's school children turned to shouts, as the water gushed out of fire hoses. "I want to see the dogs work," Bull barked, exclaiming. "Look at those niggers run." Loosened, the dogs lunged at the protesters, ripping at their clothes in search of flesh. The firemen blindly blasted at the crowd, the water tearing the bark off trees, seeking citizens, young and old. The onlookers, unassociated with the movement and untrained in nonviolence, returned Connor's force with force. From a nearby roof top, angry blacks shouted obscenities and hurled rocks and shards at the officers. The demonstrators fled the scene, finding safety in the sanctuary and the recesses of the Negro neighborhood. Yet the streams of water prevented some blacks from escaping by pinning them to the walls of the buildings which bordered Kelly Ingram Park. Connor persisted, emptying the area within half an hour. The horrifying spectacle had ended.[43]

Sickened by the photos in Saturday morning's newspapers, President Kennedy sent Burke Marshall to Birmingham to help negotiate a peace. The night before, Reverend Edward Gardner, first vice president of the ACMHR, had instructed the crowd, "this is a non-violent movement and if anybody gets mad, let it be the white man." Gardner had defiantly added, "We will overcome the dogs and the fire hoses and police brutality." Yet on Saturday morning, a rowdy crowd of blacks assembled near Kelly Ingram Park. Although Connor kept the dogs in nearby trucks, he constructed a bulwark around the block with the fire hoses. When James Bevel attempted to lead the children in another demonstration, Connor ordered the hoses on and routed the group, forcing it back into Sixteenth Street Baptist Church. Violence erupted among the onlookers, and SCLC leaders, recognizing the damaging image black retaliation projected of the movement, took to the streets with bull horns and pleaded with the bystanders to leave. Birmingham's underclass had joined the movement to the dismay of the SCLC.[44]

A two-hour prayer meeting at New Pilgrim Baptist Church concluded Sunday afternoon with the congregation deciding to march to the jail and sing to the arrested protesters. The Reverend Charles Billups, a longtime leader of the ACMHR, led several hundred blacks out of the sanctuary, which had seen many mass meetings over the years. When the group approached Bull Connor's barricade, Billups signaled the marchers and they dropped to their knees in serious prayer. The older blacks began to moan and sway as their deep faith took hold and a determination overwhelmed the demonstrators. Suddenly, Billups jumped to his feet and shouted to Connor, "Turn on your water, turn loose your dogs. We will stand here till we die."

An older woman rose from the ranks and announced: "The Lord is with this movement and we're going to the jail." Startled firemen fell back as the protesters marched through police lines. Assembling in a park near the jail, Billups led the crowd in prayer and marveled over God parting the Red Sea again.[45]

On Sunday night, May 5, 1963, the Advisory Committee met with white business leaders and discussed the movement's demands. Gaston issued "Four Points For Progress," which reiterated as the movement's demands: desegregation of the stores; equal employment opportunities for blacks; dropping the charges against the demonstrators; and creating an interracial committee to schedule the reopening of the parks, hiring black policemen, school desegregation, voter registration and removal of all city ordinances on segregation. The boycott had been effective, for not only had the merchants lost Negro trade, but also that of whites who had avoided downtown because of the demonstrations. Earlier that afternoon, Burke Marshall and Assistant Deputy Attorney General Joseph Dolan met with the merchants. By evening, the business elite, recognizing the need for the "unpleasant" negotiations, agreed to the first two demands of the movement but refused to put pressure on the city commission in order to achieve points three and four.[46]

Hundreds of school children poured out of Sixteenth Street Baptist Church to march on city hall, Monday afternoon, May 6, 1963. Connor had kept the dogs and hoses at home, opting instead to peacefully arrest the young demonstrators. School buses arrived to haul the protesters to jail, and then, once police had packed as many of the blacks into the cells as possible, to a stockade in the state fair grounds. As the children ran into the arms of policemen, Connor remarked: "Boy, if that's religion, I don't want any." By the end of the day, a disappointed onlooker hurled a bottle at the officers who had almost finished arresting the demonstrators. A black leader quickly emerged from the church before widespread violence developed and, while waving his arms, announced, "It's all over. It's all over for today." The SCLC had successfully filled the jails, but the merchants refused to concede. Monday night, the SCLC staff developed a new strategy. Up to this point, Birmingham officials had contained the demonstrations in Kelly Ingram Park. The organizers decided to circumvent Bull Connor and attack the white establishment by converging on the downtown business district. The demonstrations were scheduled for noon, two hours earlier than usual, in order to catch the police on their lunch break.[47]

Tuesday morning, May 7, began with a group of protesters leaving Sixteenth Street Baptist Church. Police moved in and arrested the decoy as hundreds of other demonstrators took fifteen different routes around the blockade. At noon, thousands of children and adults converged on Birmingham's business district. For thirty minutes, traffic stopped on busy Twentieth Street as the activists milled around cars, marched down the sidewalk and knelt in prayer. Jubilee had arrived. "We're marching for freedom," the students cheered. "The police can't stop us now. Even Bull Connor can't stop us now!" Concurrent with the demonstrations, a meeting of the white establishment's Senior Citizens Committee took place. After seeing the uncontrollable crowd of peaceful protesters, Sidney Smyer, chairman of the committee composed of Birmingham's business elite, recognized that whites could not win. Earlier in the day, Kennedy had warned Smyer that if Birmingham failed to prevent a "race riot," he would send in troops and declare martial law. Smyer apparently convinced the Senior Citizens Committee, which had probably divided between merchants seeking negotiations and corporate officers refusing to discuss the issues, to negotiate the movement's demands.[48]

As the demonstrators left the business district to return to Kelly Ingram Park, Bull Connor, obviously incensed that he had been outfoxed, placed the K-9 corps and firemen on alert. King, while hearing of the morning's successes from Walker, decided to send out a second wave of protesters. When the school children exited Sixteenth Street Baptist Church, Connor ordered his troops into action. As the high-powered hoses scattered the demonstrators, bystanders began to throw rocks and bottles at the officers. Despite pleas from movement leaders, the violence continued. The SCLC had lost control of the moment. Toward the end of the disorder, firemen focused their hoses on Shuttlesworth, who had just turned the corner of the church. The blast knocked the local leader to the ground, spinning him down the sidewalk. An ambulance arrived and took the minister, who had suffered chest injuries, to the hospital. When told of the development, Connor said: "I waited a week to see Shuttlesworth get hit with a hose. I'm sorry I missed it." The commissioner added: "I wish they'd carried him away in a hearse"[49]

While Shuttlesworth lay in a hospital bed, the movement's Advisory Committee met with representatives from the Senior Citizens Committee. Smyer led the discussions along with Pitts, Shores and Andrew Young as well as Burke Marshall and a representative from Mayor-Elect Albert Boutwell. Within a few hours, a vague agreement had been reached on some of the movement's demands, with the exception of dropping the charges filed against the demonstrators. Wednesday morning, Pitts recommended that King accept the negotiated terms, which stipulated a specific deadline that hinged on the chance that the state Supreme Court would reject the city commission and recognize Boutwell as the mayor of Birmingham. At a meeting of the advisory Committee, Pitts told King: "It is my candid opinion that if a truce is called . . . with a definite time schedule on desegregating of all store facilities and upgrading of employment practices that we would be in a good position to effect continual change in the community." King joined the black bourgeoisie in agreement and announced an end to the demonstrations.[50]

King sent for Shuttlesworth, who was convalescing at the A. G. Gaston Motel, to come to the home of John Drew in order to inform the local leader of his decision to cancel the demonstrations. "Did I hear you right?" Shuttlesworth recalled asking the civil rights leader upon his arrival. King repeated, "We have decided to call off the demonstrations." Shuttlesworth responded, "Well, Martin, *who* decided?" To which King answered, "Well, we just decided that we can't have negotiations with all this going on." Growing angrier, Shuttlesworth said, "Well, Martin, it's hard for me to see . . . how anybody could decide that without me . . . We're not calling anything off . . ." King interrupted, "Well, uh—," but Shuttlesworth continued: "Well, Martin, you know they *said* in Albany that you come in, get people excited and started, and you leave town. But I live here, the people trust me, and I have the responsibility after SCLC is gone, and I'm telling you it will not be called off." Shuttlesworth adamantly persisted: "You and I promised that we would *not* stop demonstrating until we *had* the victory. Now, that's it. That's it. And if you call it off . . . with the last little ounce of strength I got, I'm gonna get back out and lead."[51]

At this point, someone broke in to tell King of a scheduled press conference. Shuttlesworth retorted: "Oh, you've got a press conference? I thought we were to make joint statements. Well, I'll tell you what to do: you go ahead, I'm going home." An attempt by Mrs. Drew to calm Shuttlesworth failed. The leader of the ACMHR squared off with the president of the SCLC. "Now Martin, you're mister big but you're soon to be mister nothing. You're going to fall from up here to down here, and you're dead . . . let me make it plain to you . . . I'm going back home . . I'm going to wait until I see it on TV and hear it on the radio that you've called it off." Burke Marshall interrupted, "Well, I made promises to these people," to which Shuttlesworth demanded, "Burke, who gave you the authority to make any promises to any people without clearing it? But if you made promises, you can go back now and tell 'em that the demonstrations 'll be on, 'cause you can't call 'em off, President Kennedy cain't call 'em off, and there's Martin Luther King—he cain't call 'em off." In the adjoining room, John Doar had called the White House and Shuttlesworth overheard him saying, "We hit a snag—the frail one. The frail one is hanging up. Looks like it won't go through . . ." King looked at Marshall and said, "We got to have unity, Burke. We've just got to have unity." Shuttlesworth turned to King and declared, "I'll be damned if you'll have it like this. You're mister big, but you're going to be mister S-H-I-T. I'm sorry, but I cannot compromise my principles and the principles that we established." Turning his back on the crestfallen civil rights leader, Shuttlesworth left the room.[52]

At that moment, Shuttlesworth realized King's betrayal and his own mistake. For seven years, Shuttlesworth had led the Birmingham movement. His method of direct action confrontation had resulted in court cases which had defeated several facets of segregation in the city. He had fostered the student movement and his urgings had contributed to the boycott of 1962 on which the spring 1963 demonstrations were based. Despite the black bourgeoisie attempts to discredit him and destroy his work through useless negotiations, Shuttlesworth persevered, building an indigenous organization of committed Christians fighting to end segregation in Birmingham. Shuttlesworth believed that God directed his actions, and the members of the ACMHR interpreted his survival of bombings and beatings as proof that he alone led the movement. The intense religious beliefs of the ACMHR propelled the membership to volunteer for demonstrations and face Bull Connor. Shuttlesworth's followers provided the mainstay of the movement, not the middle class recruited by King. The Birmingham campaign would have collapsed in April had it not been for the ACMHR and the students.

Then Shuttlesworth invited King to Birmingham and the civil rights leader accepted the offer to lead the demonstrations. Shuttlesworth surrendered his power—his control of the people—to King. At the Dorchester retreat, Shuttlesworth mistakenly interpreted the SCLC's goal in Birmingham to be the complete destruction of segregation in the city. King did not clarify the misunderstanding. The SCLC's goal from King's perspective, that of federal commitment, had been won when Kennedy sent Burke Marshall to negotiate a settlement in Birmingham. In addition, the "Letter from Birmingham Jail" had reestablished King as the national leader of the civil rights movement. The Birmingham campaign had proved successful from a national point of view when Bull Connor repulsed school children with fire hoses and police dogs. King decided to end the demonstrations, not because of the injuries inflicted on the school children but because the SCLC could not control the violent responses of Birmingham's black underclass. Black retaliation to Bull Connor undermined the nonviolence of direct action and presented a negative image of King in the national press. Thus, when Birmingham's white establishment made overtures to accept some of the movement's demands, King readily acquiesced. He turned to his friends, the black bourgeoisie, and told them to negotiate a settlement. With Burke Marshall acting as a mediator, Birmingham's black and white elite arranged a truce. The terms of the agreement were vague enough to make the campaign appear successful. When King agreed to negotiate and call off the demonstrations, he took the power of the people entrusted to him by Shuttlesworth and gave it to the black bourgeoisie, who had craved Shuttlesworth's power since 1962.

After the fight with King, Shuttlesworth recognized his defeat. He could call together his supporters and lead a march, but without King's support he would ultimately fail. Shuttlesworth's association with King went back to the 1956 Montgomery bus boycott. His friend's deception deeply hurt him, but Shuttlesworth knew he was powerless to act, so he later returned to King and accepted the negotiated truce.

Before King's press conference announcing the end of demonstrations, Bull Connor attempted to destroy the negotiations by arresting King and Abernathy. A. G. Gaston bailed them out of jail and the press conference occurred Wednesday night. As a concession to Shuttlesworth, King threatened to resume demonstrations on Thursday if the movement's demands were not met by 11 a.m. Thursday morning, King told the press that the deadline had been extended because the negotiations were nearing a conclusion. White leaders still refused to drop the charges against the arrested protesters, so the Kennedy administration asked national union officials to pay the $160,000 in bond money. The unions agreed to post the money and King considered the demand met. A second conflict concerning equal employment opportunities for blacks remained unresolved. The negotiators worked out an unclear interpretation of the demand and the discussions ended.[53]

In a final stroke of irony, Shuttlesworth read the negotiated truce at a press conference held at 2:30 p.m. Friday, May 10, 1963, in the courtyard of the A. G. Gaston Motel. Claiming that "Birmingham may well offer for 20th-Century America an example of progressive race relations," Shuttlesworth listed the terms of the agreement:

1. The desegregation of lunch counters, rest rooms, fitting rooms and drinking fountains in planned stages within the next 90 days. Cooperative prayerful planning is necessary to insure smooth transition.
2. The upgrading and hiring of Negroes on a nondiscriminatory basis throughout the industrial community of Birmingham. This will include the hiring of Negroes as clerks and salesmen within the next 60 days, and the immediate appointment of a committee of business, industrial and professional leaders for the implementation of an area wide program for acceleration of upgrading and the employment of Negroes in job categories previously denied to Negroes.
3. Our movement has made arrangements for the release of all persons arrested in demonstrations on bond or on their personal recognizance. Our legal department is working on further solutions to this problem.
4. Through the Senior Citizens Committee of the Chamber of Commerce, communications between Negro and white will be publicly reestablished within the next two weeks. We would hope that this channel of communication between the white and Negro communities will prevent the necessity of further protest action or demonstrations.

After the local leader finished reading the prepared statement of the accord, King began a lengthy speech during which an emotionally and physically exhausted Shuttlesworth collapsed. Sidney Smyer released a statement for the Senior Citizens Committee later in the afternoon that recognized the settlement and urged peace.[54]

Despite bombings by the Ku Klux Klan and subsequent riots by Birmingham's repressed black underclass, the truce held and the city began to desegregate. With its new power, the black bourgeoisie restored order to the black community. As Andrew Young later recalled, "The leadership fell right back into the hands of the middle class, and had they not been involved at all through the process, they wouldn't have been prepared to bring leadership in the period of reconciliation that followed." After the Birmingham campaign, A. G. Gaston continued to accumulate vast amounts of wealth and he wrote a book about his success, entitled *Green Power*. The white establishment appointed Arthur Shores to the Birmingham City Council in 1968. Shuttlesworth returned to his church in Cincinnati, Ohio. Although he remained the president of the ACMHR, he was no longer recognized as a principal local leader. After Birmingham, King went on to direct other campaigns as the undisputed leader of the civil rights movement. And, thanking Bull Connor for Birmingham, President John F. Kennedy proposed a civil rights bill which became the Civil Rights Act of 1964.[55]

Conclusion

The turning point in the civil rights struggle occurred in Birmingham during the spring demonstrations of 1963. Indigenous groups, loosely connected with the Southern Christian Leadership Conference or some other civil rights organization, had been waging war across the south against a common enemy for more that a decade. By 1963, Birmingham stood as the symbolic stronghold of the enemy: segregation. The Reverend Dr. Martin Luther King, Jr., whose national reputation had been jeopardized by the failure of Albany, believed that a victory in Birmingham would spell the defeat of segregation in the South. King reasoned that if he generated enough "creative tension" in Birmingham, then the national press would swing public opinion behind the movement and thus force the Kennedy administration to intervene on behalf of the SCLC.

The leader of the Birmingham movement, Reverend Fred L. Shuttlesworth, had built the Alabama Christian Movement for Human Rights into a dedicated group of militant Christians, and as a result, these religious fanatics provided the mainstay of the spring 1963 demonstrations. During a boycott of white merchants in the spring of 1962, Shuttlesworth realized that the ACMHR could not defeat Bull Connor and segregation in Birmingham without some dramatic event to unify the black masses behind the effort. Shuttlesworth invited King and the SCLC to Birmingham to help lead demonstrations. The president of the SCLC initially refused. After Albany ended in failure with King being blamed for the movement's inability to achieve its demands, the president of the SCLC reconsidered and decided to accept Shuttlesworth's invitation. King approached Birmingham with the objective of achieving "federal commitment" to the civil rights movement. Thus, a complete victory in Birmingham did not matter to King, as long as the movement appeared successful nationally and forced the Kennedys to act. During the campaign, with local victory in reach but national victory in hand, King stopped the demonstrations in order to negotiate a settlement. By doing so, King betrayed Shuttlesworth, for he had led Shuttlesworth to believe that the SCLC would fight until the movement's demands were met.

The demands made by the SCLC during the spring, 1963, demonstrations were a culmination of the goals Shuttlesworth and the ACMHR had fought for since 1956. Shuttlesworth's autocratic leadership, which stemmed from his belief that he was acting under the direction of God, and the fanatical support of the ACMHR membership, which followed the charismatic Shuttlesworth and believed that, in fact, he had direct access to the Divine, created an organization that successfully challenged segregation in Birmingham. While Shuttlesworth was the undisputed leader of the ACMHR, several other ministers played important roles in the operations of the movement. As a result, the organization remained functional during Shuttlesworth's absence. Before the spring, 1963, campaign, the ACMHR had achieved the desegregation of the city's buses and the terminal train station. The ACMHR had forced Birmingham to allow blacks to take civil service examinations—although the city continued to refuse to hire blacks for any position other than menial work—and the organization had sought the integration of Birmingham's white schools. The ACMHR had joined the Miles students in a boycott of white merchants, which for a brief period achieved the desegregation of department stores. And a court challenge to park segregation by the ACMHR led to the closing of Birmingham's recreational facilities.

With the park desegregation case came an awakening of the white community to the need for reform in the city and an attempt by the black bourgeoisie to control the movement. Up to this point, Shuttlesworth had supported the idea of negotiations, but by 1962 he realized that whites in Birmingham would never desegregate anything voluntarily, hence his distrust of negotiations and his unwillingness to compromise. Connor played an excellent foil to Shuttlesworth. Both men were equally determined to achieve their goals, with the police commissioner defending segregation and the black minister advocating integration. Only a fanatical leader such as Shuttlesworth could have defeated the entrenched system of segregation in Birmingham. But Shuttlesworth had failed to achieve a complete victory, only winning successes piecemeal. Thus, Shuttlesworth invited King to lead the demonstrations in Birmingham with the expectation that King's charisma would rally mass-based support for the movement within the black community and that the resulting demonstrations would force whites to capitulate to the initial demands of the movement.

King viewed the Birmingham campaign as a success, not because the local white establishment agreed to the movement's demands—which it never did—but because John F. Kennedy sent Burke Marshall to Birmingham to negotiate a peace. King had already achieved recognition as the leader of the national movement with his "Letter from Birmingham Jail." Also the SCLC could no longer control the demonstrations in Birmingham and the subsequent violence threatened the peaceful image of King. Therefore, he called off the demonstrations. In the process, King settled an underlying struggle for power within Birmingham's black community.

As a result of segregation, blacks in Birmingham had been forced to develop a separate community with distinct institutions that were controlled by the black bourgeoisie. When Shuttlesworth and four other activist ministers formed the ACMHR out of a chronic need for leadership within the black community, the black bourgeoisie offered only token opposition because they did not see the new movement as a threat. With the closing of the parks in 1962, the white establishment recognized Shuttlesworth as a challenge to their power, so they turned to the black bourgeoisie to get them to quiet the black community. Traditionally holding the black bourgeoisie in contempt, the black masses rejected their offers of leadership and followed Shuttlesworth. Rebuffing the black bourgeoisie, the charismatic minister refused to negotiate and invited King to lead demonstrations in Birmingham. But the black bourgeoisie had the ear of King and they convinced him to postpone the protests. When King did arrive to lead the campaign, he gave the authority to negotiate the movement's demands to an advisory committee composed of the black bourgeoisie. By controlling the negotiations, the members of the black bourgeoisie limited reforms to those directed from above. In addition, the white establishment recognized the black bourgeoisie as the leaders of the black community. When King agreed to the negotiated truce, he gave the power of the people entrusted to him by Shuttlesworth to the black bourgeoisie, who used the power to control the black masses. Instead of reforms from below, an alignment of the city's black and white upper classes limited the success of the local movement. In effect, King disarmed a struggle by the people, replaced their leader with his friends, and left town with the national victory, while claiming a local success.

The American public accepted King's interpretation and the Birmingham campaign was correctly viewed as a victory for the national civil rights movement. The violence of Bull Conner produced northern supporters who poured money into the coffers of the SCLC. Making good on his promise of federal commitment, President John F. Kennedy in the summer of 1963, before his assassination, proposed what became the Civil Rights Act of 1964.

93

The act outlawed segregation and job discrimination in public facilities and public employment and used the threat of withholding federal funds to force the South to comply. Birmingham had led to a national awakening to the evils of segregation and a need for reforms in the region. But Birmingham also exhibited signs of the direction the movement would take in the years ahead.

The riots of Birmingham's underclass, which followed the bombings of the A. G. Gaston Motel and Sixteenth Street Baptist Church, foreshadowed the destruction of Watts and Detroit. While the demands of the Birmingham movement failed to address the needs of the underclass, the campaign itself led to the involvement of these poor and powerless blacks in the struggle. The victory of the black bourgeoisie in Birmingham assured that little would be done to improve the condition of the black underclass in Birmingham. The Student Nonviolent Coordinating Committee and the Congress of Racial Equality charged King with having "sold out" to the white establishment in Birmingham. The infighting among the various civil rights activists had surfaced in Albany, and although SCLC controlled Birmingham, SNCC and CORE had representatives there who observed the campaign. By the end of 1963, the private war between SCLC and SNCC had become public. The national civil rights movement was no longer unified.

In 1964, while attempting another victory such as Birmingham, King and the SCLC were routed in St. Augustine. Mississippi Freedom Summer was under way and although SNCC succeeded in upsetting the National Democratic Convention of 1964, the movement never quite caught the attention that Birmingham received. In Selma in 1965, the SCLC attempted to implement a strategy similar to the one used in Birmingham, but it failed to work, prompting the decision to march on Montgomery. The march took place without King's blessings, and Sheriff Jim Clark, who had observed the Birmingham demonstrations first-hand, ordered the posse into action. Selma provided the climax to Mississippi Freedom Summer as both campaigns emphasized voter registration, the final goal of the original movement. As a result, President Lyndon B. Johnson signed the Voting Rights Act of 1965. With these two acts, white America considered the South's problems solved as the federal government began implementing the reforms. For the next three years, the movement turned to the roots of the unrest within the black community: poverty and isolation. Watts and Detroit underlined the need for national reforms that would benefit not the black middle class, but the black community as a whole. The long, hot summers of 1965-1967 demonstrated the paradox of Birmingham. King's victory ultimately removed the superficial barriers of segregation, but it exposed the realities of racial oppression and then prevented any genuine reforms from taking place. Thus, the "perpetual promise" remained in Birmingham, as in the rest of the country.

Notes

INTRODUCTION

1. George R. Leighton, "Birmingham, Alabama: The City of Perpetual Promise," *Harper's Magazine*, August 1937, pp. 225-242; Robert J. Norrell, "Caste in Steel: Jim Crow Careers in Birmingham, Alabama," *Journal of American History*, 73 (December 1986), pp. 669-694.
2. Norrell, "Caste in Steel," p. 686; Geraldine Moore, *Behind the Ebony Mask* (Birmingham, Ala.: Southern University Press, 1961), p. 28; Robert Gaines Corley, "The Quest for Racial Harmony: Race Relations in Birmingham, Alabama, 1947-1963," (Ph.D. dissertation, University of Virginia, 1979), p. 11; Lee Edmundson Bains, Jr., "Birmingham 1963: Confrontation Over Civil Rights" (B.A. honors thesis, Harvard College, 1977), p. iv; Aldon D. Morris, *The Origins of the Civil Rights Movement: Black Communities Organizing for Change* (New York: The Free Press, 1984), p. 6.
3. Morris, *Origins*, pp. 4-6, 88, 96-99; Adam Fairclough, "The Preachers and the People: The Origins and Early Years of the Southern Christian Leadership Conference, 1955-1959," *Journal of Southern History*, 52 (August 1986), pp. 405-409.
4. Pittsburgh *Courier*, 14 February 1959, Reverend Fred L. Shuttlesworth Papers, Box Three, Martin Luther King, Jr., Center for Nonviolent Social Change, Archives, Atlanta, Georgia; *Christian Science Monitor*, 21 August 1958, and New York *Times*, 11 May 1963, both in Southern Educational Reporting Service, Facts on Film (hereafter cited as SERS, FOF).
5. E. Franklin Frazier, *Black Bourgeoisie* (Glencoe, Ill.: The Free Press, 1957), pp. 234-237. Membership Records, National Association for the Advancement of Colored People Papers, Birmingham Files, 1951-1955, on microfilm, Birmingham Public Library, Department of Archives and Manuscripts, Birmingham, Alabama (hereafter cited as BPL, DAM).
6. Corley, "Quest," pp. 48-49; Membership Records, NAACP Papers, Birmingham File, 1951-1955; Numan V. Bartley, *The Rise of Massive Resistance* (Baton Rouge, La.: Louisiana State University Press, 1969), pp. 215-216; New York *Times*, 2 June 1956, in SERS, FOF; Morris, *Origins*, p. 34.
7. Jacquelyn [Johnson] Clarke, "Goals and Techniques in Three Civil Rights Organizations in Alabama" (Ph.D. dissertation, Ohio State University, 1960), Appendix B, pp. 134-136 (Clarke later published this work, which analyzes the Birmingham, Montgomery and Tuskegee movements, under the title *These Rights They Seek*; however, the appendixes were omitted. Appendix B contains an essay written by Shuttlesworth in 1959 entitled "An Account of the Alabama Christian Movement for Human Rights."); Jacquelyn Johnson Clarke,

These Rights They Seek (Washington, D.C.: Public Affairs Press, 1962), p. 32; Birmingham *News*, 30 September 1955, in SERS, FOF.

8. Clarke, "Goals," Appendix B, p. 136-139.

9. *Ibid.*

10. New Orleans *Times-Picayune*, 7 June 1956; Birmingham *News*, 6 June 1956; Chattanooga *Times*, 7 June 1956; all in SERS, FOF; Birmingham *World*, 8 June 1956, p. 1; Morris, *Origins*, p. 71; Clarke, "Goals," Appendix B, pp. 139-140.

11. New Orleans *Times-Picayune*, 7 June 1956, in SERS, FOF; Clarke, "Goals," Appendix B. pp. 146-147; Morris, *Origins*, pp. 45-46.

12. Birmingham *World*, 5 June 1956, p. 6, Fairclough, "The Preachers and the People," p. 418.

13. Clarke, "Goals," Appendix B. pp. 146-147; Morris, *Origins*, p. 45; Clarke, *These Rights They Seek*, p. 66.

14. Fairclough, "The Preachers and the People," pp. 404-405, 426; Clarke, "Goals," Appendix B, p. 146.

15. Reverend Fred L. Shuttlesworth's Address at the May 17, 1957 Prayer Pilgrimage in Washington, D.C., Shuttlesworth Papers, Box Four; David J. Garrow, *Bearing the Cross; Martin Luther King, Jr., and the Southern Christian Leadership Conference* (New York: William Morrow and Co., Inc., 1986), pp. 20-24; Morris, *Origins,* pp. 20, 43, 62, 68-69; Fairclough, "The Preachers and the People," pp. 426, 411.

16. Morris, *Origins,* pp. 50, 71-72; Clarke, *These Rights They Seek*, pp. 34-35; Fairclough, "The Preachers and the People," p. 411.

17. Morris, *Origins*, pp. 8-10, 72 (Morris, a black sociologist, disagrees with Max Weber's view that "charisma and organizational dynamics are antithetical." Morris convincingly argues that the two can work together. Morris writes that the SCLC's real power stemmed from its ability effectively to combine organizational dynamics (movement centers [such as the MIA and the ACMHR]), with charismatic leadership [by King and Shuttlesworth])." See n. 36, pp. 303-304; Clarke, "Goals," Appendix B, p. 152; Garrow, *Bearing the Cross*, pp. 56-58; Fairclough, "The Preachers and the People," p. 411; "People in Motion," Shuttlesworth Papers, Box One. (This xeroxed history of the Birmingham movement was published in 1965 by the ACMHR and the Southern Conference Educational Fund, Inc.)

CHAPTER ONE

1. Jacquelyn [Johnson] Clarke, "Goals and Techniques in Three Civil Rights Organizations in Alabama" (Ph.D. dissertation, Ohio State University, 1960), Appendix B, p. 136-139. Clarke later published this work, which analyzes the Birmingham, Montgomery and Tuskegee movements, under the title *These Rights They Seek*; however, the appendixes were omitted. Appendix B contains an essay written by Reverend Fred L. Shuttlesworth in 1959 entitled "An

Account of the Alabama Christian Movement for Human Rights"; Jacquelyn Johnson Clarke, *These Rights They Seek* (Washington, D.C.: Public Affairs Press, 1962), pp. 60-65; Montgomery *Advertiser* and Birmingham *News*, 12 June 1956, in Southern Educational Reporting Service, *Facts on Film*, (hereafter cited as SERS, FOF).

2. Birmingham *News*, 10 July 1956, Birmingham *World*, 26 July 1956, 1 August 1956, all in SERS, FOF.

3. Clarke, "Goals," Appendix B, pp. 134-135; Aldon D. Morris, *The Origins of the Civil Rights Movement: Black Communities Organizing for Change* (New York: The Free Press, 1984), p. 71; "A Chronicle of Violence in Birmingham, Alabama, 1954 to mid-1958," Southern Regional Council Papers, Folder 41.2.1.3.6, Birmingham Public Library, Department of Archives and Manuscripts, Birmingham, Alabama (hereafter cited as BPL, DAM); Birmingham *News*, 23 June 1955, in SERS, FOF.

4. Birmingham *News*, 20, 22, 27 August 1956, in SERS, FOF; Robert Gaines Corley, "The Quest for Racial Harmony: Race Relations in Birmingham, Alabama, 1947-1963," (Ph.D. dissertation, University of Virginia, 1979), pp. 73-77; Clarke, "Goals," Appendix B, pp. 148-149.

5. David J. Garrow, *Bearing the Cross: Martin Luther King, Jr., and the Southern Christian Leadership Conference* (New York: William Morrow and Co., Inc., 1986), p. 82; Clarke, "Goals," Appendix B, p. 149; Birmingham *World*, 26, 29 December 1956; Birmingham *News*, 20, 21 December 1956.

6. Birmingham *World*, 26 December 1956; Birmingham *News*, 22 December 1956.

7. Birmingham *News* and Nashville *Banner*, 25 December 1956, in SERS, FOF; Garrow, *Bearing the Cross*, p. 81.

8. Birmingham *News*, 26 December 1956; Birmingham *World*, 29 December 1956; *Christian Science Monitor*, 21 August 1958, all in SERS, FOF.

9. Birmingham *News*, 26 December 1956; Morris, *Origins*, p. 70.

10. Birmingham *News*, 26 December 1956.

11. Birmingham *News*, 26 December 1956; Birmingham *World*, 29 December 1956; "People in Motion," Reverend Fred L. Shuttlesworth Papers, Box One, Martin Luther King, Jr., Center for Nonviolent Social Change, Archives, Atlanta, Georgia. (This xeroxed history of the Birmingham movement was published in 1965 by the ACMHR and the Southern Conference Educational Fund, Inc.)

12. Clarke, "Goals," Appendix B, p. 150; *Christian Science Monitor*, 27 December 1956, in SERS, FOF.

13. Birmingham *News*, 26 December 1956; Clarke, "Goals," Appendix B, p. 150; *Christian Science Monitor*, 27 December 1956, in SERS, FOF.

14. Birmingham *News*, 26 December 1956; Birmingham *World*, 29 December 1956; *Christian Science Monitor*, 27 December 1956, in SERS, FOF.

15. Birmingham *World*, 26, 29 December 1956; *Christian Science Monitor*, 27 December 1956, in SERS, FOF.

16. Birmingham *News*, 26 December 1956; Birmingham *World*, 29 December 1956.

17. *Ibid.*, *Christian Science Monitor*, 27 December 1956, in SERS, FOF.
18. Morris, *Origins*, p. 82; Garrow, *Bearing the Cross*, pp. 83-90; Adam Fairclough, "The Preachers and the People: The Origins and Early Years of the Southern Christian Leadership Conference, 1955-1959," *Journal of Southern History*, 52 9 August 1986), pp. 423-425.
19. Birmingham *News*, 5 March 1957, in SERS, FOF; Birmingham *World*, 9 March 1957, in Shuttlesworth Papers, Box Four.
20. Birmingham *World*, 9 March 1957, and Birmingham *Mirror*, 6 March 1957, both in Shuttlesworth Papers, Box Four.
21. Birmingham *World*, 9 March 1957, in Shuttlesworth Papers, Box Four; *Christian Science Monitor*, 10 September 1957, in SERS, FOF; Clarke, "Goals," Appendix B, p. 149.
22. Birmingham *News*, 12, 18 March 1957, in SERS, FOF.
23. Birmingham *News*, 18, 21 March 1957, SERS, FOF.
24. Program from the ACMHR's first anniversary, 1957, Shuttlesworth Papers, Box One; Birmingham *News*, 15 October 1956, in SERS, FOF; Corley, "Quest," pp. 158-162.
25. Birmingham *News*, 29 August 1957, in SERS, FOF; Corley, "Quest," pp. 133-136.
26. Corley, "Quest," pp. 133-137; Numan V. Bartley, *The Rise of Massive Resistance* (Baton Rouge, La.: Louisiana State University Press, 1969), pp. 291-292.
27. Birmingham *News*, 9 September 1957, *Christian Science Monitor*, 10 September 1957, in SERS, FOF.
28. *Ibid.*; Corley, "Quest," pp. 138-139.
29. *Ibid.*; Anthony Lewis, *Portrait of a Decade: The Second American Revolution* (New York: Bantam Books, 1971, paperback edition), p. 41.
30. Birmingham *News* and *Christian Science Monitor*, 10 September 1957, in SERS, FOF.
31. Birmingham *News*, 10 September 1957, in SERS, FOF.
32. "Emory F. Via's Field Report on Birmingham, 2-4 April 1958," SRC Papers, Folder 41.2.16.3.41, BPL, DAM; Montgomery *Advertiser*, Birmingham *News*, Atlanta *Journal*, and Greensboro *Daily News*, 30 June 1958, all in SERS, FOF. Newspapers published outside of Alabama usually ran Associated Press or United Press International copy, so the accounts differed from the local stories. Birmingham's newspapers often played down racial indicents by burying the accounts on the back pages. The Birmingham *News* represented the view of the white establishment and was "politely" racist as opposed to the more extremist Birmingham *Post-Herald*.
33. Birmingham *News*, 15 January 1957; Montgomery *Advertiser*, 5 July 1958, in SERS, FOF.
34. Birmingham *News*, 28 April 1958, 1 July 1958 in SERS, FOF.
35. Corley, "Quest," pp. 55-56; Birmingham *News*, 18, 20 July 1958; Atlanta *Journal*, 19 July 1958, in SERS, FOF.
36. Bob Hughes to Frank W. Baldan, 15 September 1958, SRC Papers, Folder 41.1.1.1.15, and "Birmingham High School Mob Scene," late 1958, SRC

Papers, Folder 41.2.1.3.6 both in BPL, DAM; Birmingham *News*, 31 August 1958, in SERS, FOF.

37. Birmingham *News*, 14, 17 October 1958, in SERS, FOF.
38. Birmingham *News*, 17 October 1958, in SERS, FOF.
39. Birmingham *News*, 20, 21 October 1958; Nashville *Tennessean*, 21 October 1958, in SERS, FOF; William Kunstler, *Deep in My Heart* (New York: William Morrow and Co., Inc., 1966), pp. 80-81.
40. Birmingham *News*, 21 October 1958; Montgomery *Advertiser*, 21, 22, October 1958, in SERS, FOF.
41. Birmingham *News*, 23 October 1958, in SERS, FOF; Corley, "Quest," pp. 223-225.
42. Birmingham *News*, 22, 24 October 1958; Montgomery *Advertiser*, 24 October 1958, in SERS, FOF; Bob Hughes to Fred Routh, 29 October 1958, SRC Papers, Folder 41.1.1.1.15, BPL DAM.
43. Birmingham *News*, 25, 26 October 1958, in SERS, FOF; Hughes to Routh.
44. Birmingham *News*, 27 October 1958; Montgomery *Advertiser*, 28, 29 October 1958, in SERS, FOF; Hughes to Routh; Bob Hughes memo to Leadership Personnel of Alabama Council on Human Relations, 6 November 1958, SRC Papers, Folder 41.1.1.1.15, BPL, DAM.
45. Birmingham *News*, and Montgomery *Advertiser*, 28 October 1958, in SERS, FOF; Hughes to Routh.
46. Hughes to Routh; Nashville *Banner*, 1 November 1958, in SERS, FOF.
47. Hughes to Routh; Clarke, "Goals," Appendix B, p. 142; Geraldine Moore, *Behind the Ebony Mask* (Birmingham, Alabama: Southern University Press, 1961), p. 33.
48. Bob Hughes to syndicated columnist Jack Anderson, 12 November 1958, SRC Papers, Folder 41.2.16.3.41, Hughes memo to Leadership Personnel, both in BPL, DAM; Clarke "Goals," Appendix B, p. 142; Birmingham *News*, 18, 25 November 1958, in SERS, FOF.
49. Baltimore *Afro-American*, 22 November 1958, in Shuttlesworth Papers, Box Four; Birmingham *News*, 13 December 1958, in SERS, FOF; Clarke, "Goals," Appendix B, p. 142.

CHAPTER TWO

1. "President's Annual Report," 5 June 1959, Reverend Fred L. Shuttlesworth Papers, Box One, Martin Luther King Jr., Center for Nonviolent Social Change, Archives, Atlanta, Georgia.
2. *Ibid.*; Jacquelyn [Johnson] Clarke, "Goals and Techniques in Three Civil Rights Organizations in Alabama" (Ph.D. dissertation, Ohio State University, 1960), Appendix B, p. 153; Police report, 8 March 1961, Eugene "Bull" Connor Papers, Folder 9-24, Birmingham Public Library, Department of Archives and Manuscripts, Birmingham, Alabama (hereafter cited as BPL, DAM).

3. Jacquelyn Johnson Clarke, *These Rights They Seek* (Washington, D.C.: Public Affairs Press, 1962), pp. 23, 71-72; Clarke, "Goals," Appendix B, p. 145.

4. Clarke, *These Rights They Seek*, pp. 55-58.

5. Clarke, "Goals," Appendix D, pp. 163-173. Appendix D contains Clarke's statistical information gathered at the ACMHR mass meeting. She breaks the data down into various graphs; Geraldine Moore, *Behind the Ebony Mask* (Birmingham, Ala.: Southern University Press, 1961), pp. 33-35.

6. Clarke, "Goals," Appendix D, pp. 163-173.

7. *Ibid.*

8. "President's Annual Report," 5 June 1959, Shuttlesworth Papers, Box One; Clarke, "Goals," Appendix B, p. 152; Program from the June 1962 anniversary of the ACMHR, Shuttlesworth Papers, Box One; Adam Fairclough, "The Preachers and the People: The Origins and Early Years of the Southern Christian Leadership Conference, 1955-1959," *Journal of Southern History*, 52 (August 1986), pp. 423-424.

9. Clarke, *These Rights They Seek*, pp. 60-63; Moore, *Behind the Ebony Mask*, p. 201; Pittsburgh *Courier*, 7 February 1959, Shuttlesworth Papers, Box Four.

10. Birmingham *News*, 15 June 1959, in Southern Educational Reporting Service, Facts on Film (hereafter cited as SERS, FOF); Clarke, *These Rights They Seek*, pp. 65-66.

11. Birmingham *News*, 13, 27 July, 31 August, 1 September 1959, in SERS, FOF; Bob Hughes to Harold Fleming, 27 August 1959, with extensive postscript written 28 August 1959, Southern Regional Council Papers, Folder 41.1.1.1.17, BPL, DAM.

12. Montgomery *Advertiser*, 8 September 1959, in SERS, FOF; Aldon D. Morris, *The Origins of the Civil Rights Movement: Black Communities Organizing for Change* (New York: The Free Press, 1984), p. 32; David J. Garrow, *Bearing the Cross: Martin Luther King, Jr., and the Southern Christian Leadership Conference* (New York: William Morrow and Co., Inc., 1986), 116-120; Fairclough, "The Preachers and the People," p. 436.

13. Birmingham *News*, 20 October 1959, in SERS, FOF; Shuttlesworth to Connor, 26 October 1959, Shuttlesworth Papers, Box Three.

14. Birmingham *News*, 23 November, 21 December 1959, in SERS, FOF; Statement adopted 14 December 1959 by ACMHR, fliers on how to ride desegregated buses, Shuttlesworth Papers, Box One.

15. Birmingham *News*, 29 December 1959, 21 February 1960, in SERS, FOF; "Registration of Negro Voters in Alabama in 1954," and voting statistics, 1956, in SRC Papers, Folder 41.1.6.2.31.

16. Birmingham *News*, 8 December 1959, in SERS, FOF; Garrow, *Bearing the Cross*, p. 124; Clarke, *These Rights They Seek*, pp. 43, 75.

17. Morris, *Origins*, p. 201; Bob Hughes to Harold Fleming, 1 March 1960, SRC Papers, Folder 41.1.1.1.19; Garrow, *Bearing the Cross*, p. 138.

18. Birmingham *News*, 1, 13 March 1960; New York *Times*, 12 April 1960, in SERS, FOF.

19. Birmingham *News*, 1 April 1960; New York *Times*, 12 April 1960, in SERS, FOF; "ACMHR Press Release," 30 March 1960, Shuttlesworth Papers, Box

One; Shuttlesworth's statement to the United States Commission on Civil Rights, Spring 1961, Shuttlesworth Papers, Box Four.

20. New York *Times*, 12 April, 4 May 1960, Charleston *News & Courier,* 21 April 1960, Birmingham *News*, 20 April 1960, in SERS, FOF.

21. "Birmingham: Integration's Hottest Crucible," *Time*, 15 December 1958, p. 16; Pittsburgh *Courier*, 26 April 1960, Shuttlesworth Papers, Box Four.

22. Birmingham *News*, 15 April 1960, in SERS, FOF.

23. "History of the Alabama Christian Movement Choir," Shuttlesworth Papers, Box One; Bernice Reagon, "Songs of the Civil Rights Movement, 1955-1965: A Study in Cultural History" (Ph.D dissertation, Howard University, 1975), pp. 146-148, 178; Police report, 28 March 1961 and 15 August 1961, Connor Papers, Folders 9-24 and 9-25 respectively.

24. Montgomery *Advertiser* and Chattanooga *Times*, 18 August 1960, in SERS, FOF; updated and unidentified newspaper clipping on arrest of Shuttlesworth's children, Shuttlesworth Papers, Box Four.

25. Morris, *Origins*, pp. 141-145; Frank Adams, *Unearthing Seeds of Fire: The Idea of Highlander* (Charlotte, N.C.: John F. Blair, 1975), pp. 97-99; Police report, 17 January 1961 and 15 August 1961, Connor Papers, Folders 9-24 and 9-25 respectively.

26. Birmingham *News*, 8 September, 22 November, 6 December 1960, in SERS, FOF; Transcript of *Shuttlesworth and Billups* v. *Connor and Moore*, Shuttlesworth Papers, Box Three.

27. Morris, *Origins*, pp. 46-47, 74-75; Clarke, *These Rights They Seek*, p. 64; Garrow, *Bearing the Cross*, p. 238. Information concerning an average mass meeting gathered from a reading of the police reports located in the Connor Papers.

28. Clarke, *These Rights They Seek*, pp. 65, 73; Morris, *Origins*, pp. 66-71; undated and unidentified magazine clipping on Shuttlesworth and the ACMHR, and *Shuttlesworth* v. *Connor*, both in Shuttlesworth Papers, Boxes Two and Three respectively. Information concerning the collection at an average mass meeting taken from the police reports located in the Connor Papers.

29. *Shuttlesworth* v. *Connor*, Shuttlesworth Papers, Box Three; "People in Motion" and ACMHR to Birmingham City Commission, 1 December 1958, both in Shuttlesworth Papers, Box One.

30. Clarke, *These Rights They Seek*, pp. 74-75; Address at the 17 May , 1957, Prayer Pilgrimage in Washington, D.C., Shuttlesworth Papers, Box Four; Police report, 23 January 1961, Connor Papers, Folder 9-24.

31. Police report, 11 May 1961, Connor Papers, Folder 9-24; George R. Osborne, *Nation*, 5 May 1962, p. 399; Morris, *Origins*, p. 231.

32. CBS, "CBS Reports," 18 May 1961, "Who speaks for Birmingham?" Howard K. Smith. Transcript in the Tutwiler Collection of Southern History and Literature, BPL; Police report, 16 May 1961, Connor Papers, Folder 9-24; Garrow, *Bearing the Cross*, p. 156.

33. Clayborne Carson, *In Struggle: SNCC and the Black Awakening of the 1960s* (Cambridge, Mass.: Harvard University Press, 1981), pp. 34-36; Montgomery *Advertiser*, 20 May 1961, in SERS, FOF.

34. Garrow, *Bearing the Cross*, pp. 156-158; undated and unidentified newspaper clipping, Shuttlesworth Papers, Box Four; Police report, 24 May 1961, Connor Papers, folder 9-24.
35. Police report, 14 March 1961, Connor Papers, Folder 9-24; CBS, "Who Speaks for Birmingham?"
36. CBS, "Who Speaks for Birmingham?"
37. Pittsburgh *Courier*, 10 June 1961, and undated and unidentified newspaper clipping, Shuttlesworth Papers, Box Four; Police reports, 24 May, 27 June 1961, Folder 9-24 and 19 July, 3 October 1961, Folder 9-25, Connor Papers.

CHAPTER THREE

1. Benjamin Muse Field Report, "Dangerous Situation in Birmingham," 11 January 1962, Southern Regional Council Papers, Folder 41.1.3.2.8, Birmingham Public Library, Department of Archives and Manuscripts (hereafter cited as BPL, DAM); Reverend Norman Jimerson to Paul Rilling, 5 January 1962, SRC Papers, Folder 41.2.1.3.9; Mary-Helen Vick, "A Survey of the Governing Body of Birmingham, Alabama, 1910-1964" (M.A. thesis, Alabama College in Montevallo, 1965), pp. 93-95.
2. Montgomery *Advertiser*, 30 September 1959, in Southern Educational Reporting Service, *Facts on Film* (hereafter cited as SERS, FOF); Jimerson to Rilling, 11 December 1961, SRC Papers, Folder 41.1.1.1.23.
3. Jimerson To Rilling, 27 December 1961, SRC Papers, Folder 41.1.1.1.23; Jimerson To Rilling, 5 January 1962, SRC Papers, Folder 41.2.1.3.9; Muse Field Report, 11 January 1962, SRC Papers, Folder 41.1.3.2.8; "That's What'll Happen," *Time*, 22 December 1961, p. 15; Charles Morgan Jr., *A Time to Speak* (New York: Harper & Row Publishers, 1964), p. 60.
4. Muse Field Report, 11 January 1962, SRC Papers, Folder 41.1.3.2.8; Police Report, 20 December 1961, Eugene "Bull" Connor Papers, Folder 9-25, BPL, DAM.
5. George R. Osborne, "Boycott in Birmingham," *Nation*, 5 May 1962, p. 400; Kevin Anderson Cassady, "Black Leadership and the Civil Rights Struggle in Birmingham, Alabama, 1960-1964" (Undergraduate thesis, Georgetown University, 1986), p. 28; "This We Believe," Reverend Fred L. Shuttlesworth Papers, Box Three, Martin Luther King, Jr., Center for Nonviolent Social Change, Archives, Atlanta; Muse Field Report, 11 January 1962, SRC Papers, Folder 41.1.3.2.8.
6. Robert Gaines Corley, "The Quest for Racial Harmony: Race Relations in Birmingham, Alabama, 1947-1963" (Ph.D. dissertation, University of Virginia, 1979), p. 232; David J. Garrow, *Bearing the Cross: Martin Luther King, Jr., and the Southern Christian Leadership Conference* (New York: William Morrow and Co., Inc., 1986), p. 199; Cassady, "Black Leadership," pp. 28-29, 33-34; Muse Field Report, 11 January 1962, SRC Papers, Folder 41.1.3.2.8

7. Cassady, "Black Leadership," pp. 33-34; Linda Dempsey Cochran, "Arthur Davis Shores: Advocate for Freedom" (M.A. thesis, Georgia Southern College, 1977), pp. 75, 96. Cochran writes of an interesting relationship between Shores and Bull Connor: "Shores relates that although Connor was a 'loud-mouthed, political opportunist,' he often cooperated with individual blacks in private conferences, unknown to his white masters. Publicly, he used Shores as a 'whipping boy' in his election campaigns, but advised officers at the Birmingham City Jail that if Shores represented one who was arrested, he was to be released immediately without bond." See footnote 50, p. 112; Howell Raines, *My Soul Is Rested* (New York: G.P. Putnam's Sons, Bantam Books paperback edition, 1978), p. 172; Andrew J. Young, "And Birmingham," *Drum Major*, 1 (Winter 1971), p. 23. The SCLC only published a few issues of *Drum Major* and the King Center in Atlanta has copies; Adam Fairclough, "The Preachers and the People: The Origins and Early Years of the Southern Christian Leadership Conference, 1955-1959," *Journal of Southern History*, 52 (August 1986), pp. 403-404.

8. Muse Field Report, 11 January 1962, SRC Papers, Folder 41.1.3.2.8; Jimerson to Rilling, 5 January 1962, SRC Papers, Folder 41.2.1.3.9; Muse Field Report on North Alabama, 13 July 1961, SRC Papers, Folder 41.1.3.2.7

9. Police Report, 24 January 1962, Connor Papers, Folder 12-17.

10. William Kunstler, *Deep In My Heart* (New York: William Morrow and Co., Inc., 1966), pp. 82-85; Pittsburgh *Courier*, undated clipping, Shuttlesworth Papers, Box Four.

11. Corley, "Quest," p. 232; Jimerson to Rilling, 5 February 1962, SRC Papers, Folder 41.1.1.1.24; *Nation*, 5 May 1962, pp. 400-401.

12. Rilling, "Interoffice Memo," 28 Frbruary, 5 March 1962, SRC Papers, Folder 41.1.1.1.24; Corley, "Quest," p. 232.

13. *Nation*, 5 May 1962, pp. 397, 401; Corley, "Quest," pp. 233-234; Jimerson, "Confidential Report," 5 April 1962, SRC Papers, Folder 41.1.1.1.24.

14. *Nation*, 5 May 1962, p. 401; Corley, "Quest," p. 234.

15. Undated and unidentified newspaper clipping, "NAACP Offers Help In Food Program, If . . . ," and undated Birmingham *News* clipping, "Birmingham: Face Facts," both in Shuttlesworth Papers, Box Two; Jimerson, "Confidential Report," 5 April 1962, SRC Papers, Folder 41.1.1.1.24; *Nation*, 5 May 1962, p. 401.

16. *Nation*, 5 May 1962, p. 401; Jimerson, "Confidential Report," 5 April 1962, SRC Papers, Folder 41.1.1.1.24; "Selective Buying: Right of Protest," flier distributed during boycott, Shuttlesworth Papers, Box One; Fairclough, "The Preachers and the People," p. 414.

17. Martin Luther King, Jr., *Why We Can't Wait* (New York: Harper & Row, Publishers, 1964), p. 45; Garrow, *Bearing the Cross,* p. 198; "More Race Pressure on Business," *Business Week*, 12 May 1962, p. 130; Jimerson, "Confidential Report," 5 April 1962, SRC Papers, Folder 41.1.1.1.24; *Nation*, 5 May 1962, p. 398.

18. Cassady, "Black Leadership," p. 39. Both Cassady and Corley believe the boycott failed because the city commission cut off the surplus food program;

"Selective Buying: Right of Protest," and "A Statement of Facts," both undated and in Shuttlesworth Papers, Box One; Police Report, 13 June 1962, Connor Papers, Folder 12-18.

19. Jimerson to Rilling, 3 October 1962, and John J. Brewbaker to Leslie W. Dunbar, 29 October 1962, both in SRC Papers, Folder 41.1.1.1.25; Police Report, 25 July 1962, Connor Papers, Folder 12-18; Garrow, *Bearing the Cross*, p. 220; Corley, "Quest," pp. 235-237.

20. Garrow, *Bearing the Cross*, p. 220; Corley, "Quest," pp. 235-237; King, *Why We Can't Wait*, p. 45.

21. Garrow, *Bearing the Cross*, p. 221; King, *Why We Can't Wait*, p. 47; Vincent Harding, "A Beginning in Birmingham," *Reporter*, 6 June 1963, p. 14.

22. Jimerson to Burke Marshall, 19 October 1962, SRC Papers, Folder 41.2.1.3.9; Jimerson to Rilling, 25 October 1962, SRC Papers, Folder 41.1.1.1.25; Jimerson to Rilling, 19 November 1962, SRC Papers, Folder 41.2.1.3.9; Mary Phyllis Harrison, "A Change in the City Government of the City of Birmingham: 1962-1963" (M.A. thesis, University of Montevallo, 1974), pp. 21-23, 37-39; Garrow, *Bearing the Cross*, pp. 224-225.

23. John A. Ricks III, "'De Lawd' Descends and is Crucified: Martin Luther King, Jr., in Albany, Georgia," *Journal of Southwest Georgia History*, 2 (Fall 1984), pp. 12-14; King, *Why We Can't Wait*, p. 48; Garrow, *Bearing the Cross*, pp. 201-216, 226.

24. Aldon D. Morris, *The Origins of the Civil Rights Movement: Black Communities Organizing for Change* (New York: The Free Press, 1984), pp. 252-253; Garrow, *Bearing the Cross*, p. 228; Harvard Sitkoff, *The Struggle for Black Equality, 1954-1980* (New York; Hill and Wang, 1981), pp. 128-129, 144; Raines, *My Soul Is Rested*, p. 143.

25. King, *Why We Can't Wait*, pp. 47-48; See also Coretta Scott King, *My Life With Martin Luther King, Jr.* (New York: Holt Rinehart and Winston, 1969), p. 217; Morris, *Origins*, pp. 250-251, 258. Morris takes issue with Garrow's interpretation of the SCLC's strategy behind the Birmingham movement. Garrow believes King went to Birmingham for "federal commitment," or for the national movement. Morris believes King went to Birmingham to defeat local segregation, or for the local movement. As I have explained, I believe Shuttlesworth viewed the campaign as a local movement and King as a national movement.

26. Garrow, *Bearing the Cross*, pp. 229-231; King, *Why We Can't Wait*, p. 48.

27. Harrison, "Change inCity Government," p. 45; Garrow, *Bearing the Cross*, pp. 231-235; King, *Why We Can't Wait*, p. 55; C. S. King, *My Life With Martin Luther King, Jr*, p. 219.

28. Harrison, "Change in City Government," pp. 46-51.

29. ACMHR press release announcing the demonstrations, 4 April 1963, Connor Papers, Folder 13-2; Garrow, *Bearing the Cross*, pp. 236-237.

30. King, *Why We Can't Wait*, p. 56; Garrow, *Bearing the Cross*, pp. 236-239; Morris, *Origins*, pp. 262-263; Michael Dorman, *We Shall Overcome* (New York: Delacorte Press, 1964), p. 146.

31. Garrow, *Bearing the Cross*, p. 237; Fairclough, "The Preachers and the People," pp. 438-440. Fairclough asserts in footnote 150 on page 440 that "SCLC eventually formulated an operating assumption that about two percent of a given black community could be persuaded to volunteer for jail." Discounting the school children, this statistic appears to be high for Birmingham.

32. King, *Why We Can't Wait*, pp. 64-65; Morris, *Origins*, p. 263; Young, "And Birmingham," p. 25; Fairclough, "The Preachers and the People," p. 426.

33. *Reporter*, 6 June 1963, p. 14; Garrow, *Bearing the Cross*, pp. 238-240; Morris, *Origins*, p. 256; Pittsburgh *Courier*, 7 February 1959, Shuttlesworth Papers, Box Four; Muse Field Report, 11 January 1962, SRC Papers, Folder 41.1.3.2.8. Perhaps Ware wanted to prevent Shuttlesworth from being seen as the leader of the black community.

34. Young, "And Birmingham," p. 23. Both Garrow (*Bearing the Cross*, p. 227) and Morris (*Origins*, pp. 261-262) quote Young as fact on this matter. I have concluded that neither Porter and Cross nor their churches were involved in the ACMHR by noting the locations of the mass meetings—a sign of support for the movement—according to the police reports in the Connor Papers. After King arrived, they began to hold meetings in these two churches. One exception is a meeting held on February 12, 1962, at Sixteenth Street Baptist. Shuttlesworth and Phifer were incarcerated, so King had come to address the mass meeting. Apparently Ware, who had introduced King at an Emancipation Day meeting back in 1956 held in Sixteenth Street Baptist used his influence to have King speak at Sixteenth Street again. On the 12 February 1962 meeting, Gaston and Pitts shared the rostrum with King. ACMHR treasurer W.E. Shortridge also spoke and criticized the "several churches all over town [that] had refused the movement the use of their church"; Bertha Bendall Norton, *Birmingham's First Magic Century* (Birmingham, Alabama: Lakeshore Press, 1970), p. 48; Police Reports, 6 and 20 February 1962, Connor Papers, Folder 12-17; Garrow, *Bearing the Cross*, p. 224.

35. Garrow, *Bearing the Cross*, pp. 199, 237-238.

36. Young, "And Birmingham," p. 23.

37. Garrow, *Bearing the Cross,* pp. 240-241; Police Report, 12 April 1963, Connor Papers, Folder 13-4.

38. Garrow, *Bearing the Cross*, pp. 241-242; Raines, *My Soul Is Rested*, p. 143.

39. Garrow, *Bearing the Cross*, pp. 242-244; Birmingham *Post-Herald*, 13 April 1963, p. 10; David Levering Lewis, *King: A Biography* (Urbana, Illinois: University of Illinois Press, 1979), p. 184; Police Report, 12 April 1963, Connor Papers, Folder 13-4; Transcript of King's phone conversation with his wife taped by police, 15 April 1963, Connor Papers, Folder 13-3.

40. Lewis, *King*, p. 186; King, *Why We Can't Wait*, pp. 77-100; Birmingham *Post-Herald*, 13 April 1963, p. 10; Garrow, *Bearing the Cross*, pp. 246-247; Sitkoff, *The Struggle for Black Equality*, p. 132; Young, "And Birmingham," p. 26.

41. Garrow, *Bearing the Cross*, pp. 246-247; Morris, *Origins*, pp. 253-254, 265; August Meier and Elliott Rudwick, *CORE: A Study in the Civil Rights Movement, 1942-1968* (New York: Oxford University Press, 1973), p. 219.

42. Morris, *Origins,* p. 267; Garrow, *Bearing the Cross,* pp. 247-248; Police Report, 3 May 1963, Connor Papers, Folder 13-5; Fairclough, "The Preachers and the People," p. 440.
43. Police department memo on King's press conference, 3 May 1963, Connor Papers, Folder 13-5; Dorman, *We Shall Overcome,* pp. 149-150; Garrow, *Bearing the Cross,* p. 249.
44. Garrow, *Bearing the Cross,* pp. 249-251; Police Report, 3 May 1963, Connor Papers, Folder 13-5; Dorman, *We Shall Overcome,* p. 150.
45. Dorman, *We Shall Overcome,* p. 150; King, *Why We Can't Wait,* pp. 107-108; Young, "And Birmingham," p. 27; Morris, *Origins,* p. 268; Lewis, *King,* p. 194.
46. Garrow, *Bearing the Cross,* pp. 251-252; Morris, *Origins,* p. 269.
47. Garrow, *Bearing the Cross,* p. 252; Sitkoff, *The Struggle for Black Equality,* pp. 139-140; Dorman, *We Shall Overcome,* pp. 151-153; Anthony Lewis, *Portrait of a Decade* (New York: Bantam Books, Inc., 1971), p. 159.
48. Garrow, *Bearing the Cross,* pp. 252-254; Dorman, *We Shall Overcome,* pp. 153-154; Raines, *My Soul Is Rested,* pp. 148, 163.
49. Garrow, *Bearing the Cross,* pp. 254-255; Raines, *My Soul Is Rested,* pp. 190; New York *Times,* 11 May 1963, in SERS, FOF.
50. Garrow, *Bearing the Cross,* pp. 255-256.
51. Raines, *My Soul is Rested,* pp. 172-174; Garrow, *Bearing the Cross,* pp. 256-257. The exchange between Shuttlesworth and King stemmed from deeper causes than Shuttlesworth's sedation following his hospital stay and the fact that he was still under the effects of tranquilizers when the argument took place, Shuttlesworth's anger at not being notified that the demonstrations had been called off, his distrust of Burke Marshall and his irritation that King had failed to visit him in the hospital, as Garrow suggests. Shuttlesworth explained to Raines, "I don't think that the man [King] was a liar, I really don't. I have seen him talk in ways to make people think that he might would have done it another way, but I do not think that Martin Luther King, Jr., was a liar. I don't think that. I don't think that . . ."
52. *Ibid.*
53. Garrow, *Bearing the Cross,* pp. 257-258; Dorman, *We Shall Overcome,* pp. 159-162.
54. Garrow, *Bearing the Cross,* p. 259; Dorman, *We Shall Overcome,* pp. 162-165.
55. Young, "And Birmingham," p. 23; Raines, *My Soul is Rested,* p. 175; Garrow, *Bearing the Cross,* pp. 269-271. August Meier and Elliott M. Rudwick argue in *From Plantation to Ghetto: An Interpretative History of American Negroes* (New York: Hill & Wang, 1966), p. 236, that the truce in Birmingham brought blacks "not 'Freedom Now' but token concessions that later were not carried out." After the bombing of Sixteenth Street Baptist Church on September 15, 1963, which resulted in the deaths of four innocent black girls and renewed riots, King threatened to return to Birmingham and lead demonstrations. After hearing of King's threat, Gaston and Shores issued a press release which stated: "We want to make it perfectly clear that we give full support to the leadership of Dr. Martin Luther King, Rev. F. L. Shuttlesworth, and the Alabama Christian Movement for Human Rights. We heartily agree in their guiding

principles and commitment, that the Negro community should see some results within a reasonable time to ease the tension and oppression we suffer." "If we are not able to solve our problems through negotiations, we are glad to know that the resources of Dr. King and his organization are available . . ." Statement of Dr. A. G. Gaston and Atty. Arthur D. Shores, 30 September 1963, Shuttlesworth Papers, Box Three.

Selected Bibliography

I. MANUSCRIPT COLLECTIONS

Atlanta, Ga. Martin Luther King, Jr., Center for Nonviolent Social Change, Archives. Reverend Fred L. Shuttlesworth Papers.

Birmingham, Ala. Birmingham Public Library Department of Archives and Manuscripts (hereafter cited as BPL, DAM). Eugene "Bull" Connor Papers.

Birmingham, Ala. BPL, DAM, National Association for the Advancement of Colored People, Birmingham File, 1951-1955.

Birmingham, Ala. BPL, DAM. Southern Regional Council Papers. The archives, under the excellent direction of Dr. Marvin Y. Whiting, has xeroxed the SRC papers that pertain to Birmingham. The original collection is in Atlanta, Ga.

II. UNPUBLISHED DISSERTATIONS, THESES AND OTHER MANUSCRIPTS

Bains, Lee Edmundson, Jr. "Birmingham 1963: Confrontation Over Civil Rights." B.A. honors thesis, Harvard College, 1977.

Cassady, Kevin Anderson. "Black Leadership and the Civil Rights Struggle in Birmingham, Alabama, 1960-1964." B.A. thesis, Georgetown University, 1986.

Clarke, Jacquelyne. "Goals and Techniques in Three Civil Rights Organizations in Alabama." Ph.D. dissertation, Ohio State University, 1960.

Cochran, Lynda Dempsey. "Arthur Davis Shores: Advocate for Freedom." M.A. thesis, Georgia Southern College, 1977.

Corley, Robert Gaines. "The Quest for Racial Harmony: Race Relations in Birmingham, Alabama, 1947-1963." Ph.D. dissertation, University of Virginia, 1979.

Harrison, Mary Phyllis. "A Change in the Government of the City of Birmingham: 1962-1963." M.A. thesis, University of Montevallo, 1974.

Reagon, Bernice. "Songs of the Civil Rights Movement, 1955-1965: A Study in Cultural History." Ph.D. dissertation, Howard University, 1975.

Vick, Mary-Helen. "A Survey of the Governing Body of Birmingham, Alabama, 1910-1964." M.A. thesis, Alabama College of Montevallo, 1965.

III. BOOKS

Adams, Frank. *Unearthing Seeds of Fire: The Idea of Highlander.* Charlotte, N.C.: John F. Blair, 1975.

Bartley, Numan V. *The Rise of Massive Resistance: Race and Politics in the South During the 1950's.* Baton Rouge, La.: Louisiana State University Press, 1969.

Carson, Clayborne. *In Struggle: SNCC and the Black Awakening of the 1960s.* Cambridge, Mass.: Harvard University Press, 1981.

Clarke, Jacquelyne Johnson. *These Rights They Seek.* Washington, D.C.: Public Affairs Press, 1962.

Dorman, Michael. *We Shall Overcome.* New York: Delacorte Press, 1964.

Frazier, E. Franklin. *Black Bourgeoisie.* Glenco, Ill.: The Free Press, 1957.

Garrow, David J. *Bearing the Cross: Martin Luther King, Jr., and the Southern Christian Leadership Conference.* New York: William Morrow and Co., Inc., 1986.

King, Coretta Scott. *My Life With Martin Luther King, Jr.,* New York: Holt Rinehart and Winston, 1969.

Kunstler, William. *Deep in My Heart.* New York: William Morrow and Co., Inc., 1966.

Lewis, Anthony. *Portrait of a Decade: The Second American Revolution.* New York: Bantam Books, Inc., 1971.

Lewis, David Levering. *King: A Biography.* Urbana, Ill.: University of Illinois Press, 1979.

Meier, August and Rudwick, Elliott M. *CORE: A Study in the Civil Rights Movement, 1942-1968.* New York: Oxford University Press, 1973.

_____. *From Plantation to Ghetto: An Interpretive History of American Negroes.* New York: Hill and Wang, 1966.

Moore, Geraldine Hamilton. *Behind the Ebony Mask.* Birmingham, Ala.: Southern University Press, 1961.

Morgan, Charles Jr. *A Time to Speak.* New York: Harper and Row, Publishers, 1964.

Morris, Aldon D. *The Origins of the Civil Rights Movement: Black Communities Organizing for Change.* New York: The Free Press, 1984.

Norton, Bertha Bendall. *Birmingham's First Magic Century.* Birmingham, Ala.: Lakeshore Press, 1970.

Raines, Howell. *My Soul Is Rested.* New York: Bantam Books, Inc., 1978.

Sitkoff, Harvard. *The Struggle For Black Equality.* New York: Hill and Wang, 1981.

IV. ARTICLES

"More Race Pressure on Business." *Business Week*, 12 May 1962, pp. 130-131.

Fairclough, Adam. "The Preachers and the People: The Origins and Early Years of the Southern Christian Leadership Conference, 1955-1959." *Journal of Southern History* 52 (August 1986): 403-440.

Harding, Vincent. "A Beginning in Birmingham." *Reporter*, 6 June 1963, pp. 13-19.

Leighton, George R. "Birmingham, Alabama: The City of Perpetual Promise." *Harper's Magazine*, August 1937, pp. 225-242.

Norrell, Robert J. "Caste in Steel: Jim Crow Careers in Birmingham, Alabama." *Journal of American History* 73 (December 1986): 669-694.

Osborne, George R. "Boycott in Birmingham." *Nation*, 5 May 1962, pp. 397-401.

"That's What'll Happen." *Time*, 22 December 1961, p. 15.

"Birmingham: Integration's Hottest Crucible." *Time*, 15 December 1958, p. 16.

Young, Andrew J. "And Birmingham." *Drum Major* 1 (Winter 1971): 21-27.

V. NEWSPAPERS AND OTHER SOURCES

Birmingham *News*, 1956-1963.
Birmingham *Post-Herald*, 1963.
Birmingham *World*, 1956-1963.
New York *Times*, 1960.

Smith, Howard K. "Who Speaks for Birmingham?" "CBS Reports," 18 May 1961, CBS. Transcript in the Tutwiler Collection of Southern History and Literature, Birmingham Public Library.

Southern Educational Reporting Service. *Facts on Film*, 1955-1963. SERS, FOF is an excellent collection of newspaper clippings (on microfilm) from papers across the country concerning race relations in the South.

Fred L. Shuttlesworth:
Indigenous Leader

LEWIS W. JONES

The Reverend Mr. Shuttlesworth is President of the Alabama Christian Movement for Human Rights. He *is* the leader of that organization. He sends no one; he goes himself, the five feet six inches and one hundred thirty pounds of him. When the organization was founded in Birmingham in May 1956 against the warnings from other Negro leaders of dire consequences for those involved, he promised his followers: "If anybody gets arrested, it'll be me; it anybody goes to jail it'll be me; if anybody suffers it'll be me; if anybody gets killed, it'll be me." Everything but killing has happened to him and on several occasions he has not been far from death. The consequence is: he is the leader of his organization, an optimistic leader of inexhaustible energy and a contagiously happy man.

Restive disadvantaged people who are determined to take action to improve themselves and their way of life look for leaders to guide them in securing for themselves those things to which they aspire. In many places leaders are persons who have recently come into a community, but Reverend Shuttlesworth is a product of Birmingham whose people identify with him as he speaks for them and they follow his lead. He knows what to expect of the adversaries of his people and to this opposition he also speaks in unmistakable terms. He brings no philosophy that his followers must be taught or when uncomprehending they must accept on faith. Reverend Shuttlesworth's faith is that of his followers compounded of fundamentalist religion, utilitarian education, and united action for the common good.

The word "dynamic" applies accurately to Fred Shuttlesworth. The first impression of this slightly built man is that he is restless, never still even when standing or sitting. Seated on a platform, he conveys the impression that he is on the verge of doing something. He leans forward, leans back, crosses and recrosses his legs. At the same time he gives intent attention to another person speaking, and he is the most appreciative audience anyone could wish. He is always responding to what is being said with a "yes," "amen," or an approving burst of laughter. As the speaker makes a telling point he slaps his thighs, throws his head back to chuckle or laugh. His bright birdlike eyes dart about the audience too, as if he were constantly taking an impressionistic poll of audience reaction.

When he speaks, which he does as frequently as he can to satisfy the many demands for him, he talks with assurance that his hearers are with him. His voice is clear and loud without any suggestion of mannerism or act. He is just talking, Fred Shuttlesworth talking, and what he says is all Fred Shuttlesworth. He is obviously not trying to assume a pose but what he says is impressive. The cliches he uses become peculiarly his own and his awkward sentences communicate. The audience quickly identifies with this man who can so cheerily report being mistreated or abused, and seethes for him with the indignation he does not express.

He has a great deal to say about God and you soon envy him his happy camaraderie with God. God is for him a powerful, reliable friend. There is nothing fearsome or mystical or intellectual about God as he talks. If you are disposed to be skeptical you are soon amazed by his unfeigned simplicity and convinced of the honesty of his belief. His brown face glows, his eyes sparkle, his total expression, a happy one that may be readily associated with his uncomplicated faith.

At the end of February 1961, Reverend Fred L. Shuttlesworth, Pastor of the Bethel Baptist Church, Birmingham, Alabama, was a litigant in 14 lawsuits involving 17 million dollars. He was free on bond awaiting hearings on his appeals on two convictions that carried jail sentences and fines. His automobile had been taken and sold at public auction to satisfy a judgment of one-half million dollars against him.

None of this litigation is related to the affairs of his church, whose building has been twice wrecked by bombs. In the vacant space alongside Bethel Church the parsonage stood until it was demolished by bombs. He has been beaten with brass knuckles in open daylight on the streets of Birmingham. His wife has been stabbed by a member of a mob. As his youngest daughter, then age 7, was being taken from the bombed parsonage to the hospital, she looked up at her father and said, "They can't kill us can they, Daddy?"

116

Fred was born in Montgomery County, Alabama, in 1922, but memory begins for him when he became "Shuttlesworth" in Oxmoor, a woebegone coal-mining village ten miles from Birmingham, at the age of three when his mother married Tom Shuttlesworth.

"Shuttlesworth is a step-name," he says; "it was my step-father's name. He reared me from the time I was small size and I took his name. Mama said one time that the man who takes care of you and brings you up is your father. I'm proud to praise him by honoring the name Shuttlesworth."

This candor and lack of concern about the paternal blood tie is a characteristic that identifies Fred Shuttlesworth with rural Negroes who accept the fact of having been born with a simplicity that more sophisticated people find difficult to appreciate. Getting born is not the business of these people when they have such an arduous task surviving and being somebody. The attitude taken can really make the question "What's in a name?" one to ponder.

One young man cheerily confused a census enumerator who was trying to get his name by saying, "I go by Alex Simpson but some folks call me 'Alex Smith' cause that was my mama's name before she married Josh Simpson but my sure 'nough daddy is Rufus Jones and sometime I went by Jones." People with no heritage or prospects of inheritance are on their own and the name they wear is pure convenience. For them a parent is the person who plays the role of parent.

Fred Shuttlesworth's "Daddy," Tom Shuttlesworth, was a sick man. Like the Oxmoor settlement he was a victim of the abuses of coal mining. Fred says, "This ore dust on his lungs" (silicosis) had "retired him." The Shuttlesworth family was poor "though we were never starving." Fred says that the boyhood he knew made him "learn to sympathize with the underdog." This sympathy was really identity because young Fred Shuttlesworth was by any criteria an underdog.

In Oxmoor he sold papers, *The Birmingham News* and *The Birmingham Post*, walking miles morning and night earning money to buy a bicycle. By the time he was twelve Fred had his bicycle to pedal into Birmingham to the food distribution office on 24th Street. The Shuttlesworths were "on welfare" and shared with their neighbors the shibboleth, "Let Roosevelt feed you and the good Lord lead you." Somehow the people were not downcast in an area acutely impoverished before "depressed area" became a familiar term.

Oxmoor had been a mining town but its mine had been worked out and its smelting plant dismantled. With them the town had disappeared. Calling themselves Oxmoor were two neighborhoods, one white and one Negro, separated by three or four miles. Only one white family lived in the Negro neighborhood and this was the family of the keeper of the general store.

The important Negro neighborhood institutions were an elementary school and two churches, the Methodist Church Fred attended and a Baptist Church. Fred completed the elementary school in 1935 when he was thirteen. In the fall of that year he enrolled in the Wenonah School to which he walked eight miles each way daily. The next year he transferred to the Rosedale High School from which he graduated Valedictorian of his class in 1940.

One of his Oxmoor teachers, Miss Windham, is given special mention for "making me get my lessons. When I had a lesson for Miss Windham I didn't get over it, I got it." He idolized two of his other teachers, Miss Worth and Mr. Ramsey. "I believed in them and they believed in me. These were the people from whom I learned to analyze things. This has been very helpful in dealing with some of these Southern politicians. Pay attention to what they do; not what they say."

The relationship of a teacher and a bright-eyed busy lad such as Fred is unnoticed high drama in dull depressed places like Oxmoor. The smart pupil who has a recognizable "something special" finds it being carefully nurtured by the teacher. For the child the teacher becomes what sociologists call the "significant other." Praise and approval from the teacher become the stuff of life for the pupil. And the admiration of the pupil, his "hanging around," asking questions other pupils don't ask, can give the teacher a sense of meaning in the midst of the monotony of routine teaching. The Oxmoor teachers fanned the spark of ambition in Fred and nudged him out of the heavy drag of poverty and defeat that was Oxmoor.

Dramatic personalities were preachers or deacons whose eloquence stirred the emotions of those who heard them preach or pray. Playing preacher by small boys is second in popularity only to playing house in such places as Oxmoor where there are so few roles for children to take in make-believe. Fred, like many other boys, found a model he wanted to pray like and one to preach like. There was Mr. Hawthorne of whom Fred says, "I would rather hear Mr. Hawthorne pray than to eat; I always wanted to pray like that." Fred wanted to preach in sonorous tones creating images that excited people as Reverend Tompkins did when he came to Oxmoor to "run revivals."

Fred says, "I learned in coming up not to imitate; to do what I could do according to my own special gift but the good I saw in people I certainly wanted to imitate. Oxmoor was a community like that; there were no great people in the sense of the word except that there can be little people who do big things. I think that is the greatness of Oxmoor." The romanticized aura of childhood hangs over Fred's memories of Oxmoor because with completion of high school he was to move from Oxmoor, swiftly precipitated into manhood.

His path from Oxmoor was a familiar one and the journey short. He continued to live at home but his activities were in the city. His first job was at the old Southern Club building on Fifth Avenue at 20th Street in Birmingham. On Wednesdays, Thursdays, and Fridays he worked as a handyman in the offices of doctors where people applying for relief were examined.

A young girl who was a nursing student at Tuskegee Institute worked in these offices in the summer of 1940 earning money to return to college in the Fall. She and Fred met and Fred began walking her home from work pushing his bicycle as they strolled along. She didn't return to college and in October 1941 they were married. He was 19 and she was 18.

With a wife, Fred decided he needed a better job than he had and found one at the Alpha Portland Cement Company. Out in Fairfield, Hayes Aircraft offered instruction in auto mechanics and Fred enrolled for this training. His wife worked in the doctors' offices and they moved into a small house to make their home.

In July 1943 with three of his friends who also had taken the training at Hayes Aircraft, Fred went to Mobile seeking employment in a defense industry. The day after they reached Mobile, the four of them were employed at Brookley Air Force Base. Fred began as a truck driver and later was a machine operator at the base until 1947.

Fred considers his move to Mobile as a critical point in his life. There were many temptations in the boom town that Mobile was in these years. However, his marriage had been a satisfying companionship from the beginning with his wife constantly with him. His friends from Birmingham were older men and "steady." He prides himself in not "getting with a wild and rowdy crowd." Instead he "felt the call" to enter in the ministry and decided to make his call known.

The Shuttlesworths had been Methodists at Oxmoor so he began attending a Methodist Church in Mobile. He can't explain why, but says that in the Methodist Church he just didn't get the spirit. He visited the Corinthian

Baptist Church with a friend and found the service "so invigorating" that he came home and told his wife how much he liked that church. He was not sure that this was the church for him and began visiting other churches to make comparisons. None of them had the spirit he felt at Corinthian so he returned there, joined the Church and was baptized. He declared his call to preach and went through the process necessary to receive a license to preach.

The license to preach has nothing to do with pastoring a church except that a minister must have the license in order to become a pastor. The license is given by a board of already licensed ministers who interrogate the candidate to determine his fitness. The candidate must convince this board of his unquestioning Christian faith, his complete subscription to Baptist doctrine, and his determination to uphold high standards of morals and manners. If the board is satisfactorily convinced, the candidate is prayed over, consecrated to God's service and given a certificate or license declaring him acceptable as a witness for God through preaching. Fred still had much to learn about his chosen profession, license for which did not require formal education or any systematic training.

With the enthusiasm so characteristic of him, Fred set about the study of his Bible. As he describes the period: "When I was licensed to preach at Corinthian in Mobile, I hadn't had a lot of special training in the Bible or a lot of theological studies. I was blessed with a job with which I had a lot of leisure; I would drive a truck out a block or two to deliver workmen, park it all day and didn't have anything to do until time to bring the men back but live and sleep so I took time to read the Bible. I had a chance to read it through two or three times. I was seeking for that Light, for understanding and the Bible is read with the idea of finding what God wants a person to do instead of finding fault with others. I learned the Bible generally that way."

Fred was a busy young man during these years. He was working full time at Brookley Field, preaching whenever he had an opportunity, using his spare time to build a house for his family, and studying to improve himself. He had not charted a career for himself but his activities showed his personality taking form as that of a man of action. He behaved as a person of ambition, however unfocused that ambition might be.

As a licensed "local" preacher for whom the ministry was an avocation he was surprised but gratified by the reaction of his fellow church members when occasionally he was asked to speak to them.

"At the church people would gladly hear me speak, so like a rocket I got up, and in no time I was a very popular preacher. That in itself is a bad thing if you don't know how to govern yourself. Always I somehow had that spirit of humility and understanding that God's way is sacred, however sinful we might find ourselves sometimes. God's purposes are eternal and change neither for me nor anybody. We have to bring ourselves up to fit them; they don't come down to fit us. So the Lord blessed my Ministry." Shuttlesworth was thus encouraged to greater effort in his preaching.

He and one of his friends bought adjacent lots beginning with $10 down payments. They planned to help each other construct houses on these lots. Fred had a truck. They would buy salvage building materials in Mobile and haul them to the building site and work on their houses. When two rooms built out of concrete blocks were completed, the Shuttlesworths moved into their home. The two rooms were only a beginning of a continuing job that added rooms until they had a rather comfortable six-room house.

Fred was not satisfied with his accomplishments or his prospects in Mobile. He had a good job making $1.25 an hour and had become a favorite of his supervisors so that his assignments were to less arduous tasks. But he did not see his future in this employment.

He was soon going to school at night. In Pritchard, a suburb of Mobile, there was a small school called Cedar Grove Seminary operated by the Mobile Sunlight Association. Fred enrolled for basic English, mathematics and simple elementary courses. He was encouraged by the Goodwill Missionaries to Negroes from the Southern Baptist Convention. These were an aged white couple, Dr. Maynard and his wife. They encouraged Fred to become better prepared for the ministry and promised to help him if he would sacrifice and go to college.

There is a small Negro Baptist college at Selma, Alabama, called, hopefully, Selma University. Fred went there from Cedar Grove Seminary as a participant in an oratorical contest in which the applause and compliments he got made him decide that he would like to study at that institution. The decision was not easy because the Shuttlesworths now had two children, a home about paid for and Fred's permanent job at Brookley Field.

Fred had security in his job despite difficulties he had made for himself on the job. He was a pleasant well-liked fellow but was known to be outspoken and for a small man, uncommonly fearless. In the department where he worked there was a fellow employee, white Mississippian, who took satisfaction from badgering the Negroes. His favorite entertainment was to tell stories of the stern control of Negroes where he came from. He enjoyed the discomfort of the Negro workers who had to listen to these stories which they heard without retort.

One day this man was telling a story that described Negroes who came into the white section of his town taking off their hats and walking in the streets bareheaded until they left the neighborhood. He drew the moral that the Negroes knew their places, all of them observed this practice and whites and Negroes "got along just fine."

Fred did not remain quiet but addressed this tormentor, "You want to know how you got along fine? Because you didn't have no Negroes in your town with guts. I haven't been in your town and if I ever get there you will see a Negro with his hat on walking on your sidewalks. That'll be one time a Negro won't be walking in the street bareheaded." He swaggered away before the white man could reply, a hero of his Negro fellow workers.

A more serious situation was precipitated when Fred took action on behalf of some of his fellow workers he felt were being treated unfairly. He was then driving a truck for a group of workers who were constructing a runway on the airfield at a wage of $.65 an hour. Somehow he knew the civilian head of this operation was being paid $24 a day. This inequity bothered Fred and when one of the workers who had six children was threatened with a pay cut he went into action. He got the men on the job together and took them to protest to the Captain who was the responsible military official on the operation.

This was a really involved situation. The head of the construction department insisted that he be fired as a troublemaker. Fred's own foreman who supervised the truck drivers did not want Fred fired even if he had agitated among the construction laborers. He took him off the truck and had him work in the office for six weeks. When the furor subsided the foreman talked to Fred before reassigning him to his truck.

"Fred," he explained, "you aren't supposed to stick your neck out like this. This is a government job and you can't teach men to strike here."

Fred said he hadn't advocated a strike. He assured his foreman that he "just went to the head official and told him these men deserve a job and the right pay for doing it."

"I knew I was jeopardizing my position but somebody had to do it and there wasn't anybody else." As a result of the protest the laborers fared better and some got raises in pay. The man against whom the protest had been made was a perceptive man. When Shuttlesworth wasn't fired he remarked, "Well he's a crusader now."

Fred, however, had no more crusades planned for Mobile. His future was in the ministry and he was determined to move into it.

He began to give expression to his unrest and dissatisfaction. He discussed their situation with his wife. "We have less than a hundred dollars saved since we built this house and we have been here three years," he told her. "I could pick up sticks and save more money than this."

Then he told her of his plans. "We came down here to help the defense effort and save money and we don't have any so I have decided to go to school."

"I feel as if God has a greater purpose for me than just making a living. I feel that my life is to come in contact or influence many lives."

His whirlwind energy gets things done when he decides to act and in this case he moved fast. He wrote to the President of Selma University saying that he wanted to come there to further his training.

President Dinkins replied that if he came to Selma University he would do all he could to help him get through the course of study. He offered him one of the houses then being built on the campus for married students. This provided a place for the Shuttlesworth family which now included three children.

Preparations to leave Mobile went ahead. He resigned his job and got fulsome recommendations from officers at Brookley Field. There were no assurances of earnings in Selma so Shuttlesworth and wife decided to buy a cow to be slaughtered to provide them with meat for the winter. Four-hundred pounds of beef were dressed out of the cow.

The Shuttlesworth family had a dwelling in Selma, meat for the winter and Fred was going to see that they kept warm. He had installed a butane gas heating system in the Mobile house. Now he dug up the tank and pulled out the pipes. He was ready to move.

He rented a truck which he loaded with his butane tank and pipes, a deep freeze full of beef, his household effects, and his family. The Shuttlesworths were off to Selma three weeks after his first discussion of the idea with his wife.

They were the first married student family to occupy one of the houses on Selma University campus. Fred installed his butane system himself and got his family settled. The children needed milk and he made a deal with the president of the college to get a cow. Dinkins was to buy the cow,

Shuttlesworth would make the money to repay him by selling milk to the school, and for his good offices the President was to be given a quart of milk a day.

Shuttlesworth hadn't been at Selma long before he and President Dinkins disagreed. He was studying determinedly but there was the questioning of maintaining his family. He began doing odd jobs and soon his wife found useful the nurse's training she had interrupted to marry. She was employed by the Good Samaritan Hospital, a Catholic institution. Dr. Dinkins disapproved and authoritarian that he was, he called Shuttlesworth to his office to express his opposition to Baptists working for Catholics.

Fred Shuttlesworth was already a formidable, quick-thinking opponent in argument. He first countered with the basic proposition that, "It's my business to tell my wife where to work," not the President's. The next point was that the school was not furnishing his living so he was free to make a living. Thirdly, his wife was working honestly and he was not going to tell her to quit working for the Catholics. "And by the way," he added, "I don't think religion has anything to do with it."

As Shuttlesworth tells it, President Dinkins didn't try to answer these arguments. He was evidently overwhelmed by the rush of words if not by the difficult logic. He mumbled, "You should have more pride in yourself," and Shuttlesworth delightedly parried this with, "the Bible says pride goes before destruction." His wife continued to work at the hospital and President Dinkins never again mentioned the subject.

The Shuttlesworth family was settled at Selma and life was running smoothly. One small cloud hung over the first year—that 400 pounds of beef they brought with them. Shuttlesworth muses, "I don't care much for beef now." Mrs. Shuttlesworth chimes in, "I just don't eat any beef."

Fred calls his two years at Selma "glorious years." He was president of his class and became a popular chapel speaker. He crowded his schedule with extra subjects with no regard for the normal student load. He liked languages and took Greek, Latin and French. When he returned recently to give the Baccalaureate sermon at Selma, the Dean introduced him as the student who "made the highest marks in the 75-year history of this institution."

While a student at Selma University, Shuttlesworth undertook his first pastorate. In July 1948, the Everdale Baptist Church, 10 miles in the country outside of Selma, called him for two Sundays a month. The next month he was called by the Mount Zion Baptist Church, four miles below Selma for the other two Sundays a month. Already he had preached occasionally in

Selma churches. He says that he would have been perfectly satisfied "if the Lord had led me to keep these rural churches and go ahead getting my certificate at Selma University, but God has his own purposes."

As Shuttlesworth divined God's purposes, the time had come for him to make another move. Studying his words when written down does not convey the faith that he communicates so effectively when they are spoken. He seeks to explain his decision—making with God's help.

"I have always believed in idealism, and I've always been the kind to take the Scripture where the Lord says, 'Try and prove me.'" When I am preaching I say that this is God's challenge: try and see if I tell a lie, try to make a liar out of me if you can. It is impossible to do that. When we find ourselves getting over on faith he does even more than he promised." When Shuttlesworth decided a move was in order, he moved, secure in his faith that God would take care of him.

Shuttlesworth, in the midst of his studies and having his first pastorates, had not yet made a firm career decision. His unanticipated successes had strengthened his mystical religious fundamentalism. By this time there is no doubt on his part that his success comes through communication with his God and his willingness to follow the revelations he receives on unquestioning faith. He is a man of action as his insight reveals the divine purpose for him. His thinking is not cluttered by theology or philosophy he has been taught at Selma. Subsequent experiences appear to fix the decisions he made at this period in his life as having been divinely inspired. Exultation over his surrender to God's will that he change despite his satisfaction with his condition marks him as a man not to reason why but to move as he is guided.

There was an advertised shortage of public school teachers in Alabama in 1949. Shuttlesworth found out that the need for teachers was such that persons were being hired on teaching permits who did not even meet the requirements for the lowest grade of teaching certificate, the "C" certificate. He reasoned that if he earned a "C" certificate he could teach and support his family more comfortably. He was now preaching every Sunday but the country churches he pastored hardly paid him ten dollars a Sunday.

Selma University didn't offer work that would qualify him for a certificate. So Fred discussed the idea with his wife and decided the thing to do was to go to Alabama State College in Montgomery and earn the teacher's certificate he wanted. Within two weeks the Shuttlesworths were in Montgomery. He didn't bother to tell the people at Selma he was leaving; he was just gone.

He felt that there would be efforts to dissuade him when no logic could refute his inner direction. The kind of faith Shuttlesworth expressed in his move to Montgomery was that he could sacrifice the security he had at Selma to give his family greater security and comfort when no immediate advancement to a better pastorate was offered him. His wife gave up her job at the hospital in Selma and the small income from the two country churches would sustain the family for his period of study at Alabama State College.

Shuttlesworth says, "We were almost vagabonds. We rented a house on a ditch and when it rained you could hardly get out to go to school or do anything else. But my family stuck with me and while we were in Montgomery our fourth child was born. Some weeks I didn't have ten dollars because there's not much money in these rural churches."

Fred took the transcript of his grades at Selma to register at Alabama State. He talked with J. T. Brooks, assistant to the president at the State College. Brooks looked at this record and said, "Mr. Shuttlesworth, I've never seen a student with such consistent high marks. Are you that good?"

Shuttlesworth answered, "Mr. Brooks, I believe in getting my lessons and if you give me a chance, I will try."

Brooks said, "If you come to school here we'll have to break you back to a C average; you can't maintain the average here that you did at Selma."

Shuttlesworth took the challenge. The first year his grades were all As and Bs. He went to see Brooks who congratulated him with, "You made it. You have been on the honor roll each quarter." Shuttlesworth said, "All it shows is I mean business about studying. But I didn't have time to study like I wanted to because I had to be away preaching every Sunday at one of my churches."

When Shuttlesworth first went to Selma, he had associated himself with a town church on that temporary basis the Baptists call "watch care" and occasionally he had preached for the congregation. Soon after he moved to Montgomery, this church lost its pastor. One of the deacons came to Shuttlesworth with a proposition. His proposal was that Shuttlesworth preach for them until they could secure another pastor. He wanted Shuttlesworth to preach at the Selma church in the morning if he could arrange to preach at the rural churches in the afternoon. This idea didn't flatter Shuttlesworth who was given to know that he was not regarded as being of acceptable status as a pastor but a fill-in while they sought a pastor.

He accepted their proposition after his two rural churches agreed to shift their hours for services. In October 1949, he began preaching on this schedule. He would preach in town and rush out to his rural church. But, he says, the town church paid him $10 a Sunday "and in these days $10 was $10." In the Spring of 1950 he tired of this routine and told them to get busy finding themselves a pastor.

Meanwhile the First Baptist Church in Selma, the oldest Baptist Church in Dallas County, became without a pastor. This congregation called Shuttlesworth to become its pastor. He promptly accepted and moved his family into the beautiful parsonage the church provided. He now had made the grade as preacher. He remained at this post for three years but these were not the most harmonious of years. He immediately found himself having difficulties with the church officials. He describes the situation better than anyone else can.

"The First Baptist is an old historic, front line church and some people call themselves front line and forget to stay up in the front ranks, to the extent that the buildings were decaying and so forth and the deacon board had become old. This is no reflection, just facts. The youngest man on the board was old enough to be my daddy and most of them were old enough for my grandfather.

"Here was a clash; a new idealist and those old and ultra radical conservatists. I had serious problems and am coming to the point which I think fits me for the struggle here. They weren't paying a lot of money and they were impressed with the idea that prestige is a great thing so that they wouldn't even cut the grass around the parsonage. Worse than that they had agreed that the board had the power of the church and they didn't have to make reports, so that and several other things were a clash. That was one of the main things; they believed that the deacon board should do everything in the church and not even tell the church about it. If they decided to hold a meeting and buy Mr. X's property, it was their privilege even with the church's money. This was the basic conflict."

The growth of the ego of the Reverend Mister Shuttlesworth had reached the dimension where God spoke not only to him but through him to the degree that he did not hesitate to make decisions about a circumstance in which he found himself or about conduct of the affairs of a church with which he was in disagreement. Before this time when he found a circumstance incompatible for him he moved; now he would try to alter a circumstance. This change in his life view was not an easy transition to make by a person who depended so strongly on spiritual guidance. He obviously wanted to act in a situation where he needed guidance more than ever before in his decision-making.

Reverend Shuttlesworth describes this as the first major crisis in his career. The other changes he has reported were soon decided and almost abruptly made.

"We had a board meeting once a month and I found myself getting nervous and upset for two or three days before and afterwards. I believe God leads people into difficult circumstances in order to get them hardened for something else. When the National Baptist Convention was held in 1952 in Oklahoma City, I had become so upset worrying about how to get along with this old system that looked like you couldn't like and couldn't help. There were such deep roots and preaching doesn't solve all problems. A devil at heart is a devil on the outside." The conflict between Shuttlesworth and his church officials had brought him to another fundamental decision: the opposition to a man of God must be allied with the devil if not little devils themselves beyond the moral suasion of preaching.

On the Baptist Convention Special Train the delegates had finally gotten to sleep by 2:00 a.m. and Shuttlesworth was still sleepless. He says that he hadn't slept well for weeks and here on the train he went into one of his serious conferences with God.

"I said to the Lord, 'I don't know why you sent me to First Baptist. I had rural churches and I was doing good but you brought me here. I don't know why it is but I want you to do one thing: I'm willing to take hardships and suffer like all your disciples, John, Peter, and all in the Bible. If the Bible is true then all have to suffer and I'm willing, but fix me so I won't worry so much. I'm willing to sacrifice my family and everything because this load is too heavy.'

"That same night it seemed like the weight of the train had lifted off me and I knew then that I had gotten so I didn't worry. All through the bombing and crashes I have been through, I never worried. Any decision I have to make, I make it. I see first what the Lord wants and I do it.

"I went back to First Baptist and started to work me up a program because I couldn't go along any longer with any group, two or three groups, having the authority of several hundred members to whom you can't give a report. I decided you can't do this, so I took all the power and put it in the body of the church. I gave my first recommendation that the power of this church remain in the body of the church. I had to take over signing checks so that checks would not be written without my consent. These were basic decisions but you have to get ready for it and I understand now that God was getting me ready for Birmingham. I have always come out one step ahead of my enemies. The church went with me and they started picking up. The old board tried making trouble but I was never one to worry from that night, as I have told you."

Shuttlesworth did not take the circumstances in the First Baptist Church lightly. He could see no end to the contention with the church officers. "I thought I was going to be in a fight all the time." In December he resigned the pastorate of First Baptist Church. His experiences there brought him to realize there were new developments taking place in his personality. "I was getting to the place where I didn't mind fighting although I am not a fighter by nature." This realization disturbed him.

Being engaged in a struggle for power with his church officials did not fully occupy Shuttlesworth. He had gone to Alabama State College to earn a teacher's certificate and he would use it. In September he was employed as a teacher in Mentor Street Manual Training School. His financial status reached a high. Teaching and preaching brought him an income of $425 per month.

This state of things lasted very briefly. His antagonists, the officers of his church, informed him that he couldn't teach and pastor the church; he would have to choose. He took the issue to the membership of the church and they supported him, agreeing that there was nothing wrong with his having two jobs.

He went through a soul-searching that his conflicts at First Baptist forced on him. He has a simplicity that may not appropriately be termed humility. When he finds himself in a developing situation he becomes concerned about what he must do even if the doing is merely a statement that rationalizes the stance he takes or the role he is playing. As pastor of the First Baptist Church and a teacher he was proud of his achievements but apparently he had not translated what he was doing into such status terms as who he had now become. As he has said above, this church considered itself a prestige church whose officials were concerned about the public image of their pastor even if he had no consciousness about the figure the pastor of First Baptist should be. One of his deacons found it desirable to counsel him about his friends and associates in a way that forced him to a consideration of his status. The deacon came to him one day and said, "You are pastor of First Baptist now: you are a Big Nigger, you have to quit associating with these little fellows."

He replied to his deacon, "J. D., God must have loved little niggers; he made so many of them." Viewing his position he recognized that his strength lay in the support of his lower status following and not with those who would set themselves apart as higher status. His sympathies were to be clearly with the underdog and he now made his identification a philosophic one where heretofore it had been unthinking affinity.

In this same period he arrived at his belief concerning worldly possessions. He says, "I've never been against anybody having anything. As I thought it out my philosophy became what it is now: People should get all they can get honestly. I think this country has one advantage over the Communist country; it encourages creativity and initiative to get and enjoy. You can do a lot of things if you have the initiative," he says.

His resignation from the First Baptist Church of Selma did not jeopardize his reputation as a preacher. Soon he had invitations to be a guest minister that booked him for six months ahead. He liked Florida and took opportunities to preach at Florida churches and view the possibilities there. He had an appointment to preach at a Florida church on the second Sunday in February, 1953, when a friend telephoned him for help.

This friend, a Reverend Martin, had been called to the pastorate of the Bethel Baptist Church in Birmingham. He hadn't decided to accept Bethel but he had promised to preach for them on the second Sunday in February. Now, he discovered that on that Sunday the church he was currently pastoring had a scheduled Annual Day and he couldn't fill his engagement at Bethel. He called Shuttlesworth to ask him to go to Bethel in his stead.

Shuttlesworth protested, "Brother, I have an engagement in Florida that Sunday and I want to go to Florida."

Martin said, "If you go to Bethel, I'll give you forty dollars." Shuttlesworth says forty dollars was forty dollars so he changed his plans and went to Bethel. The next week Reverend Martin telephoned again asking him to return to Bethel.

After his second sermon, officers of the church spoke to him saying, "We want *you* for our pastor."

Shuttlesworth could not in good conscience violate the ethics of the situation, but he liked the response the members of Bethel made to his preaching. He did not flatly reject the officers' proposition when he explained the ethics of it to them. "I came here to preach for Reverend Martin and he has promised to meet you-all on this coming Friday night and give you his answer. I can't say anything about pastoring Bethel until Reverend Martin has had his say."

The spokesman inquired, "Are you interested?"

Shuttlesworth dodged, "I would be but I have no business being interested in a church another man has."

The Friday night of decision came and instead of Reverend Martin appearing he sent a telegram reporting his decision not to accept the offer. The church meeting proceeded then to call Reverend Fred Shuttlesworth who accepted to assume his duties on March 1, 1953.

According to his school contract he would have to continue teaching until the session ended in May. The school authorities were reluctant to release him and tried to work out an arrangement to have him continue teaching. The offer they worked out was that his weekends would be free to carry out his church duties, he would be released from school to attend his church conventions, and they would give him the first principalship opening in the schools. To teach in Selma and preach in Birmingham was not a practical arrangement. Shuttlesworth submitted his resignation from the teaching job explaining that, "My first calling was the ministry."

Fred Shuttlesworth returned to Birmingham where soon he would become the most publicized crusader in the history of the city. His social consciousness had reached the stage of development that made him ready for social action. He is puzzled by the fact that he had not engaged in such activity before beginning his ministry in Birmingham.

Now, he insists that he had been long aware of the evils against which he was to campaign. "I think I came to the conclusion that something had to be done first when I was a kid out in Oxmoor. Our deputy sheriff would come out there and beat up people. I did try to do something when I was at Brookley Field. It is hard for me to see why all the things I witnessed in Dallas County when I was teaching didn't bring out the social protest in me."

He says, "There was enough in Dallas County to protest about. Just teaching in the schools showed it to you. You couldn't get to some of the schools when it rained hard. The creeks would rise and some of the kids couldn't get to school for weeks. All the buses they would give to Negro children were those that the white children had worn out. Depending on these buses, sometimes the Negro children wouldn't get to school until two or three o'clock in the day. I would pick children up waiting on the road in the rain for the bus."

"I remember one school that was almost like a school in Abraham Lincoln's day. In Dallas County, Alabama, in the fifties they had a log school with little square shutters over holes for light. They had logs spread with hay for these children to sit on. These were terrific conditions. I said, 'This is the trouble; the idea of the white man's superiority has got to go.' In my church I started preaching against it but that was as far as I went." At this time Shuttlesworth met his pastoral responsibility through his preachments that amounted to complaining to the limited group that his congregation was. As a leader in direct action when he makes appraisal of his preaching he indicates his feeling that preaching alone was ineffective in bringing about social change.

Reverend Shuttlesworth now dates his aggressive role in social affairs from the United States Supreme Court decision in 1954 on school desegregation. He says, "The Supreme Court decision stirred up in me what I knew all the time. I remember standing on the corner at the Birmingham Post Office reading that the Supreme Court had ruled out segregation in the schools and to me that was a new birth right there on that corner. I told myself, 'This means that we have the same right everybody else has and I am going to give my attention to it.'"

In his "new birth," Shuttlesworth had no positive focus but he began expressing himself by challenging his fellow ministers. There was a Negro ministers' group in Birmingham to which he began talking. "I started raving at the Ministers' Conference that the ministers ought to do something and say something.

"I always have felt that the preacher is God's first man. Part of our struggle is because the ministers of God are not leading the people. The prophets of old give us vivid examples of how the church stands up and when they stand up the walls must fall. I think that's what Christ meant by the 'gates of Hell shall not prevail.' It didn't mean, in my opinion, a man or gambler or wicked institution triumphant over the Church but it meant the Church triumphant over them because the people would be inspired to go out and crusade against it."

Shuttlesworth soon had an issue without his being the initiator in the question of hiring Negro policemen in Birmingham. Several white civic groups had discussed the matter and encouraged the placing of Negroes on the police force. Shuttlesworth took the idea to the conference of Negro ministers in a meeting at Bethel Church. He offered a resolution in support of the employment of Negro policemen which the conference refused to pass as a body. He told the conference, "A petition is going to the city commissioners asking for the policemen whether you endorse it or not." He was confident that he could get other signatures than those of ministers. After the meeting several ministers decided they would sign the petition as individuals.

Shuttlesworth formed a committee that got the signatures of seventy-seven ministers on his petition. Presentation of the petition to the city commissioner made headlines in the Birmingham newspapers. Shuttlesworth's committee of five talked with the commissioners and he began to learn fast about politicians, about whom he observed that when one waits for another one to vote with him he's not sure it's the thing to do. The meeting was pleasant but Shuttlesworth says, "I learned right then that a white man smiles like he means 'yes' but he means 'hell, no.'" But meeting with the commissioners was only the first step.

Then Shuttlesworth went to Montgomery where Negro policemen had been put on the force and talked with the Montgomery Police Commissioner. Police Commissioner Birmingham gave him pamphlets from Miami, Florida, in which the Chief of Police set forth the advantages of having Negroes on the police force. The Commissioner wrote to the city of Birmingham (coincidence of names of city and the Police Commissioner of Montgomery) officials in support of Negro policemen. Shuttlesworth had the letter photostated and circulated with another petition. This time the signatures of 4,500 Negroes and 119 white people were secured and Shuttlesworth's committee went again to the city commissioners to present this petition. The commissioners agreed in this meeting to reach a decision within ten days. Before these ten days passed, the Emmett Till case in Mississippi hit the headlines of Southern newspapers and Commissioner Morgan, the Mayor of Birmingham, told the committee when it returned on the day appointed for the decision, "I don't think now is the time to discuss it."

With the tactlessness that his associates deplore in him, Shuttlesworth bluntly told the commissioner, "Emmett Till's death had nothing to do with Negro police. You are telling us that you won't give them to us; we'll have to fight to get them." He says he understood what he was doing. "I knew I'd lose some smiling faces, smiling faces of supposed-to-be friends. But I knew we had to fight."

Shuttlesworth increased his following in Birmingham as a result of the leadership he took in the effort to get Negro policemen. He accepted the chairmanship of the Membership Drive for the NAACP.

He was the speaker at the NAACP sponsored Emancipation Day celebration January 1, 1956. Then the NAACP was outlawed in Alabama by a court decision in Montgomery in May, 1956, and nobody seemed to know what to do in the circumstances. Many sought Shuttlesworth's opinion and he didn't have one, but felt that the ministers should offer leadership only to realize the Ministers' Conference was hopelessly divided.

Shuttlesworth describes his reaching a decision to do something. "I was pondering over our problem one morning about three o'clock. I sat straight up in bed. I had decided to call a mass meeting in Birmingham. Just like that." The next day he secured the support of five other ministers in issuing a call to the Negroes of Birmingham to attend a mass meeting on Tuesday night, June 5th.

Crowds came to fill the church with many milling about outside who couldn't get in. This action by Negroes in Birmingham was news and reporters came to cover it. Shuttlesworth had decided to form an organization to replace the NAACP. His opponents in the Ministers' Conference who had opposed action he proposed for that body came to the mass meeting. When Shuttlesworth had spoken to the meeting and had the people worked up to a high pitch of enthusiasm he made his new organization proposal and asked them to vote on it.

Several of the ministers took the floor to oppose the organization. A prominent minister with great prestige in the city, Reverend M. W. Witt, immediately clashed with Shuttlesworth.

As Shuttlesworth reports it, "Of course I was presiding and he told us we didn't have any sense and didn't know what we were doing, and were going to get somebody killed. The people really wanted to throw him out but I told them we couldn't do that. I said, 'Doctor, you have three minutes,' and he said, 'Who are you to give me three minutes?' I said, 'In here tonight I am the presiding officer and we want to be respectful but take three minutes. You're taking your own time talking back to me. Say what you want to way in three minutes.' So he said we didn't need any organization like this. I said the people think we need it and there have been people talking about leading it but where are they? Now is the time for us to move up. They have said that we can't fight legally; they are trying to kill our hope. We are determined to keep it alive if I'm the first man going to jail."

Shuttlesworth says, "That's history now. We organized that night."

"The problem in Birmingham had been the ministers of the city. Some of them had been here a long time, they had prestige, they were the leaders and here I came, a little upstart. I can understand that but *the people* followed *me*. The Alabama Christian Movement for Human Rights was organized and the people have continued to follow me for five years."

Fred Shuttlesworth would lead where many would be reluctant to follow but he would go in their names. Going in Birmingham would be rough; people met on the way would be mean. Birmingham vies with Memphis for the distinction of being the toughest city for Negroes in the South and Birmingham carries off the dishonor. The two cities differ basically: Memphis is a "market town" for an extensive plantation area. It is old, has traditions of the Old South including that paternalism that mitigates the lot of its Negro population. Birmingham is a "company town," young, a quickly grown oaf of a city. As in the worst of company towns of whatever size it has a raffish population from the classes of people who knew no polite tradition or who escaped in revolt against the humane niceties. The absentee owners of the city, among whom the steel interests predominate, are apparently happy to leave it to their agents, the managers and foremen, a hard-driving, rough-handling lot of men.

Segregation and subordination of Negroes was not so old a custom here that people didn't think about it or were troubled when it was forced to their attention. Birmingham whites thought about it all the time. Maintenance of it was essential to their conceptions of themselves and a measure of their well-being because they were the whites, nobodies who came from nowhere, in a situation of which they were not masters but overseers. Unlike the aristocrats, who took a benevolent attitude and encouraged the aspirations of competent Negroes who could never challenge their status, the Birmingham whites had memories of competition with Negroes for a secure place in the South and still saw in him a competitor who should not be given the least opportunity to compete. By trickery, violence or whatever power they could lay hold on they had to keep Negroes in their places and frequently give them a violent reminder of how far they were determined to go to protect a whiteness on which they had a precarious hold.

Here was the battle ground and opponents Shuttlesworth had chosen. He belonged to the class of Negroes who would challenge white Birmingham. His faith now added the U. S. Supreme Court to God as a protagonist. His followers came from the "field hand" type of Negro who reciprocated the enmity of the white "overseer" type. They knew that they would not be joined by, and sometimes would be actually opposed by, the "house servant" Negro type who abhorred the thought of their gratuities being placed in jeopardy. The smart, well-fed Negro who enjoyed the few preferred places within the Birmingham-defined Negro status would not be joining them in their rude unmannerly behavior toward the good white folks.

These facts of social life did not deter Shuttlesworth and his cohorts who were determined to make their move praying to all-powerful God and appealing to a most powerful Caesar awakening in Washington.

When the Supreme Court decision removing bus segregation in Montgomery was announced, Shuttlesworth called, "Let's go." He announced that Negroes would move to desegregate buses in Birmingham, notified the city commissioner that they should desegregate the buses but "if you don't we are going to ride anyway."

The first regular meeting of the Alabama Christian Movement for Human Rights was scheduled for Christmas Eve but had been moved to Wednesday because of the holiday. Word had gotten around that Negroes would sign pledges at this meeting to begin unsegregated bus riding on Thursday. The police department of Birmingham ordered up a special detail of fifty officers for Thursday to obstruct the anticipated move. Newspaper reporters came to the meeting to get the story of the Negroes' plans. There were no plans. President Shuttlesworth called the meeting to order and then announced adjournment to the buses of the Birmingham Transit Company. The reporters telephoned the police commissioner, "These Negroes are riding today!" and hurried after them to bus stops.

What a riding there was that day. Twenty-two Negroes were arrested but there were too many riding for the police to take them off. Shuttlesworth couldn't enjoy the fun because one of his daughters had been burned in a household accident and he had to visit her at the hospital. Returning from the hospital he took a bus and with his flair for the dramatic sat up front only to rise and offer a young white woman his seat a few blocks farther on when it had become crowded.

Fred Shuttlesworth's coup on the bus issue made him a man marked for danger. He preached his Christmas Day sermon on "The Wonderful Jesus." During the course of his sermon he remarked that any day a stick of dynamite might be thrown at his house. He didn't know how prophetic he was; that night twelve sticks of dynamite blew his house apart.

"The old parsonage was setting where the vacant lot is now;" he explains, "there was a space of about two feet between the house and the church, so you'd have to turn sideways to get in there. Somebody came to the corner of the church and house which were parallel and put this dynamite there. The head of my bed sat there in that corner, and I was in bed. That bomb blew the floor out of the house, the wall down between my head and the dynamite; it blew the wall into the street, the porch columns, the floor out from under the mattress and we've never been able to find the springs to this day. The mattress sank down into that hole, and I didn't get a scratch. I never was harmed in any way in that blast which should have killed me and I don't know yet how it didn't, except for the grace of God. Where I was I had to get up and bend over to creep out from under there where the corner of the roof had come down.

"My trustee, Brother Revis, lived next door and one of the policemen came around to the back and he was wondering if I was dead, so I called out of the wreckage to tell him I was all right.

"I couldn't find my pants and I wasn't coming out naked in my underclothes. The policeman wanted me to come out. 'Reverend, come on out; this thing is going to fall,' and he didn't want Brother Revis to come in. Brother Revis said, 'I'm going in to get my pastor.' And he said, 'You can forget it.' So I said to him, 'If you are nervous, just give Brother Revis the light because I'm not coming out until I find my pants.' The policeman hollered, 'I'm just trying to help you, Shuttlesworth.' I called back, 'I've already been helped by the Lord, I'm all right, soon as I find my pants.'

He passed the light in and I came out wearing my pants and pajama top.

"When I got out there was a terrific crowd all around, and one little ruddy-faced policeman was cursing out a Negro and I saw the Negro had a switchblade knife in his hand and the blade was sticking out. He had the advantage on the policeman at that time. The policeman had been rough with him, trying to make him move and everybody was mad seeing that thing that had happened. The Negro said, 'If you put your hand on me again, I'll cut your throat to death. You are the cause of this thing; you policemen call yourself God and are the ones who are the cause of it. You all are the Klan.'

"The policeman was red and I just came up and patted the young fellow on the back and said, 'What are you so mad about? I came out of this; God spared me and I'm not mad at all. I want you to shut your knife up and there won't be any trouble.'

"To the policeman, I said, 'There won't be any shooting or beating either. If you can't control yourself and you're out here to keep order, I'll go and call the commissioner and have you pulled from out here. You calm down, these people are people just like you and they are excited because of this. So you pipe down, brother.' He didn't say anything and the Negro shut up his knife and went on.

"I spoke to the crowd, 'All right, people, let's clear the street. The officers are supposed to keep order so let's be orderly. If I'm alive and not angry I don't think you should be. This proves to us that we have a job to do and I have been spared alive to lead this fight. We aren't going to leave town but the fight is on from here on in. There won't be anymore of this in Birmingham because I'm going to see to it.'

"This policeman who was nervous said to me, 'Reverend, this thing is mighty bad. If I were you I would leave town as quick as I could.' I said, 'I'm not you, and you're not me so that's why I'm not going to leave. This is all the more reason why I should stay here and work it out. If anyone wants to have hard feelings it's all right; they tried to kill me but they missed me. That shows there's a stronger Man in town than they are. I'm going to stay and help Him work this thing out.'

"He said, 'Well, you sure must believe in God.' I said, 'Can you say that anybody else saved me? What do you give it credit to?' He said, 'I think it was dumb luck.' I said, 'If it was, then I'm going to trust dumb luck, only I call it God.'

"This crowd backed up but they wouldn't leave. The officers wanted us to tear down the house next day but I said, 'No, we'll take it down this week but let the folks see what's happening.' So thousands of people passed to see it."

Bethel Church began promptly to build a new parsonage for Reverend Shuttlesworth and his family. A guard house was built too for the guards who constantly protect Shuttlesworth. For a long time he had been guarded. There had been a guard seated in a chair in his bedroom when the parsonage was dynamited so it was decided that adequate protection required guards outside of the house. The church itself was dynamited for a second time and a guard was posted to protect it. No arrests have been made in the dynamitings but the church guards have been arrested for carrying firearms without a permit.

The weekly mass meetings have continued and Shuttlesworth has continued his battle against segregation. He tested the new bus ordinance in

Birmingham and was arrested. He sat with a couple in the white waiting room of a railroad station and was arrested. Harassment, arrest and suits became familiar to him but his next spectacular experience came when he moved to desegregate the Birmingham schools.

In September 1957, Shuttlesworth accompanied by his wife and a friend, Reverend Phifer, took several children, including the Shuttlesworth children, to enroll in the all-white Phillips High School. The children were refused enrollment, and when they came out of the building a mob had gathered. The children were put in the car and Mrs. Shuttlesworth was stabbed in the hip as she was entering the car but it was her husband who took the punishment. He says this was the first time he had ever seen brass knuckles and he was being struck with them. Another man had a length of heavy chain.

"I was struck several times and I was in a kind of semi-conscious state or a little bit worse. I was in a daze but I could discern this fellow maneuvering to strike me again. I knew if he hit me again it would be all over. I just ran into him. I just sprang and butted him in the belly. As I went by somebody kicked me in the kidney that suffered damage. Another man was in my way and I just pushed him and he fell over. I don't know if it was super-human strength or what but I seem to have understood in that moment of extreme weakness and near death that the Lord said, 'You can't die here, get up, you have a job to do.' I got up and made it to the car and went on to the hospital."

Three members of the mob, including the man with the chain, were arrested when the police arrived but the grand jury did not indict them.

Shuttlesworth was so well-battered in this encounter that he was taken to the hospital. He says that he nearly fainted about twenty times, but reasoned that if he fainted he would be kept in the hospital and he was afraid to remain there because he would not be protected from people determined to do him harm. If he could get back home he would be secure with all of the protection his followers and friends could give him.

While he was in the emergency waiting room, nurses, orderlies and "just white folks" moved past the door looking at him. "They were looking for a big man, a real black fellow, and there was nobody there but little me."

The doctor who came to attend him was courteous and pleasant. "How do you feel?" he inquired. "Fine, how are you?" Shuttlesworth replied. In fact, the patient was a sight to behold. His face was bruised. Skin had been kicked off his face, his ears were peeled. He bled from wounds in the back of his head, from his nose and other wounds.

The doctor said, "Reverend, we're going to have to x-ray you." "That's all right, help yourself," Shuttlesworth agreed.

"My, Reverend, you are awfully calm to have come through a mob. You don't even seem to be mad about it," the physician commented.

The doctor took Shuttlesworth's blood pressure. It was normal. "I couldn't take it and not be mad," he said.

Shuttlesworth even in this extremity could make his little speeches. "Doctor, when God has a job to be done, he has to fix somebody to do it and he fixed me for this one. I'm not angry with the people who beat me; they are doing what they think serves an order which you and I both know is headed out."

Careful examination of Shuttlesworth's head failed to find the fracture the physician expected. He commented on the good fortune that none of the blows had fractured Shuttlesworth's skull.

Shuttlesworth did not appear surprised. "God knew I had to have a thick skull, Doctor. He knew what he was going to send me into."

The physician patched Shuttlesworth and treated his bruises and dismissed him with, "You sure do have faith," a judgment in which was the most satisfying one Shuttlesworth would have asked.

Shuttlesworth's goodbye was, "I do Doctor, I do, and you can tell your white friends that killing people can't frustrate God's plan." His smarting bruises were a small price to pay for his moral victory recognized by the doctor.

Shuttlesworth assumes an air of equanimity, and the more experiences he has with critical situations the better able he seems to maintain calmness. "If I am killed today or tomorrow," he says, "so long as it served the cause of Jesus Christ, then I know I'm doing a good job. If death be my destiny then freedom would be the result. I may die in Birmingham but I think Birmingham is very close to hell itself; the Johannesburg of the South, and hell couldn't be over an inch-and-a-half away. There's no better place to go to heaven from.

"I don't worry. If I knew the police or a mob were coming right now, that wouldn't bother me. I might take steps to meet it but it wouldn't worry me. I've learned to relax while working. When the horse is saddled and harnessed, there's nothing to do but go."

Shuttlesworth's primary adversary is Police Commissioner Eugene "Bull" Connor of Birmingham. His officers are alert to arrest Shuttlesworth and have done so repeatedly. In one altercation, Bull Connor challenged Shuttlesworth to take a lie detector test. Shuttlesworth agreed to take the test *IF* Bull Connor took one also. Commissioner Connor declined. Shuttlesworth is now suing the Commissioner for assigning officers to cover his weekly mass meeting.

Each week there are two plain-clothes police officers at the mass meeting. One stands in the vestibule of the church while the other stands inside taking notes of the proceedings. Speakers sometimes find these presences annoying.

One minister made allusions to the officers' presence. "These men writing something down every now and then" and pointing upward continued, "but I know *Somebody* who is writing about them all the time. I would hate to go to meet God and have to explain to Him what I was doing in His house with a pistol on my hip."

When the President's turn came to make remarks at the end of the meeting, Shuttlesworth showed the face of sweet reason he is determined to present in all circumstances by saying, "Don't bother these gentlemen with us here. They're doing their job, they're making a living, they were sent here." Then he laughed and added, "Folks, we don't have to worry about getting a message to Mr. Connor; he's paying our messengers himself."

On one of his arrests, Shuttlesworth says that the next morning police officers came to his cell all red-eyed and tired. One of them said, "We came to interview you."

"I said, 'Now you know I can't say nothing, you know I have my rights and I'm arrested so I'm a defendant now. If I knew anything, I wouldn't say it now. That's one right I'm going to use.'"

One of the officers said, "Tell us how you feel."

"I said, 'I feel fine.'"

He said, "We've been up all night."

"I said, 'I was back there asleep. There's no use of me staying up and Bull Connor, too. Somebody had to get some sleep.'"

Shuttlesworth went on, "I felt sorry for them. They were up all night worrying about what I'd done or what they thought I'd done and what they thought I was going to do when I got out.

"If you stay calm, cool and easy in this dire situation, this evil climate with wicked police, you make them look silly."

"One of the nightmares you have to go through is these people that arrest you and harass you and then drop the charges. My philosophy on that, and here again I am an actionist, I am an active pacifist, not a full pacifist; that is using nonviolence to resist segregation. I believe in action. I don't think you can sit down and wait. My philosophy is that if they swing and miss you, then you sue them.

"I'm thinking now about suing some officers here in the city that arrested me in March when the sit-ins occurred. They had a warrant for my arrest already drawn up forty days ahead of time on a charge of giving false information to the police. This charge grew out of the fact that there was another attempt at castration here. Four men saw the evidences of it and testified in court and the jury found me guilty. This man admitted in court that he had told three different lies about it, so when the appeal trial came up in circuit court, the man and his wife didn't show up. Somebody said he left town so the city had to drop the case.

"If I wasn't in so much, I would already have had them sued and I still think I'm going to sue them. Because police officers have no right to violate your rights and get away with it. It is the only way to restrain the other policemen who would come up and do it. The Supreme Court just ruled yesterday that policemen who violate public rights are subject to suit. If you can't get the city, then get the city's boys. That's my philosophy.

"They're even after my children. Since the Gadsden affair the police in Birmingham have arrested some children they thought were my children, sitting in the front of the bus, for disorderly conduct. They were trying to get some arrests to make them out delinquents. We've had a time."

The "Gadsden Affair" is the most recent major crisis for Reverend Shuttlesworth. Three of his children were arrested in Gadsden, Alabama, in August, 1960 for refusing to move to the rear of an interstate bus on which they were passengers when the bus driver directed them to do so.

The oldest Shuttlesworth daughter, age 16, telephoned her father long distance to tell him the three of them, herself, her sister and her brother, had been arrested and that a white mob was gathering outside the police station.

Shuttlesworth alerted the State Police and the Sheriff of Etowah County in which Gadsden is located. He got bail-bonds from a Birmingham bonding company and with several friends, set out for Gadsden to get his children released from jail.

The Alabama Highway Patrol, whom Shuttlesworth himself had alerted, met the party enroute to Gadsden, stopped them and gave them tickets for speeding. As a result, Shuttlesworth's driver's license was taken from him for a year. Shuttlesworth decided, "If I can't drive, I can be driven. Segregation has to go, either way. If you can't take it, you can't make it, so be ready to take it."

Word had been circulated that the Chief of Police had advised his officers, "If Shuttlesworth comes up here with a gang, shoot first and ask questions later." Gadsden police cars met the Shuttlesworth party at the city limits and trailed them to the police station.

At one point the police cars stopped them to give tickets for running a red light. Shuttlesworth asked the officer, "How are you going to give a man a ticket for running a red light at one o'clock in the morning when the traffic lights are cut off?"

Shuttlesworth walked into the Police Station and said to the officer on duty, "Captain, I'm Reverend Shuttlesworth, you have my children here. I came to get the children if I can."

"You'll have to make bond," he said.

Shuttlesworth drew from his pocket the bonds he had brought with him. The officer said, "These bonds are no good; they're Birmingham bonds." Then he said, "You came up here with a gang, did you?"

Shuttlesworth replied, "I do not have a gang; I like company and people like to accompany me. So long as you have my children here in Gadsden, I will be here. I know I have that constitutional right. Now, you seem to be angry, Officer."

The Gadsden police officers were not pleased because Shuttlesworth had called the State Police and the County Sheriff's Office. When Shuttlesworth returned to the police station from securing bonds signed by citizens of Gadsden, one of his friends was there under arrest. This friend had forgotten his billfold in his haste to accompany Shuttlesworth and couldn't produce the identification the police officers had asked from all of the members of the party from Birmingham who waited outside the police station. Shuttlesworth walked over to the officer who said, "We're going to put this man in jail for a vagrant."

Shuttlesworth said, "Now listen, Officer, you have better sense than that. In your madness I am sure you are going to use discretion. You can't put this man in jail for a vagrant when he's with us. Now, you put him in jail, I challenge you to do it. You all want to be rough and we can play it rough. What you're expecting is for us to come up here and do something so you can beat us up and we've got more sense than that. Go ahead and put him in jail. The arresting officer said something to the captain who had rejected our bonds, who told him to turn the man loose.

"But the captain said to the man who had been driving the car, 'Well, we're going to give you a ticket for running a red light.' He said, 'What red light? When I pulled over here I got to the light.'

"I said, 'Johnson, take the ticket, what difference does it make. We didn't come up here to argue with these policemen. We don't want to give them any occasion for stumbling. They are having as difficult a time of it as we are. Let's be Christians and take the ticket whether you deserve it or not.'"

Shuttlesworth had gone out into Gadsden and found a Negro businessman and a Negro physician who signed the bonds of the Shuttlesworth children. That was a surprise for the police authorities who didn't think Shuttlesworth could get bonds in Gadsden in the middle of the night. Still they didn't accept them. The police captain took them remarking, "We'll see you in the morning if these bonds are any good."

As Shuttlesworth came out of the police station this time, the Police Captain told his waiting friends, "You won't loiter in the street here; we have loitering laws and we'll use them."

Shuttlesworth said, "Gentlemen, get in the cars. Let's not give the captain any occasion for offense. We want the captain to be the same man after we leave as he was when we came. We don't want to give any occasion for his anger."

The captain turned to Shuttlesworth and said, "You act like you're scared." Shuttlesworth said, "Scared of what?"

The captain answered, "You had to call the highway patrol; don't you know that we have efficient police here?" Shuttlesworth replied, "Most efficient; too efficient in fact. Your policemen have all the arms. I've never seen a riot gun before. What are you going to do with it? You've read of me before you saw me and you know I'm not scared of anything."

"That isn't the point; you have my children locked up and I'd appreciate any help you'd give me to get them." The police officer then said, "My advice to you would be to take your gang and get out of town." Shuttlesworth said, "I don't have a gang. I never had one. They are my company; I like to have company where I go. They don't have any arms and you don't believe they have because you haven't searched them. As long as these children are here in jail, I'll be here getting them out. It's my constitutional right. I brought a bond, got two citizens to sign it and you still won't accept it. If you're going to wait here til morning to find out if the bonds are all right, I'll wait here with you."

The group went to a taxi stand where Shuttlesworth told all the men to go back to Birmingham except James Armstrong, whose children, along with Shuttlesworth's, are plaintiffs in the school suit in Birmingham. Armstrong went with him to a motel for the rest of the night. The police car followed them to the motel and then took off.

The next morning bail was made and the children put in their father's custody.

Shuttlesworth tells the story of the trial of his children. "We had to go back to trial on September 6th, and that's when the big crowd gathering was. The courtroom was half full of white people and this young lawyer from Virginia, Len Holt, distinguished himself. He was our lawyer and they really didn't have anything and admitted it in the trial. We got the testimony that the children didn't do anything, and one white passenger on the bus tried to say that the girl had her foot in the aisle. The bus driver said it wasn't so; they had her arrested when she disobeyed his order to move to the back. That was it but the jury instead of giving a not guilty verdict directed her case to come up with the cases of the other two children who were younger than she.

"All were to be tried in juvenile court and when we got to the juvenile court, the judge didn't expect the lawyer to be there but he was. We went back for the trial in juvenile court the judge wouldn't let the trial come in that day. He said, 'I wasn't expecting a lawyer, and these kind of cases don't have to be represented by counsel; with juveniles we are informal.' We said we could be informal and they would find them guilty of being delinquents. During the trials we told the kids not to talk because the Gadsden folks would build a case on what they said. They wouldn't talk to the probation lady and they didn't say a word to the judge in the chambers. They were little soldiers. The jury said they wouldn't talk and they were found delinquents. They asked what we were going to do and we said we were going to appeal. The judge was shocked and turned to me and said, 'Nobody ever appealed from this court before.' And I said, 'I think you all should welcome another chance for the jury to agree with you.' He said that was our system of government, and to go ahead and appeal, that $5,000 bond apiece would be set. I said to the lawyer to tell him that we will appeal. I know they were on the spot more than I was. The lawyer said, 'Your Honor has the responsibility of putting these children in jail and keeping them there while the parents try to make bond, because they are going to appeal.' The judge saw we weren't going to yield, that we had an appeal so he let them make bond for $500. From $5,000 to $500, and it is on appeal now."

A suit has been filed in the name of the Shuttlesworth children against the Greyhound Bus Company for $9,000,000 damage. Reverend Shuttlesworth said he didn't agree to such a high figure but the lawyers wanted it to be that.

Reverend Shuttlesworth mused, "Yes sir, I'm in fourteen lawsuits about segregation now." He chucked, "But I remember what Mama told me: 'Never set a hen on one egg; it just wastes the hen's time.'"

The Shuttlesworth actions have drawn no support of white people in Birmingham. He says he has had offers of help from one or two white people but these were people who had been treated badly by their own people and were mad at them and wanted to get back at them through the Negro movement. "I don't want that kind of help," he said, "we aren't mad with white folks. The white man is just upholding an evil system which we are out to destroy."

"I'm convinced that segregation will not destroy itself because no snake commits suicide. The washing always comes before the rinsing. No baseball team every strikes itself out; you've got to put it out."

Shuttlesworth is careful to point out that this status in Birmingham is not a lowly one despite his maltreatment. "I have the utmost respect, most of the white people respect me. I have triple A credit to get anything I want in this town. At first the papers portrayed me as a radical but they found out that wouldn't work. Bull Connor used to swing at me and call me everything until he challenged me to a lie detector test and I told him I'd take one if he took one. That was in all the newspapers and he dropped it like a hot potato."

Shuttlesworth has announced that in the future he is going to act as his own legal counsel. He says the Alabama Christian Movement for Human Rights has paid out in four years more than $60,000 in bonds, court costs and fees. "The decision handed down this week in the Railroad Terminal case is our first victory. The basic fee for this case was $3,000 and another $2,000 in expenses, and it took four years. The lawyers don't push the cases. They just don't act. These lawyers need to get in the fight and realize they are in the fight."

In contrast to his opinion of Birmingham lawyers, he is well pleased with the young lawyer who had been handling the case of his children. "This young fellow, Len Holt, from the firm of Jordan, Gall and Holt in Virginia, is seen by some people as a radical but sometimes radicals will help your cause and I'm concerned about the cause, not about the radicals. He has been really reasonable in his fees even coming all the way here from Virginia.

"This lawyer has come down here for the Gadsden case twice, and while he was down here the second time on September 17th, is when we filed those suits against the airport limousine and the airport restaurant and we filed the Bull Connor suit. All three suits were filed in September and I have had a hearing on the Bull Connor suit, and that was in November and the others have come up for motion. Now we haven't paid him a thousand dollars and he's been down here five times. The Gadsden case, the first time in court would cost me about $500 under a lawyer here and the second trial would have been the same with the appeal still to come. I've got three cases in court of my own, plus these of my children, plus these five suits against Greyhound, which taken at the regular rate would be about $25,000."

The world of Fred Shuttlesworth is a good world in 1961. God is not remote in His heaven but at Shuttlesworth's side. He is convinced that segregation neither dignifies man nor glorifies God and that his struggle against it is a blessed activity.

He is proud of the Alabama Conference and the leadership he is giving to it. "My philosophy is that we organized to fight segregation, not just to hold meetings; that is the reason for our success."

The night I visited one of his weekly mass meetings was a rainy night, following a dreary day. The church was full and Shuttlesworth boasted in an interview, "You wouldn't find another organization with its members standing around the church and packing the aisles like they were last night in the rain. They do in the snow because I have given them the drive."

As to his leadership, he regards handling of the funds of the organization as a test of his stewardship. "The world should see the leaders in the fight for freedom as not profiteering. I don't want to live myself at other men's expense. I convinced the income tax man of that when he came around checking up on me not long ago. The cause needs money and I go out and speak and I accept what they give me for the work, not for myself."

Reverend Shuttlesworth is not cowed by labels of "radical," "red," or "Communist," secure as he is in his conscience that he is none of these. He works with groups and organizations that in his reasoning are "doing good things" in the best interest of his people. Anyway, the people who bad-name groups are the same people who have persecuted him or who have stood by, giving him neither aid nor comfort, when he has been persecuted. Such people, of whatever power or prestige, certainly are ignored when they disparage his friends and allies. Denunciation of anyone by Senator Eastland or Governor Patterson or Commissioner Connor is for Shuttlesworth a big laugh. He knows better after an attack from these sources than before who is Christian-spirited and democratic-minded.

He is a member of the board of directors of the Southern Conference Educational Fund where he is associated with Negroes having national prestige and fine, long-suffering white Southerners. Aubrey W. Williams, President of SCEF, would be a great figure to Shuttlesworth if he knew nothing else about him but that Senator Eastland went from White Citizens Council meetings to "investigate" him. Shuttlesworth is a popular leader of workshops at the Highlander Folk School which he enjoys as an oasis of compatible interracial association, even better because Attorney General Bruce Bennett of Arkansas came over into Tennessee to assist it getting the school closed down. As he sees it, the best interests of his followers are his best interests and he feels pity for Negroes who serve the interest of the opposition whether from fear or for personal gain.

Shuttlesworth knows he is not a communist because he believes in enjoyment of the rewards from personal initiative, private enterprise, freedom of speech, and God. The individuality of his inspired leadership is utterly hostile to an apparatus that would attempt to manipulate him. His is a *leader* to whom the role of cog in a machine is unthinkable. After all, his work gives him a place among the saints and martyrs of an enduring movement against which the gates of hell shall not prevail and the most vigorous efforts of men have no remote chance. The true Christian is in great company; there can be no greater and no man or men can bring you in or put you out. He reads his ideology from the Holy Bible and there has been no confusing change of line in The Word.

All humanity are Shuttlesworth's brothers and sisters, redeemed or to be redeemed, without emphasis on a new internationalism. In nearby Montgomery he has the sad object lesson in what can happen to a movement and the fortunes of the people when the leader becomes a world figure. He is concerned about how all of the great things happening in this country and in the world may benefit Birmingham where his hard job is to see that the people of Birmingham enjoy the new dispensation in his United States and move with the advancing ranks of Africans and Asians. He "glories" in the good news from far places that pushes him to greater effort to make his Christian Movement for Human Rights effective against Bull Connor, the White Citizens Council, and the Ku Klux Klan in Birmingham. It takes a lot of prayer and a lot of work to keep an organization united in aggressive action. "We have to be different leaders in this movement from the old Negro leaders, who get something started, to fall out squabbling about the money. That has happened here in Birmingham. That is why this organization is so amazing. We don't have squabbles. Those who like it can join and those who don't can stay out and we're still going on."

Shuttlesworth was one of the ministers in Alabama who was sued along with *The New York Times* for an advertisement judged in an Alabama court as libeling Alabama public officials. This court found against them and the ministers could not appeal with *The Times*. The judgment against them was satisfied by taking their property for sale. Shuttlesworth's automobile was taken and his followers are raising money to buy another car for his use.

Shuttlesworth praises his wife and children as "jewels." "Of course I am the type of person who believes that if something can be done, I go on and move. I think my wife understood that. She has not been a burden to me in the sense that she is trying to get out of this. She has gone on with me from place to place and we've stuck together thus far. The kids have come up in this thing and I have never sat down yet and expounded this doctrine to them. They have understood it and I've noticed that they are quite religious in their lives, quite mannerable, although I won't brag on them because what is in the future remains to be seen. But I do know that they are dedicated to the cause of freedom; they are little soldiers. They are not afraid of anything. We've gotten a million calls and threats and the kids take it as a joke. Some Klansmen called, 'This is the KKK, and you have ten minutes to get out.' That is a dangerous thing at one o'clock in the morning. They are little soldiers. All that has helped me to know that when the Lord is in control, he will handle the situation. You walk with him and he'll get something done."

Fred Shuttlesworth's faith in God and in his fellow man is of such simplicity as to make him a complicated personality, difficult for more sophisticated people to appreciate. In his family he is an old-fashioned patriarch, but he would be the last to use that figure in describing himself. He recognized the nervous strain under which his wife lives and sends her away for holidays outside of the South. She is his wife for whom "better or worse" is not a sentimental phrase or a cynical cliche.

Reverend Shuttlesworth fits none of the common stereotypes of the preacher. He is not the ascetic deeply immersed in another world; he has a lusty, sensuous quality expressed by sharing with his followers the good feelings of the flesh. He is not a repository of wisdom to be drawn on when he needs an answer to a question; he answers in a folk figure of speech his questioner is sure to understand. He certainly is not a mountebank who preys on the credulity, fears, and hopes of others; the beliefs, fears, and hopes of his fellowman are his own to be regarded with gravity. He is busy, happily, God's man confident of being about his business even when that business has become a rough and terrible enterprise. He has become more leader than preacher because he is not the prisoner of his ambitions nor the instrument of any group of men. He is not an acrobat toiling through the labyrinths of an intricate ideology.

Reverend Shuttlesworth explains his daring and his being more outspoken than his fellow ministers in Birmingham on the grounds that he is free and they are not. "They belong to somebody and can't listen to the voice of God. They have personal debts or their churches are mortgaged or they owe something to somebody they have to take orders from." Shuttlesworth sees himself as taking orders only from God who speaks to him and through him.

Shuttlesworth describes the difference in the leadership he is giving and that the older generations of leaders gave in the following terms:

"The old Negro leader used to make deals with somebody on the other side. There are no deals now. The Negroes in this movement have to prove that is our system, you can have democracy if you earn it. We can earn it in a righteous and dignified way. I think when this struggle is over the Negro people will be better fitted to be good citizens than if they didn't have to struggle. It is glorious; that for which we struggle is sacred.

"By struggling we are getting more than we planned to seek. Six years ago the white man could have gotten away with 'separate but equal' but he is so low-down, so dogmatic, he wouldn't do that when he said he was and now he can't. In this struggle God is not only using us to bring about his purposes but his purposes in our own lives."

Birmingham, 1963:

Confrontation over

Civil Rights

LEE E. BAINS, JR.

To

Lee E. Bains

and

Ruel Baines

Contents

Preface—1989

The preparation of this senior thesis was a true learning experience for me. At the time of the 1963 direct action program in Birmingham, I was seven years old and not really aware of what was taking place in the city where I lived. The process of researching and writing the thesis helped me understand those important historical events. The process also gave me an opportunity to learn about segments of the Birmingham population that I never knew.

The thesis was written in 1976 and 1977, when I was twenty-one years old. I have neither attempted to up-date the research in light of materials that have become available during the last twelve years, nor undertaken substantial revisions.

My work has been cited in a number of significant works dealing with the civil rights movement, including David Garrow's *Bearing the Cross*, Taylor Branch's *Parting The Waters*, and the PBS television series, *Eyes On the Prize*. I hope that it will be helpful to others who are interested in learning about the Birmingham events. I also hope that the thesis, which focuses on the activities during a six-week period in Birmingham, will provide assistance in a broader study of the civil rights movement in Birmingham.

Birmingham has been indelibly marred by some of the events of the 1963 direct action program. Pictures of police dogs attacking black demonstrators and water hoses being used to disperse protesters are still dusted off and used in connection with discussions of the city. But the Birmingham of 1989 is quite different from the Birmingham of a quarter century ago. Birmingham is now led by its first black mayor, Dr. Richard Arrington, who is currently serving his third term. Six of the nine Birmingham city council members are black. A majority of the Birmingham population is now black. Progress has also been made in reducing racial discrimination and in providing economic opportunity to blacks.

I would like to thank Ralph Carlson for spear-heading this worthwhile project. I would also like to thank my wife for encouraging me to pursue publication and for her helpful comments on the proofs. Finally, I would like to thank my wonderful parents, to whom this thesis is dedicated. The financing of my Harvard education, during which this thesis was prepared, was but a small example of their life-long support.

Lee E. Bains, Jr.
Birmingham, Alabama
July 20, 1989

Preface–1977

There were many factors working before 1954 for change in American race relations: the urbanization and industrialization of the South, bringing with them social anonymity and security; the weakening of regional differences in the United States through the impact of the mass media; compulsory service in unsegregated armed forces; a slow growth in legal and political protection for blacks. But, the initiation of change often requires a spark, a catalyst. For the change in American race relations this was the decision by the U.S. Supreme Court in *Brown v. Board of Education of Topeka, Kansas* on May 17, 1954.

When the decision came, the white South reacted with bitterness. Racism flourished in ugly new forms such as the White Citizens' Council. Politicians preached the doctrine of defiance and interdiction; states passed threadbare statutes in futile efforts to preserve the past. Southern police and even judges misused their power and manipulated the law to repress the Negro. There was mob violence.

The school segregation decision was also a catalyst for the blacks. The law was on their side—often a faraway law, offering little immediate protection against the local pressures of white supremacy but still giving hope of ultimate justice. Overcoming fear, Southern blacks made the effort to enroll their children in white schools. It was an effort that cost many parents a great deal, in physical and economic reprisals; the burden was even greater for the children.

In city after city in the South, racial disturbances arose as a result of school desegregation attempts. In Little Rock, Arkansas, white youth outside Central High School shouted, "Niggers, keep away from our school, go back to the jungle," and a mother just kept screaming "nigger." In New Orleans, in the fall of 1960, a white mob shouted "nigger-lover" at a Catholic priest who helped bring a white Methodist minister's young daughter to a newly integrated school in the face of a white boycott.

The courage of the little children who were the pioneers of school desegregation inspired Southern blacks. The struggle to carry out the Supreme Court's decision created a climate that encouraged blacks to challenge the segregated society in which they lived.

On the evening of December 1, 1955, a middle-aged black seamstress, Mrs. Rosa Parks, got on a bus in Montgomery, Alabama to ride home. She was tired so she took a seat near the front of the bus in a section reserved by custom for whites. When a white man got on the bus, the bus driver ordered Mrs. Parks to give up the seat. She refused. She was arrested, jailed briefly, then tried on the charge of violating segregation laws. Montgomery's black community, rallying around a young minister in town, Martin Luther King, Jr., began a boycott of the city's buses that lasted a year. Legal action, combined with the boycott, was successful in ending bus segregation in the city.

On February 1, 1960, four black college freshmen in Greensboro, North Carolina staged a sit-down strike in a downtown Woolworth store and vowed to continue it in relays until blacks were served at the lunch counter. By the fourth day the four young men were joined by other students. Outside Greensboro, the power of what they were doing began to be recognized. Other students sat at other lunch counters, and a movement was born.

In the spring of 1961, blacks and whites associated with the Congress of Racial Equality (CORE) began to ride buses in the South to protest segregation at the terminals. In three Alabama cities, the Freedom Riders were savagely beaten, stomped on the ground, and slashed with chains. One bus was stoned and then burned. As a result of the publicity surrounding the Freedom Riders, the Interstate Commerce Commission outlawed segregation in all trains, buses, and terminals.

The protest against segregation on buses, the demand for coffee at a lunch counter, and the violence of Southern white mobs were all elements in the struggle of Southern blacks to obtain freedom.[1]

A critical episode in the civil rights struggle in the South occurred in Birmingham, Alabama between April 3 and May 12, 1963. During this six-week period, officials from the Southern Christian Leadership Conference (SCLC), working in conjunction with the Birmingham black community, used a non-violent direct action program as a means of achieving desegregation of local retail stores. The purpose of this study is to analyze the Birmingham events. Prior to the analysis, it is informative to have a brief demographic analysis of Birmingham.

Alabama's largest city, which was founded in 1871, is located in the middle of the state. Protected by mountains to the southeast and northwest, Birmingham lies within narrow Jones Valley. The city's residential environs spread over the mountain slopes and into the valleys beyond.

In 1960, the city had a population of 340,000, of which 40% was black.[2] About one-third of Birmingham's adult population had completed high school, while less than 7% of the population had a college degree.[3] The median family income in Birmingham was $1,200 less than the national urban average.[4] The occupational structure in Birmingham included highly-skilled workers—represented by professionals and technical workers, managers, proprietors, craftsmen and foremen—who comprised 34.8% of the active labor force; medium-skilled workers—clerical and sales workers, operatives and service workers—constituted 52.1% of the city's workers; low-skilled workers—household workers and laborers—comprised 13.1% of Birmingham's workers.[5]

The differences in education, income, and occupation between blacks and whites in Birmingham were striking. As late as 1960, three times as many local whites had completed high school as had blacks; the median number of school years completed by blacks was 7.7 as contrasted with 12.5 years for whites.[6] The median income for black families in Birmingham was $3000, which fell quite short of the $6,200 mark for the relatively smaller white families.[7] Blacks generally held lower-skilled jobs than did whites. For example, although 2.9% of the city's white workers were employed in low-skilled positions, 38.0% of the black labor force worked in these jobs.[8]

The Birmingham economy, from which these racial differences arose, was unlike any other in the southeastern region. Most of the major metropolitan areas in the South had developed strong diversified economies.[9] Manufacturing functions, however, dominated the Birmingham economy; the city had been unable to attract other economic activities that generally accrue to areas with large concentrations of population.[10]

The metal industry accounted for over one-half of the city's manufacturing employment.[11] Secondary industries that used a great deal of steel in their production processes, such as machinery and transportation equipment, had not developed in Birmingham; less than 12% of the city's workers were actually employed in these particular secondary industries.[12] Birmingham's proximity to Atlanta and the established pattern of air travel focused on

Atlanta also made it difficult for the city to attract the regional headquarters of major national companies.[13] As a result of its inability to develop a strong, diversified economy, Birmingham was dependent upon its iron and steel industry.

With this brief demographic analysis of Birmingham, it is easier to understand the 1963 direct action program. The framework that will be employed in this analysis was developed by Stephen E. C. Hintz in his 1971 Yale dissertation, "Citizenship And Race: Confrontation In Rhodesia And Alabama." The process of confrontation over the desegregation demands by blacks is seen as consisting of relationships among four major sets of actors: the local governing officials, the external governments, the overwhelmingly white electorate, and the black populations. These four major sets of actors are categories of people who by status or function are differentiated from each other. Use of these categories does not imply that all people in a particular category behaved in the same manner. There were often significant differences in behavior within these sets. The use of this framework also does not imply that all the actors in the Birmingham events are discussed. For example, the local labor unions, which maintained a very low official profile during the demonstrations, will not be discussed.[14]

In order to correctly gauge the behavior of these different actors, an analysis will be made of each. Three inter-related factors will be discussed for each of the actors involved in the Birmingham events: the goals sought by each group, the strategies employed to achieve these goals, and the resources marshalled to implement the strategies. These three factors—goals, strategies, and resources—provide a consistent structure within which the actors' positions and actions can be viewed.

This thesis is composed of seven chapters. The first chapter discusses the background of the 1963 events. The chronology of the direct action program, from the time of the decision to enter Birmingham until the bombings on May 12, 1963, is covered in the second chapter.

The third chapter analyzes the actions of the local governing officials. In November, 1962, the voters of Birmingham voted to change the form of city government from a City Commission to a Mayor-Council. After the election for the new Mayor and City Council, the City Commission refused to leave office. From April 15, 1963, when the new Mayor and Council were sworn into office, until May 23, 1963, when the Alabama Supreme Court ruled that the new Mayor and Council were the legitimate city government, Birmingham had two separate sets of governing officials. Each of these groups of local officials—the City Commission and the Mayor-Council—is studied in the third chapter.

There is a discussion of the external governments—state and federal—in the fourth chapter. The white business leaders, white liberal activists, and white racists are the three elements of the white electorate that are discussed in the fifth chapter. The national black civil rights leadership and the city's black community are the two groups discussed in the sixth chapter. The conclusion of this study appears in chapter seven.

An important source of information for this study was the interviews that were conducted in the summer of 1976 with many of the people involved with the civil rights demonstrations. In any oral history project, there is always a possibility that the interviewees will develop "retrospective amnesia;" especially thirteen years after an event, memories tend to blur. For this reason, a cautious approach was taken toward information derived from interviews. This oral information was normally used in this study only if it could be substantiated either by printed documentation or by more than one person providing the same information.

This thesis would not have been possible without the assistance of many people. Dr. Marvin Whiting and Ms. Mary Bess Kirksey of the Birmingham Public Library's Southern History Department were more than generous with their time. They were extremely helpful in providing me with leads on information and in securing materials in which I was interested. Mr. David Allsobrook, of the Alabama Department of Archives and History, was very helpful in pinpointing material in the Official Papers of Governor George Wallace. The research I did at the Martin Luther King, Jr. Center for Social Change was facilitated by the kind assistance of Ms. Minnie H. Clayton. Ms. Marge Manderson's knowledge of the news-clipping files of the Southern Regional Council aided the research I did there.

Mr. Mike Nichols, who wrote a senior thesis at Brown University in 1973 about Birmingham, was extremely kind to give me access to his research materials; the interview that Mr. Nichols conducted with Reverend Wyatt Tee Walker in October, 1973, was absolutely brilliant and significantly aided my analysis.

Three people were extremely helpful with their suggestions concerning the text of this thesis. Dr. Edward S. LaMonte, of the University of Alabama in Birmingham, helped me immensely throughout the research and writing of this thesis. He helped define the scope of this study and thereby saved me from doing a great deal of tangential research; his detailed comments on each chapter were extremely helpful in the preparation of this final draft. My discussions with Dr. Robert Coles provided me with more insight into the civil rights movement that did hours of interviews and months of reading. Dr. Coles is exactly what I think a Harvard faculty member should be, but rarely is. Rather than residing in an ivory tower, Dr. Coles lives and works with real people. Dr. Marty Peretz was simply amazing. I had never run into a Harvard faculty member who cared about me as a person; my only regret is that I did not meet him three years earlier. Dr. Peretz's assistance to this thesis went far beyond his incisive criticisms.

Ms. Shelia Davidson saved my life by working tirelessly on the preparation of this final draft. Although many people have helped me in this study, the responsibility for its faults rests with me.

ONE

Background

Being a black in Birmingham, Alabama, prior to the mid-1960's meant that you had a strange status. You were born in a Negro hospital to parents who lived in a black neighborhood. You attended an all-Negro school. You spent your childhood playing mainly in the streets because the "colored" parks were abysmally inadequate. You rode in a certain section of the street car, used special elevators in public buildings, drank from water fountains marked "colored," and could not eat from lunch counters in department stores. You could cook for white people, nurse their babies, handle all of their possessions and their household belongings as you went about your chores in their homes, but you could never forget that you had a "place" in relationship to them, and that "place" made you inferior, no matter how intimate your relationships with them might be.[1]

In Birmingham, blacks had an inherited position in a social organization that was based on their labor and yet noticed their skin color before any individual accomplishments.[2] In addition to suffering social oppression, blacks in Birmingham were exploited economically and relegated to the position of second-class citizens in political matters.

In 1960, the median family income for Birmingham blacks was less than one-half that of whites.[3] This wide disparity existed as a result of the rigid restrictions on job opportunities available to blacks. As a result of racially discriminatory official hiring practices, there was not a single black policeman, bus operator, or fireman in Birmingham. The city's leading department stores did not hire Negroes as salesmen and salesladies. There were no blacks employed as cashiers or clerks in Birmingham banks, or large white-owned supermarkets. Black secretaries could not work for white businessmen or professionals.[4]

In 1960, only one out of every six blacks in Birmingham was a skilled laborer; three out of four whites were skilled.[5] While blacks constituted almost 35% of Birmingham's labor force, they were only 5% of the sales employees and only 7% of the managerial workers; on the other hand, over

95% of Birmingham's domestic workers were black.[6] When a cut-back in production necessitated labor lay-offs, black employees were the first to be fired. As a result, the unemployment rate for blacks in Birmingham was two and one-half times the rate for whites.[7]

In effect, blacks remained at the bottom of the economic ladder in Birmingham. They lived within two concentric circles of segregation. One imprisoned them on the basis of color, while the other confined them within a separate culture of poverty. The social prejudice and economic injustice had a malignant kinship.[8]

The segregationist attitude held by the vast majority of whites in Birmingham provided the basis for local segregation codes. These local laws prohibited blacks and whites from playing cards, checkers, or pool together.[9] Birmingham restaurants were prohibited from serving blacks and whites in the same room, "unless such white and colored persons are effectually separated by a solid partition extending from the floor upward to a distance of seven feet or higher, and unless a separate entrance from the street is provided for each compartment."[10]

Blacks could not hope to change this situation through participation in the political sphere; only 9.5% of the eligible black voters in Birmingham had overcome the obstacles to registration.[11] Democracy was a concept for Birmingham blacks rather than a reality.

The number of whites in Birmingham who were sympathetic to the plight and desires of the blacks was limited. The cultural background of the white community was based on segregation. Birmingham was deeply rooted in southern customs and traditions regarding the Negro and his "place" in American society. Birmingham whites were indoctrinated with the belief that blacks were inherently inferior, shiftless, and lazy.[12]

Interracial social contact was severely limited. The only informal dialogue between the white and black communities was between servant and master.[13] As late as the 1950's, unofficial interracial groups sought to facilitate communication between the races. As a result of intimidation and economic pressure, however, these groups were phased out of existence.[14] Birmingham city officials did not try to establish an organized system of communication with the black community. The Birmingham City Commission had only sporadic, informal contact with Birmingham blacks.[15]

This limited communication between the races, which was the outgrowth of the rigidly segregated social system, significantly exacerbated the problems which arose during the 1963 demonstrations.[16]

Before 1963, Birmingham was composed of two separate, closed communities. Blacks in Birmingham suffered social, economic and political oppression at the hands of local whites. Even the poorest, ill-educated white in Birmingham was accorded a higher social status than the most prominent local black. Desiring a more equitable social system, Birmingham blacks began their slow and arduous process of organizing to combat this oppression.[17] During the early 1950's, the NAACP was the primary organization through which the civil rights movement was conducted in Birmingham. The state of Alabama, however, enjoined the NAACP in the mid-1950's from performing its civil rights work by declaring it a "foreign corporation" and rendering its activities illegal.[18]

Wanting to continue the struggle for civil rights, Reverend Fred L. Shuttlesworth, a black Baptist minister in Birmingham, gathered a few ex-members of the NAACP and formed an organization called the Alabama Christian Movement for Human Rights (ACMHR).[19] Although not receiving the publicity that the Montgomery Improvement Association got during the Montgomery bus boycott, the ACMHR spearheaded the successful attempt to desegregate Birmingham buses.[20] Trying to effect social reform primarily through legal methods, the ACMHR instituted a large number of court cases which challenged the constitutionality of local segregation ordinances. In conjunction with the recently formed Southern Christian Leadership Conference (SCLC), the ACMHR also sponsored several workshops on non-violence.[21]

These attempts at desegregation by local blacks met with strong resistance from the white community. Many of the blacks who were active in the civil rights struggle were fired from their jobs by local industrialists, businessmen and housewives.[22] In addition to economic pressure, other more violent methods were employed by strict segregationists. Between 1957 and 1962, there were seventeen unsolved bombings of Negro churches and homes in the Birmingham area. The most frequent targets were the churches, which welcomed the weekly civil rights mass meetings, and the homes of blacks with high visibility in the civil rights struggle.[23] For example, the home of Reverend Shuttlesworth, the president of ACMHR, was bombed on Christmas Eve in 1962.[24]

At times, whites sought to beat and to torture individual blacks for no reason other than racial hatred. In 1956, three whites attacked the popular singer, Nat King Cole, during the middle of his concert at the Birmingham Municipal Auditorium. A more heinous crime occurred on Labor Day, 1957,

167

when a young Negro handyman, Judge Aaron, was abducted from a Birmingham street corner by a car full of white men. Mr. Aaron was taken to a dirty shack and was castrated; the whites attempted to increase his torturous pain by pouring turpentine on his wound.[25]

In addition to the extra-legal and illegal pressure that was applied by whites against Birmingham blacks, legal harassment was exerted by Birmingham city officials. The first years of the 1960's witnessed a hardening of racial attitudes by the three-member City Commission, which was composed of three arch-segregationists—Art Hanes, T. Eugene "Bull" Connor, and James T. "Jabo" Waggoner.[26] The City Commissioners tried to thwart the civil rights efforts of the ACMHR by sending detectives from the Birmingham Police Department to the weekly civil rights mass meetings.[27]

When the ACMHR requested that segregation practices be ended, the requests were summarily dismissed by city officials. For example, when Reverend Shuttlesworth and Reverend F. S. Phifer were incarcerated for violating segregation ordinances in February of 1962, they sent a petition from jail to the City Commissioners asking desegregation of City Hall drinking fountains and rest rooms. Birmingham's Mayor, Art Hanes, immediately sent an answer to the Negro ministers saying:

> This letter acknowledges receipt of your ridiculous so-called petition, and to let you know that action is being taken immediately, that is to throw it in the wastebasket.
> My advice to you is to do the best job you can on K.P. duty while confined in City Jail and I will do my best to do my duty in running the Mayor's office.[28]

The City Commission adamantly adhered to its segregationist stance throughout its tenure in office. When a Federal Court ordered Birmingham to desegregate its park and recreation programs in 1962, the City Commission chose instead to close its sixty-eight parks, thirty-eight playgrounds, six swimming pools, and four golf courses.[29]

The City Commission's opposition to desegregation and the civil rights struggle was not bound by legal means, however. An example of the commission's blatant disregard for the law occurred in 1961. The U.S. Justice Department had informed the City Commission of the estimated arrival time in Birmingham of the Freedom Riders on Mother's Day, 1961. With this advance knowledge and knowing that the Freedom Riders had encountered significant violence from Southern mobs, the City Police still arrived at the bus terminal fifteen minutes late, allowing members of the Ku Klux Klan and other groups enough time to beat unmercifully the civil rights demonstrators. It was recently reported that Senate investigations revealed that two Birmingham policemen—Lt. Tom Cook and Detective W. W. Self—arranged for the late arrival of police.[30] A local newspaper reported that Bull Connor indicated in a private conversation prior to "Bloody Mother's Day" that he was aware of the arrangements being made to aid the Klansmen.[31]

As a prelude to the 1963 confrontation, tension arose between the city officials and local civil rights leaders over a black boycott of downtown retail stores in 1962. Black students at Miles College, Daniel Payne College, Booker T. Washington Business College, and some white students at Birmingham-Southern College initiated a staggered series of selective buying campaigns against downtown white merchants.[32]

Reverend Fred Shuttlesworth and the other ACMHR leaders joined with the students in mobilizing Birmingham's blacks in a determined withdrawal of business from the segregated retail stores.[33] The selective buying campaign was designed to achieve three objectives—desegregation of lunch counters, rest rooms, and drinking fountains; hiring of blacks as clerks and sales personnel; and a general upgrading of employment for blacks.[34]

Handbills and pamphlets were distributed and radio appeals were made in order to encourage blacks to use the millions of dollars that they spent in the downtown area as a leverage to obtain "freedom, justice and equality."[35] The boycott was between 80% and 95% effective.[36] As a result of the campaign, business at some downtown stores fell off as much as 40%, thereby inflicting serious economic losses on the white merchants.[37]

The City Commission was determined to punish the blacks for their actions. Commissioner Bull Connor threatened to "sic the dogs" on Negroes unless the boycott was lifted.[38] The City Commission finally agreed on a policy with a much more negative effect; the city of Birmingham withdrew its $45,000 appropriation to the county surplus-food program, which was patronized primarily by blacks.[39] The city's action did a disservice to the low-income black families but aided the boycott by arousing the black community in Birmingham.[40]

Because they were being hurt by the boycott and because they were afraid that Martin Luther King, Jr. would come to Birmingham and further stimulate the boycott, the merchants in Birmingham met for the first time with Reverend Fred Shuttlesworth and other civil rights leaders.[41] In the course of the negotiations, certain limited promises were made by the white merchants—for example, to remove the stores' humiliating racial signs. On the basis of these promises, Reverend Fred Shuttlesworth and the leaders of the ACMHR agreed to a moratorium on the boycott.[42]

The agreements were soon broken, however, as the jim-crow signs reappeared in the stores. Two reasons contributed to the breaking of the agreements. First, most of the merchants, who shared the prevalent white segregationist's attitudes, were not enthusiastic about desegregation. Second, Bull Connor, who as Public Safety Commissioner had broad powers over the enforcement of city regulations, began to harass the merchants who had agreed to desegregate. Connor's inspectors were suddenly able to find unsafe elevators and stairs, inadequate fireproofing and other violations at the compliant businesses. Local blacks felt that the token action had been taken by the merchants in order to stop the boycott and to avoid the possible involvement of Dr. Martin Luther King, Jr. The abrogation of agreements by white merchants was the final factor that convinced national civil rights leaders to enter Birmingham with a direct action program in the spring of 1963.[43]

While the primary civil rights group in Birmingham increased its activities and the City Commission remained dedicated to its strong segregationist stand, white moderates in Birmingham began to make some progress in limiting the excesses that had been employed in attacking desegregation attempts. Most of the white moderates were still dedicated to segregation as a social system, but they believed that the hard-line approach taken by the City Commission was counterproductive. The first significant successful reform achieved by white moderates involved the change in the form of Birmingham's government in 1962 from a three-member City Commission to a Mayor and a nine-member City Council.

The drive to change the form of Birmingham's city government was initiated by the Birmingham Chamber of Commerce.[44] The city's business leaders had three main goals which prompted them to seek the change in governmental form. First, they were increasingly dismayed by the inflammatory and inflexible actions of the commissioners in race relations. Changing the form of government was a convenient way of removing the occupants of office prior to the next regularly scheduled election in 1965.[45] Second, the business leaders preferred a less adamant position toward the rising demands of black leaders.[46] Third, the Chamber officials wanted to achieve the elusive goal of merging the suburban communities with the central city; they believed that a new governmental structure was necessary to meet the outlying areas' demands for a more representative form of government.[47]

Although endorsing the change in government, Chamber leaders felt that since they lived in outlying suburbs they could not publicly initiate the effort to change the form of government. With this problem in mind, Mr. Sidney Smyer, the president of the Birmingham Chamber of Commerce, approached the Birmingham Bar Association in February, 1961, with the request that the Bar Association appoint a committee to study the present and future governmental needs of Birmingham.[48]

The Bar Association group studied the situation and voted in December, 1961, to recommend that the city adopt the Mayor-Council form of government.[49] Having secured the desired recommendation for change from a respected professional organization, the Chamber again felt that it was not an appropriate group to mount a public campaign to implement the Bar Association's Report. The Young Men's Business Club provided a solution to this problem by adopting the report as a project for its membership, which was comprised of young business and professional men in Birmingham. Two young attorneys assumed major responsibility for promoting the new governmental structure—Erskine Smith and David Vann.[50]

The Young Men's Business Club held a public meeting at which the supporters of the change in government decided to form a new group—Birmingham Citizens For Progress—whose purpose was to spearhead the petition drive. In order to hold a referendum on the form of government, it was first necessary to secure a petition with the signatures of 7,500 registered voters.[51] The all-white Citizens For Progress group manned petition booths at a city-wide election on August 28, 1962. This tactic ensured that the petition signers were in fact registered voters. In order to avoid charges of manipulated black vote, no booths were placed in predominantly black precincts. Even without the support of blacks, the petition drive was extremely successful, gathering the support of between 11,000 and 12,000 registered voters; November 6, 1962, was set as the date for the referendum.[52]

Prior to the referendum election, there was a significant amount of campaigning. Calling the City Commission form of government outmoded, proponents of the Mayor-Council form saw change as necessary in order to

171

establish both executive leadership and a representative legislative branch. The Citizens For Progress also argued that a change in governmental form might induce voluntary merger by outlying suburbs. Opponents of the change in government advanced a significantly different argument. Bull Connor, utilizing racist rhetoric, tried to tie the change of government proposals to the integration movement.[53]

Final referendum election returns gave a small majority to the Mayor-Council form. Although the Citizens For Progress made no appeal to blacks for support, studiously avoided getting their signatures during the petition drive, and publicly supported the status quo in race relations, black voters overwhelmingly supported the change. Analysts have concluded that the black voters actually provided the margin of victory for change.[54]

In the ensuing mayoral and city council campaign, three major issues emerged: the city's proper response to desegregation demands, the condition of the city's economy, and the bad "image" of the city presented in the national media.[55] Although seventy-six candidates vied for the nine city council posts, chief interest was focused on the four men who sought to become mayor. Tom King, the most liberal of the four, had lost a mayoral run-off to Art Hanes in 1961 after being pictured shaking hands with a black man. Albert Boutwell, a former Lt. Governor of Alabama, had co-authored the state's "freedom of choice" amendments that were designed to negate the effect of the 1954 Supreme Court decision on school desegregation; but, Boutwell was still seen as a racial moderate. Two old-line leaders, City Commissioners Bull Connor and Jabo Waggoner, ardently adhered to their hard-line segregationist positions.

The special election on March 5, 1963, ended with no candidate receiving a majority of the ballots cast. The run-off election scheduled for April 2, 1963, had a field of eighteen candidates, including two blacks, vying for the nine City Council seats; Bull Connor and Albert Boutwell faced each other in the mayoral race.

During the month of campaigning prior to the run-off, Bull Connor indicated his willingness to violate the law rather than to permit desegregation. Boutwell promised "to defend the long standing traditions of the City," but to defend it with "absolute enforcement of the law and the total maintenance of order."[56] Birmingham voters were provided a choice between alternative means of opposing desegregation; a choice between segregation and desegregation was not provided.

Boutwell won a significant victory over Connor by amassing a victory margin of 29,630 to 21,648. A large percentage of the registered black voters cast ballots in the election, and they overwhelmingly supported Boutwell. For example, one predominantly black precinct supported Boutwell over Connor by a vote of 1,679 to 2.[57] As in the referendum on governmental change, the black vote appeared to be the deciding factor in electing the reformers.[58] While rejecting as Mayor the chief proponent of the hard-line segregationist position, Birmingham voters also defeated those City Council candidates who took adamant stands against any accommodation in race relations.[59]

By their support of the change in government and their rejection of ardent segregationists in the subsequent city election, the voters of the city rejected the intransigence of the Commission and indicated a willingness to seek moderation in race relations.[60] But by no means, did the citizens of Birmingham indicate a willingness to abandon segregation as a way of life. For example, two black candidates for City Council had sufficient support from the black community to make the final field of eighteen candidates: but the white supporters of defeated council candidates rallied behind the sixteen white candidates in the run-off. With practically no support from white voters, the two black City Council candidates finished last in the run-off.[61]

Rather than supporting the extension of civil and social rights to blacks, whites in Birmingham continued to favor segregation. White support for governmental change and moderate city officials simply indicated the choice of a new strategy; they felt that moderation was the key to maintaining the racial, social and economic status quo.[62] A change in white attitudes did not occur along with the change in government. Rather than showing signs of real progress in race relations, Birmingham retained the dubious distinction of being one of America's most racially bigoted city. It was said that Birmingham's heart was hard like the steel it manufactured and black like the coal it mined.[63]

When members of SCLC came to Birmingham to plan the direct action program of 1963, they saw the welcome signs to the Magic City, which read, "It's Nice to Have You in Birmingham;" but, insofar as the majority of whites were concerned, it was nice to have you in Birmingham *if* you were one who believed only in the status quo in race relations; *if* you were satisfied to exist with things as they were, without seeking to change them; *if* you only *believed* that the Negro was a human being deserving civil rights without *acting* on your belief.[64]

TWO

Chronology

In the late spring of 1962, Reverend Fred Shuttlesworth met in Tennessee with the Board of Directors of the Southern Christian Leadership Conference (SCLC). At that time, Reverend Shuttlesworth suggested that SCLC join with his organization in Birmingham, the Alabama Christian Movement for Human Rights (ACMHR), in a massive campaign against segregation. With the support of Martin Luther King, Jr. and Ralph Abernathy, the SCLC Board decided to enter Birmingham in early 1963.[1]

In preparation for the direct action program, Dr. King called a three-day retreat and planning session with about twenty-five to thirty members of the SCLC staff and Board of Directors at their training center in Dorchester, Georgia. At that time, they agreed that the operations in Birmingham—known as Project C (for "confrontation")—would be launched during the first week in March, 1963, in order to cripple the business community's Easter sales.[2] Since the Birmingham Police and Alabama State Troopers were suspected of tapping the phones of ACMHR leaders, it was agreed that Project C would be kept secret.[3] The civil rights leaders realized that if plans were discovered, Birmingham whites might react by electing Bull Connor in the city elections that were planned for the spring.[4] A variety of code names for people, places and events were thus formulated and regularly used in communications in order to ensure secrecy.[5]

Two weeks after the retreat at Dorchester center, Dr. King went to Birmingham with Reverend Ralph Abernathy and Reverend Wyatt Tee Walker in order to meet with ACMHR leaders. The meeting occurred in room 30 of the Gaston Motel, which served as the headquarters for all the strategy sessions in subsequent months. At this Birmingham meeting, the leaders from SCLC and from ACMHR discussed ways of coordinating their efforts in preparing for the direct action program.[6]

The extensive preparations, which occurred prior to the start of the direct action program in Birmingham, were conducted on two levels, national and local. Dr. King bore primary responsibility for the national planning. Soon after leaving the meeting with ACMHR officials in Birmingham, Dr. King began a whirlwind speaking tour during which he made twenty-eight speeches in sixteen cities. Reminding his sympathetic audiences that "as Birmingham goes, so goes the South," Dr. King was able to recruit volunteers and line up pledges of cash bonds for the eventuality of arrests during Project C in Birmingham.[7]

In New York City, Dr. King's long-time friend, Harry Belafonte, sponsored a meeting of seventy-five Eastern liberals in his apartment. Dr. King and Reverend Shuttlesworth told this group about the existing situation in Birmingham and their plans for the direct action program. With Mr. Belafonte's continued assistance, the financial backing of these Eastern liberals was soon forthcoming.[8] A similar meeting was held in Los Angeles with one of SCLC's strongest affiliates—the Western Christian Leadership Conference; the Western Conference, with the assistance of the NAACP and other local organizations, was eventually able to funnel $75,000 to the SCLC for use in Project C.[9]

Seeking to solidify support from national civil rights groups, SCLC leaders wrote confidential letters to the NAACP, the Congress of Racial Equality (CORE), the Student Nonviolent Coordinating Committee (SNCC), and the Southern Regional Council telling them of the plans for Birmingham in the spring of 1963.[10] President John F. Kennedy was also advised by a letter from Dr. King of the impending direct action program.[11]

Since Dr. King was handling the national planning for Project C, he placed Reverend Wyatt Tee Walker in charge of the local planning effort.[12] Traveling very frequently to Birmingham during the months of preparations preceding the start of Project C, Reverend Walker and other SCLC aides, worked closely with Reverend Shuttlesworth and his staff.[13] While in Birmingham, Walker organized a transportation corps to facilitate mobilization of demonstrators; he conferred with local attorneys concerning the city code provisions dealing with picketing and demonstrations; legal representation was arranged for demonstrators who would be arrested and jailed; and, the probable bail bond situation was explored.[14] Walker, Shuttlesworth, and their staff held endless conferences about the mood of the city, its strengths, its weaknesses, and its public personalities.[15]

Wyatt Walker made a thorough reconnaissance of downtown Birmingham, at which the demonstrations were to be directed. In commenting about the extent of his preparations, Walker said:

I knew how long it took for an old person to walk from the Sixteenth Street Baptist Church to downtown. I knew how long it took a kid to walk . . .

I had counted every stool, every table, every chair in these stores . . .

I had picked out two or three different routes to go . . .[16]

In addition to the primary targets downtown, Walker established a secondary target and a tertiary target for demonstrations.[17] As a result of the extensive preparations, the Birmingham Project was all laid out before the start of Project C.[18]

The remaining factor that was needed to complete planning for Project C was people. It was necessary to have at least 300 Birmingham citizens who were willing to go to jail.[19] Reverend Walker and Reverend Shuttlesworth relied on the most loyal and fearless ACMHR members as their recruits.[20]

The city elections that were being held in Birmingham in the early spring of 1963 caused the start of Project C to be delayed twice. Dr. King initially wanted to start the direct action program in early March, 1963, about six weeks before Easter. But city elections for the new Mayor and City Council were set for March 5.[21] In order to avoid having the direct action program turn into a political issue, the civil rights leaders planned to begin demonstrations on March 14.[22]

The March 5th election results posed a serious new problem to Project C. No mayoral candidate had won a clear majority. Bull Connor, the arch-segregationist Commissioner of Public Safety, and Albert Boutwell, a more moderate segregationist, were to face each other in the run-off. Realizing that Connor would capitalize politically if the direct action program began during the run-off campaign, SCLC and ACMHR officials decided to postpone the demonstrations until after the run-off.[23] The local ACMHR members, who had volunteered to be jailed, were kept informed of the status of Project C.[24] It had been decided in advance that regardless of the winner in the mayoral run-off, the direct action program would begin immediately after the election.[25]

On Wednesday, April 3, 1963 less than twenty-four hours after Albert Boutwell had been elected as Birmingham's new mayor over Bull Connor, the direct action program began. The first phase of Project C was directed at the lunch counters of downtown retail stores. Sit-ins were staged at the lunch counters which refused to serve Negroes; pickets outside the targeted stores encouraged shoppers to boycott the establishments. Twenty Negroes were arrested the first day on charges of trespassing after warning in five retail stores.[26]

ACMHR officials attempted on April 3 and on April 5 to secure permits for picketing and parading "against the injustices of segregation and discrimination." Bull Connor responded to the request by saying, "you will not get a permit in Birmingham to picket. I will picket you over to the City Jail."[27] This refusal, however, did not cause civil rights leaders to change their plans.

As the boycott, picketing, and sit-ins continued, the second phase of Project C—street demonstrations—was initiated on Saturday, April 6, 1963, with a march on City Hall. Over thirty demonstrators led by Reverend Shuttlesworth marched two abreast from Kelly Ingram Park toward the Birmingham City Hall. Bull Connor intercepted them and with "amazing politeness" had them escorted to police vans.[28] The next day, Palm Sunday, April 7, marked the first open conflict between Negro demonstrators and white policemen. A peaceful prayer march led by Reverend A. D. King, younger brother of Dr. King, developed into violence when policemen waded into the crowd with night sticks and police dogs.[29]

A more dangerous weapon was soon employed against the civil rights demonstrators. Acting upon a bill of complaint filed by city officials, Circuit Judge W. A. Jenkins, Jr. on April 10, issued a sweeping injunction barring 133 civil rights leaders from participating in or encouraging any kind of protest, mass demonstration, boycott, or sit-in.[30] Shortly before 1:00 A.M. on April 11, the state court injunction was served on Reverends King, Abernathy, Walker, and Shuttlesworth.[31]

Even before the start of Project C, the national and local black leaders had anticipated that an injunction would be issued to thwart the demonstrations.[32] They viewed the injunction method as a "pseudo-legal way of breaking the back of legitimate moral protest."[33] The civil rights leaders' decision to violate the state court injunction was made with full awareness of the possible legal consequences.[34]

There were two reasons that the injunction was violated—moral and practical. In statements concerning their conscious decision to violate the injunction, the black leaders voiced their moral objection:

> This injunction is raw tyranny under the guise of maintaining law and order. We cannot in all good conscience obey such an injunction which is an unjust, undemocratic and unconstitutional misuse of the legal process.

We view this injunction as one of the inevitable torpedoes thrown in our way; but on the road to freedom, justice, and equality, Negroes can have but one slogan: Damn the torpedoes! Full speed ahead![35]

The decision to violate the court order was also premised on the practical point that the direct action program would lose its momentum and effectively end if the injunction were obeyed.[36]

Dr. King was one of the first demonstrators who willingly violated the injunction. After an emotional meeting with a group of his closest advisors and friends in Room 30 of the Gaston Motel, Dr. King decided to go to jail on Good Friday, April 12, only one day after being served with the injunction.[37] After marching less than one-half mile from the Sixteenth Street Baptist Church toward the downtown section, Dr. King and Reverend Ralph Abernathy were arrested and jailed, along with more than fifty demonstrators, for violating the state court injunction.[38]

Three days after Dr. King's arrest, Albert Boutwell and the new City Council were sworn into office; the old City Commission, however, refused to leave office. Proceedings were initiated to remove the old Commission from office, but a decision was not rendered by the Alabama Supreme Court until May 23.[39] Thus, during the remainder of the direct action program, two city governments shared power in Birmingham.

It was during his eight day imprisonment that Dr. King issued his famous "Letter From Birmingham Jail" in response to objections raised to the direct action program by eight white clergymen.[40] By remaining in jail, Dr. King aroused people throughout the United States to send money to Birmingham to build up reserves for bond payments that would be used to obtain the release of demonstrators, who were jailed in Project C.[41] On April 20, 1963, however, Reverends King and Abernathy had the $300 bail paid for each of them and quickly left for Room 30 of the Gaston Motel in order to confer both with SCLC attorneys about the impending contempt case and with ACMHR officials over strategies for the direct action program.[42] Project C had all but ground to a halt during Dr. King's incarceration.[43] It was decided on April 20th that in order to stimulate the direct action program, it was necessary to have a massive infusion of volunteers who were willing to be jailed; it was necessary to introduce children into the demonstrations.[44] But, first Dr. King had to face trial on the contempt charges arising out of his violation of the state court injunction.

The contempt trial, which began April 22nd, lasted only two days. Judge Jenkins held that legal and orderly processes required the black defendants to attack the validity of the injunction through a motion to dissolve it, rather than violate it without thus testing its validity.[45] Consequently, eleven defendants were convicted of criminal contempt, sentenced to five days in jail and fined $50. All eleven were allowed to remain at liberty pending an appeal to the Alabama Supreme Court.[46]

Throughout the period between Dr. King's arrest on Good Friday, April 12th, and the end of the contempt trial on April 24th, the picketing and sit-ins had continued in the downtown business district. This was a small-scale operation, however, involving only about a dozen or so people each day.[47] Such tactics as kneel-ins by black demonstrators who were refused the right to worship at white churches and marches on the Jefferson County Court House by blacks wanting to register to vote were employed during this period.[48] The primary efforts of SCLC and ACMHR officials during the last ten days in April, however, were directed at the preparation for the third and most controversial phase of Project C—the introduction of children.[49]

SCLC staff members, headed in their efforts by James Bevel, Andrew Young, Bernard Lee, and Dorothy Cotton, initiated contact with Birmingham children through the public schools. Going into the classrooms and libraries, SCLC members urged the school children to go to the Movement's churches to see films—*Walk to Freedom* and *The Nashville Story*—and to hear King and Bevel, among others, explain nonviolence.[50] By Thursday, May 2, some 6,000 children were organized and ready to march; James Bevel, who was in charge of this "D-Day", had the children assemble at the Sixteenth Street Baptist Church.[51] For forty-five minutes, Martin Luther King, Jr., and other SCLC leaders addressed the first contingent of 300 youngsters who ranged in age from six to eighteen. In clusters of ten to fifty, the children began to stream down the street at intervals; as they did so, a steady flow of children arrived at the church, ready to march. As the children marched, they were given directions by older youths with walkie-talkies, a system instituted by Wyatt Tee Walker. Police soon ran out of patrol wagons and began using school buses to transport the students to jail or to juvenile court. Over a period of four hours, ten large waves of children surged downtown.[52]

The next morning, Friday, May 3, Dr. King announced to groups of assembled students, "Yesterday was D-Day in Birmingham. Today will be Double D-Day."[53] Wave after wave of children were sent into the streets; for the first time since Palm Sunday, Bull Connor ordered that police dogs and clubs be used. Water bursts from high-powered fire hoses bowled over the young demonstrators, some no older than six or seven.[54]

The black community became emotionally keyed up when they saw the children being attacked as they demonstrated non-violently. Adult onlookers responded with a barrage of bricks and bottles directed at the Birmingham policemen and firemen.[55] The next day, Saturday, May 4, Negro spectators were seen brandishing knives and pistols along the fringes of the demonstrations. James Bevel, fearing the possibility of black violence, borrowed a policeman's bullhorn and announced to the crowd, "Everybody get off this corner. If you're not going to demonstrate in a nonviolent manner, then leave."[56] After the crowd dispersed, it was decided to call off further demonstrations for the day.

On Monday and Tuesday, May 6 and 7, the demonstrations reached unprecedented intensity. Birmingham jails, filled with some 2,000 demonstrators, were strained to the breaking point. Young black demonstrators were held in the jails of nearby towns and in barracks at the State Fairgrounds.[57]

During the course of the demonstrations, white downtown retail merchants who were being hurt financially by the continuing black boycott, began to meet together each day. Out of these daily meetings came the decision to initiate negotiations with local black leaders. The white merchants asked David Vann, who had led the drive to change the form of government, and Sidney Smyer, who was an influential Birmingham realtor, to be their primary negotiators with local blacks.[58] Contact with the black community was made through Arthur Shores, a prominent black Birmingham attorney, who represented SCLC and ACMHR[59] The black negotiating committee at the merchants' insistence consisted solely of local blacks; but, the black negotiators served merely as the mouthpiece for Dr. King, taking their orders directly from him.[60]

The black and white negotiating committees met together secretly at night and then reported back to the larger group of leaders of each race during the day in order to detail the progress that had been made and to get further instructions.[61] Mr. Burke Marshall, head of the Civil Rights Division of the U.S. Justice Department, helped facilitate these interracial negotiations by acting as an intermediary.

The local white retail merchants were unwilling to finalize agreements with local blacks, however, without the support of Birmingham's entire business community. It was with the purpose of securing this broader backing that the merchants turned to the Senior Citizens Committee.[62]

The Senior Citizens Committee was a group of seventy business leaders who represented companies that accounted for more than 80% of Birmingham's employment; although they had no official standing, this group of business leaders could make decisions on behalf of the private sector and had enough economic power to ensure that the decision would be implemented.[63] When a meeting of the Senior Citizens Committee was convened on Tuesday, May 7, Jefferson County Sheriff Mel Bailey reported that it would be necessary to impose martial law if the demonstrations were not ended; Assistant Attorney General Burke Marshall stressed the need for negotiations in good faith. Reacting to this counsel, the Senior Citizens Committee empowered a special subcommittee, chaired by Sidney Smyer, to take over the negotiations that had been started by the white merchants.[64] With the full force of the Birmingham business community behind the negotiations, preliminary agreements were quickly reached. Black leaders, satisfied with the terms of the initial offer made by the special Senior Citizens subcommittee, called off the massive demonstrations planned for May 8.[65]

The final terms of the agreement were announced on Friday, May 10, at two simultaneous news conferences. The morally binding agreement provided for:

1. desegregation of lunch counters, rest rooms, fitting rooms, and drinking fountains in all downtown stores within ninety days;
2. placement of blacks in clerical and sales jobs in stores within sixty days;
3. release of prisoners in jail on low bail; and
4. the establishment of permanent communications between white and black leaders.[66]

In order to fulfill the third part of the agreement, it was necessary to raise $237,000 in bail funds; the United Auto Workers, the National Maritime Union, the United Steelworkers Union, and the AFL-CIO quickly contributed the money in order to obtain the release of the 790 demonstrators left in the jails.[67]

With the settlement came an end to the demonstrations, but not an end to the violence. In the early morning hours of Sunday, May 12, only hours after a Ku Klux Klan meeting had ended on the outskirts of town, two bombs exploded at the Ensley home of Reverend A. D. King, Dr. King's younger brother. Within minutes another bomb exploded near Room 30 of the Gaston Motel, which housed the national civil rights leaders.[68] Although the crowd at A. D. King's home was quickly calmed, the neighborhood around the Gaston Motel erupted into violence.

The motel bombing occurred just as the bars in the Negro district were closing; the Saturday-night drinkers hit the streets and began to throw rocks and bottles. Reverend Wyatt Tee Walker began pleading with the mob, "Please go home. This is no good. Throwing rocks won't help"; but the black rioters were in no mood to listen to Walker's entreaties.[69] Finally, after Bull Connor's policemen had been supplemented by Colonel Al Lingo's State Troopers, the area was cleared of civilians. During the two-hour riot, thirty-five blacks and five whites were injured; seven stores and homes were destroyed by fire.[70]

Fearing the outbreak of further racial violence, President Kennedy dispatched Federal troops to bases near Birmingham.[71] Pledging to prevent the biracial agreement from being "sabotaged by a few extremists on either side who think they can defy both the law and the wishes of responsible citizens by inciting or inviting violence," Kennedy also ordered all necessary preliminary steps be taken to call the Alabama National Guard into Federal service.[72]

State troopers and conservation officers, who had been sent to Birmingham to quell the riot, continued to patrol the street in a twenty-eight-block Negro business and residential area. The carbines and shotguns that had been brought out during the riots were put away.[73]

Dr. Martin Luther King, Jr., upon learning of the riots, returned to Birmingham from Atlanta. He conducted a pool-hall pilgrimage in the black areas of Birmingham to preach the doctrine of nonviolence. The blacks, who had rioted, responded to Dr. King's pleas and remained calm in the midst of the tense situation.[74]

A further confrontation did not arise between blacks and whites. The Federal troops did not enter Birmingham; the state forces were slowly withdrawn; local blacks did not react to provocation. The city settled down and began to implement its four-point agreement.

THREE

Governing Officials

The direct action program began on April 3, 1963, less than a day after former Lt. Governor Albert Boutwell had been elected mayor. For the next twelve days, the lame-duck City Commission dealt with the demonstrations, boycotts and sit-ins. On the morning of April 15th, the new mayor and nine-member council were sworn into office; but, they did not begin to exert sole control over the city government until five weeks later.[1] The reason for this lag between the official and actual change-over in governmental control was that the old City Commission simply refused to leave office. Arguing that a 1959 state legislative act implied that the switch should not occur until October, 1965, Mayor Art Hanes said, "We're sitting right here, we're not moving, and we're going to continue to govern this city as we have been doing until the Supreme Court says otherwise."[2] Between April 15, 1963, and May 23, 1963, when the Alabama Supreme Court ruled that the City Council was the legitimate government in Birmingham, the City Commission and the Mayor-Council shared control of the Birmingham government.[3] During the period of the direct action program, April 3rd to May 11th, Birmingham was probably not the city with the best government in the world, but it did have the most government—with two complete sets of governing bodies in City Hall.[4] The local joke during this time was that Birmingham was the only city in the United States with two mayors, a King and a parade every day.[5]

The relationship between the City Council and the City Commission remained amiable during the five-week period of dual government.[6] Office space was quickly arranged in City Hall for Mayor Boutwell's use.[7] Although a slight conflict arose because both governments attempted to hold their weekly meetings at the same time in the same room, a generally satisfactory working relationship existed between officials in the two governments.[8] The City Council's weekly meetings would immediately follow the City Commission's meeting; the same agenda would be discussed and acted upon by the two groups.[9] During the five weeks of shared power, none but the most routine matters necessary for the day-to-day operation of the city's business was considered for adoption by either the Commission or the Council; thus, no significant disagreements arose during this period.[10] In order to avoid any difficulties, paychecks to city employees were also signed by both Mayors.[11]

Complete coordination did not exist, however, between the City Commission and the Mayor-Council. There was virtually no communication between the three-member commission and the nine-member council.[12] The primary lines of communication were between Mayor Boutwell and the City Commission; thus, the City Council was only indirectly in contact with the City Commission.[13]

Throughout the duration of the direct action program, Commissioner Bull Connor remained in firm control of the Birmingham Police and Fire Departments.[14] The new City Council and Mayor failed to challenge this control, thereby abdicating their potential for influence over the handling of the demonstrations.[15] It is informative to analyze separately the positions and actions taken by the two Birmingham city governments in relation to the direct action program.

City Commission

The racial attitudes held by the individual City Commissioners significantly affected the official position they adopted toward the direct action program. Each of the three Commissioners was a product of the Southern segregated social system; each was dedicated to upholding that social system by the use of every available means. It is informative to review briefly the racial attitudes held by the three City Commissioners—Public Improvements Commissioner James T. "Jabo" Waggoner, Public Safety Commissioner T. Eugene "Bull" Connor, and Mayor Arthur J. Hanes.

In his 1956 campaign for the City Commission, Jabo Waggoner cashed in on the segregationist sentiments of the white electorate in Birmingham. Proclaiming that he was "the grandson of two Confederate veterans—a true son of Dixie [who had been] born and bred in the traditions of our South," Mr. Waggoner reiterated his dedication to the preservation of segregation. During his tenure in office, Waggoner maintained a low profile and only infrequently spoke out on racial issues. In the mayoral campaign of 1963, however, Mr. Waggoner again revealed his racist tendencies. Commenting that Birmingham had suffered from a cholera epidemic or "black plague" in 1873, Waggoner told an assembled audience that, "next Tuesday [in the mayoral election], the black plague can sweep this city unless you choose wisely."[16]

Undoubtedly the best known of the three-member commission was T. Eugene "Bull" Connor. Commissioner Connor had earned his nickname of "Bull" while announcing simulated play-by-play baseball games for a Birmingham radio station in the late 1920's. In this method of broadcasting, the plays only came in every few minutes; Connor, however, had to announce as if the game were going on before his eyes. Thus, when there was a break in the information, he had to "shoot the bull" in order to maintain the pretense of live broadcasting.[17]

Although otherwise astute observers have argued that Connor, "was first a politician and only secondarily a racist . . . [who] used racism for political purposes rather than as an ideology," it would be much more accurate to argue that Bull Connor was a long-time racist who believed in strict segregation.[18] Seven pieces of evidence can be used to prove Bull Connor's long and consistent history as a racist. First, as early as 1942, Bull Connor revealed his blatantly racist attitudes. In a letter to President Franklin D. Roosevelt, Connor posed a rhetorical question and then responded to it:

> When the downfall of the doctrine of white supremacy is advocated and taught by agitators and federal officials, who know absolutely nothing about the Negro problem in the South, what happens? Negroes become impudent, unruly, arrogant, law-breaking, violent and insolent . . . Amalgamation of the races will result in lawlessness, disunity and probable bloodshed.[19]

Second, after pledging to walk out of the 1948 Democratic Convention if a civil rights plank were adopted, Connor won the state-wide election for delegate-at-large on the basis of strong support in the conservative Black Belt counties.[20] When a civil rights plank was adopted, Bull Connor and half the Alabama delegation walked out of the convention; Connor was confident that a dramatic gesture of this kind would, "help roll back the attempt of meddlers, agitators and communist stooges to force down our throats, through our own Democratic Party, the bitter dose they are now offering us under the false name of Civil Liberties."[21]

Third, determined to uphold both the tradition and the laws of segregation, Bull Connor brazenly arrested and jailed Henry Wallace's

Progressive Party Vice-Presidential candidate, Senator Glen Taylor, when the Senator entered a Birmingham building through the "colored" entrance.[22]

Fourth, Connor utilized the Red Scare in his continuing attempts to oppose any breaks in segregation. In an article published in 1950, Connor argued that, "Communist elements are responsible for stirring up all the trouble between white people and colored people, especially in the South."[23]

Fifth, Connor utilized all the tactics of a professional race-hater in his successful 1957 campaign for Commissioner of Public Safety.[24] Sixth, Connor received the open support of the Ku Klux Klan in his 1960 state-wide race for Democratic national committeeman.[25] Seventh, Bull's close ties with the Klan led to the Birmingham Police Department's failure to prevent the beating of the Freedom Riders by Klansmen on Bloody Mother's Day, 1961.[26]

From observing Bull's long history of statements and actions, it must be concluded that Connor actually did adhere to racism as an ideology. This ideology was shared by Birmingham's Mayor during the early 1960's—Arthur J. Hanes. Mayor Hanes spoke more openly than Connor in public forums concerning his racial attitudes.[27] Describing integration and Communism as "one and the same," Mayor Hanes lamented the fact that the Negroes, who were a "simple, happy people," were being exploited in the Communist scheme to topple the United States.[28] According to Hanes, the 1963 direct action program was planned and executed in part by Communists[29] and professional agitators.[30] Hanes thus felt justified in advocating that, "The Nigger King ought to be investigated by the Attorney General."[31]

The City Commissioners in 1963 were blatant racists; they had been elected on strict segregation platforms and had committed themselves to maintaining complete segregation of the races. Thus, the goal sought by the City Commission during the 1963 direct action program was the preservation of the status quo in race relations. Rather than recognizing that change was inevitable, the City Commission remained adamantly opposed to any modification in Birmingham's rigid patterns of racial segregation.[32] In their unrelenting advocacy of segregation the City Commission utilized a series of varied strategies against the black demonstrators.

Since each City Commissioner was assigned a separate functional area of government, Bull Connor, as Public Safety Commissioner, had independent control of the police and fire departments.[33] During the 1963 demonstrations, Mayor Hanes and Commissioner Waggoner had no voice in determining police strategies; in effect, Bull Connor exercised dictatorial control over the police and fire department throughout Project C.[34]

In deciding how to handle the demonstrations in the spring of 1963, Bull Connor had two strikingly different alternatives. First, he could bring his police reserves to every black demonstration, show no mercy, and beat the participants back into their ghettos. This method would result in bad publicity, but it would prevent the downtown business district from serving as the scene of confrontation. Second, he could order his policemen to non-violently herd the protestors into groups and to take them off to jail quietly.[35] Commissioner Connor's past actions would have suggested that the first alternative would have been pursued throughout the demonstrations. But, Bull Connor and his Chief of Police, Jamie Moore, had observed the success with which Chief Laurie Pritchett of Albany, Georgia, had pursued a non-violent police strategy when demonstrations occurred there.[36] In order to achieve his goal of preserving segregation, Bull Connor was willing to adopt at least initially a non-violent strategy toward demonstrations.

The first few days of the direct action program were unique in Birmingham for the civility of the police; Commissioner Connor demonstrated an unsuspected judiciousness in his work. Demonstrators were warned away from their targets and then quietly arrested. Although Connor allowed police dogs to be used to control crowds on Palm Sunday, April 7, he continued to behave like the comparatively benign Laurie Pritchett.[37]

This calm, reasoned approach was in evidence when the City Commission acted upon an official request by Reverend Fred Shuttlesworth for a parade permit. Rather than publicly proclaiming that it would throw the request in the wastebasket, as Mayor Hanes had done in 1962, the Commission passed a unanimous resolution stating that, "the public welfare, peace, safety, good order, and convenience of the people of the City of Birmingham, both white and colored, require that the application for said [parade] permit be denied."[38]

Throughout the demonstrations, Bull Connor and police officials utilized their extensive contacts to dissuade the Ku Klux Klan from entering Birmingham and exacerbating the situation.[39] The issuance of the state court injunction barring civil rights leaders from encouraging or engaging in demonstrations was also an outgrowth of Connor's non-violent counter-strategy. He hoped that a legal approach of this nature would defuse the demonstrations.

Two factors prevented the continued use of this non-violent police strategy. First, this method of handling demonstrations ran counter to every previous action that Bull Connor had taken as Public Safety Commissioner. Over the course of twenty years, Connor had built up an image of being an arch-segregationist who would tolerate no attempt to change the racial status quo. To continue to pursue the non-violent strategy would have destroyed that image.[40] Second, the massive size of the demonstrations also caused Connor to abandon his relative restraint.[41] When Double-D Day occurred—Friday, May 3—with hundreds of black youths marching toward the downtown business district, Bull Connor reacted by using police dogs, policemen with nightsticks, and pressure fire hoses against the demonstrators.[42]

The non-violent police strategy practiced for a month gave way to an oppressive use of police power against the demonstrators. After hoses, dogs, and clubs had been used on demonstrators for several days, Commissioner Connor remarked that, "We've just begun to fight."[43] When Reverend Fred Shuttlesworth, president of the local ACMHR, was injured by a blast of water from the pressure fire hoses and had to be taken away in an ambulance, Bull Connor commented, "I wish they'd carried him away in a hearse."[44] In general, black demonstrators suffered a wide range of injuries from Birmingham police during the final week of demonstrations.[45]

Once negotiations between local whites and blacks began, the City Commission refused to cooperate. Mayor Hanes adamantly refused to discuss the possibility of abolishing local segregation ordinances with black leaders while the demonstrations were occurring.[46] Bull Connor unsuccessfully attempted to prevent any interracial negotiations during this period.[47]

When the desegregation agreement between the Senior Citizens Committee and black leaders was announced, Mayor Hanes reacted by calling the white negotiators, "a bunch of quisling, gutless traitors."[48] Connor and Hanes unsuccessfully advocated that a counter-boycott be organized by Birmingham whites against downtown retail merchants who were willing to desegregate, in order to demonstrate which race had the real economic power.[49]

In implementing the strategies against civil rights demonstrators, Bull Connor was able to use the full police power of Birmingham. During the early 1960's, the Birmingham police generally held racial attitudes that were similar to those of Commissioner Connor.[50] With no official lines of communication with the black community, the Birmingham police displayed a general lack of understanding of the problems faced by blacks in a segregated urban area.[51]

The general lack of understanding led to police brutality toward blacks. Many of the Birmingham police viewed blacks as being indolent, immoral, criminal, and intellectually inferior; these views led the police to adopt different methods of policing the black and white communities. Blacks would often be arrested for minor offenses, such as traffic violations and gambling; very serious crimes, committed by one black against another, were treated very lightly.[52]

With these attitudes, the Birmingham police felt relatively comfortable when stringent methods were employed against demonstrators during the direct action program. Although Chief Jamie Moore was supposedly in control of the Birmingham Police Department during the demonstrations, Bull Connor normally controlled police activity at the scene of the demonstrations.[53] There was no conflict between the values of the man who determined police strategies and those who executed them. Thus, with a compliant, even eager police, the City Commission could easily put its strategies to work.

City Council

The newly-elected Mayor and City Council did not share the strict segregationist views of the City Commissioners. As a result, the goals and strategies pursued by the City Council did not coincide completely with those of the City Commission. The position taken toward the direct action program by the City Council can perhaps be better understood by a brief review of the racial attitudes of the Mayor and the Councilmen.

Mayor Albert Boutwell was an extremely cautious politician, who had served as the sole state Senator from Jefferson County and as Lt. Governor of Alabama.[54] After the 1954 Supreme Court Decision in *Brown v. Board*, Albert Boutwell played a prominent role in attempts to prevent school desegregation. As chairman of a state interim legislative committee, Boutwell initially recommended that the Alabama legislature vote to abolish the constitutional provision that the state maintain a public school system. When this idea was rejected, he co-authored the "freedom of choice" bills, which permitted parents to request that their children be transferred to schools other than the ones to which they were assigned by the school board.[55]

Throughout his political career, Boutwell endorsed legal resistance as the only acceptable method of opposing desegregation attempts.

Working with Mayor Boutwell in the new city government was a nine-member, all-white City Council, which was described by one of its members as a very conservative body.[56] Although the mayor and the City Councilmen were dedicated to segregation, it was anticipated that they would adopt a more moderate method of defending the status quo in race relations.[57] Rather than viewing the maintenance of segregation as the primary goal of local government, as did the City Commission, the new City Council felt that lawful behavior was more important. In a statement that was consistent with his previous attempts to prevent school desegregation, Albert Boutwell stated, "I am determined that we are going to defend, I hope maintain, segregation, but we are not going to be a city of unrestrained and unhampered mockery of the law."[58]

By valuing legality above the preservation of segregation by any means, the City Council disagreed with the goals of the City Commission; the newly-elected officials, however, did not attempt to moderate the police strategies toward demonstrators. The Council failed to exert any influence over the handling of the demonstrations for three reasons. First, the Council realized that Bull Connor had control over the police and fire departments.[59] Second, since the Alabama Supreme Court did not rule until May 23 on the issue of which was the legitimate form of government in Birmingham, the newly-elected City Council was unsure of its status. Thus, they were hesitant to try to exert any significant influence over police strategies.[60] Third, the City Council basically agreed with both the restrained method and later the violence with which the Birmingham police were handling the demonstrations. In a unanimous resolution, the City Council commended the law enforcement agencies of Birmingham for their actions during the demonstrations.[61] The City Council also praised Colonel Al Lingo, the racist head of the Alabama State Troopers, who had brutally quelled the disturbances following the bombings on May 12, 1963. In a letter to Lingo, the Council stated:

> . . . Your men met every expectation as to firmness, restraints and alertness.
> All of us do appreciate the fine services and protection of your Troopers. We shall never forget it.[62]

In addition to agreeing with the police tactics adopted by the City Commission, the City Council concurred on major policy decisions. For example, Mayor Boutwell suggested that the City Council deny the parade permit requested by Reverend Shuttlesworth because, "such a parade would be a provocation to further disorder and to possible, indeed probable violence along its route or in other areas of the city."[63] The City Council responded by unanimously rejecting the request for a parade permit; the language of the resolution adopted by the City Council was identical to the one adopted by the Commission.[64]

The primary difference in the strategies adopted by the two city governments involved negotiations with the local black leaders. While the City Commission adamantly refused to meet with blacks while the demonstrations were continuing, the City Council quietly met with local black leaders. The Council members felt that if they could convince local blacks to begin negotiations, then the demonstrations would end, and the Council's goal of maintaining law and order would be achieved.[65]

The communications and negotiations between Birmingham blacks and the newly-elected city officials were conducted primarily on an individual, informal basis.[66] During the demonstrations, Councilman Alan T. Drennen, who had received strong black support in the city election, met periodically with local black leaders in an attempt to resolve major differences.[67] When Burke Marshall, the head of the Civil Rights Division of the U.S. Justice Department, entered Birmingham to assist in negotiations, a representative of the City Council worked with Marshall and local blacks.[68] Although the Council later denied any role in the negotiations, Mayor Boutwell and some Council members attended the larger negotiating meetings with the Senior Citizens Committee.[69] But the newly-elected city officials did not play a very prominent role in the final stages of negotiations which resulted in the desegregation agreement.

Summary

The City Commission adhered so strongly to their segregationist stands that they could not or would not realize that change in race relations was inevitable. In seeking to prevent desegregation, Bull Connor initially adopted a non-violent police strategy toward demonstrators. The massive size of the demonstrations and the image he had developed through his previous actions as Public Safety Commissioner, however, caused Bull Connor to unleash the full force of local police powers against the demonstrators. The Birmingham

Police Department responded to Bull Connor's commands and provided a significant resource in the Commission's attempts to fight desegregation.

The conservative, cautious City Council wanted to maintain law and order, but it was continually impeded by Connor's continued control of the police force and its own uncertain status as the legitimate government of Birmingham. Although more moderate in their racial attitudes than the Commissioners, the Mayor and City Councilmen primarily agreed with the Commission's handling of the demonstrations. The Council's willingness to negotiate at least covertly with local blacks constituted the only significant difference in strategy between the Council and the Commission. Between the swearing-in of the newly-elected city officials on April 15, 1963, and the Alabama Supreme Court decision on May 24, 1963, the City of Birmingham had too many governors, but no recognized government.[70] The lack of strong local governmental leadership during this crucial period had a detrimental effect on Birmingham.[71] The city faced the direct action program during the throes of a leadership crisis; because of the intransigence of the City Commission and the inactivity of the Mayor-Council, a political vacuum existed in Birmingham during a period in which it needed strong, progressive leadership.

FOUR

External Governments

During the course of the direct action program, a strained relationship existed between the federal and the state government. This conflict, which was to last for several years, arose as a result of differing views of the proper role the federal government should play in relation to the state, especially in civil rights matters. President John F. Kennedy, who was personally committed to ending segregation, felt that the federal government should insure that federal statutes were upheld and federal court orders were obeyed. He advocated the use of mediation and persuasion as the proper federal action to protect civil rights; when those methods failed, lawsuits and court actions should be used.[1] Kennedy, however, rejected proposals by the U.S. Civil Rights Commission that federal funds be withheld from areas that denied civil rights to blacks.[2] By the spring of 1963, after two years in office, Kennedy had also neither proposed nor strongly advocated progressive civil rights legislation.

In running for governor of Alabama in 1962, George Wallace defeated two candidates who were relatively moderate on the race issue.[3] He built his victory on a promise never to compromise on desegregation.[4] In his inaugural address, Wallace reaffirmed his position by thundering to the assembled crowd, "Segregation now, segregation tomorrow, segregation forever."[5] The governor remained unalterably opposed to any strong initiative by the federal government in the area of civil rights. Talking the words of defiance and interdiction, Wallace called on Alabamians to "rise to the call of freedom-loving blood that is in us and send our answer to the tyranny that clanks its chains upon the South. I draw the line in the dust and toss the gauntlet before the feet of tyranny."[6]

With such widely disparate views, it was inevitable that Kennedy and Wallace would strongly disagree over the proper position that should be taken during the direct action program in Birmingham. The most severe conflict occurred after the settlement was announced between the Senior Citizens Committee and the civil rights leaders. As a result of the bombings of Reverend A. D. King's home and the Gaston Motel and the ensuing riots, President Kennedy deployed riot-control army troops to military bases in Alabama in order to prepare for the possibility of further racial disturbances in Birmingham.

Rather than thanking Kennedy for his assistance, Governor Wallace denounced the President's actions by saying:

> We must preserve liberty and freedom in Alabama and in the nation. This military dictatorship must be nipped in the bud. These federal military troops must be removed from Alabama at once if free government is to continue.[7]

This ironic statement was the political basis for Alabama's legal attempt to thwart Kennedy's actions. The state of Alabama tried to file an original bill of complaint in the U.S. Supreme Court against the United States and the Secretary of Defense, seeking relief from the deployment of troops to federal installations in the Birmingham area. The Supreme Court denied the state of Alabama's motion for leave to file the bill of complaint, ruling that the President's actions were "purely preparatory measures" affording no basis for judicial relief.[8]

The antagonism between the federal and state governments, which was very apparent in the controversy over the deployment of federal troops, existed throughout the duration of the direct action program. In order to better understand this federal-state relationship, it is informative to analyze the goals, strategies, and resources of the federal government and of the state government.

Federal Government

Having been informed in advance of the planned demonstrations in Birmingham, President Kennedy adopted a very cautious policy toward the direct action program.[9] Both the President and Attorney General Robert Kennedy initially called the demonstrations "ill-timed" because they perceived the in-coming Boutwell city administration to be more moderate on racial issues than the City Commission had been.[10] When Dr. King was jailed on Good Friday, April 12, 1963, pressure was exerted on Kennedy to intervene; rather than taking action, the Kennedy administration stated that, "the federal government has no authority to take legal action to intervene in Birmingham as the situation now stands."[11] Kennedy also refused to introduce federal troops to protect civil rights demonstrators during the latter stages of the direct action program when Bull Connor began to use police dogs, fire hoses and nightsticks against blacks. The failure of the Kennedy administration to take formal action in Birmingham was premised on the belief that no federal statute had been violated there and thus action was not warranted.[12]

The goal of the federal government in relation to the direct action program was not solely to end the demonstrations. Instead, President Kennedy sought just and equitable remedies to the "very real abuses too long inflicted on the Negro citizens of that community."[13]

In its attempts to aid in the settlement of disputes in Birmingham, the Kennedy administration relied primarily on informal action.[14] Trying to define its own proper role, the administration argued that the primary responsibility for peace in Birmingham rested with the "leaders of business, labor and the bar, as well as city officials themselves."[15] Thus, the Kennedy administration basically tried to stimulate and facilitate, rather than dominate, serious negotiations between black and white leaders in Birmingham.[16]

Two basic informal strategies were utilized by the federal government. First, the Kennedy administration both directly and indirectly tried to pressure influential Birmingham business and industrial leaders into lending their support to the negotiations. President John Kennedy, Attorney General Robert Kennedy, Secretary of the Treasury Douglas Dillon, and Defense Secretary Robert McNamara, made dozens of phone calls to old friends and to political and business contacts in Birmingham, stressing the need for a quick settlement of the disputes in the city.[17] Eugene V. Rostow, Dean of the Yale Law School, urged one of his graduates, Roger Blough, Chairman of the Board of U.S. Steel, to intercede with the president of his corporation's Birmingham subsidiary; Blough quickly called his Birmingham associates and emphasized the importance of their involvement in reaching a negotiated settlement.[18]

The second informal strategy involved direct attempts to solve the difficult task of mediating the differences between blacks and whites in Birmingham. When Assistant Attorney General Burke Marshall entered Birmingham in early May, 1963, there was very little communication between the black and white communities.[19] As a result of this lack of interracial communication and the down-playing of the demonstrations by the local newspapers, white leaders literally did not know the goals of the direct action program.[20] Burke Marshall sought to open lines of communication between the races, to inform each race of the positions of the other, and to arrange negotiations between blacks and whites.[21] Meeting with groups and with individual leaders in the black and white communities, Burke Marshall began to succeed at his task.[22]

Marshall spoke bluntly to each group. He reminded whites of the limited demands of the blacks—the right to have a cup of coffee, the right to token jobs, amnesty for demonstrators. He posed the possibility of real violence developing in the black community if Dr. King's non-violent methods were unsuccessful.[23] Marshall warned black leaders against the strategy of trying to provoke intervention by federal troops.[24]

Benefitting from Marshall's persistent prodding, local leaders finally reached the settlement. The Kennedy administration immediately hailed the agreement as "a tremendous step forward for Birmingham, for Alabama, and for the South."[25] President Kennedy felt that the agreement was an important advance, not simply because it ended the Birmingham demonstrations, but because, "it recognized the fundamental right of all citizens to be accorded equal treatment and opportunity."[26]

The federal government had formidable resources that it could muster in implementing its strategy of informal action.[27] It was by relying upon the power of its prestige that the federal government was able to convince many conservative businessmen to support the negotiations. In addition, Burke Marshall proved to leaders of both races that he could deal openly and fairly with them. Although Mayor Hanes criticized Marshall for "negotiating behind our backs," leaders of both races praised the assistant attorney general's diplomacy and noted his indispensable efforts in bringing about the agreement.[28]

State Government

The favorable attitude held by the federal government toward the civil rights movement was not shared by the state government in Alabama. Governor George Wallace was an arch-segregationist who viewed Negroes as being "easy going, basically happy, unambitious, [and] incapable of much learning."[29] Wallace's opposition to desegregation efforts was paralleled by his staunch opposition to federal intervention; he pledged his efforts to fight the "continued usurpation of state sovereignty."[30]

When the direct action program began in Birmingham, Wallace labelled the demonstrators as "lawless Negro mobs," who had received assistance from Communists.[31] Having covertly supported Bull Connor in the recent mayoral race, Wallace backed up the strategies that Connor employed against the demonstrators.[32] Wallace increased the police power that Connor could use against demonstrators by sending Colonel Al Lingo, head of the state troopers, into Birmingham with a few hundred men. Governor Wallace also phoned Sheriff Jim Clark of Dallas County and asked if he could furnish some assistance to Connor. Sheriff Clark agreed to take part of his regular force of eight deputies and about a hundred members of his "irregular posse" to Birmingham.[33]

These two law enforcement officials had absolutely no understanding of urban problems or the civil rights struggle.[34] Although the Birmingham police welcomed their presence, local blacks felt that Lingo was a beast; the state troopers, the city police, and the deputized white irregulars were perceived by local blacks as constituting little more than an organized vigilante mob operating under the protective shield of authority.[35] Although Lingo and Clark were a standing insult to blacks, Governor Wallace nevertheless kept them in Birmingham for several weeks.[36]

Governor Wallace felt that the entire crisis in Birmingham was precipitated by the Kennedy administration.[37] Wallace protested that, "when Negro mobs demonstrate and bring about property damage and injury to constitutional authorities, they are given sympathy and tacit approval by the high officialdom in Washington."[38] The governor tried to frighten Alabamians into believing that the Kennedy administration wanted "to surrender [Alabama] to Martin Luther King and his group."[39]

When negotiations began between white business leaders and local blacks, Wallace lined up with Commissioner Connor and Mayor Hanes, by stating "I, as governor . . . will not be party to any such meeting to compromise on the issues of segregation."[40] In addition to denying any participation in the negotiations, Wallace denounced the white negotiators by saying, "The so-called bi-racial negotiating group of appeasers . . . have played right into the hands of Martin Luther King and his cohorts."[41]

The Alabama legislature was very supportive of Wallace's actions in Birmingham. The legislature also condemned civil rights leaders by labelling the direct action program as one of "calculated hate, planned unrest, useless destruction of private and public property, and needless agitation between the white and colored races."[42] In reaction to the Birmingham crisis, the legislature created a Commission to Preserve the Peace and empowered it to investigate and interrogate groups engaging in activities that were "detrimental to the peace and dignity of the State of Alabama."[43] Soon after enactment of the enabling legislation, the legislature revealed the bill's intent by requesting that the Commission investigate the Senior Citizens Committee, which had negotiated the Birmingham settlement.[44]

Summary

The federal government sought reasoned and reasonable solutions to the problems plaguing blacks in Birmingham. Refusing to take official or legal action, President John F. Kennedy did use the influence of the national government to aid in the establishment of serious negotiations between leaders of both races in Birmingham.

By sending Colonel Al Lingo and Sheriff Jim Clark to Birmingham, Governor Wallace provided a significant addition to the police forces which were at Bull Connor's disposal; this action also indicated Wallace's lack of concern for the welfare and safety of the Birmingham black community. As an extension of his staunch support of segregation, Governor Wallace criticized the role played by the federal government in facilitating negotiations. The Alabama legislature joined Wallace in opposing the negotiating efforts of white business leaders in Birmingham.

It is evident that the federal and state governments were working at cross-purposes during the direct action program in Birmingham. While the federal government sought to mediate differences in Birmingham, the actions of the state government exacerbated the problems.

FIVE

White Electorate

Every segment of Birmingham's white electorate was concerned with the direct action program which occurred in the spring of 1963. Although a new city government had just been elected, no local official exerted sufficient influence to unify the different elements of the white electorate during the civil rights demonstrations. By viewing the actions and reactions of three different elements in the white community during the direct action program, it is possible to gauge the range of racial attitudes held by Birmingham's white electorate.

The first group of whites favored the preservation of the status quo in race relations. Their desire to maintain segregation, however, was bound by their unwillingness to use violence. These whites supported the change in Birmingham's governmental form from a City Commission to a Mayor-Council; this group also rejected Bull Connor's hard-line approach to preserving segregation in favor of the more moderate approach advocated by Albert Boutwell.

The actions taken and positions advocated by Birmingham's business leaders adequately reflected the prevalent racial attitudes of the city's white community. The powerful Senior Citizens Committee, which served as the voice of the entire Birmingham business community during the direct action program, flatly stated its opposition to desegregation.[1] This committee had suggested in 1962 that all Birmingham businesses distribute a bulletin which stated in part, "all employees are advised and requested to refrain from any participation, direct or indirect . . . in public demonstrations in connection with racial, social or other controversies."[2] In effect, Birmingham business leaders, like the majority of the white community, identified themselves with the racial status quo and regarded any rupture in it with apprehension.[3]

A second racial attitude was held by the most enlightened members of Birmingham's white community. These whites were willing to admit, at least to themselves, that the purpose of segregation was to perpetuate the economic, social, and political oppression of blacks. Although this attitude was privately acknowledged by many whites in Birmingham, it was rarely publicly proclaimed. It was the "age-old fear of ostracism, of being not merely an outsider, but an outcast from your own community" that caused many "white liberals" to remain quiet.[4] Those whites who fearlessly fought for significant racial and social change often came under intense personal and economic pressure.[5]

A third racial attitude held by a significant number of Birmingham citizens was one of white supremacy. This segment of the population adamantly opposed any moderation on the issues of segregation. The citizens who held these racist attitudes often joined extra-party, pro-segregation groups such as the Ku Klux Klan. Working through these organizations, the white extremists advocated and employed extra-legal and illegal means to achieve their goal of complete racial segregation. In the political sphere, they supported the actions of Mayor Art Hanes, Commissioner Bull Connor, and Governor George Wallace.[6]

Although all three racial attitudes—moderate segregationist, liberal, and white supremacist—were held by different segments of the Birmingham white electorate, there was an uneven numerical distribution along the spectrum. The vast majority of Birmingham whites, including most of the city's business leaders, held moderate segregationist attitudes. Since most white liberals refused to state their racial attitudes publicly, it is difficult to estimate their number in 1963; but, it is safe to assume that the number was limited. Bull Connor's ability to draw over 20,000 votes in the 1963 mayoral run-off was a valid indication that a significant segment of the electorate was ardent racist.

It is difficult to accurately explain the social classes from which these three groups in the white electorate drew their members. There were often personal and psychological factors that caused an individual to hold a specific racial attitude. Thus, there was not a direct correspondence between an individual's social class and his position on segregation.

The ranks of Birmingham's business leaders were composed of native citizens, who were associated with familial enterprises, and corporate nomads, who were assigned to Birmingham by their national corporations.[7] As a relatively new city, Birmingham did not have a layer of aristocratic families like Mobile and Charleston. Instead, most of the upper-class families in Birmingham had profited from the city's mineral wealth. The city's wealthy natives had grown up in a segregated society and had enjoyed all the benefits of being the dominant class; the corporate nomads accepted or adjusted to the social system.[8] The business leaders benefitted in two ways from segregation. First, by playing on the racist tendencies of the white workers, Birmingham business leaders were able to prevent the unification of black and white workers; by dealing with what was effectively two separate labor markets, the local business leaders were able to exploit their workers. Second, since the employment opportunities for blacks were extremely limited, many were forced to work as domestics for low wages; it was in the homes of the city's wealthy families that the blacks worked. Since the white businessmen accrued personal and economic benefits from segregation, most of them endorsed the racial status quo.

The white liberals who did challenge the existing racial situation were often the well-educated upper-middle-class professionals.[9] In part as a result of their education and cosmopolitan experiences, these individuals realized the injustices arising from a system that judged a person on the color of his skin rather than on his individual accomplishments. Several of the city's young white professionals were in the forefront of attempts to effect important political reforms.[10] Although most of the wealthy individuals in Birmingham were unwilling to challenge segregation since they benefitted from it, a few of these upper-class individuals openly expressed their opposition to segregation.[11] A few members of the city's three white colleges also adopted relatively liberal positions on the race issue.[12]

At the opposite end of the ideological spectrum from the white liberals were the white racists. Although individuals in every social class held hard-line segregationist positions, the individuals who joined the white extremist organizations were primarily industrial workers and rural farmers.[13] During the early-1960's, these lower-class whites were assured that no matter how poor or ill-educated they were, the blacks would always occupy an even lower status. The black's lowliness often served to distract the bigot from a sense of worthlessness; the black's proclaimed bestiality and carnality warded off the bigot's dim awareness that he, too, had to deal with the impulses he decried in others; the black's demands, or forsaken ambitions, reflected the bigot's envies and feelings of loss or weakness. The white extremists saw the civil rights movement as a distinct challenge to their social and economic status. If racial barriers were lowered, then these whites would no longer have the artificially maintained buffer of blacks beneath them. The violent reaction of white extremists to the advances made by the civil rights movement was a result of this fear of losing status.[14]

In order to better understand the Birmingham white electorate, it is beneficial to review the goals, strategies, and resources of the Birmingham business leaders, white liberal activists, and white extremists in relation to the 1963 direct action program.

Business Leaders

An arresting fact about Birmingham's business leaders in 1963 was that most of them did not live in the city. Instead, they lived in the outlying suburbs. But the fact that they were not Birmingham voters did not prevent the local businessmen from periodically playing prominent roles in the city's political affairs. For example, these businessmen initiated and encouraged the drive for the change in Birmingham's governmental form.[15] The 1963 direct action program was another incident in which the business leaders played a crucial role.

The local business leaders were unified in their opposition to the direct action program. At the beginning of Project C, weeks before the really massive street demonstrations began, several groups condemned the civil rights protests. The Young Men's Business Club, a relatively moderate organization of young professionals and businessmen, passed a resolution that stated in part: "We urge all citizens in Birmingham to co-operate in preventing the growth of racial tensions by ignoring the current demonstrations."[16] The board of directors of the Birmingham Chamber of Commerce expressed a much stronger opposition to the demonstrations by "condemning the efforts of Martin Luther King and his outside lieutenants to create hate and dissension among our citizens."[17] The local newspapers, which were tied to the city's business community, questioned the motivation of the national black leaders. For example, the Birmingham Post-Herald criticized "the outside agitators [who] make a profession of trouble-making and take from it profitable returns."[18] The entire business community was distressed over the initiation of Project C.

The business community in Birmingham was not a single entity, however. Instead, the businesses, as in any large town, could be divided into two economic groups. First, there were the retail merchants, who dealt directly with the consuming public.[19] Second, there was a group of bankers and industrialists who had only infrequent contact with individual consumers.[20]

As a result of their different economic functions, the two groups often had different perspectives on issues.

During the 1963 direct action program, the retail merchants and the banking-industrial leaders were affected in different ways. As a result, the two groups were motivated by different concerns. In order to have a complete understanding of the role played by Birmingham's business leaders, it is necessary to analyze the actions and reactions of both groups.

The downtown retail merchants were directly hurt by the black boycott, which was a central strategy of Project C.[21] But since the Birmingham black community possessed a relatively limited share of the city's total purchasing power, the effect of the boycott alone did not have a critical effect on the local merchants.[22] Instead, the demonstrations and marches had the most significant negative economic effect because white shoppers were afraid to go downtown.[23] This suspension of white purchasing power, in addition to the black boycott, caused retail sales in Birmingham department stores to decline by 15% to 20%.[24] It was this significant decrease in retail sales that stimulated local merchants to seek a negotiated settlement with civil rights leaders.[25] In effect, the merchants acted in order to preserve their own economic interest.[26]

Although the direct action program had a direct negative economic effect on the local retail merchants, the demonstrations and boycotts only indirectly affected the banking-industrial leaders in Birmingham. A less immediate, but equally damaging economic problem confronted the city's bankers and industrialists. As a result of a general economic slow-down in Birmingham during the early 1960's, the banking-industrial leaders had been suffering financial losses for some time. During the years preceding the 1963 direct action program, new plant investment in Birmingham had declined by more than three-quarters; because of this lack of infusion of new capital investments, the number of jobs available in Birmingham had grown less than in any of the major cities in the southeast.[27] Thus, the city slipped in its relative economic standing in the region.

Birmingham's banking-industrial leaders slowly began to realize that the city's negative image throughout the United States was the primary contributing factor to the area's slow-down in economic growth.[28] The city's image was one of "reaction, rebellion and riots, bigotry, bias, and backwardness."[29] Potential investors simply refused to locate in a city with such a long history of poor race relations.[30] The businessmen came to understand that in order to revitalize the local economy it would be necessary to seek modifications in Birmingham's strictly segregated social system.[31] A prime example of this re-orientation in thought involved Mr. Sidney Smyer, who was instrumental in the 1963 negotiations with local blacks.

Mr. Smyer, like most Birmingham businessmen, was a staunch supporter of segregation; as a delegate to the 1948 Democratic national convention, he had participated in the walk-out over the Convention's adoption of a civil rights plank.[32] While he was president of the Birmingham Chamber of Commerce in 1961, Mr. Smyer went on a trip to Tokyo with a large number of American businessmen. During the trip, Smyer learned of the negative image that Birmingham had throughout the U.S. and the hesitancy of businessmen to make investments in the city. When Smyer returned to Birmingham, he was convinced that in order for the city to prosper economically, it was necessary to seek moderate racial and social change.[33]

The direct action program and the possibility of serious violence quickly raised the salience of the racial issues for many of Birmingham's banking and industrial leaders.[34] Although not suffering direct financial losses, these business leaders realized that racial unrest perpetuated the city's negative image, which in turn compounded Birmingham's economic problems.[35] It was this realization that "civil unrest [was] bad for business" that convinced the banking-industrial leaders to accept many of the social changes sought by the civil rights demonstrators.[36] Thus, during Project C, Birmingham's most powerful business leaders took positive action in hopes of reversing the city's trend toward economic decay.

In trying to attain their goals of minimizing their economic losses and promoting the local economy, the Birmingham business leaders—both the merchants and the bankers-industrialists—pursued the strategy of negotiating with local black leaders.[37] The negotiations were initiated by the downtown retail merchants, who were directly affected by the direct action program.[38] Instead of negotiating directly with local blacks, the store-owners had certain representatives who held discussions with the leaders in the city's black community.[39]

Realizing that their retail establishments would be vulnerable to a counter-boycott by whites who opposed desegregation, the merchants were unwilling to finalize agreements with the local blacks unless they had the support of the broader business community in Birmingham.[40] In order to obtain this backing, the merchants acted as a catalyst to involve the banking-industrial leaders in the negotiations.[41]

Responsibility for the negotiations begun by the merchants was assumed by the Senior Citizens Committee, which had top executive representatives from companies that employed 80% of the labor force in Birmingham.[42] With Birmingham's economic power structure endorsing the negotiations, a settlement was quickly reached with local blacks, who in turn called off the demonstrations.[43] Fearing violent reprisals for the role they played in the negotiations, members of the Senior Citizens Committee refused for a week to have their names released to the public.[44]

It was the participation of members of Birmingham's economic power structure—the industrial, banking and other important business leaders on the Senior Citizens Committee—that provided the most significant resource in the negotiations.[45] The entire Birmingham community benefitted from the actions taken by these powerful and prominent business leaders. It was inaccurate to assert, however, as the civil rights leaders did, that the business community had "reached an accord with its conscience."[46] Instead of being interested in advancing the cause of racial equality, most of the Birmingham business leaders were merely willing to moderate their segregationist stands in order to avoid both direct economic losses and the further decay of the city's general economy.

White Liberal Activists

The vast majority of Birmingham's white electorate accepted without question the segregated society in which they lived in 1963. It seemed completely natural to native Birmingham citizens that blacks should drink from different water fountains, use different rest rooms and dine in different restaurants. The thought of dealing with blacks as equals was foreign to most Birmingham whites.

A few enlightened members of Birmingham's white community, however, believed that segregation was wrong. Because they feared economic, physical and social reprisals, only a small number of these enlightened whites were willing to act on their beliefs.[47] Those white liberals, who overcame fear and did act, played a far more important role in the 1963 direct action program than their numerical strength would have suggested.

While most whites sought solely to end the civil rights demonstrations, the goal of Birmingham's white liberal activists was to seek just and meaningful solutions to the problems facing the city's black community.[48] National civil rights leaders acknowledged the honorable intentions of the white liberals by praising their "work and courage in attempting to help the white community accept change toward racial justice in Birmingham."[49]

Even before the demonstrations reached massive intensity, the city's white liberal activists began meeting with black leaders in hopes of aiding the drive for desegregation.[50] These few whites were the only Alabama residents who willingly met with Dr. Martin Luther King, Jr. and his SCLC aides during the direct action program.[51] Refusing to trumpet their negotiating efforts, the liberal whites used their connections with the local black leadership in order to lay the groundwork for the negotiations between Birmingham business leaders and local blacks.[52]

Before the Senior Citizens Committee entered the negotiations, the white liberals, representing the retail merchants, served as the prime negotiators with local blacks.[53] The white business leaders were willing to trust these activists because they had worked together in the early 1960's to change the form of Birmingham's government.[54] Initially working alone, the Birmingham liberals were joined in their efforts by Assistant U.S. Attorney General Burke Marshall.[55] Holding secret nightly meetings with blacks in downtown buildings or in individual homes, the white liberals and Mr. Marshall were able to make significant advances in the negotiations.[56] As a result of the efforts of the white activists, Birmingham's business leaders were able to learn the goals of the direct action program and the limited concessions that it would be necessary for them to make.[57]

Even though the Senior Citizens Committee used a subcommittee of its own members to finalize agreements with the local blacks, the white liberals were an essential element in the resolution of Birmingham's pressing racial difficulties.[58] Although aided by two other liberal attorneys, the primary credit for the initiation of efforts to resolve Birmingham's racial difficulties belongs to Mr. David Vann.[59] A former law clerk to the late Supreme Court Justice Hugo Black, Mr. Vann worked tirelessly throughout the direct action program and proved himself a man of good will.[60] If it can be said of any actor in a complicated political struggle, it can be said of the liberal white activists that they were motivated by idealism.

White Extremists

While the Birmingham white liberals sought to effect social change in order to improve the situation for local blacks, certain segments of the Birmingham white electorate were unwilling to accept any change in the racial status quo. These ardent white racists magnified their individual opposition to racial moderation by joining any of a number of pro-segregation pressure groups.

The most moderate of these organizations was the White Citizens' Council, which had been established throughout the South in response to the 1954 U.S. Supreme Court decision on school desegregation.[61] While professing to reject racist beliefs, the national letterhead of the Citizens' Council stated only one principle, "The Only Nationwide Organization Dedicated to Preserving the Integrity of the White Race."[62] Although adamantly opposed to desegregation, the Citizens' Council varied in three significant ways from the more extreme racist groups like the Ku Klux Klan.

First, the Council normally rejected the anti-Semitic conspiratorial theories concerning the civil rights movement.[63] Second, the Council endorsed legal resistance as the only acceptable method of opposing desegregation; economic boycotts and sanctions were strategies often employed by the Citizens' Council in order to "persuade" individuals to oppose desegregation.[64] Third, the membership of the White Citizens' Council varied significantly from the more extreme organizations. Instead of being composed primarily of lower-class whites, the Council's membership included bankers, planters, businessmen and politicians drawn from the respected levels of Southern life.[65]

Membership in the White Citizens' Council reached a peak in about 1956. After this period organized Council activity subsided: economic sanctions and pressures against blacks became infrequent; attendance at mass meetings dropped sharply; the renewals of membership and financial contributions dropped sharply.[66] Birmingham's White Citizens' Council lost significant power during the 1950's after an anti-Semitic racist had served as the group's executive director.[67] By 1963, the White Citizen's Council had only limited strength in Birmingham.[68]

During the midst of the civil right demonstrations, Council spokesmen condemned Martin Luther King, Jr. as an "out-of-town professional Negro agitator," who orchestrated "the great fraud of 'passive' protest."[69] Later, when the Birmingham desegregation agreement was announced, the White Citizens' Council criticized the "small, self-appointed, so-called committee of

Birmingham businessmen pretending to represent the people of Birmingham and the city government in negotiating with the Negro agitators."[70] But public pronouncements comprised the full extent of the White Citizens' Council's involvement with the direct action program.

Although the White Citizens' Council effectively exercised no power, a number of more extreme white supremacist groups were quite active in the Birmingham area. The National State Rights Party, which proclaimed itself the "Largest White Racist Political Party in America," had its national headquarters on the outskirts of Birmingham.[71] Five different Ku Klux Klan organizations were also operating in Alabama in 1963.[72] The United Klans of America, with Imperial Wizard Robert Shelton, had the largest membership in Alabama and in the United States.[73]

Although inter-Klan skirmishes periodically erupted, there were no basic philosophical differences between the white extremist organizations.[74] The actual goals sought by the white extremists were shaped by their views of blacks and the civil rights movement.

Blacks were perceived as being at least 200,000 years behind the Caucasian race in evolutionary development.[75] White supremacists asserted that "the superficial divergence in physical form between 'modern' apes and negroid racial stock is a relatively recent occurrence."[76] As a result of this perceived evolutionary lag, Negroes were seen as a "primitive [sic], low I.Q., backward race."[77] White extremist leaders openly argued that blacks were biologically inferior and asserted in their literature that the black race exhibited certain inherent traits such as laziness, unreliability, immorality, criminal inclination and incapability of sustained mental activity.[78]

The Ku Klux Klan and the National States Rights Party believed that the major civil rights organizations were actually controlled by Jews, who sought to "mongrelize the White Christian people with the Black race."[79] Blacks were merely tools used by Jews in their highly organized and planned invasion of the United States.[80] Judaism and Communism were viewed as being synonymous; the goal of each was to promote racial integration, thereby destroying America.[81] If the Jews and Communists succeeded in lowering racial barriers, there would be a "decline in productivity, high academic levels, cultural standards, and national wealth."[82] In order to prevent this downfall of civilization, white extremist organizations were united in their ardent opposition to desegregation.[83]

Since the purpose of the direct action program was to end segregation practices, which were cherished by the white extremists, it was inevitable that the Klan groups would be horrified at the events occurring in Birmingham. Dr. Martin Luther King, Jr., who led the direct action program, was especially hated by the white supremacists. The black minister was viewed as a race-hate merchant, who was a front-man for the Communists and Jews.[84] Dr. King was hanged in effigy in front of the headquarters of the National States Rights Party.[85]

The white supremacists vilified the demonstrators and marchers in Birmingham; but, they did not place all the blame on Dr. King, instead, the "Kennedy Dictators" had to assume responsibility along with "the NAACP, the Americans for Democratic Action, wealthy organizations like the Ford Foundation and the Rockefeller Foundation, the American Federation of Labor and many other such groups who have poured untold millions into the hands of enemies of the South."[86]

In opposing the goals of the direct action program, the white extremist organizations employed a wide variety of strategies. Many of the activities were designed to harass civil rights organizations and those who were willing to accept moderate racial change. White extremists would often call those who were playing prominent roles in the direct action program during the middle of the night; when the person awoke and answered the phone, the caller would hang up.[87] In order to gain advance knowledge of the planned civil rights activities, the Ku Klux Klan also used one of its members to infiltrate the civil rights movement.[88]

During the spring of 1963, the extremist organizations in Birmingham published and distributed a large amount of free literature, which presented their racial views. It was by this method and by mass rallies, attended by crowds of over 2,000 that extremist groups sought to "educate" the white majority of the threats of desegregation.[89]

When the negotiated settlement between local blacks and the Birmingham business leaders was announced, the white extremists severely criticized the "local Jew dominated Chamber of Commerce" for its willingness "to surrender Southern traditions and heritages."[90] Unwilling to limit their activities to criticizing the negotiations, white extremist groups initiated boycotts of all stores that agreed to desegregate.[91] This counter boycott met with only limited success.

The ardent pro-segregation groups allegedly used violence as part of their strategy. The white extremist leaders adamantly denied ever advocating the use of violence by their organizations' members.[92] But, strong evidence indicates that Klansmen were linked with many acts of racial intimidation.[93]

211

For example, during the trial of four white men for the castration of Judge Aaron, a Birmingham Negro handyman, testimony revealed that all four were Klansmen. The violent act against Mr. Aaron had been a test for proving one of the individual's worthiness "of becoming Assistant Exalted Cyclops."[94]

Although Klan leaders piously disavowed violence and denied its use, they used rhetoric designed to incite such reactions by their members. For example, in addressing a mass rally of Klansmen on the outskirts of Birmingham the day after the desegregation pact was announced, Robert Shelton, the United Klans' Imperial Wizard, said:

> We have had to deal with King and Abernathy and those known Communists this month . . . We now know who the men are who are selling out our country . . . tonight is the darkest night we have ever faced. Tonight we, as God-fearing men and women, can turn Alabama upside down for God . . .[95]

Within hours after Shelton used this emotional stimulus to incite the Klansmen, bombs exploded at the Reverend A. D. King's home and the Gaston Motel.

The primary resource that the white extremist groups marshalled in the implementation of their strategies was the element of hard-core racists in the Birmingham white electorate. Although the extremist organizations refused to give information about the extent of their membership, it was estimated that there were 10,000 to 12,000 members of the United Klans in Alabama.[96] The extremist groups grew in size during the 1963 direct action program; once the civil rights demonstrations ended, the white extremist organizations lost much of their following; in effect, there was a dynamic interaction between the two movements—the integration and white supremacist movements.[97]

Summary

During the 1963 direct action program, two separate governing bodies claimed to be Birmingham's legitimate government. As a result of this disputed governmental control, a political vacuum existed. The different segments of the white electorate acted and reacted without direct guidance from local city officials.

Birmingham's business leaders, representing most closely the prevalent racial attitudes of the white electorate, filled the leadership vacuum. Suffering financial losses as a result of the black boycott and demonstrations, Birmingham retail merchants initiated negotiations with local blacks. Unwilling to assume sole responsibility for a desegregation agreement, the merchants enlisted the support of the broader business community. Birmingham's economic power structure, which was represented in the Senior Citizens Committee, saw the demonstrations as having a negative impact on the city's general economy. Realizing that Birmingham's economic decay had to be halted, the Senior Citizens Committee assumed responsibility for negotiations with local blacks and quickly finalized desegregation agreements.

In establishing the negotiations, the white liberal activists in Birmingham played an essential role. Relying upon the confidence gained from business leaders in their earlier joint efforts to change the form of Birmingham's government, the white liberals began negotiating with national and local black leaders before the massive demonstrations began. Seeking just and meaningful solutions to the problems plaguing Birmingham blacks, white liberals played a role far more important than their number would have suggested.

While the white liberals sought equitable solutions to Birmingham's racial problems, the white extremists adamantly opposed any attempt at desegregation. Relying upon extra-legal harassment and possibly racially-motivated violence, the hard-core white extremists significantly exacerbated the problems that Birmingham faced in the spring of 1963.

SIX

Blacks

Rather than being a monolithic mass, as some white observers have argued, the Birmingham black community was significantly divided along social and economic lines in 1963.[1] The most accurate indicator of divisions within the black community was its diverse reaction to the local civil rights movement. The Alabama Christian Movement for Human Rights (ACMHR), which was the central civil rights organization in Birmingham during the late 1950's and early 1960's, did not have complete support from a unified local black community. Although the ACMHR had token support from the black middle-class, it was not a truly heterogeneous group of blacks.[2] Instead, the vast majority of the relatively wealthy blacks in Birmingham failed to support the efforts of the ACMHR.[3]

There were primarily two reasons for the failure of the black elite to take an active part in the civil rights struggle in Birmingham.[4] First, the actions and attitudes of the president of the ACMHR, Reverend Fred L. Shuttlesworth, alienated many of the city's middle-class blacks.[5] There was a general feeling among the city's black elite that Reverend Shuttlesworth was more interested in garnering personal publicity than in advancing the cause of racial equality.[6] Second, most of the city's middle-class blacks feared that they would suffer economically if they advocated desegregation. Many of the middle-class blacks, such as the school teachers and principals, were directly dependent on the white power structure for their livelihood.[7] If they challenged the segregated social system they could suffer economic reprisals.[8] Many blacks in Birmingham were indirectly tied to the white power structure. Black lawyers practiced before white judges and juries; black beauticians and barbers had to receive state licenses in order to operate their establishments; black owners of restaurants and bars had to satisfy a number of health standards administered by the city. These members of the black middle-class knew that governmental pressure would be applied against them if they actively participated in the civil rights struggle.[9] Many black businessmen actually profited from segregation.[10] Black undertakers, insurance agents and small store-owners had a captive market in the local black community.[11] With this powerful economic position, many black businessmen exploited the black masses as ruthlessly as did white ones.[12] If segregation barriers were lowered, then the city's blacks would be able to deal more easily with white businessmen. Thus, in order to maintain their captive market, most black businessmen did not endorse, let alone lead, desegregation attempts.[13] In general, most of Birmingham's middle-class blacks felt a sense of economic security within the segregated society, even though they suffered overt racial discrimination from the city's white community.[14] This sense of their own position, in addition to the profit they could earn in a segregated society, contributed to the failure of the relatively wealthy segment of the Birmingham black community to work with ACMHR.[15]

Another extremely powerful segment of the black community—the local ministers—failed to provide complete support to the civil rights movement.[16] This failure to support the efforts of the ACMHR was premised on the rejection of the social gospel by many of the older black preachers.[17] By trying to avoid controversial issues regarding race relations, these black ministers fostered the complacent acceptance of racial inferiority and second-class citizenship.[18]

The surface acceptance of the existing social system by the majority of the local black community was the most significant obstacle which the ACMHR faced in its attempts to achieve desegregation. Many local blacks had lived their entire lives in the South. They had been held back so long that many of them no longer had any ambition to participate in a social reform movement. Birmingham blacks were also very susceptible to economic and physical reprisals from the white community. Discrimination, segregation, and intimidation had destroyed their spirit.[19] Since they passively accepted segregation, the great mass of blacks were unwilling to get actively involved in the civil rights struggle.[20]

Although the ACMHR was relatively unsuccessful in rallying the support of the middle-class blacks, most of the local ministers, and the large segment of apathetic blacks, the local civil rights organization was able to gather a small dedicated group of followers. In a city with a black population of about 140,000, the ACMHR had a membership in the early 1960's that held at about 1,200.[21] Thus, the civil rights movement had only limited support in the black community.

It was primarily among the city's lower middle class that the ACMHR recruited its members.[22] The typical member of the ACMHR was a middle-aged married woman, who was a long-time resident of Alabama; she had a high school education and was a member of the Baptist church.[23] Almost all of the ACMHR members were members of a black church.[24] The leadership of the ACMHR was composed of local black ministers who advocated an active role for religion in the civil rights movement.[25]

With this core of dedicated leaders and followers, the ACMHR followed a relatively conservative course in its advocacy of civil rights. Prior to the selective buying campaign conducted in conjunction with the students at Miles college in 1962, the ACMHR sought social reform primarily through legal channels.[26] A survey conducted in 1959 revealed that only about one-third of the ACMHR membership felt that picketing, boycotts or mass marches were appropriate means of protesting segregation.[27]

The divisions that existed in Birmingham's black community were highlighted by the beginning of the direct action program on April 3, 1963.[28] Those black businessmen, professionals and ministers, who had failed to support the efforts of the ACMHR, provided a tremendous amount of initial resistance to Project C.[29] This staunch opposition was based on four major factors. First, many of the city's middle-class blacks felt that massive civil rights demonstrations would jeopardize their own standing in the community.[30] These blacks identified with the status quo and viewed any rupture in the social system with apprehension. Second, a significant portion of the black community felt that the timing of the demonstrations was poor.[31] According to these black leaders, the new Boutwell city government should have been given a chance to effect racial and social reform.[32] Another element of the local blacks' opposition to the timing of the demonstrations was the fact that most of them were not informed of the impending direct action program; the national civil rights leaders, wanting to maintain complete secrecy in order not to affect the local mayoral election, had failed to inform many of the city's black elite of their plans.[33]

A third factor contributing to local black opposition to Project C was jealousy. Many of the city's local black leaders felt that if any action were to be taken, then they should be the ones to direct it; they did not want "outsiders" to be the dominant force.[34] This attitude was evident in an editorial of the local black newspaper, which stated, "Our hometown leadership represents the basic leadership. No other leadership should be more responsible for bringing about the removal of racial segregation."[35] Fourth, many of the city's prominent black leaders opposed the tactics of Project C.[36] Feeling much more comfortable with the legal avenues for

217

change that had been previously employed, these blacks urged caution rather than action. Expressing the concern of the relatively wealthy blacks, the local black newspaper argued that, "In penetrating Alabama and Mississippi with their mass tactics, Negro leaders are forcing issues in areas where their demands are the most difficult to grant. They should exercise patience."[37]

Facing these deep divisions in the black community at the onset of the direct action program, the ACMHR and the Southern Christian Leadership Conference (SCLC) sought to unify the local black community in support of Project C. During the months of secret joint preparation for Project C, the SCLC and the ACMHR had formulated general goals and strategies.[38] The primary difference between the orientation of the national civil rights leaders and the local leaders was the level of their focus. The national black leadership sought much broader objectives than did the local blacks. Rather than being content with achieving local reforms, the SCLC officials wanted to use the Birmingham events as a base for stimulating national sympathy and action in favor of civil rights.

Although the national and local civil rights leaders agreed on the strategies that should be employed in Birmingham, they took different approaches in the determination of those strategies. The SCLC officials had long advocated a series of general strategies in their civil rights activities throughout the South. The local civil rights leaders were able to suggest specific strategies within the general framework that was formulated by the SCLC officials. Learning from the SCLC's mistakes in the Albany, Georgia direct action program of 1962, civil rights leaders decided to avoid the scatter-gun attack on segregation.[39] Instead, they would concentrate on a few vulnerable targets and utilize black economic power to achieve their goals.[40]

During the actual demonstrations, the method of determining strategies became routinized. Each evening after the general mass meeting, the Central Coordinating Committee would meet in Room 30 of the Gaston Motel.[41] Dr. Martin Luther King's closest advisors and many of the conservative local middle-class blacks served on this committee, which would map out strategy for the next day.[42] It was by allowing the local middle-class blacks to have an input into policy decisions that Dr. King was able to gather support from segments of the local community that had previously failed to support the civil rights movement.[43]

In order to better understand the way in which the national civil rights leaders and the local black leaders worked together in Project C, it is informative to analyze the goals, strategies, and resources of each group.

National Black Leadership

Several national civil rights organizations were indirectly involved in the 1963 direct action program in Birmingham. Although the National Association for the Advancement of Colored People (NAACP) had been effectively outlawed in Alabama, the New York-based NAACP Legal Defense Fund, Inc. provided legal representation for the black demonstrators during Project C.[44] Two other national organizations had field workers in Birmingham during April and May of 1963—the Congress of Racial Equality (CORE) and the Student Non-Violent Coordinating Committee (SNCC)[45] Although aided by the efforts of these other groups, the SCLC was the primary national civil rights organization that was involved with the direct action program in Birmingham.[46]

The goals of the national black leadership extended beyond Birmingham's city limits. The SCLC officials did not want to merely desegregate a few department stores in Birmingham. Instead, they wanted to "nationalize" the local racial conflict.[47] By centering national attention on Birmingham, SCLC officials hoped to gain national sympathy for the plight of Southern blacks and to stimulate the Kennedy administration to take progressive action in the area of civil rights. With national support for the cause of racial equality, the SCLC could achieve its broad goal of "full citizenship rights and total integration of the Negro in American life."[48] It was for this purpose of ending racial discrimination throughout the United States that the SCLC began the direct action program in Birmingham.[49]

There were several factors that were present in Birmingham that qualified it to be the target city for SCLC's direct action program. First, it was the largest segregated city in the United States; SCLC officials felt that if segregation barriers in Birmingham were broken then the South would go the same way.[50] Second, it was necessary to have creative local leadership, which would work in conjunction with SCLC.[51] Birmingham's SCLC affiliate, the ACMHR, satisfied this condition because it was anxious to work with the parent organization in order to promote the local civil rights efforts. Third, it was essential that a target city have governmental officials who "responded clumsily and arrogantly."[52] Bull Connor, who was the symbol of official racism and police brutality in the South, fulfilled this condition admirably.[53] As a result of the presence of these factors, Birmingham was chosen for the intensive effort by the SCLC.

The strategies that were employed by the SCLC in Birmingham were directed toward creating a crisis-packed racial situation. It was upon this primary strategy of establishing and perpetuating a creative tension that all other strategies were based.[54]

Two strikingly different alternatives existed with which the national civil rights leadership could foster this creative tension—a violent and non-violent approach. The option of using violent means to create a tense environment was rejected for both practical and ideological reasons. On a purely pragmatic level, violent actions by blacks would have caused even more violent reactions by local authorities; thus, violence would have been counter-productive.[55] On a philosophical level, a violent approach was incompatible with the general moralistic orientation of the civil rights movement; Dr. King elaborated on the basis of this objection by writing that, "The Negro turned his back on force . . . because he believed that through force he could lose his soul."[56]

The national civil rights leaders were firmly convinced that non-violent direct action was the most effective method with which to establish a creative tension to end segregation.[57] This method was "a way of overcoming injustice without becoming unjust, a way of fighting hatred without hating others, a way of conquering fear without being overcome by it."[58] It was upon this principle of non-violent direct action that the civil rights movement was based.[59] The techniques of non-violent direct action were an essential element of the creative tension approach.

The doctrine of nonviolence, however, was a very difficult one for the blacks in Birmingham to accept.[60] For several years, the local black community had been subjected to bombings and beatings by white racists. Many blacks in Birmingham believed that there was no alternative to a violent approach in seeking to achieve desegregation.[61] Confronted by this attitude which was prevalent among the city's black population, the SCLC began educating the local blacks about the benefits of non-violent direct action.[62]

All potential demonstrators in Birmingham were required to attend workshops on non-violence.[63] These training sessions, which were conducted by the SCLC staff members, included socio-dramas designed to prepare the volunteers for some of the confrontations they could expect to face during the demonstrations.[64] The volunteers were taught "to resist without bitterness, to be cursed and not reply, to be beaten and not hit back."[65] Those individuals who were unwilling to accept the doctrines of nonviolence were not allowed to demonstrate.[66]

The doctrine of nonviolence, to which the SCLC officials so strongly adhered, was strongly rooted in Christian philosophy.[67] The non-violent doctrine, which was preached by many of the younger Southern black ministers, was not one "that made their followers yearn for revenge but one that called upon them to champion change. It was not a doctrine that asked an eye for an eye but one that summoned men to seek to open the eyes of blind prejudice."[68] In effect, Christian philosophy and the tenets of nonviolence were closely linked.

The Christian religion made three significant contributions to the direct action program in Birmingham. First, the civil rights movement was often portrayed as God's movement.[69] The interracial confrontations, which were an outgrowth of the direct action program, were aimed at making "the God of love in the white man triumphant over the Satan of segregation that is in him."[70] The demonstrators were actually requested to adhere to certain commandments which included, "Meditating daily on the teachings and life of Jesus [and] pray[ing] daily to be used by God in order that all men might be free."[71] One reason the civil rights demonstrations were planned for the Easter season was the religious symbolism of individual suffering in order to promote a greater cause; the decision of Reverends King and Abernathy to be jailed on Good Friday was also made with full knowledge of the religious symbolism of their action.[72] By posing the civil rights struggle in these religious terms, black leaders were able to gather an enthusiastic following among many church members.[73]

The second contribution made by religion was the institutional structure of the church. The black church in Birmingham was a very viable vehicle for organizing the mass protests and stimulating individual involvement.[74] Although most of the black churches had been hesitant to get involved with the ACMHR, many became spearheads of reform during Project C.[75] Organizational meetings and workshops on non-violence were often conducted in various black churches in Birmingham.

The Christian religion contributed a third important factor to the direct action program—the black preacher. As a result of the central role in black life that the church occupied, the black preacher had enormous power in the community.[76] Since he was paid by the church's congregation, the black minister was generally free from white economic domination.[77] There was a growing awareness, especially among the younger black ministers, that religion should play a prominent role in rectifying social, economic and political problems.[78] Basing their actions on an advocacy of this social gospel, many of the local black preachers played very active roles in Project C.

In order to raise the Birmingham civil rights demonstrations to the level of national significance, it was necessary to have very massive confrontations between the local police and large groups of demonstrators. In trying to recruit demonstrators, the SCLC discovered that two general factors discouraged all Birmingham black adults from participating in the demonstrations. First, since many civil rights demonstrators had been fired by their white employers, most black adults feared similar economic reprisals.[79] A second factor that discouraged adult participation was the fear of being jailed. For years, the threat of being jailed and receiving the racially-biased form of southern justice had been used to keep blacks in their "place."[80] It was an extremely difficult task to convince local blacks that going to jail was a positive act. As a result of these two factors, most of the black adults in Birmingham were unwilling to participate in the demonstrations.

Because of the dearth of adult volunteers and the absolute necessity of a large number of demonstrators, the national civil rights officials decided to use children in the direct action program.[81] Through informal discussions and workshops on non-violence, the SCLC officials were able to recruit a large number of school children, who were willing to be jailed.[82] With the introduction of children into the demonstrations on D-Day, May 2, 1963, the creative tension, which SCLC officials had hoped to establish in Birmingham, immediately reached a high intensity.[83] Equally important, the participation in the demonstrations by the children caused more of the city's black adults to get involved in the direct action program.[84] The result was massive demonstrations which precipitated the desired confrontation between civil rights demonstrators and local governing officials. On the second day of the massive street demonstrations by the children, Bull Connor ordered that police dogs and fire hoses be used to control the crowd.

Although the national black leadership was able to create a tense racial environment in Birmingham by relying on children to implement the non-violent techniques, one final factor was necessary to achieve its goal of nationalizing the local racial conflict—publicity.[85] The national media readily responded to the massive demonstrations by converging on Birmingham. Scenes of dogs snapping at civil rights demonstrators and fire hoses with high-pressure streams of water pounding at the bodies of black women and children were telecast throughout the United States and the world.[86] It was the particular brutality of Birmingham that pushed the general situation of Southern blacks onto the previously indifferent whites throughout the country.[87] The national publicity surrounding the Birmingham events also stimulated the federal executive to intervene directly in Birmingham by sending Burke Marshall to aid in the interracial negotiations.[88] By gaining national sympathy and stimulating federal intervention, the SCLC was able to "subpoena the conscience of the nation to the judgement seat of morality."[89]

Dr. Martin Luther King's organizational and advocacy abilities constituted an extremely powerful resource that could be used in the implementation of the strategies of the SCLC. As previously mentioned, most of the middle-class blacks in Birmingham refused to get involved in the local civil rights struggle and initially failed to support the direct action program.[90] Realizing that problems did exist within the black community, Dr. King made a concerted effort during the first week of Project C to garner the support of the local black businessmen.[91] Meeting with several groups of businessmen each day, Dr. King explained to them the goals and strategies of the non-violent direct action program.[92] The local ministers, who were considered by SCLC officials as the individuals in the black community with the greatest economic freedom, were also targeted for intensive recruitment.[93] To the ministers, Dr. King stressed the need for a social gospel to supplement the gospel of individual salvation.[94] He also urged the projection of strong, firm leadership by the black ministers.[95]

In order to increase the interest of the middle-class blacks and the conservative local ministers in the direct action program, Dr. King appointed a number of them to the Central Coordinating Committee which determined the daily strategies for Project C.[96] By delegating responsibility to these powerful segments of the black community and by listening to their ideas, Dr. King succeeded, where Reverend Shuttlesworth had failed, in mobilizing significant support from the city's black elite.

In addition to leading the organizational meetings with local leaders, Dr. King provided an intangible asset to Project C—his personality. Referred to at times as the "epitome of Christ" or as a "prophet", Martin Luther King, Jr., was held in high esteem by the blacks in Birmingham.[97] As a result of his charismatic personality and his organizational efforts, Dr. King was able to mend some of the deep divisions that existed in Birmingham's black community.[98]

Besides his successful actions in relation to the local black community, Dr. King played a vital role in ensuring that the Birmingham events would have a national impact. He very effectively communicated the aspirations of Southern blacks to the nation's white population and thereby gained their sympathy and support.[99]

Although most of the national publicity was riveted on the role played by Dr. King, the entire SCLC staff was extremely talented. Described by Reverend Wyatt Tee Walker as having a "better administration than General Motors," the SCLC assumed primary responsibility for coordinating the participation of Birmingham's school children in the demonstrations.[100] Students were invited to attend meetings at which the SCLC staff taught them the philosophy of nonviolence.[101] The SCLC staff members used emotional and religious appeals to get support from the city's youth. For example, in trying to convince a group of adolescents that they should protest nonviolently and willingly be jailed, Reverend James Bevel said:

> You get an education in jail, too. In the schools you've been going to, they haven't taught you to be proud of yourselves . . . they haven't taught you the price of freedom . . . The white man has brainwashed us, tricked us; but Mr. Charlie's brainwashing is washing off now . . . And the most important thing in the struggle is to stay together . . . We've got to start learning to love one another enough to say: as long as one Negro kid is in jail, we all want to be in jail. If everybody in town would be arrested, everybody would be free, wouldn't they?[102]

These appeals were successful. Birmingham's black children refused to accept the prevailing values of the city's segregated society. They became committed to action, dedicated to affirming new values.[103] Inspired by Dr. King's example, the city's black children in massive numbers agreed to demonstrate and to go to jail.[104] This willingness to participate immensely aided the direct action program.

Ironically, SCLC officials relied in the conceptualization and implementation of their strategies on Birmingham Public Safety Commissioner Bull Connor. The local black community viewed Connor as the primary symbol of segregation in the city.[105] He was a perfect adversary for the national civil rights leaders.[106] By refusing to grant any concessions to the demonstrators, Connor both inspired the local black community to act and provided the confrontation which was necessary to nationalize the local conflict.[107] Many civil rights leaders firmly believed that if Bull Connor had simply allowed the civil rights demonstrators to conduct their peaceful marches, then the direct action program would not have succeeded.[108] In effect, by his unwillingness to allow the civil rights demonstrations, Bull Connor contributed to the success of the movement.[109]

Birmingham Blacks

Rather than viewing the direct action program as a means of ending segregation throughout the South, Birmingham blacks were much more interested in the practical local reforms that could be achieved. There were four major local goals of the direct action program. First, local blacks sought the desegregation of lunch counters, rest rooms, fitting rooms and drinking fountains in department stores. Second, they wanted the employment opportunities available for blacks to be immediately upgraded and non-discriminatory hiring policies to be implemented. Third, all charges against jailed demonstrators were to be dropped. Fourth, local blacks wanted a biracial committee to be created in order to work out timetables for desegregation in other areas of the community.[110] Thus, the goals of the local black leadership were more narrow than those of the national black leadership.

Project C was essentially directed at the section of the local power structure that was directly involved in the areas of the desegregation demands—the downtown retail merchants.[111] The local black leaders felt that if enough pressure were applied, the local merchants would be motivated to gather white support for the civil rights demands.[112]

Blacks used two converging strategies against the downtown retail establishments. First, since the black community in Birmingham possessed a significant amount of economic power, a black boycott of white-owned stores was conducted during the direct action program.[113] "Don't Buy Segregation!" was the basis of the appeal made by the local civil rights leaders to the city's blacks.[114] A close monitoring of the effectiveness of the boycott revealed that very few local blacks continued to patronize the downtown retail stores.[115] The second strategy which had a significant effect on the local stores was the mass demonstrations. By generating a great deal of civil rights activity in downtown Birmingham, the local black leaders were able to discourage whites from shopping at the local stores.[116] The effect of these two strategies—boycott and demonstrations—was a significant decrease in the retail sales of local stores.[117]

Several other non-violent strategies were employed by the Birmingham blacks. Each Sunday during the direct action program, well-dressed blacks attempted to worship at white churches; when they were refused admittance, they held kneel-ins on the steps of the church.[118] Marches were also made on the Jefferson County Courthouse as part of a voter-registration drive.[119]

All the non-violent strategies were designed to create a local situation in which white leaders would agree to participate in negotiations with Birmingham blacks.[120] By creating and perpetuating a tense racial environment, the civil rights demonstrators forced the city's white businessmen to agree to discussions. The negotiations, in which only local leaders participated, were very successful in achieving the four specific goals sought in the direct action program.[121]

In the determination of specific strategies to be employed in the direct action program, there were certain disagreements within the local black community.[122] The most significant opposition arose over the use of children in the demonstrations.[123] The local black newspaper, *The Birmingham World*, expressed the deep concern of most of the city's black adults by arguing that the "technique [of] pressing children to the fore is questionable."[124]

The most effective means of mobilizing the support of local blacks involved the mass meetings. Based on an established format, these meetings were held every night during Project C in various churches in Birmingham.[125] The mass meetings, which were primarily religiously oriented, began with a prayer meeting of thirty minutes duration.[126] The rest of the three-hour meeting was filled with a series of freedom songs and pep talks.[127] Toward the end of the mass meeting, Dr. King, Reverend Abernathy, or Reverend Shuttlesworth would extend an emotional appeal to the congregation for volunteers to participate in the demonstrations.[128] In generating support among local blacks, these meetings were very important.[129]

It was primarily the lower middle-class blacks in Birmingham who provided the human resources for the civil rights demonstrations.[130] Many of the local black demonstrators were unemployed and thus did not risk direct economic reprisals from the white economic power structure.[131] Local students, who had few economic ties with the white community, were also active in the demonstrations.[132] These demonstrators were primarily "church people," who responded positively to the non-violent religious appeals of the civil rights leaders.[133] As a result of their deeply-held religious beliefs, the demonstrators were very well disciplined and closely adhered to the tenets of nonviolence.[134]

Although most of the city's middle-class blacks initially opposed the direct action program, a significant segment of the black elite came to support the demonstrators. This change in orientation occurred as a result of four factors. First, as previously mentioned, Dr. Martin Luther King, Jr., was able to win the support of many of the middle-class blacks, who had failed to support the efforts of Reverend Shuttlesworth and the ACMHR.[135] Second, the situation in Birmingham became so intense and well-publicized that many of the black elite wanted to join the excitement surrounding the moral confrontation.[136] Third, the lower-class blacks began to exert a great deal of pressure on the black elite to get involved in Project C; the general black community during the period of crisis was very critical of "Uncle Tom-ism."[137] Fourth, it is quite possible that the black elite was motivated to act out of a fear of losing their dominant position in the black community to the civil rights leaders, who were developing a strong following. Responding to these various factors, many of the city's black middle-class became involved in the direct action program.[138]

A few of the city's prominent black leaders participated in the protest marches and willingly went to jail.[139] But, the black elite usually participated in other ways. For example, many members of the black middle-class served on a bond committee; these relatively wealthy blacks used their property holdings in lieu of cash bonds in order to obtain the release of demonstrators from jail.[140] Several middle-class blacks were members of the Central Coordinating Committee, which established the daily strategies for Project C, and the local Negotiating Team, which met with the city's white businessmen.[141]

In order to better understand the city's black elite, it is informative to briefly review the actions and attitudes of one of its members—Dr. A. G. Gaston. A long-time resident of Birmingham, Gaston was the wealthiest black in Alabama.[142] His business empire included several funeral homes, an insurance company, a business college, a motel, and a bank.[143] Although Gaston was committed to the cause of racial equality, he was not entirely in sympathy with Project C.[144] Gaston did not agree with the strategies employed in the non-violent direct action program.[145] Believing that nothing justified disrespect for law and order, Gaston favored negotiations rather than demonstrations as the proper means of presenting the civil rights demands.[146] Gaston also opposed the use of children in Project C because he felt that

227

their education was more important than their participation in demonstrations during school hours.[147]

Despite his objections to the strategies, Dr. Gaston contributed a great deal to the direct action program.[148] Having been informed of the plans for Project C, Gaston worked closely with the civil rights leaders during the months of preparation.[149] He provided free living quarters for the SCLC officials and supplied most of the office equipment that they needed.[150] During the demonstrations, Gaston also gave a great deal of the money that was necessary to cover the bail for jailed demonstrators.[151] According to Reverend Wyatt Tee Walker, Gaston's contributions were absolutely essential to the success of Project C.[152]

It is difficult to determine exactly the reason that Gaston was willing to provide significant economic resources to Project C, since he disagreed with many of the strategies. The most likely explanation is that he feared the consequences of not participating. If he had failed to get involved with the direct action program, two detrimental effects could have occurred. First, he probably could not have had any influence on the decisions made by the civil rights leaders. Since he did actively contribute to the direct action program, he was made a member of both the Central Coordinating Committee and the Negotiating Team; thus, he could have an effect on policy decisions.[153] Second, the attitude of the general black population during this period was very negative toward any "Uncle Tom-ism."[154] If Gaston had failed to get actively involved in Project C, his business interests, which were primarily dependent on the city's black population, would have suffered significantly. It was probably for these reasons that Gaston felt compelled to support the program even though he disagreed with the general strategies.

The 1963 direct action program was marred by occasional bursts of violence by blacks. The tensest situation occurred when riots erupted after the bombing of Reverend A. D. King's home and of the Gaston Motel during the early morning hours of May 12, 1963. The blacks who reacted violently to the naked provocation were not disciplined people of the Movement; instead, they were the segment of the black community that had refused to accept the doctrine of nonviolence.[155] It was primarily the young adult, lower-class black males, who participated in the riots.[156] The rioters, who were variously described by civil rights leaders as "wineheads" or "riff-raff," were members of the lowest social strata in the black community.[157] Having been oppressed their entire lives and relegated to the lowest socio-economic positions within the social system, these blacks were members of what might be called the desperate class.[158] These blacks fought their entire lives—with their fists, knives, or guns—boisterously aggressive or sullenly silent, in either case violently protecting themselves against anything white that crossed them. They had no respect for law made by or for them. They expected no justice from the courts; they received no consideration from the police.[159] The angry mood of this desperate class motivated them to react violently to the brutal bombings on May 12th. In addition, the anonymity afforded by mob action during the night allowed the individual blacks to act without fear of personal reprisals.[160]

The reluctance of the lowest-class blacks to accept the non-violent doctrine was but one example of the continued divisions in the black community over the direct action program. Several observers of the Birmingham events have failed to realize these divisions. In a relatively recent study of Project C, it was argued that "Martin Luther King had almost monolithic support from the black community . . . the black business and religious local leaders in Birmingham totally supported King and his actions . . . This movement was a monolithic group of the poor and the rich, the ignorant and the college-educated."[161] Even observers in 1963 did not perceive these continued divisions. Several argued that the city's black community was united in a classless revolt against segregation.[162] Bayard Rustin's enthusiastic endorsement of the demonstrations as an unmatched symbol of grass roots protest involving all strata of the black community was also somewhat excessive.[163]

The direct action program failed to enlist unified support from two major segments of the black community. First, although many of the city's middle-class blacks were drawn into Project C by Dr. King's presence, the excitement surrounding the events, and the pressure from the black masses, most of the city's black middle-class refused to participate. The black business leaders, who were content with their social and economic position, feared that they would suffer economic losses from the turmoil that was created by the protests.[164] Many of the local ministers, who were either jealous of Martin Luther King, Jr., or were sincerely opposed to the tactics of Project C, also refused to participate in the demonstrations.[165] The local black newspaper reflected this attitude of continued opposition by editorializing that "much of this direct action program seems to be both wasteful and worthless . . . there would be no need for marching if there would be found a meeting of the minds."[166] Second, only a small segment of Birmingham's lower-class blacks was involved in Project C. Most of the city's black population had suffered constant oppression and discrimination in Birmingham's segregated society. They generally felt that the efforts to achieve social change were foredoomed. These individuals also feared the very real possibility of economic and physical reprisals from the white community if they participated in the protests. For these reasons, they refused to get involved in the direct action program.[167]

The actual level of participation by the Birmingham black community in the direct action program is difficult to state. The vast majority of the city's blacks did not try to break the boycott of the downtown retail stores. The decision to participate in the boycott, however, was a passive decision rather than an active one; it took little effort to refuse to patronize the downtown stores for a few weeks. Indeed, it would have been an indication of overt opposition to the direct action program, if blacks had been willing to cross the picket lines around the downtown stores. But, the individuals who were willing to become actively involved in the civil rights protests—to participate in the marches and to man the picket lines—constituted a very small minority of the city's black community. Although estimates vary, there were about 3,000 arrests and jailings arising from the civil rights demonstrations.[168] Many of the demonstrators were jailed several times; some as many as six times.[169] Thus, the number of individuals who were jailed was about 2,500.[170] Although this was quite an impressive figure by itself, it represented only about 2% of Birmingham's total black population of 140,000.[171] Even if it is assumed that as many as 15,000 actually marched or worked behind the scenes, this figure still represents only about 10% of the city's black population. Several of the local civil rights leaders estimated that the actual percentage of the black community that was actively involved in the direct action program was very small, perhaps around the 10% mark.[172] From this analysis, it is evident that there was more apathy than involvement in the Birmingham black community. The vast majority of the city's blacks was unwilling to get actively involved in the direct action program.

Summary

During the months of preparation preceding Project C and the six weeks of civil rights demonstrations, the SCLC and the ACMHR worked together very effectively in formulating strategies and marshalling resources to implement the strategies. The SCLC basically took a broad view of the

Birmingham events. The national black leadership wanted to use the direct action program in Birmingham as a means of generating national sympathy and action in favor of civil rights. Although aware of the potential national effects of Project C, the local black leadership was more interested in securing significant local reforms.

Using non-violent strategies that were designed to create a tense racial environment, the black leaders were able to force two groups to act. First, responding to the black economic boycott and the mass demonstrations that scared away white shoppers, the local retail merchants enlisted the support of the white economic power structure in negotiations with local blacks. Second, the federal government reacted to the confrontation between the civil rights demonstrators and the local police by sending representatives into Birmingham to aid and facilitate interracial negotiations. By precipitating these reactions, the black leaders were able to achieve both their national and local goals.

Dr. Martin Luther King, Jr., played a very prominent role in rallying the support of a significant segment of the city's black population. However, as a result of their dependence on the white power structure and the profits they derived from operating in a segregated society, most of Birmingham's middle-class blacks refused to participate in the demonstrations. The much larger group of lower-class blacks, having lived and worked for many years in a segregated social system felt that the demonstrations had very little chance of success and thus did not actively participate. In effect, only a very small minority of the local black community was actively involved in the direct action program.

SEVEN

Conclusion

During the early 1960's, Birmingham, Alabama was a city in which the leaders of both races refused to seriously challenge the racial status quo. The prominent white business leaders were dedicated to the preservation of segregation. They had been indoctrinated with the belief that blacks were neither fit to sit beside them at a luncheon counter nor fit to drink from the same water fountain. As a result of being the dominant class in the society, the white business leaders benefitted from segregation.

Although they suffered overt discrimination from the white community, the Birmingham black middle-class felt a certain degree of social and economic security within the segregated society. As a result of their fears of economic and physical reprisals from the white power structure, to which they were linked, and the profits they derived from dealing with a captive black market, the black elite failed to push strongly for significant racial reforms.

The only segments of the local population that seriously questioned the advisability of segregation were the liberal white activists and the dedicated members of the local civil rights organization—the Alabama Christian Movement for Human Rights. The actual number of those who challenged the racial status quo was insufficient, however, to effect significant local reforms.

It was the external intervention of the national civil rights leaders that finally forced Birmingham to confront the issue of desegregation. Relying on non-violent techniques developed during its South-wide civil rights struggles, the Southern Christian Leadership Conference (SCLC) motivated many local blacks to participate in the demonstrations that were designed to achieve desegregation of local retail stores. In absolute terms, a large number of Birmingham's blacks actively participated in the direct action program, but it was still a small minority of the local black community. Although some of the local middle-class responded to Dr. Martin Luther King, Jr.'s appeals, the general excitement surrounding the moral confrontation, and the fear of losing status in the black community, most of the city's black elite did not get actively involved in Project C. The lower-class blacks, who constituted the vast majority of the local black population, feared that they would suffer economic and physical reprisals if they took an active part in the demonstrations; having lived most of their lives in a segregated society, they also felt any efforts to change the existing social order were foredoomed; thus, they did not participate in the civil rights protests. By relying on local volunteers including a massive number of the city's school children, the SCLC officials established a tense racial environment in Birmingham that motivated several groups to take action.

The responses of the various non-black actors to the direct action program can be divided into two categories—actions that helped solve the racial problems plaguing the city and actions that exacerbated those problems. There were basically four groups that added to the city's racial problems as a result of their attitudes and actions. First, consistent with their advocacy of a hard-line segregationist position, the City Commission tried to prevent the blacks from realizing their goals. Birmingham's Public Safety Commissioner Bull Connor initially adopted a non-violent police strategy toward demonstrators.[1] As part of this moderate approach to demonstrations, Bull Connor sought and received a broad state court injunction that barred civil rights leaders from participating in or encouraging any kind of protest, mass demonstration, boycott, or sit-in. Connor finally abandoned this moderate approach as a result of the massive size of the demonstrations and his desire to perpetuate the racial image he had developed from his past actions as Public Safety Commissioner; during the final week of the direct action program, the full force of local police powers were brutally unleashed against the demonstrators.

Second, the newly-elected Mayor and City Council did not actually exacerbate the racial problems in the city, but they did fail to take positive action to maintain law and order. During the period of shared governmental powers in Birmingham, the Mayor and City Council did not try to moderate the City Commission's handling of the demonstrations. The Council's willingness to negotiate at least covertly with local blacks constituted their only significant disagreement with the Commission over strategy.

Third, the state government in Alabama agreed with the strategies adopted by Bull Connor. In order to supplement the police forces under Connor's control, Governor George Wallace sent Colonel Al Lingo, with a large contingent of State Troopers, and Sheriff Jim Clark, with about 100 of his deputized irregulars, to Birmingham. By sending these two brutal racists to deal with the civil rights protest, Governor Wallace demonstrated a lack of concern for the welfare and safety of the Birmingham black community. As an extension of his staunch support of segregation, Governor Wallace also criticized the role played by the federal government in facilitating negotiations.

Fourth, the hard-core white racists adamantly opposed any attempt at desegregation. Basing their actions on their self-perceived role as protectors of the white race, the local white extremists relied upon extra-legal harassment and possibly racially-motivated violence. Although the guilty party was never apprehended, it is quite possible that white racists were responsible for the bombings of Reverend A. D. King's home and the Gaston Motel on May 12, 1963.

There were three groups that tried to counteract the negative influences exerted by the state and local governing officials and the white racists. First, the liberal white activists believed that the effect of maintaining segregation was the perpetuation of the economic, social, and political oppression of blacks. In acting upon their belief that such oppression was wrong, the local liberals played a very important role in the direct action program; they served as liaison between the local merchants and the black community in the initial stages of negotiations.

Second, meeting with local black leaders, the city's white business leaders concluded agreements that ended the civil rights demonstrations. As a result of the financial losses they were suffering from the black boycott and demonstrations, the Birmingham retail merchants initiated the negotiations. Since they were unwilling to assume sole responsibility for a desegregation agreement, the merchants enlisted the support of the banking and industrial leaders. Birmingham's economic power structure, which was represented in the Senior Citizens Committee, believed that the demonstrations were having a negative impact on the city's general economy. Although they favored segregation, Birmingham's Senior Citizens Committee finalized desegregation agreements with local blacks in order to reverse the city's economic decline.

The third group whose actions had a positive effect on solving the city's racial problems was the federal government. Stimulated to action by the sympathetic national reaction to the massive confrontations between Birmingham police and civil rights demonstrators, the federal government intervened directly in Birmingham. Assistant Attorney General Burke Marshall was sent to the city in order to facilitate negotiations between white business leaders and local blacks. By stressing the need of accepting the desegregation demands to the white business leaders, the federal government played an instrumental role in concluding the agreements.

The confrontation in Birmingham occurred as a result of the conflicting goals and strategies of the various actors. The direct action program ended when the city's leaders of both races finally agreed to discuss and to settle the issue of desegregation.

The 1963 direct action program had both local and national effects. On the local level, the four specific agreements—desegregation of downtown stores, improved employment opportunity for blacks in the retail stores, release of jailed demonstrators on low bail, and the establishment of a permanent interracial committee—were implemented within three months with relatively little difficulty.[2] The attitudes of the city's black and white citizens did not change as rapidly, however. The direct action program did not stimulate local blacks to become militant in their demands for further desegregation.[3] A survey conducted among blacks in Birmingham in 1964 indicated that over 80% was conservative or moderate in their response to the civil rights struggle.[4] For example, a majority of Birmingham's blacks felt that members of their race should spend more time praying and less time demonstrating.[5]

The civil rights demonstrations also had the effect of stiffening white resistance.[6] Rather than calmly preparing to accept the desegregation of local public schools in September of 1963, Birmingham's white citizens remained intransigent in their opposition. Working under a court-approved plan that permitted black parents to apply for the transfer of their children to white schools, the Birmingham city government prepared to integrate two high schools and one elementary school. Although a partial white student boycott developed at the integrated schools, the school plan seemed to be successful. The possibility of peaceful desegregation quickly evaporated, however, when the home of a prominent black attorney in Birmingham, Arthur Shores, was bombed for the second time in two weeks and a riot broke out.[7]

Reacting to the violence, the Birmingham Board of Education temporarily closed the three schools involved in the desegregation plans. When the schools were reopened, Alabama State Troopers, following orders from Governor Wallace, prevented five black students from attending the three white schools. The school issue was soon settled when President Kennedy federalized the Alabama National Guard to ensure both the implementation of the plan and the safety of the five black children.[8]

Birmingham's white citizens were still unwilling to accept desegregation. One more local event was necessary to change the attitudes of the white population. That event occurred on Sunday, September 15, 1963. The explosion that day blew most of the stained glass windows of the Sixteenth Street Baptist Church out of their frames. The one remaining window, which was damaged, showed Jesus Christ leading little children. But the ranks of His followers had been depleted by four, because beneath tons of broken concrete and shattered glass lay the crushed, lifeless bodies of four little girls who had unknowingly committed what to some demented person was an awful, unpardonable crime—they had been born black.[9] Governor Wallace commented that he was not sure that the bombing "was the work of white persons. It could very easily have been done by Communists or other Negroes who had a lot to gain by the ensuing publicity."[10] Most of Birmingham's white citizens rejected this explanation; the bombing horrified them and reinforced their growing realization that violence was bad ethics as well as bad politics.[11]

There were no more bombings in Birmingham; there were no more marches. The city slowly accommodated itself to the inevitable changes in race relations. But, serious racial reforms still were not generated on the local level. Federal action was required to stimulate progress.

In that fact lies the particular irony of the Birmingham events. The primary impact of the 1963 direct action program was national rather than local.[12] It is informative to analyze the status of civil rights on the national level before and after the demonstrations in Birmingham.

Prior to the spring of 1963, the Kennedy administration had at best a mixed record on civil rights. Although more blacks were appointed to important federal positions than in any previous administration and a large number of legal cases were instituted in order to safeguard the constitutional rights of blacks, civil rights remained in the rear ranks of the Kennedy administration's early priorities.[13] President Kennedy's civil rights program was more limited than his campaign rhetoric would have suggested. As a candidate, Kennedy had promised that an active President could integrate federally assisted housing with "a stroke of the Presidential pen." After he was elected, supporters had to wait over one and one-half years and mount an "Ink for Jack" campaign, which inundated the White House mails with ink bottles, before President Kennedy finally signed a weak, non-retroactive order.[14]

In the spring of 1963 in the principal Southern states there were no black circuit court judges, no black district court judges, no black U.S. commissioners, no black jury commissioners and no black U.S. marshals.[15] Instead of appointing competent blacks to openings arising in the federal judiciary in the South, Kennedy filled no fewer than 25% of the federal judgeships in the Fifth Circuit with segregationists.[16] Judge W. Harold Cox of Jackson, Mississippi, who was appointed in June of 1961, was perhaps the most outrageous appointee. From the bench Cox referred to black litigants as "niggers" and posed such humiliating questions as "Who is telling these people they can get in line [to register to vote] and push people around acting like a bunch of chimpanzees?"[17] By appointing these segregationist judges, Kennedy dealt a severe blow to the civil rights movement.

The primary involvement of the Kennedy administration in civil rights prior to the spring of 1963 was through events rather than planning, through necessity rather than philosophy, through emergency rather than deliberation. Federal challenges to local Southern authorities arose mainly during periods of crisis—federal protection provided to the Freedom Riders in 1961 when local police refused to prevent attacks by Southern mobs and to James Meredith in his attempt to desegregate the University of Mississippi in 1962.

The events in Birmingham led President Kennedy to reconsider his position on civil rights. Assistant Attorney General Burke Marshall, who was the federal government's representative in Birmingham, explained that after Project C had ended, President Kennedy "wanted to know what he should do—not to deal with Birmingham, but to deal with what was clearly an explosion in the racial problem that could not, would not, go away."[18] Reacting to the Birmingham events, President Kennedy expressed a deep personal concern over the race issue by stating:

> We preach freedom around the world and we mean it. And we cherish freedom here at home. But are we to say to the world—and much more importantly to each other—that this is the land of the free, except for the Negroes; that we have no second-class citizens, except Negroes; that we have no class or caste system, no ghettoes, except with respect to Negroes.[19]

But even more important than Kennedy's personal commitment to civil rights was the change in national attitudes toward civil rights. Before the events in Birmingham there had been a lack of agitation by the white population in the United States for federal action. The national publicity surrounding the massive confrontation in Birmingham awakened the middle-class conscience.[20] To oversimplify somewhat, the effect of the demonstrations was to rally sympathetic Northern opinion against Southern whites in freeing Southern blacks.[21] President Kennedy alluded to this effect when he said somewhat sarcastically, "The civil rights movement should thank God for Bull Connor. He's helped it as much as Abraham Lincoln."[22]

It was the national reaction to the Birmingham demonstrations and to George Wallace's well-publicized attempt to prevent blacks from registering at the University of Alabama, which followed within a month of the Birmingham events, that finally led President Kennedy to endorse progressive civil rights legislation.[23] Kennedy publicly admitted the effect of the increased national pressure for civil rights legislation by stating, "The events in Birmingham and elsewhere have so increased cries for equality that no city or state or legislative body can prudently choose to ignore them."[24]

When John Kennedy died on November 22, 1963, the federal government had a legal, political and moral commitment to the cause of civil rights. In his first address to Congress, President Lyndon B. Johnson expressed his own commitment to ending racial discrimination by calling for passage of the civil rights bill in order to bring alive "the dream of equal rights for all Americans whatever their race or color."[25] The bill passed the Senate exactly one year from the day President Kennedy had proposed the legislation by saying that it should be enacted, "not merely for reasons of economic efficiency, world diplomacy and domestic tranquility—but above all because it is right."[26] President Lyndon Johnson signed the Civil Rights Act of 1964 on July 2, 1964.

Once this act went into effect, it forced desegregation in Birmingham far beyond anything previously accomplished.[27] Local black and white leaders, who had been very hesitant to deal with significant racial problems, found that the city's racial patterns of conduct began to change slowly as a result of the legislative action.

The events in Birmingham in 1963 represented a very significant turning point in the civil rights struggle.[28] The demonstrations produced a national awareness of the Southern racial problems that spurred the introduction and passage of the Civil Rights Act of 1964.[29] But it was not until these federally-imposed reforms were actually implemented that local progress in race relations accelerated. Thus, the impact of the 1963 direct action program was not limited to Birmingham, but was truly national in scope.

Notes

PREFACE

1. The description of the civil rights activities in the South during the late 1950's and early 1960's is drawn directly from Anthony Lewis and *The New York Times, Portrait of a Decade* (New York: Random House, 1964).
2. U.S. Bureau of the Census. *U.S. Census of Population and Housing: 1960. Census Tracts.* Final Report PHC (1)-17. U.S. Government Printing Office, Washington, D.C., 1961, p.15.
3. *Ibid.*
4. The median family income in Birmingham was $4947 as compared with the national urban average of $6166. *Ibid.*; U.S. Bureau of the Census. *U.S. Census of Population: 1960.* Vol. I, *Characteristics of the Population.* Part 1, United States Summary. U.S. Government Printing Office, Washington, D.C., 1964, p. 1-225.
5. Hammer, Greene, Siler Associates, *The Economy of Metropolitan Birmingham* (Atlanta: Hammer, Greene, Siler Associates, 1966), pp. 99-100.
6. Carl T. Grindstaff, "The Negro, Urbanization, and Relative Deprivation in the Deep South," *Social Problems* 15 (Winter, 1968): 345.
7. *Ibid.*, p. 348.
8. Hammer, Greene, Siler Associates, *supra* note 5, preface, at p. 100.
9. Table 1.

EMPLOYMENT PROFILES FOR THREE SOUTHEASTERN METROPOLITAN AREAS, 1965

	Birmingham	Atlanta	New Orleans
Manufacturing	30.3%	22.9%	17.1%
Construction	5.8	6.6	7.9
Mining	2.0	——	3.6
Transportation, Communications and Utilities	7.7	9.3	12.8
Trade	22.9	26.0	23.7
Finance, Insurance, and Real Estate	7.1	7.3	5.7
Services	12.8	14.1	16.2
Government	11.4	13.8	13.0
TOTAL	100.0%	100.0%	100.0%

Table 1 is drawn form Hammer, Greene, Siler Associates, *supra* note 5, preface, at p. 74.

10. *Ibid.*
11. U.S. Bureau of the Census, *supra* note 2, preface, at p. 39.
12. *Ibid.*; Hammer, Greene, Siler Associates, *supra* note 5, preface, at p. 13.
13. Hammer, Greene, Siler Associates, *supra* note 5, preface, at p. 80.
14. The members of local labor unions were often found in the ranks of the white racists. A discussion of this relationship will appear in Chapter 5. Local labor unions as a separate organized entity, however, will not be discussed. One general observation can be made of the role of local labor unions in the movement for racial equality. Although there were differences among the unions in Birmingham, most of the local unions did not support the civil rights movement; by adopting this position, the local unions were thrust into an antagonistic relationship with the national unions, with which they were affiliated. The AFL-CIO and other national unions generally provided financial and moral support to the civil rights movement.

CHAPTER ONE

1. Geraldine Moore, *Behind The Ebony Mask* (Birmingham, Alabama: Southern Univ. Press, 1961), pp. 11-12; Martin Luther King, Jr., *Why We Can't Wait* (New York: The New American Library, 1963), pp. ix, 47-48; Rev. Abraham L. Woods, Jr., recorded interview by Addie Pugh, October 1975, pp. 4-5, Birmingham Civil Rights Project (U.A.B., 1975); Mike Nichols, "Cities Are What Men Make Them" (Senior thesis, Brown University, 1973), p. 84.
2. Moore, *Behind The Ebony Mask,*, p. 12; interview with J. Mason Davis, Bessemer, Alabama, 16 August 1976 (RR 157, 253); telephone interview with Rev. Fred L. Shuttlesworth, from Cambridge, Massachusetts to Cincinnati, Ohio, 19 October 1976 (RR 100); Robert Coles, *Children of Crisis: A Study of Courage and Fear* (Boston: Little, Brown and Company), p. 4; Andrew Young, "The Day We Went To Jail In Birmingham," *Friends*, 9 February 1964, p.5.
3. Grindstaff, *supra* note 6, preface, at pp. 348, 351.
4. Moore, *Behind The Ebony Mask*, p. 211.
5. Grindstaff, *supra* note 6, preface, at p. 347; David L. Lewis, *King: A Critical Biography* (New York: Praeger Publishers, Inc., 1970), p. 172.
6. U.S. Bureau of the Census, *supra* note 2, preface, at pp. 39, 47.
7. Grindstaff, *supra* note 6, preface, at p. 347.
8. King, *Why We Can't Wait*, pp. 23-24.
9. *The General Code of the City of Birmingham, Alabama,* 1944, Sec. 597, 939; interview with J. Mason Davis (RR 166-195).
10. *The General Code of the City of Birmingham, Alabama,* 1944, Sec 369.

11. Burke Marshall, *Federalism and Civil Rights* (New York: Columbia University Press, 1964), p. 27.
12. Moore, *Behind The Ebony Mask*, p. 205; interview with Charles Zukoski, Jefferson County Planned Parenthood, Birmingham, Alabama, 23 August 1976 (RR 577).
13. Fred L. Shuttlesworth, "Birmingham Shall Be Free Some Day," *Freedomways*, Winter 1964, p. 17; interview with Arthur Hanes, Frank Nelson Building, Birmingham, Alabama, 26 August 1976 (RR 186); interview with Rev. Nelson Henry Smith, Jr., New Pilgrim Baptist Church, Birmingham, Alabama 31 August 1976 (RR 253); interview with William Spencer III, Motion Industries, Birmingham, Alabama, 2 Sept. 1976 (RR 431); interview with Charles Zukoski (RR 522); interview with Dr. Arthur George Gaston, Sr., Citizen's Federal Bank, Birmingham, Alabama, 20 Sept. 1976 (RR 012).
14. Alabama Christian Movement for Human Rights, *They Challenge Segregation at Its Core!*, pamphlet, p. 4; Edward S. LaMonte, "Politics and Welfare in Birmingham, Alabama: 1900-1975" (Ph.D. dissertation, University of Chicago, 1976), p. 231.
15. Joe David Brown, "Birmingham, " *Saturday Evening Post*, 2 March 1963, p. 13; interview with Duard LeGrande, *Birmingham Post-Herald*, Birmingham, Alabama, 25 August 1976 (RR 118); interview with M. Edwin Wiggins, City Hall, Birmingham, Alabama, 30 August 1976 (RR 125); interview with William Spencer III (Rr 509-14); interview with Don A. Hawkins, Central Bank Building, Birmingham, Alabama, 10 Sept. 1976 (RR 499).
16. Interview with Dr. E.C. Overton, 5 Points West, Birmingham, Alabama, 1 Sept. 1976 (RR 284); interview with Charles Zukoski (RR 155); interview with Thad Holt, Southern Natural Gas Building, Birmingham, Alabama, 25 August 1976 (RR 564); Charles Morgan, Jr., *A Time to Speak* (New York: Harper and Row, 1964), p. 68.
17. Nichols, *supra* note 1, chapter 1, at p. 86.
18. King, *Why We Can't Wait*, p. 48; Moore, *Behind The Ebony Mask*, p. 200.
19. Nichols, *supra* note 1, chapter 1, at p. 90; interview with Orzell Billingsley, Jr., Masonic Temple Building, Birmingham, Alabama, 3 Sept. 1976 (RR 560); Emma Gelders Sterne, *I Have A Dream* (New York: Knopf, 1965), p. 172.
20. Nichols, *supra* note 1, chapter 1, at p. 107; oral history with Rev. Woods, *supra* note 1, chapter 1, at p. 8.
21. Southern Christian Leadership Conference and Alabama Christian Movement for Human Rights, "Third State-Wide Institute Non-Violent Resistance to Segregation," pamphlet, August 1960, Shuttlesworth Papers, Box 4, The Martin Luther King, Jr. Center for Social Change (hereafter abbreviated "KCSC"), Atlanta, Georgia; Rev. Wyatt Tee Walker, recorded interview by Mike Nichols, New York, New York, October 1973 (RR1-70); Jacquelyne Johnson Clarke, *These Rights They Seek* (Washington, D.C.: Public Affairs Press, 1962), p. 55.
22. Nichols, *supra* note 1, chapter 1, at p. 107.
23. Coretta Scott King, *My Life with Martin Luther King, Jr.* (New York: Avon, 1970), p. 217; *New York Times,* 16 Sept. 1963, file "Birmingham September,

1963," Southern Regional Council (hereafter abbreviated "SRC"), Atlanta, Georgia; LaMonte, *supra* note 14, chapter 1, at pp. 251-52.

24. Brown, *supra* note 15, chapter 1, at p. 13; Rev. Fred L. Shuttlesworth, recorded interview by James Mosley, September 1968, pp. 16-17, Civil Rights Documentation Project.

25. *Birmingham News,* 3 April 1959; interview with Duard LeGrande (RR 230); interview with Thad Holt (RR 264-67). As a result of pouring turpentine on Aaron's wound, the whites unwittingly saved Aaron's life by stopping the flow of blood. The attackers were tried and convicted on charges of mayhem and were sentenced to 20 years in prison. During the trial of the accused whites, it was discovered that the castration was made as part of a Ku Klux Klan initiation. One of Mr. Aaron's attackers had been among the three men who attacked Nat King Cole the year before.

26. LaMonte, *supra* note 14, chapter 1, at p. 236; interview with Arthur Hanes (RR 117).

27. Interview with George Wall, City Hall, Birmingham, Alabama, 30 August 1976 (RR 288); interview with J. Mason Davis (RR 041); Nichols, *supra* note 1, chapter 1, at p. 106.

28. *Birmingham News,* 7 February 1962.

29. LaMonte, *supra* note 14, chapter 1, at p. 236.

30. *Birmingham Post-Herald,* 3 December 1975, p. 1.

31. *Birmingham Post-Herald,* 20 December 1975.

32. King, *Why We Can't Wait,* pp. 51-52; Mary Phyllis Harrison, "A Change in the Government of the City of Birmingham: 1962-1963" (M.A. thesis, University of Montevallo, 1974), p. 16. The program of black economic withdrawal from retail stores was termed a "Selective Buying Campaign" rather than a "boycott" because Alabama law prohibited boycotts. See *Code of Alabama,* 1940, Title 14, Sections 54, 56, 61.

33. King, *Why We Can't Wait,* pp. 51-52.

34. Harrison, *supra* note 32, chapter 1, at p. 16; George R. Osborne, "Boycott in Birmingham," *The Nation,* 5 May 1962, p. 397.

35. Harrison, *supra* note 32, chapter 1, at pp. 16-17; The Miles College student body, et al. "Join the Glorious Struggle for Freedom," 1962 (mimeographed).

36. William Robert Miller, *Miller Luther King, Jr.* (New York; Weybright and Talley, 1968), p. 131; Jim Bishop, *The Days of Martin Luther King, Jr.* (New York: Putnam, 1971), p. 269.

37. King, *Why We Can't Wait,* pp. 51-52; Miller, *Martin Luther King, Jr.,* p. 131.

38. Connor is quoted in a mimeographed sheet entitled, "Selective Buying—Right of Protest."

39. "Confidential Memorandum," Birmingham, Alabama, 5 April 1962 (typewritten); Harrison, *supra* note 32, chapter 1, at p. 17.

40. Osborne, *supra* note 34, chapter 1, at p. 401; Harrison, *supra* note 32, chapter 1, at p. 17.

41. Oral history with Rev. Shuttlesworth, *supra* note 24, chapter 1, at pp. 52-58.

42. Harry Holloway, *The Politics of the Southern Negro* (New York; Random House, 1969), p. 161; Martin Luther King, Jr., "Letter from Birmingham Jail,"

in *What Country Have I?*, ed. Herbert J. Storing (New York: Harper and Row, 1970), p. 118.

43. King, *Why We Can't Wait*, pp. 53-54; Holloway, *The Politics of the Southern Negro*, p. 161; interview with Emil Hess, Parisian, Inc., Birmingham, Alabama, 1 Sept. 1976 (RR 060); interview with Rev. Abraham Woods, Jr., St. Joseph Day Care Center, Birmingham, Alabama, 7 Sept. 1976 (RR 2-410 to 2-420); Brown, *supra* note 15, chapter 1, at p. 18; F.L. Shuttlesworth and N. H. Smith, "The Birmingham Manifesto," *Freedomways,* Winter 1964, pp. 20-21.

44. LaMonte, *supra* note 14, chapter 1, at p. 237.

45. *Ibid.*; interview with Thad Holt (RR 318-20); interview with William Spencer III (RR 370).

46. LaMonte, *supra* note 14, chapter 1, at p. 237; interview with Dr. E.C. Overton (RR 169).

47. LaMonte, *supra* note 14, chapter 1, at p. 237.

48. LaMonte, *supra* note 14, chapter 1, at pp. 238-39; Nichols, *supra* note 1, chapter 1, at p. 218.

49. Nichols, *supra* note 1, chapter 1, at p. 219.

50. LaMonte, *supra* note 14, chapter 1, at p. 239; interview with Duard LeGrande (RR 006).

51. *Birmingham Post-Herald*, 20 August 1962.

52. LaMonte, *supra* note 14, chapter 1, at pp. 240-41; Nichols, *supra* note 1, chapter 1, at pp. 222-23.

53. LaMonte, *supra* note 14, chapter 1, at p. 241; Nichols, *supra* note 1, chapter 1, at pp. 226-27.

54. LaMonte, *supra* note 14, chapter 1, at pp. 242-43; Holloway, *The Politics of the Southern Negro*, p. 59.

55. LaMonte, *supra* note 14, chapter 1, at p. 245.

56. Nichols, *supra* note 1, chapter 1, at pp. 232-34.

57. Birmingham, Alabama, "Recapitulating Sheets of 1963 City Elections," (Birmingham City Clerk's Office); Jefferson County, Alabama, "Registration Figures by Precinct, 1962 and 1964," (Board of Registrars—Jefferson County).

58. LaMonte, *supra* note 14, chapter 1, at pp. 247-49; Harrison *supra* note 32, chapter 1, at p. 45; interview with Arthur Shores, Citizen's Federal Bank, Birmingham, Alabama, 20 Sept. 1976 (RR 485-549); Jefferson County, Alabama, *supra* note 57, chapter 1.

59. LaMonte, *supra* note 14, chapter 1, at p. 248; Reese Cleghorn,"'Bustling' Birmingham," *New Republic*, 20 April 1963, p. 9.

60. LaMonte, *supra* note 14, chapter 1, at p. 244.

61. Birmingham, Alabama, *supra* note 57, chapter 1; Jefferson County, Alabama *supra* note 57, chapter 1.

62. Nichols, *supra* note 1, chapter 1, at p. 230; Harrison, *supra* note 32, chapter 1, at p. 61.

63. Shuttlesworth, *supra* note 13, chapter 1, at p. 16; Shuttlesworth and Smith, *supra* note 43, chapter 1, at pp. 20-21; King, "Letter from Birmingham Jail," p. 118.; Holloway, *The Politics of the Southern Negro*, p. 152.

64. Shuttlesworth, *supra* note 13, chapter 1, at p. 16.

CHAPTER TWO

1. King, *My Life with Martin Luther King, Jr.*, p. 217; Nichols, *supra* note 1, chapter 1, at p. 249; Bishop, *The Days of Martin Luther King, Jr.*, p. 268; interview with Rev. Carter Gaston, Jr., Beth-El Baptist Church, Birmingham, Alabama, 24 August 1976 (RR 020); oral history with Rev. Shuttlesworth, *supra* note 24, chapter 1, at pp. 51-53; interview with Rev. Shuttlesworth (RR 108); interview with Rev. John Thomas Porter, Jr., 6th Avenue Baptist Church, Birmingham, Alabama, 31 August 1976 (RR053); "Shuttlesworth Declares Birmingham Must Show Progress," press release from Birmingham, Alabama on 3 October 1962, KCSC, Box 10-27-63; Lerone Bennett, Jr., *What Manner of Man—Martin Luther King, Jr.* (Chicago: Johnson Publishing Co., 1968), p. 131.
2. King, *Why We Can't Wait*, pp. 54-55; oral history with Rev. Walker, *supra* note 21, chapter 1 (RR 2-275); Lewis, *King: A Critical Biography*, p. 174; Bishop, *The Days of Martin Luther King, Jr.*, p. 269; Miller, *Martin Luther King, Jr.*, p. 132.
3. Alan F. Westin and Barry Mahoney, *The Trial of Martin Luther King* (New York: Thomas Y. Crowell, Co., 1974), pp. 48-49; Nettie Fleming, recorded interview by Cornelius Brown, 2 May 1976, Daniel Payne College Oral History Project; Sterne, *I Have a Dream*, p. 184.
4. Interview with Rev. Nelson Henry Smith, Jr. (RR 015).
5. Westin and Mahoney, *The Trial of Martin Luther King*, pp. 48-49; Miller, *Martin Luther King, Jr.*, p. 132; Bishop, *The Days of Martin Luther King, Jr.*, p. 269.
6. King, *Why We Can't Wait*, p. 55; Miller, *Martin Luther King, Jr.*, p. 133; Lewis, *King: A Critical Biography*, pp. 174-75; King, *My Life with Martin Luther King, Jr.*, pp. 217-18.
7. Miller, *Martin Luther King, Jr.*, p. 134; Bishop, *The Days of Martin Luther King, Jr.*, p. 281; Lewis, *King: A Critical Biography*, p. 176; Westin and Mahoney, *The Trial of Martin Luther King*, p. 51.
8. King, *Why We Can't Wait*, pp. 57-58; Nichols, *supra* note 1, chapter 1, at p. 257.
9. Bishop, *The Days of Martin Luther King, Jr.*, p. 281; Lewis, *King: A Critical Biography*, p. 176.
10. King, *Why We Can't Wait*, p. 57.
11. King, *My LIfe with Martin Luther King, Jr.*, p. 219; Bishop, *The Days of Martin Luther King, Jr.*, p. 270. The correspondence between the national civil rights leaders and the Kennedy administration continued throughout the direct action program. For example in a letter dated 16 April 1963, Wyatt Tee Walker wrote the following to Assistant Attorney General Burke Marshall:

> Let me take this opportunity to alert you that we will be moving into the second phase of our campaign—that is, changing the enthusiasm built up into voter registration efforts.

> We trust that the Justice Department will keep a close eye on our activities.

12. Bennett, *What Manner of Man—Martin Luther King, Jr.*, p. 132; interview with Rev. John Thomas Porter, Jr. (RR 355); oral history with Rev. Walker, *supra* note 21, chapter 1 (RR 1-102); interview with Rev. Carter Gaston, Jr. (RR 040); interview with Rev. Abraham Woods, Jr. (RR 499).
13. Interview with Rev. Fred Shuttlesworth (RR 374-84); interview with Rev. Carter Gaston, Jr. (RR 053-090); oral history with Rev. Walker, *supra* note 21, chapter 1 (RR 3-303).
14. King, *Why We Cant' Wait*, pp. 55-56; Nichols, *supra* note 1, chapter 1, at p. 256; *Billingsley v. Eskridge* Case No. 75-3121, (5th Cir. 1974); interview with Orzell Billingsley, Jr., (RR 538-633).
15. Bishop, *The Days of Martin Luther King, Jr.*, p. 280.
16. Oral history with Rev. Walker, *supra* note 21, chapter 1 (RR 3-326); Nichols, *supra* note 1, chapter 1, at p. 256; Miller, *Martin Luther King, Jr.*, pp. 133-134; Bishop, *The Days of Martin Luther King, Jr.*, p. 280.
17. Oral history with Rev. Walker, *supra* note 21, chapter 1 (RR 3-336 to 3-340). The secondary target was the Federal Post Office complex near Kelly Ingram Park; the tertiary target was an outlying suburban shopping center.
18. Oral history with Rev. Walker, *supra* note 21, chapter 1 (RR 2-244).
19. Ibid., (RR 2-250).
20. Interview with Rev. Abraham Woods, Jr. (RR 070); oral history with Rev. Walker, *supra* note 21, chapter 1 (RR 3-323); Nichols, *supra* note 1, chapter 1, at p. 256; Theodore White, *The Making of the President—1964* (New York: Atheneum, 1965), p. 168; Bishop, *The Days of Martin Luther King, Jr.*, p. 281.
21. Holloway, *The Politics of the Southern Negro*, p. 162.
22. King, *Why We Can't Wait*, p. 55; "Tentative Schedule For Project X Birmingham, Alabama" (typewritten), KCSC, box 10-31-63; Sterne, *I Have A Dream*, pp. 184-85; King, "Letter from Birmingham Jail," p. 119.
23. King, *Why We Can't Wait*, pp. 56-57; Shuttlesworth and Smith, *supra* note 43, chapter 1, at p. 21; Rev Fred L. Shuttlesworth, "Why We Must Demonstrate," special news bulletin, 19 March 1964 (mimeographed); Lewis, *King: A Critical Biography*, pp. 176-77; Alabama Christian Movement for Human Rights, *People in Motion*, pamphlet, 1966, p. 17.
24. Wyatt Tee Walker to Freedom Fighters, 11 March 1963, KCSC, Box 10-31-63.
25. King, *Why We Can't Wait*, p. 57; interview with Albert Boutwell, John A. Hand Building, Birmingham, Alabama, 21 Sept. 1976 (RR 152). Although Birmingham blacks overwhelmingly supported Boutwell in the run-off, they viewed the former Lt. Governor as merely a dignified Bull Connor. Interview with Rev. Abraham Woods, Jr. (RR 2-565 to 2-575); King, "Letter from Birmingham Jail," p. 120; Vincent Harding, "A Beginning in Birmingham," *The Reporter*, 6 June 1963, p. 14.
26. King, *Why We Can't Wait*, p. 60; White, *The Making of the President—1964*, p. 169; oral history with Rev. Woods, *supra* note 1, chapter 1, at pp. 15-17;

Birmingham Post-Herald, 4 April 1963, p. 5. The twenty Negro demonstrators were tried, convicted and sentenced to 180 days in jail and fined $100 in Birmingham's Recorder's Court. *Birmingham Post-Herald*, 5 April 1963, p. 4.

27. Westin and Mahoney, *The Trail of Martin Luther King,* pp. 65-66.

28. King, *Why We Can't Wait*, p. 68; *New York Times*, 7 April 1963, p. 55; *Birmingham News,* 6 April 1963.

29. Bennett, *What Manner of Man—Martin Luther King, Jr.*, p. 136; *New York Times*, 8 April 1963, p. 31; *Birmingham News*, 8 April 1963; *Birmingham Post-Herald*, 8 April 1963, p. 2. After this first encounter, the police dogs were not used again in crowd control until Friday, May 3rd (Double-D Day) when massive numbers of Negro children were used in demonstrations.

30. Westin and Mahoney, *The Trial of Martin Luther King,* pp. 69-71; Bennett, *What Manner of Man—Martin Luther King, Jr.*, p. 136; *Race Relations Law Reporter,* 1963, p. 436; *New York Times*, 12 April 1963, p. 1; *Birmingham Post-Herald*, 12 April 1963, p. 4.

31. Westin and Mahoney, *The Trial of Martin Luther King*, p. 72.

32. King, *Why We Can't Wait*, p. 70; oral history with Rev. Walker, *supra* note 21, chapter 1 (RR 2-287).

33. King, *Why We Can't Wait*, p. 70.

34. *Wyatt Tee Walker et al. v. City of Birmingham*, 18 L. Ed. 2d 1210, 1221 (1967); interview with Arthur Shores (RR 267); interview with John Drew, Alexander and Co., Inc., Birmingham, Alabama, 2 Sept. 1976 (RR 496); interview with Orzell Billingsley, Jr. (RR 2-018).

35. *Wyatt Tee Walker et al. v. City of Birmingham,* 181 So. 2d 493, 496 (Alabama Sup. Ct., 1965); "Statement by Rev. F.L. Shuttlesworth," 14 April 1963, Shuttlesworth Papers, Box 1, KCSC; Sterne, *I Have A Dream*, p. 186; LaMonte, *supra* note 14, chapter 1, at p. 186. U.S. Supreme Court Justice Brennan agreed with the civil rights leaders' assessment of the injunction by labelling it a "blatantly unconstitutional restraining order." *Wyatt Tee Walker et al. v. City of Birmingham*, *supra* note 34, chapter 2, at p. 1231.

36. Interview with Orzell Billingsley, Jr. (RR 2-002).

37. Interview with Rev. Abraham Woods, Jr. (RR 3-365 to 3-427); interview with Rev. Nelson Henry Smith, Jr. (RR 032); King, *Why We Can't Wait*, p. 71.

38. *New York Times*, 13 April 1963, p. 1; *Birmingham Post-Herald*, 13 April 1963, p. 10; Westin and Mahoney, *The Trial of Martin Luther King*, p. 85.

39. *Connor v. State*, 153 So. 2d 787 (Alabama Sup. Ct., 1963); *Birmingham Post-Herald*, 15 April 1963, p. 1; *Ibid.*, 16 April 1963, p. 1; *New York Times*, 16 April 1963, p. 1.

40. *Birmingham Post-Herald*, 13 April 1963, p. 10; see King, *Why We Can't Wait*, pp. 76-95; see also King, "Letter from Birmingham Jail," *supra* note 42, chapter 1.

41. Interview with Arthur Shores (RR 275).

42. King, *Why We Can't Wait*, p. 96; *New York Times*, 12 April 1963, p. 70.

43. Bishop, *The Days of Martin Luther King, Jr.*, pp. 295-99; Lewis, *King: A Critical Biography*, p. 185.

44. Miller, *Martin Luther King, Jr.*, p. 140.
45. *Race Relations Law Reporter*, 1963, pp. 439-40; Westin and Mahoney, *The Trail of Martin Luther King*, pp. 121, 122, 141; Bishop, *The Days of Martin Luther King, Jr.*, p. 300; *New York Times*, 23 April 1963, p. 20; *Ibid.*, 24 April 1963, p. 19; *Ibid.*, 25 April 1963, p. 20; *Birmingham Post-Herald*, 23 April 1963; *Ibid.*, 24 April 1963.
46. *New York Times*, 27 April 1963, p. 9; *Birmingham Post-Herald*, 27 April 1963, p. 5; *Birmingham News*, 26 April 1963. The case involving the violation of the state court injunction involved a landmark U.S. Supreme Court decision, *Wyatt Tee Walker et al. v. City of Birmingham*, 388 U.S. 307, 18 L. Ed.2d 1210, 87 S. Ct. 1824 (1967). In a 5-4 decision, the U.S. Supreme Court, in an opinion by Justice Stewart, held that since the Circuit Court had jurisdiction over the petitioners and over the subject matter of the controversy, the petitioners could properly be held in contempt for disobeying the injunction, even though the injunction and the parade ordinances were unquestionably subject to substantial constitutional question. In a minority opinion, Chief Justice Earl Warren correctly discerned that the reason that Birmingham city officials sought the injunction was "to immunize the unconstitutional statute and its unconstitutional application from any attack." (18 L. Ed. 2d 1210, 1227). In a separate opinion, Justice William O. Douglas argued that "an ordinance—unconstitutional on its face or patently unconstitutional as applied—is not made sacred by an unconstitutional injunction that enforces it." (18 L. Ed. 2d 1210, 1230)
    But, the black defendants, receiving only minority support from the U.S. Supreme Court, had to return to Birmingham and serve their 5-day jail sentence.
47. Westin and Mahoney, *The Trial of Martin Luther King*, pp. 142-43; *Birmingham Post-Herald*, 22 April 1963, p. 6.
48. *New York Times*, 15 April 1963, p. 1; *Ibid.*, 18 April 1963, p. 21; *Ibid.*, 6 May 1963, p. 59; *Birmingham Post-Herald*, 15 April 1963, p. 6; *Ibid.*, 22 April 1963, p. 6; *Ibid.*, 29 April 1963, p. 1.
49. Miller, *Martin Luther King. Jr.*, p. 140; Lewis, *King: A Critical Biography*, p. 192.
50. Miller, *Martin Luther King, Jr.*, p. 140.
51. *Ibid.*, pp. 140-41; Bennett, *What Manner of Man—Martin Luther King, Jr.*, p. 152; oral history with Rev. Walker, *supra* note 21, chapter 1 (RR 6-006).
52. Oral history with Rev. Walker, *supra* note 21, chapter 1 (RR 5-405); *New York Times*, 3 May 1963, p. 1; *Birmingham Post-Herald*, 3 May 1963, p. 3; *Birmingham News*, 2 May 1963; Miller, *Martin Luther King, Jr.*, pp. 140-41; Bishop, *The Days of Martin Luther King, Jr.*, p. 301; Bennett, *What Manner of Man—Martin Luther King, Jr.*, p. 152.
53. King, *My Life With Martin Luther King*, Jr., p. 229.
54. Bennett, *What Manner of Man—Martin Luther King, Jr.*, p. 152; *Wyatt Tee Walker et al. v. City of Birmingham*, *supra* note 34, chapter 2, at p. 1222; *New York Times*, 4 May 1963, p. 1; *Birmingham Post-Herald*, 4 May 1963, p. 2.

55. Bennett, *What Manner of Man—Martin Luther King, Jr.*, p. 152; *New York Times*, 4 May 1963, p. 8.
56. Miller, *Martin Luther King, Jr.*, p. 142; *Atlanta Journal-Constitution*, 5 May 1963, SRC; Bishop, *The Days of Martin Luther King, Jr.*, p. 303; *New York Times*, 5 May 1963, p. 1; *Birmingham News,* 4 May 1963.
57. *New York Times*, 7 May 1963, p. 1; *Ibid.*, 8 May 1963, p. 1; *Atlanta Journal-Constitution*, 7 May 1963, SRC; *Birmingham Post-Herald*, 7 May 1963, p. 2; *Birmingham News*, 7 May 1963. The total number of persons arrested and jailed during the demonstrations is difficult to estimate; it is evident, however, that a sharp increase in arrests and jailings by the Birmingham Police Department occurred in May, 1963. Police Department, *Annual Report 1963*, Birmingham, Alabama.
58. Interview with Emil Hess (RR 236); Nichols, *supra* note 1, chapter 1, at p. 320; interview with Arthur Shores (RR 582); *New York Post*, 10 May 1963, p. 1, KCSC.
59. Interview with David J. Vann, City Hall, Birmingham, Alabama, 10 Sept. 1976 (RR 094).
60. Interview with Arthur Shores (RR 554-65); oral history with Rev. Walker (RR 6-107); *Pittsburgh Courier*, 25 May 1963, p. 1, SRC.
61. Interview with David J. Vann (RR 132); interview with Arthur Shores (RR 565). In addition to David Vann and Sid Smyer, the white negotiators included Erskine Smith, a young lawyer who along with Vann had spearheaded the drive to change the form of government, and Billy Hamilton, Mayor Boutwell's Executive Secretary. The black negotiators included Arthur Shores, Rev. Fred Shuttlesworth, Dr. A.G. Gaston, a very wealthy black businessman, Mr. and Mrs. John Drew, a local insurance executive and his wife, Mrs. Tyree Barefield-Pendleton, the wife of a prominent doctor, Dr. Lucius Pitts, president of the local Miles College, and several ministers including Reverends Harold Long, Nelson Henry Smith, Jr., John Thomas Porter, Jr., and Abraham Woods, Jr. Interview with John Drew (RR 100-250); interview with David J. Vann (RR 102); See also *New York Times*, 11 May 1963, p. 9.
62. Nichols, *supra* note 1, chapter 1, at p. 321.
63. *New York Times,* 11 May 1963, p. 1; *Birmingham Post Herald*, 10 May 1963, p. 1; interview with David J. Vann (RR 117-24); Nichols, *supra* note 1, chapter 1, at p. 328.
64. Harding, *supra* note 25, chapter 2; Westin and Mahoney, *The Trial of Martin Luther King*, p. 146; Bennett, *What Manner of Man—Martin Luther King, Jr.*, p. 153; *Birmingham Post-Herald*, 8 May 1963, p. 2.
65. Harding, *supra* note 25, chapter 2, at p. 17; *New York Times*, 9 May 1963, p. 1; *Birmingham Post-Herald*, 8 May 1963, p. 2.
66. *New York Times*, 11 May 1963, p. 8; *Pittsburgh Courier*, 25 May 1963, p. 1, SRC; King, *Why We Can't Wait*, pp. 105-6; *Birmingham Post-Herald*, 11 May 1963, p. 2; interview with David J. Vann (RR 170).
67. Miller, *Martin Luther King, Jr.*, p. 146; Victor S. Navasky, *Kennedy Justice* (New York: Atheneum, 1971), p. 208.

68. King, *Why We Can't Wait*, p. 106; *New York Times*, 12 May 1963, p. 1; *Birmingham Post-Herald*, 13 May 1963, p. 1; *Birmingham News*, 13 May 1963.
69. King, *Why We Can't Wait*, p. 147; Miller, *Martin Luther King, Jr.*, p. 147.
70. Nichols, *supra* note 1, chapter 1, at p. 346; *New York Times*, 13 May 1963, p. 24; *New York Herald Tribune*, 13 May 1963, SRC; *Birmingham Post-Herald*, 13 May 1963, p. 1.
71. *New York Times*, 13 May 1963, p. 1.
72. *Ibid.*, pp. 1, 25.
73. *Ibid.*, 14 May 1963, p. 27.
74. *Ibid.*

CHAPTER THREE

1. *Birmingham Post-Herald*, 15 April 1963, p. 1.
2. *The Examiner*, 25 April 1963, p. 1; "Statement of the Commissioners of the City of Birmingham," *Birmingham News*, 7 April 1963; *Birmingham Post-Herald*, 4 April 1963, p. 1.
3. Interview with M. Edwin Wiggins (RR 030); *Connor v. State*, 153 So. 2d 787 (Alabama Sup. Ct., 1963).
4. *The Examiner*, 18 April 1963, p. 1.
5. Interview with David J. Vann (RR 045); interview with William Spencer III (RR 426); Morgan, *A Time to Speak*, pp. 152-53.
6. Interview with Arthur Hanes (RR 080, 174); interview with M. Edwin Wiggins (RR 062); LaMonte, *supra* note 14, chapter 1, at p. 250.
7. Interview with Arthur Hanes (RR 016); interview with Albert Boutwell (RR 220); interview with M. Edwin Wiggins (RR 036).
8. *Birmingham Post-Herald*, 16 April 1963; interview with Don Hawkins (RR 451); interview with M. Edwin Wiggins (RR 055).
9. Interview with Don Hawkins (RR 461); interview with M. Edwin Wiggins (RR 052).
10. In a communication to the City Council, Mayor Boutwell wrote that "In view of this litigation [*Connor v. State*], and on advice of the City Attorney, none but the most routine matters necessary to the day-to-day operation of the city's business has been considered for adoption." Birmingham City Council, Minutes of Regular Meeting, 30 April 1963, p. 19.
11. Interview with Dr. E.C. Overton (RR 005); interview with Don A. Hawkins (RR 460).
12. Interview with Don A. Hawkins (RR 451-66); interview with M. Edwin Wiggins (RR 278-86); interview with Alan T. Drennen, Jr., Protective Life Insurance Building, Birmingham, Alabama, 20 Sept. 1976 (RR 600).
13. Interview with M. Edwin Wiggins (RR 278-86); interview with Arthur Hanes (RR 018); interview with Don A. Hawkins (RR 451); interview with Alan T. Drennen, Jr. (RR 600).

14. Interview with George Wall (RR 050-155); interview with Duard LeGrande (RR 044); interview with Albert Boutwell (RR 298); interview with Alan T. Drennan, Jr. (RR 2-038); interview with Dr. E.C. Overton (RR 070-105); interview with M. Edwin Wiggins (RR 088, 177). In view of overwhelming evidence to the contrary, it appears that the observation that Connor and Boutwell "made decisions on the handling of the demonstrations together," [Harrison, *supra* note 32, chapter 1, at p. 59] is incorrect.

15. Interview with M. Edwin Wiggins (RR 077-245); interview with Dr. E.C. Overton (RR 089); interview with Duard LeGrande (RR 042); interview with Don A. Hawkins (RR 469).

16. *Birmingham News*, 20 May 1956; *Birmingham Post-Herald*, 8 April 1962, p. 2.

17. Nichols, *supra* note 1, chapter 1, at p. 53.

18. Nichols, *supra* note 1, chapter 1, at pp. 74-75. Bull Connor in fact was a self-proclaimed white supremacist. *Wyatt Tee Walker et al. v. City of Birmingham*, *supra* note 34, chapter 1, at 1222; *Congress and the Nation 1945-1964* (Congressional Quarterly Service, 1965), p. 1604.

19. Eugene (Bull) Connor to Franklin D. Roosevelt, 6 August 1942, Official Governor's Papers—Chauncey Sparks, Drawer 180, Alabama Department of Archives and History (hereafter abbreviated "ADAH").

20. *The Birmingham Post*, 2 June 1948; William J. Barnard, *Dixiecrats and Democrats: Alabama Politics 1942-1950* (University, Alabama: The University of Alabama Press, 1974), p. 11.

21. Robert A. Garson, *The Democratic Party and the Politics of Sectionalism, 1941-1948* (Baton Rouge, Louisiana: Louisiana State University Press, 1974), p. 253; *Southern School News*, April 1963, p. 8. One member of the more liberal loyalist wing of the Alabama Democratic Party who refused to participate in the walk-out was a young state representative from Barbour County—George C. Wallace. Barnard, *Dixiecrats and Democrats: Alabama Politics 1942-1950*, p. 111.

22. Nichols, *supra* note 1, chapter 1, at p. 65.

23. Eugene (Bull) Connor, "Birmingham Wars on Communism," *The Alabama Local Government Journal*, August, 1950, p. 38; Barnard, *Dixiecrats and Democrats: Alabama Politics 1942-1950*, p. 177, note 30.

24. Nichols, *supra* note 1, chapter 1, at p. 77.

25. *Montgomery Advertiser*, 1 May 1960.

26. Interview with James Parsons, City Hall, Birmingham, Alabama, 26 August 1976 (RR 573-610); *Birmingham Post-Herald*, 3 Dec. 1975, p. 1; *Ibid.*, 20 Dec. 1975.

27. Professor Wayne Flynt of Samford University argues that when a speaker "appeals to emotions which short circuit the auditor's normal critical facilities, [then] unethical and undemocratic methods" are being employed. If this argument be accepted, then all three City Commissioners in Birmingham in early 1963 could be charged with utilizing these methods. Wayne Flynt, "The Ethics of Democratic Persuasion and the Birmingham Crisis," *The Southern Speech Journal* 35 (Fall 1969): 40.

28. Brown, *supra* note 15, chapter 1, at p. 17; "The Situation and Prospects of the Rights Argument in the South," transcript of program of news and comment by Howard K. Smith, 26 May 1963, p. 6; *Birmingham News*, 21 July 1963; *Birmingham Post-Herald*, 26 Sept. 1963.
29. Interview with Arthur Hanes (RR 2-234, 2-210); Cleghorn, *supra* note 59, chapter 1.
30. Interview with Arthur Hanes (RR 277, 2-047).
31. Navasky, *Kennedy Justice*, p. 218; Arthur M. Schlesinger, Jr., *A Thousand Days* (Boston: Houghton Mifflin, 1965), p. 959; Lewis, *King: A Critical Biography*, p. 203.
32. LaMonte, *supra* note 14, chapter 1, at pp. 233-36; interview with M. Edwin Wiggins (RR 350).
33. Interview with Arthur Hanes (RR 158-66); Nichols, *supra* note 1, chapter 1, at pp. 57-62.
34. Interview with Arthur Hanes (RR 168-80, 362-72); Nichols, *supra* note 1, chapter 1, at pp. 236, 283.
35. Bishop, *The Days of Martin Luther King, Jr.*, p. 286.
36. *Birmingham News*, 4 April 1963; Bishop, *The Days of Martin Luther King, Jr.*, p. 299; interview with James Parson (RR 427); King, *Why We Can't Wait*, p. 69.
37. Lewis, *King: A Critical Biography*, pp. 181-93.
38. Birmingham City Commission, Minutes of Regular Meeting, 30 April 1963, p. 603.
39. Interview with James Parsons (RR 593-610); interview with Arthur Hanes (RR 388-404); interview with Thad Holt (RR 282); Nichols, *supra* note 1, chapter 1, at p. 284; Gary Thomas Rowe, Jr., *My Undercover Years with the Ku Klux Klan* (New York: Bantam Books, 1976), p. 92.
40. Interview with James Parsons (RR 457); unrecorded interview with Jamie Moore, City Federal Building, Birmingham, Alabama, 27 August 1976; Bishop, *The Days of Martin Luther King, Jr.*, p. 299; Lewis, *King: A Critical Biography*, pp. 181-82.
41. Interview with James Parson (RR 436); unrecorded interview with Jamie Moore.
42. Lewis, *King: A Critical Biography*, p. 193.
43. *New York Times*, 8 May 1963, p. 29.
44. *Ibid.*; Rev. Fred L. Shuttlesworth, "Birmingham Revisited," *Ebony*, August 1971, p. 118.
45. The Inter-Citizens Committee, Inc., "Documents on Human Rights in Alabama," (mimeographed pamphlet) Official Governor's Papers—George C. Wallace, File Drawer 399, ADAH.
46. Interview with Arthur Hanes (RR 273); *The Examiner*, 9 May 1963, p., 1; *Birmingham Post-Herald*, 14 May 1963, p. 7.
47. Nichols, *supra* note 1, chapter 1, at p. 313.
48. Lewis and *The New York Times*, *Portrait of a Decade*, p. 184; interview with Arthur Hanes (RR 2-064).

49. *Montgomery Advertiser*, 8 June 1963; interviews with Arthur Hanes (RR 2-083).

50. Interview with James Parsons (RR 128.)

51. Ibid., (RR 331).

52. Ibid., (RR 128-91); see also John Dollard, *Caste and Class in a Southern Town* (Garden City, New York: Doubleday and Company, Inc. 1947), pp. 279-80. In a survey conducted in 1964, 60% of the blacks questioned in Birmingham said that the local police treated members of their race badly. In the same survey only 26% of the blacks in Northern metropolitan areas felt that they were treated badly by local police. Gary T. Marx, *Protest and Prejudice* (New York: Harper and Row, 1969) p. 36.

53. Unrecorded interview with Jamie Moore; interview with George Wall (RR 056, 188-238); interview with Duard LeGrande (RR 047).

54. Interview with Albert Boutwell (RR 2-309); interview with Alan T. Drennen, Jr. (RR 2-058); Dr. John E. Bryan, recorded interview by George Stewart, March 1972, Birmingham Public Library.

55. LaMonte, *supra* note 14, chapter 1, at pp. 203-4.

56. Interview with Dr. E.C. Overton (RR 389). The nine members of the City Council were Dr. John E. Bryan, Alan T. Drennen, Jr., John Golden, Don A. Hawkins, Nina Miglianico, Dr. E.C. Overton, George G. Seibels, Jr., Tom W. Woods, and City Council President M. Edwin Wiggins.

57. Thad Holt, "Memorandum on the Martin Luther King Demonstrations in Birmingham, Alabama," 10 May 1963, p. 3; LaMonte, *supra* note 14, chapter 1, at p. 249.

58. LaMonte, *supra* note 14, chapter 1, at pp. 245, 259; Nichols, *supra* note 1, chapter 1, at pp. 232-34.

59. Interview with Dr. E.C. Overton (RR 097-108); interview with Don A. Hawkins (RR 488).

60. Interview with Alan T. Drennen, Jr. (RR 2-053); interview with Albert Boutwell (RR 233); interview with Don A. Hawkins (RR 470-94, 2-015); interview with Dr. E.C. Overton (RR 081); interview with M. Edwin Wiggins (RR 080-172).

61. Birmingham City Council, Minutes of Regular Meeting, 14 May 1963, pp. 48-49.

62. George G. Seibels, Jr. to Al Lingo, 13 June 1963, Official Governor's Papers—George C. Wallace, File Drawer 399, ADAH.

63. Birmingham City Council, *supra* note 10, chapter 3, at p. 19; interview with M. Edwin Wiggins (RR 217).

64. Birmingham City Council, *supra* note 10, chapter 3, at p. 20; Birmingham City Commission, *supra* note 38, chapter 3, at p. 603.

65. Interview with Albert Boutwell (RR 416, 639, 2-158); interview with Alan T. Drennen, Jr. (RR 608, 2-010); interview with Don A. Hawkins (RR 2-017); Albert Boutwell, Speech to the National Conference of Christians and Jews, Birmingham, Alabama, 19 April 1963, pp. 2, 4. The City Council refused to meet with the national black leadership because they were viewed as

"irresponsible and unthinking agitators." *Birmingham Post-Herald*, 4 May 1963, p. 2; Birmingham City Council, *supra* note 61, chapter 3, at pp. 48-49.

66. Interview with Alan T. Drennen, Jr. (RR 2-018 to 2-028); interview with M. Edwin Wiggins (RR 150).

67. Interview with Alan T. Drennen, Jr. (RR 457, 2-019); interview with M. Edwin Wiggins (RR 161); interview with Don A. Hawkins (Rr 2-031). Election results from the 1963 City Council race indicated that Alan T. Drennen, Jr. marshalled stronger support among black voters than any other white candidate.

68. Interview with Dr. E.C. Overton (Rr 292, 581); interview with Albert Boutwell (RR 2-215); interview with David J. Vann (RR 102). The City Council's representative was Billy Hamilton, Albert Boutwell's executive secretary, who had extensive contact with the federal government.

69. Interview with Albert Boutwell (RR 2-228).

70. LaMonte, *supra* note 14, chapter 1, at p. 250; *Atlanta Journal-Constitution*, 11 May 1963, SRC.

71. Interview with Sidney W. Smyer, Sr., 2780 Smyer Circle, Birmingham Alabama, 9 Sept. 1976 (RR 265); interview with Charles Zukoski (RR 071, 191).

CHAPTER FOUR

1. *New York Times*, 9 May 1963, p. 16.

2. *New York Times*, 17 April 1963, p. 1; *Ibid.*, 20 April 1963, p. 1. There will be a brief critical review of the Kennedy administration's civil rights efforts in chapter 7.

3. The two leading racially moderate candidates, who were defeated by Wallace in the Democratic Party primary, were former Governor James "Big Jim" Folsom and state Senator Ryan DeGraffenreid. Numan V. Bartley and Hugh D. Graham, *Southern Politics and the Second Reconstruction* (Baltimore: The Johns Hopkins University Press, 1975), pp. 67-68.

4. In the Democratic Party primary campaign in May, 1962, Wallace promised the voters, "I shall go to jail, rather than submit to integration." *Birmingham Post-Herald*, 7 November 1962, p. 3.

5. *Birmingham Post-Herald*, 15 January 1963, p. 1.

6. *Montgomery Advertiser*, 15 January 1963, p. 1.

7. *New York Times*, 16 May 1963, p. 23. In commenting upon the riots, Wallace also said, "This is what Martin Luther King calls nonviolence and passive resistance." *New York Times*, 13 May 1963, p. 24.

8. *Race Relations Law Reporter*, 1963, p. 448; *St. Louis Post-Dispatch*, 23 May 1963, p. 2A, SRC.

9. King, *My Life With Martin Luther King, Jr.*, p. 219; Bishop, *The Days of Martin Luther King, Jr.*, p. 270.

10. Schlesinger, *A Thousand Days*, p. 959; Bishop, *The Days of Martin Luther King, Jr.*, p. 283.

11. *New York Times*, 14 April 1963, p. 46; Westin and Mahoney, *The Trial of Martin Luther King*, pp. 86-87.

12. *New York Times*, 9 May 1963, p., 16; Burke Marshall, recorded interview by Anthony Lewis, 20 June 1964, p. 104, John F. Kennedy Library Oral History Program, John F. Kennedy Library (hereafter abbreviated "JFKL"), Waltham, Massachusetts.

13. *New York Times*, 9 May 1963, p. 16.

14. This position was evident in the executive action taken when Dr. King was arrested and jailed in Birmingham. After talking with Coretta Scott King, President Kennedy arranged a phone call for her with her husband, who was being held incommunicado. King, *My Life with Martin Luther King, Jr.*, pp. 224-27; Bishop, *The Days of Martin Luther King, Jr.*, pp. 296-98; Lewis, *King: A Critical Biography*, p. 186.

15. *Washington Post*, 7 May 1963, SRC.

16. *New York Times*, 9 May 1963, p. 16.

17. Oral history with Burke Marshall, *supra* note 12, chapter 4, at pp. 101-2; Schlesinger, *A Thousand Days*, p. 959; Westin and Mahoney, *The Trial of Martin Luther King*, p. 147; Miller, *Martin Luther King, Jr.*, p. 145. The Birmingham business leaders who were contacted included Edward Norton, chairman of Royal Crown Cola, Frank Plummer, president of Birmingham Trust National Bank, and William H. Hulsey, board chairman of Realty Mortgage Company. Lewis, *King: A Critical Biography*, p. 198.

18. Miller, *Martin Luther King, Jr.*, p. 145; Lewis, *King: A Critical Biography*, p. 198.

19. Oral history with Burke Marshall, *supra* note 12, chapter 4, at p. 97; *New York Post*, 12 May 1963, KCSC; Lewis and *The New York Times, Portrait of a Decade*, pp. 182-83; Schlesinger, *A Thousand Days*, p. 959.

20. *New York Post*, 12 May 1963, KCSC; Lewis and *The New York Times, Portrait of a Decade*, p. 183. The two main Birmingham daily newspapers did not put articles concerning the demonstrations on the front page, even though they were often on the first page of the *New York Times* and other major dailies. Interview with Duard LeGrande (RR 082-088); Thad Holt, *supra* note 57, chapter 3, at p. 7.

21. *Washington Post*, 7 May 1963, SRC; Thad Holt *supra* note 57, chapter 3, at p. 5; *The Examiner*, 9 May 1963, p. 1.

22. Oral history with Burke Marshall, *supra* note 12, chapter 4, at p. 99; *New York Post*, 12 May 1963, KCSC; interview with David J. Vann (RR 080).

23. Navasky, *Kennedy Justice*, p. 218; Lewis and *The New York Times, Portrait of a Decade*, p. 187.

24. Lewis and *The New York Times, Portrait of a Decade*, p. 183.

25. *New York Times*, 11 May 1963, p. 1.

26. *Ibid.*, 13 May 1963, p. 25.

27. A wide range of resources were available to the federal government to use in Birmingham. The withholding of federal funds to the area would have provided a very powerful weapon for the federal government to use in enforcing its will. As a result of its decision to rely solely on informal action, however, the Kennedy administration was unwilling to utilize the enormous resources of the federal government.

28. Interview with Arthur Hanes (RR 2-220); interview with Albert Boutwell (RR 294); interview with David J. Vann (RR 364); Navasky, Kennedy Justice, p. 219; King, *Why We Can't Wait*, p. 103; interview with Rev. Nelson Henry Smith, Jr. (RR 307-16). Although most white civil rights advocates, while in Birmingham, stayed at the integrated A.G. Gaston Motel, Burke Marshall stayed at the segregated Holiday Inn, in order to avoid alienating Birmingham whites. Thad Holt, *supra* note 57, chapter 3, at p. 8.

29. George C. Wallace, Speech prepared for delivery at Harvard University, 4 November 1963, Official Governor's Papers—George C. Wallace, Drawer 399, ADAH, p. 4.

30. George C. Wallace to Howard G. Swafford, 28 May 1963, Official Governor's Papers—George C. Wallace, Drawer 399, ADAH.

31. *Birmingham News*, 9 May 1963; George C. Wallace to Henry G. Swafford, *supra* note 30, chapter 4; *New York Times*, 13 May 1963, p. 24.

32. *Birmingham News*, 3 March 1963; *Atlanta Constitution*, 7 March 1963, p. 3, SRC; *Birmingham Post-Herald*, 4 March 1963, p. 10; *Atlanta Constitution*, 14 May 1963, SRC; Thad Holt, *supra* note 57, chapter 3, at p. 3.

33. Bishop, *The Days of Martin Luther King, Jr.*, p. 304. Lingo and Clark joined forces again in the spring of 1965. At that time, they used tear gas and electric cattle prods against a group of civil rights demonstrators, who were attempting to begin the Selma-Montgomery march. The demonstrators were chased through the Selma streets by State Troopers and members of the Dallas County "irregulars," who were on horseback.

34. Interview with James Parsons (RR 400-15).

35. Interview with George Wall (RR 145-47); oral history with Rev. Walker, *supra* note 21, chapter 1 (RR 13-067); *The Militant*, 20 May 1963, p. 1, KCSC.

36. Bishop, *The Days of Martin Luther King, Jr.*, p. 304.

37. George C. Wallace to Harry P. Gamble, 8 May 1963, Official Governor's Papers—George C. Wallace, Drawer 399, ADAH.

38. *New York Times*, 13 May 1963, p. 24.

39. *Birmingham News*, 9 May 1963.

40. *Ibid.*; Lewis and *The New York Times, Portrait of a Decade*, p. 184.

41. *New York Times*, 13 May 1963, p. 24.

42. Alabama, *Journal of the House, 1963*, Regular Session, H.J.R. 10, pp. 104-5.

43. Alabama, *supra* note 42, chapter 4, at H.J.R. 5, p. 6. In a subsequent report to the Alabama Legislature, the Commission to Preserve the Peace stated that, "Communist subversion in America is in large measure directed through minority groups." The Commission also argued that, "S.N.C.C. is an agent for the Communist conspiracy." Alabama, *Journal of the House, 1965*, Regular Session, pp. 881, 887.

44. Alabama, *supra* note 42, chapter 4, at H.J.R. 14, pp. 106-7.

CHAPTER FIVE

1. Nichols, *supra* note 1, chapter 1, at p. 430; interview with Sidney W. Smyer, Sr. (RR 072); interview with Thad Holt (RR 208).
2. Senior Citizens Committee, "Statement of Policy to Employees," 19 Sept. 1962 (mimeographed).
3. George C. Lodge, "The Introduction of Change," Harvard Business School Case 9-371-003 (Boston: Intercollegiate Case Clearinghouse, Sept., 1972), p. 1; interview with Emil Hess (RR 330).
4. Morgan, *A Time to Speak*, p. 133.
5. It is informative to review the actions of a prominent white in Birmingham who acted upon his belief in racial equality. Mr. Charles Morgan, a liberal white attorney, felt pressured to leave Birmingham after he publicly criticized the city's white leaders for their failure to seek just solutions to problems plaguing local blacks.
6. *Thunderbolt*, tabloid published by the National States Rights Party, 51 (May 1963), p. 6; Reese Cleghorn, *Radicalism: Southern Style* (Atlanta: Southern Regional Council, 1968), p. 11.
7. An analysis of the membership of the Senior Citizens Committee reveals that about 30% of its members worked for national corporations; the remaining members were primarily local industrialists, financiers, attorneys or bankers. Those individuals who worked for national corporations usually had fewer ties to the city than did the businessmen associated with local companies. There was usually a difference in their length of residence in the city; the corporate nomads were usually neither born nor raised in Birmingham. The corporate nomads' primary allegiance was not to the city. For example, Arthur Weibel, president of U.S. Steel's Birmingham division (Tennessee Coal and Iron), stated explicitly, "I am still and always will be first loyal to U.S. Steel." [Nichols, *supra* note 1, chapter 1, at p. 191.] The normal corporate aversion to controversy led the individuals in the national corporations to limit their activity in the community to non-controversial charity organizations such as the Red Cross and the United Fund. See C. Wright Mills, *The Power Elite* (New York: Oxford University Press, 1956), pp. 41-52; M. Kent Jennings, *Community Influentials* (New York: Free Press of Glencoe, 1964), pp. 49-56.
8. Many of the corporate nomads were either born or educated in the North. Arthur Weibel was born and raised in Maryland; he received his education at Carnegie Tech. Amasa G. Smith, manager of the Chicago Bridge Co. factory in Birmingham, was born in the North and educated at M.I.T. Nichols, *supra* note 1, chapter 1, at pp. 191-93.
9. Discussion with Dr. Robert Coles, 3 March 1977; see also Dollard, *Caste and Class in a Southern Town*, p. 83.

10. Five young Birmingham attorneys—Charles Morgan, Jr., Robert S. Vance, George "Peach" Taylor, David J. Vann, and C. Erskine Smith—led several of the fights for political and social changes during the early 1960's. The role played by Vann and Smith in the change in Birmingham's form of government is discussed in chapter 1. *San Francisco Chronicle*, 19 May 1963, p. 1.

11. Mr. Charles Zukoski, the executive vice-president of the state's largest bank, publicly criticized the segregationist inaugural address delivered by Governor George Wallace in January of 1963. As a result of his public criticism, Mr. Zukoski was dismissed by the bank, although he was to retire within two years. Nichols, *supra* note 1, chapter 1, at pp. 203-4; see also *supra* note 5, chapter 5.

12. Dr. Henry King Stanford, the president of Birmingham-Southern College, refused to expel one of his students who had been active in various civil rights activities. As a result of his stand, Dr. Stanford was pressured into leaving Birmingham. Discussion with Dr. Robert Coles, 3 March 1977; Nichols, *supra* note 1, chapter 1, at pp. 205-6.

13. Interview with Robert M. Shelton, Ramada Inn-Downtown, Tuscaloosa, Alabama, 22 Sept. 1976 (RR 325); interview with Edward Fields, National Headquarters-National States Rights Party, Marietta, Georgia, 15 Sept. 1976 (RR 122-32). Since the Ku Klux Klan is a secret organization, membership lists are unavailable. Thus, the characterization of the membership of these extremist groups is based upon the leaders' evaluation. One study has been done, however, in which 153 known Klansmen were grouped into four occupational groups:

> 1) skilled workers (for example, garage mechanics, machinists, carpenters, and stonemasons);
> 2) marginal, small businessmen (for example, small building-trade contractors and proprietors of food markets, grills, and gas stations);
> 3) marginal white-collar workers (for example, grocery store clerks, service-station attendants, policemen, and salesmen); and
> 4) transportation workers (primarily truck drivers) unskilled and semi-skilled workers in the textile, construction, automotive, aircraft, coal and steel industries.

Of the 153 Klansmen who were classified according to these categories, 33.3% were skilled workers; 7.1% were marginal businessmen; 23.3% were marginal white-collar workers; and, 36% were unskilled and semi-skilled workers. James W. Vander Zanden, "The Klan Revival," *American Journal of Sociology*, 65 (March 1960): 458.

14. Robert Coles, *Children of Crisis: A Study of Courage and Fear* (Boston: Little, Brown and Company, 1964), p. 376; James W. Vander Zanden, *supra* note 13, chapter 5, at p. 460; "The Situation and Prospects of the Rights Argument in the South," *supra* note 28, chapter 3, at p. 3.; David Chalmers, *Hooded Americanism* (Garden City, New York: Doubleday, 1965), p. 373.

15. See chapter 1, pp. 11-14.
16. *Birmingham Post-Herald*, 9 April 1963, p. 2.
17. *Birmingham News*, 19 April 1963.
18. *Birmingham Post-Herald*, 5 April 1963.
19. The largest retail stores in Birmingham were locally-owned. Loveman's and Pizitz were large downtown department stores that were owned by Jews in Birmingham. [See *infra* note 26, chapter 5.] There were several retail variety stores in Birmingham that were part of national chains, including Sears Roebuck and Co., Woolworth, Newberry's, S.S. Kresge, and McCrory's.
20. The largest employer in Birmingham in 1963 was Tennessee Coal and Iron (T.C.I.), which was a division of U.S. Steel. T.C.I. employed 16,000 workers of whom about 12,000 were production and maintenance workers. The second largest employer in the area, Hayes International, began during the Korean War as an aircraft modification and repair operation; it later entered the space industry. As a result of its specialization in a technical area, Hayes employed very skilled workers—over one-fifth of the company's 9,000 workers were graduate engineers. A third major employer even in 1963 was Birmingham's Medical Center. Composed of three major parts—the Medical College of Alabama, the School of Dentistry, and University of Alabama Hospitals and Clinics—the Medical Center employed more than 4,200 workers.

    There were several major banks in Birmingham in 1963. By far the largest bank, not only in the city but also in the entire state, was the First National Bank, which had assets of $572,000,000 in 1965. The Birmingham Trust National Bank had approximately $240,000,000 in resources at that time; the Exchange Bank had assets of $100,000,000. Hammer, Greene, Siler Associates, *supra* note 5, preface, at pp. 79-85; *Birmingham News*, 31 Oct. 1293, p. 12, SRC.
21. Interview with Thad Holt (RR 079).
22. Birmingham Chamber of Commerce officials estimated that although blacks comprised about 40% of the population of metropolitan Birmingham, the Negroes' buying power was only 12.5% of the city's total. This figure not only indicates the limited effect that a black boycott could have, but also provides support to the assertion that Birmingham blacks were at a distinct economic disadvantage relative to whites. *New York Times*, 28 May 1963, 0. 24.
23. Interview with Emil Hess (RR 029, 138); unrecorded interview with Local Merchant No. 2, Birmingham, Alabama, 20 Sept. 1976; interview with William Spencer III (RR 2-058 to 2-062); oral history with Rev. Walker, *supra* note 21, chapter 1 (RR 6-005).
24. Interview with Emil Hess (RR 090); unrecorded telephone interview with Local Merchant No. 1, Bessemer, Alabama to Birmingham, Alabama, 8 Sept. 1976; unrecorded interview with Local Merchant No. 2; interview with Thad Holt (RR 229-71); interview with Charles Zukoski (RR 284); interview with Duard LeGrande (RR 155-59). The Federal Reserve Bank in Atlanta released figures indicating that in the four-week period ending May 18, 1963—during the height of the demonstrations—department store sales in Birmingham were

15% below the total for the same period in 1962. *New York Times*, 28 May 1963, p. 24.

25. Interview with William Spencer III (RR 2-053); interview with Duard LeGrande (RR 181-86); Rev. Fred Taylor and Tyrone Brooks, *The Movement*, pamphlet (Atlanta: SCLC, 1975), p. 6.

26. Since many of the owners and managers of the local retail stores were Jews, it is appropriate at this point to note the actions taken by Birmingham's Jewish community. In 1963, there were about 4,000 Jews who lived in the Birmingham area. Unlike Northern Jews who were often in the forefront of the civil rights movement, most Birmingham Jews were hesitant to get involved with integration attempts. This hesitancy was the result in part of the virulent, and at times violent, anti-Semitic sentiments of some of the city's white supremacists. The National States Rights Party and the Ku Klux Klan often distributed anti-Semitic literature in Birmingham. In addition, there had been an attempted bombing of Temple Beth El in 1958. The fear of suffering physical reprisals stopped most of the city's Jews from taking the lead in urging racial moderation in the white community.

Birmingham Jews actually tried to remove themselves completely from the civil rights struggle. The local Jewish community leadership believed that "Jews, as such, ought to stay out of the desegregation fight on the ground that it is a 'Christian problem' between whites and Negroes and not simply a racial problem." When nineteen conservative Northern rabbis flew to Birmingham to express their support of the civil rights efforts in the city on May 8, 1963, members of the local Jewish community tried unsuccessfully to convince them to leave immediately; the local Jews were able to have the news of the visit withheld from publication in the local newspapers. Mark H. Elovitz, *A Century of Jewish Life in Dixie* (University, Alabama: The University of Alabama Press, 1974), pp. 167-76; Nichols, *supra* note 1, chapter 1, at pp. 208-10.

27. Lewis and *The New York Times, Portrait of a Decade*, p. 188. Between 1950 and 1963, Birmingham had both the smallest numerical gain in employment and the smallest percentage gain in employment among the 13 largest cities in the Southeast. During that period, Birmingham slipped from having the third largest employed labor force to sixth. Hammer, Greene, Siler Associates, *supra* note 5, preface, at p. 87.

28. *Birmingham News*, 14 April 1963; interview with William Spencer III (RR 599-603).

29. *Birmingham Post-Herald*, 5 March 1963, p. 9.

30. Interview with William Spencer III (RR 369); interview with Sidney W. Smyer, Sr. (RR 112-16); unrecorded interview with Local Merchant No. 2; Alabama Christian Movement for Human Rights, *supra* note 23, chapter 2, at p. 20.

31. Interview with Charles Zukoski (RR 429); interview with Sidney W. Smyer, Sr. (RR 121-29).

32. *Wall Street Journal*, 23 May 1963, p. 18, SRC; interview with Duard LeGrande (RR 208).

33. Interview with Sidney W. Smyer, Sr. (RR 100-10); interview with Charles Zukoski (RR 380-95); oral history with Dr. John E. Bryan, *supra* note 54, chapter 3.
34. Interview with Charles Zukoski (RR 528); interview with Thad Holt (RR 260); Bayard Rustin, "The Meaning of Birmingham," *Liberation*, June 1963, p. 9.
35. Interview with Charles Zukoski (RR 2-040); unrecorded interview with Local Merchant No. 2; *Nashville Tennessean*, 23 May 1963, p. 21, SRC.
36. *Birmingham Post-Herald*, 5 March 1963, p. 9; interview with Charles Zukoski (RR 528); George C. Lodge, *supra* note 3, chapter 5, at p. 1; Alabama Christian Movement for Human Rights, *supra* note 23, chapter 2, at p. 17.
37. Oral history with Burke Marshall, *supra* note 12, chapter 4, at pp. 99-100: interview with Thad Holt (RR 100); interview with Sidney W. Smyer, Sr. (RR 147-51). The white Birmingham business leaders remained unwilling to meet with the national civil rights leaders throughout the entire period of negotiations.
38. Interview with Emil Hess (RR 225); unrecorded interview with Local Merchant No. 2.
39. See chapter 5, p. 79.
40. Interview with Emil Hess (RR 225); oral history with Burke Marshall, note 12, chapter 4, at pp. 99-100; interview with David J. Vann (RR 186); Harding, *supra* note 25, chapter 2, at p. 15.
41. Interview with Emil Hess (RR 043); unrecorded telephone interview with Local Merchant No. 1; interview with David J. Vann (RR 405); Harding, *supra* note 25, chapter 2, at p. 16.
42. Interview with William Spencer III (RR 441); interview with David J. Vann (RR 195); interview with Thad Holt (RR 097). The Senior Citizens Committee was established in August, 1962, by the Birmingham Chamber of Commerce in order to consider various community problems—including race relations. A statement by members of the Senior Citizens Committee, which was released on May 15, 1963, indicated that there were about 77 businessmen on the committee. *Birmingham News*, 16 May 1963; *Birmingham Post-Herald*, 16 May 1963, p. 1; *The Examiner*, 16 May 1963, p. 1; *Ibid.*, 23 May 1963, p. 1; *Ibid.*, 30 May 1963, p. 1; interview with Emil Hess (RR 318).
43. Interview with William Spencer III (RR 499); *The Examiner*, 30 May 1963, p. 1; Harding, *supra* note 25, chapter 2, at p. 16.
44. Interview with Sidney W. Smyer, Sr. (RR 398); interview with Thad Holt (RR 495).
45. J.H. O'Dell, "How Powerful is the Southern Power Structure?" *Freedomways*, Winter 1964, p. 78; Morgan, *A Time to Speak*, p. 88; Paul Good, "Birmingham Two Years Later," *The Reporter*, 2 Dec. 1965, p. 26; interview with Charles Zukoski (RR 260-75); interview with Thad Holt (RR 470).
46. *New York Times*, 11 May 1963, p. 8.
47. See *supra* notes 5, 11, chapter 5.
48. Harding, *supra* note 25, chapter 2, at pp. 15-18.

49. Fred L. Shuttlesworth, Ralph D. Abernathy, Martin Luther King, Jr. to David Vann, Sydney [sic] Smyer, W. Chalmers Hamilton, Burke Marshall, 17 May 1963, Box 10-31-63, KCSC.
50. Harding, *supra* note 25, chapter 2, at p. 15.
51. *Ibid.*; interview with David J. Vann (RR 253).
52. *The Examiner*, 30 May 1963, p. 2; Interview with David J. Vann (RR 034, 094); oral history with Rev. Walker, *supra* note 21, chapter 1 (RR 9-383).
53. Interview with Emil Hess (RR 236); Nichols, *supra* note 1, chapter 1, at p. 320; interview with Arthur Shores (RR 582); *New York Post*, 10 May 1963, KCSC.
54. Harding, *supra* note 25, chapter 2, at p. 15; LaMonte, *supra* note 14, chapter 1, at p. 243.
55. Interview with David J. Vann (RR 080); *Washington Post*, 7 May 1963, SRC; *New York Post*, 12 May 1963, KCSC; Thad Holt, *supra* note 57, chapter 3, at p. 5; *The Examiner*, 9 May 1963, p. 1.
56. Interview with David J. Vann (RR 102-253); interview with John Drew (RR 122-52); *New York Times*, 11 May 1963, p. 9.
57. Interview with David J. Vann (RR 132); interview with Arthur Shores (RR 565); interview with Duard LeGrande (RR 082-088); *New York Post*, 12 May 1963, KCSC.
58. Interview with David J. Vann (RR 249); interview with Rev. Carter Gaston, Jr. (RR 122).
59. C. Erskine Smith and Charles Morgan were also helpful in opening communications between the white and black communities in 1963. Interview with David J. Vann (RR 102); *The Examiner*, 30 May 1963, p. 1; oral history with Rev. Walker, *supra* note 21, chapter 1 (RR 9-383).
60. *New York Times*, 11 May 1963, p. 8.
61. Interview with Edward Fields (RR 300).
62. Norman L. Kilpatrick, "The White Citizens' Councils Move North," pamphlet, Box "Organizations," SRC.
63. Interview with Robert M. Shelton (RR 2-063); interview with Edward Fields (RR 077); Kilpatrick, *supra* note 62, chapter 5.
64. Arnold Forster and Benjamin R. Epstein, *Report on the Ku Klux Klan*, pamphlet (New York: Anti-Defamation League of B'nai B'rith, 1965), p. 18; James W. Vander Zanden, "The Citizens' Councils," *Alpha Kappa Deltan*, Spring 1963, pp. 8-9.
65. James W. Vander Zanden, *supra* note 64, chapter 5, at p. 4; Foster and Epstein, *supra* note 64, chapter 5, at p. 18; Kilpatrick, *supra* note 62, chapter 5.
66. James W. Vander Zanden, *supra* note 13, chapter 5, at p. 457; *Idem*, *supra* note 64, chapter 5, at p. 5.
67. "A Survey of the Resistance Groups of Alabama," Box "Organizations," SRC, pp. 1-10, 25-28.
68. Interview with Albert Boutwell (RR 2-390); interview with Edward Fields (RR 088).

69. *South: The News Magazine of Dixie*, 27 May 1963, pp. 1, 8. "The periodical which most clearly reflected the [White Citizens'] Council's point of view was *South: The News Magazine of Dixie*." Neil R. McMillen, *The Citizens' Council* (Urbana, Illinois: University of Illinois Press, 1971), p. 375.
70. *Birmingham News*, 12 May 1963.
71. *The Thunderbolt*, publication of the National States Rights Party (N.S.R.P.), Issue No. 203, p. 9. The N.S.R.P. was formed in the mid-1950s by members of the United White Party and rank and file states righters. In 1962, the N.S.R.P. merged with the National White America Party. *Atlanta Journal*, 24 Sept. 1963, SRC.
72. The second largest Klan group was the national Knights of the Ku Klux Klan, Inc., with headquarters in Tucker, Georgia. The head of the National Knights was James Venable, an Atlanta lawyer who had a long history as an extreme segregationist. Three Ku Klux Klan organizations operated on a very limited basis in Alabama. The Improved Order of U.S. Klans, headed by Earl E. George, had two klaverns in Alabama. The Dixie Klans, Knights of the Ku Klux Klan, Inc., ruled over by Jack and Harry Leon Brown of Chattanooga, Tennessee, had a very strong klavern in Anniston, Alabama. The Knights of the Ku Klux Klan also existed on a rudimentary level in Alabama in 1963. Forster and Epstein, *supra* note 64, chapter 5, pp. 7-8; interview with Don Black, Hueytown, Alabama, 19 Sept. 1976 (RR 380-91, 630-42); *New York Times*, 13 April 1960, p. 33.
73. Interview with Edward Fields (RR 102); interview with Robert M. Shelton (RR 500).
74. Interview with Robert M. Shelton 9RR 004-030, 507); interview with Edward Fields (RR 091-093); interview with Don Black (RR 069, 511-33).
75. *The Crusader*, publication of the Knights of the Ku Klux Klan (K.K.K.K.), Special Edition, p. 9.
76. *The Crusader*, publication of the K.K.K.K., Issue No. 9, p. 4.
77. *The Thunderbolt,* publication of the N.S.R.P., Issue No. 209, p. 1.
78. Interview with Robert M. Shelton (RR 107); interview with Edward Fields (RR 045); interview with Don Black (RR 143); *The Crusader, supra* note 76, chapter 5, at p. 9: James W. Vander Zanden, "The Ideology of White Supremacy," *Journal of the History of Ideas* 20 (June-Sept. 1959): 397. In order to support their assertions of the inherent inferiority of blacks, the white extremist groups have recently begun to use psuedo-scientific arguments based on the writings of William Shockley, Arthur Jensen, and Richard Herrnstein. The arguments of these three men are often twisted in order to support the arguments of the white supremacists. For example, an article in a 1975 issue of *The Crusader*, which is the publication of the Knights of the Ku Klux Klan, contained the following paragraph:

> Herrenstein [sic] was frank to the point of curtness speaking of ghetto riots: 'They're not rebelling because they don't have jobs they could have and are being denied. They are craxy [sic] rebels who are too dumb for

these jobs, and that's why they don't have them. So they're rebelling against their genes.'

79. Edward R. Fields, *Jews Behind Race Mixing*, pamphlet (Marietta, Georgia: The Thunderbolt, Inc.), p. 1; interview with Robert M. Shelton (RR 137); interview with Edward Fields (RR 047-089); interview with Don Black (RR 118-25).
80. Interview with Robert M. Shelton (RR 141, 171-79); interview with Don Black (RR 133, 313); *The Crusader, supra* note 75, chapter 5, at pp. 3, 8.
81. Interview with Robert M. Shelton (RR 150); interview with Don Black (RR 294); *The Crusader*, publication of the K.K.K.K., Vol. II, No. 3, p. 4.
82. *The Crusader, supra* note 75, chapter 5, at p. 6; interview with Edward Fields (RR 038); interview with Don Black (RR 436); James W. Vander Zanden, *supra* note 78, chapter 5, at pp. 385-86.
83. Robert Shelton, recorded interview by Ben Hendrix, 21 January 1975, p. 4, Samford University Oral History Program; *National States Rights Party Official Platform*, pamphlet (Marietta, Georgia: The Thunderbolt, Inc.); *The Thunderbolt,* publication of the N.S.R.P. Issue No 201, p. 1.
84. *The Examiner*, 9 May 1963, p. 1; interview with Robert M. Shelton (RR 187, 604, 2-125); *Martin Luther King's Communist Record*, pamphlet (Marietta, Georgia: The Thunderbolt, Inc.); Billy James Hargis to Fellow Country-Saver, 1961, Box "Organizations," SRC; interview with Don Black (RR 459).
85. *Thunderbolt, supra* note 6, chapter 5, at pp. 6-7.
86. *The Birmingham Bulletin*, publication of the N.S.R.P., 9 Oct. 1963; *The Leeds News*, 17 May 1963, p. 1; *Thunderbolt, supra* note 6, chapter 5, at p. 7; interview with Edward Fields (RR 167); *The Crusader, supra* note 76, chapter 5, at p. 3; *The Examiner*, 9 May 1963, p. 1; *Ibid.*, 16 May 1963, p. 15.
87. Interview with Edward Fields (RR 263). Among the individuals who received this harassment were M. Edwin Wiggins, William Spencer III, James Armstrong, and Rev. Abraham Woods, Jr.
88. Rowe, *My Undercover Years with the Ku Klux Klan, supra* note 39, chapter 3, at p. 93.
89. Interview with Edward Fields (RR 302, 336-43); Paul Anthony, "An Analysis of the Hate Literature of Resistance Groups of the South," memorandum to Harold C. Fleming, 1955, Box "Organizations," SRC.
90. *Thunderbolt, supra* note 6, chapter 5, at p. 6; interview with Edward Fields (RR 252).
91. *Thunderbolt, supra* note 6, chapter 5, at p. 6; interview with Edward Fields (RR 217-46); *The Birmingham Bulletin*, publication of the N.S.R.P., 22 August 1963; *The Thunderbolt*, publication of the N.S.R.P., August 1963, p. 6.
92. Interview with Robert M. Shelton (RR 450); *The Crusader, supra* note 75, chapter 5, p. 7.
93. Forster and Epstein, *supra* note 64, chapter 5, at p. 6; King, *Why We Can't Wait*, p. 49.
94. James W. Vander Zanden, *supra* note 13, chapter 5, at p. 456.
95. David Cort, "The Voices of Birmingham," *Nation*, 27 July 1963, p. 46.

96. Interview with Edward Fields (RR 015); Forster and Epstein, *supra* note 64, chapter 5, at p. 8.
97. Interview with Edward Fields (RR 485-90); James W. Vander Zanden, *supra* note 64, chapter 5, at pp. 5-6; Forster and Epstein, *supra* note 64, chapter 5, at pp. 6-7; "Interview with a Former Grand Dragon," *New South*, Summer 1969, p. 66.

CHAPTER SIX

1. Oral history with Rev. Walker, *supra* note 21, chapter 1 (RR 8-284); Moore, *Behind The Ebony Mask*, pp. 12, 33, 206. Mr. Mike Nichols in a senior thesis written at Brown University argued that, "the [Birmingham] black community was not at all divided on class line." Nichols, *supra* note 1, chapter 1, at p. 259.
2. Mike Nichols further argued that, "The ACMHR was from the beginning a heterogeneous group of blacks. Many were from the wealthier middle class." Nichols, *supra* note 1, chapter 1, at p. 96.
3. Interview with Rev. Fred L. Shuttlesworth (RR 037-050); oral history with Rev. Shuttlesworth, *supra* note 24, chapter 1, at pp. 49-50; oral history with Rev. Walker (RR 9-415).
4. The black community in Birmingham did not have a well-developed upper-class. In the absence of a strong upper-class, the middle-class blacks constituted the city's black elite. The upper-layer of the middle-class was composed of professionals and the owners and managers of black business enterprises, including small retail stores and a small number of insurance companies. Blacks, who worked in the skilled occupations, constituted the lower stratum of the middle-class.

   Members of the black elite constituted about 12% of the city's black population in 1960. 12.8% of the black workers in the city were in high-skilled positions—professionals, technical workers, managers, proprietors, craftsmen and foremen. 12.4% of the city's black families had a median income of over $6000, which was roughly the median income of the city's white families. Thus, about one-eighth of the city's black population was able to maintain a middle-class standard of living. Hammer, Greene, Siler Associates, *supra* note 5, preface at p. 100; U.S. Bureau of the Census, *supra* note 2, preface, at p. 47; Grindstaff, *supra* note 3, chapter 1, at p. 348; see also E. Franklin Frazier, *The Negro Church in America* (New York: Schocken Books, 1974), p. 80.
5. Nichols, *supra* note 1, chapter 1, at p. 253; Harding, *supra* note 25, chapter 2, at p. 18.
6. Interview with Rev. John Thomas Porter, Jr. (RR 030-076); interview with Arthur Shores (RR 389-407); interview with Rev. Nelson Henry Smith, Jr. (RR 177); interview with Rev. Abraham Woods, Jr. (RR 2-362). By the spring of 1963, Rev. Shuttlesworth had moved to Cincinnati, Ohio. He flew to Birmingham regularly and retained the presidency of the ACMHR. This in absentia leadership was viewed by many blacks in Birmingham as a further

indication of Shuttlesworth's lack of consideration for the welfare of the city's black community.

7. Interview with John Drew (RR 065); discussion with Dr. Robert Coles, 14 February 1977, Cambridge, Massachusetts.
8. Interview with Rev. Fred L. Shuttlesworth (RR 065, 224); interview with Rev. Abraham Woods, Jr. (RR 080-093); discussion with Dr. Robert Coles, *supra* note 7, chapter 6.
9. Discussion with Dr. Robert Coles, 20 February 1977, Cambridge, Massachusetts.
10. King, *Why We Can't Wait*, pp. 44-45; King, "Letter from Birmingham Jail," p. 124; see also Moore, *Behind The Ebony Mask*, pp. 109-110.
11. E. Franklin Frazier, *Black Bourgeoisie* (London: Collier Books, 1962), p. 42; see also Moore, *Behind The Ebony Mask*, pp. 109-110.
12. Frazier, *Black Bourgeoisie*, p. 194; see also Dollard, *Caste and Class in a Southern Town*, p. 209.
13. Discussion with Dr. Robert Coles, *supra* note 9, chapter 6.
14. King, "Letter from Birmingham Jail," p. 124; interview with John Drew (RR 065).
15. Although most middle-class blacks in Birmingham did not actively support the efforts of the ACMHR, many prominent members of the black elite did get involved in the local civil rights struggle. Mr. and Mrs. John Drew, the president of a local insurance company and his wife, were prime examples of black middle-class activists. Although not in complete accord with Rev. Shuttlesworth's attitudes and tactics, Mr. and Mrs. Drew were in the forefront of local attempts to advance the cause of racial equality. Oral history with Rev. Walker, *supra* note 21, chapter 1 (RR 9-416); interview with John Drew (RR 320-520).
16. Oral history with Rev. Shuttlesworth, *supra* note 24, chapter 1, at p. 74.
17. Interview with Rev. Fred L. Shuttlesworth (RR 634); interview with Rev. Nelson Henry Smith, Jr. (RR 072); interview with Rev. John Thomas Porter, Jr. (RR 565-93); King, "Letter from Birmingham Jail," p. 127.
18. Moore, *Behind The Ebony Mask*, pp. 130-44.
19. *Ibid.*, p. 189.
20. *Ibid.*, pp. 15, 42, 203; Coles, *Children of Crisis: A Study of Courage and Fear*, p. 289. It is difficult to determine the attitudes of black domestics toward the civil rights struggle. These individuals worked in the homes and yards of the city's wealthy white families. As a result of being directly dependent on whites for their livelihood, these domestics would almost never indicate open support for the demonstrations to their white employers. Some of these domestics really did not support the civil rights protest. But, many of these blacks had a dual personality of sorts; their deference and subservience to their white employers was a social mask; with members of their own race, these domestics were willing both to admit their support of the civil rights movement and to participate in certain activities. Dollard, *Caste and Class in a Southern Town*, pp. 257-58, 440; James Weldon Johnson, *The Autobiography of an Ex-Coloured Man* (New York: Alfred A. Knopf, 1927), pp. 21-22, 78; Moore, *Behind The Ebony Mask*, pp. 188-89.

21. Clarke, *These Rights They Seek*, pp. 26-27. The black population in Birmingham in 1960 was 135,267. U.S. Bureau of the Census, *supra* note 2, preface, at p. 47.
22. Interview with Rev. Fred L. Shuttlesworth (RR 039-056); interview with Rev. Abraham Woods, Jr. (RR 2-028); Harding, *supra* note 25, chapter 2, at p. 18.
23. Clarke, *These Rights They Seek*, p. 37.
24. *Ibid.*; interview with John Drew (RR 321).
25. Alabama Christian Movement for Human Rights, "Seventh Annual Celebration," program for 5 June 1963, Shuttlesworth Papers, Box 1, KCSC.
26. See *supra* note 21, chapter 1.
27. Clarke, *These Rights They Seek*, p. 56.
28. King, *Why We Can't Wait*, p. 67; *Washington Post*, 12 May 1963, SRC.
29. King, *Why We Can't Wait*, p. 65.
30. Interview with Arthur Shores (RR 340); oral history with Rev. Walker, *supra* note 21, chapter 1 (RR 9-415).
31. King, *Why We Can't Wait*, p. 65; interview with Rev. Carter Gaston, Jr. (RR 225-34).
32. King, *My Life with Martin Luther King, Jr.*, p. 221; Pat Watters, *Down to Now* (New York: Pantheon Books, 1971), p. 266.
33. Southern Christian Leadership Conference, Minutes of Staff Conference held at Dorchester, 5-7 Sept. 1963, Box 10-32-64, KCSC; King, *Why We Can't Wait*, pp. 65-66.
34. Interview with Rev. Abraham Woods, Jr. (RR 637, 2-315); interview with John Drew (RR 059); interview with Rev. Fred L. Shuttlesworth (RR 587).
35. *Birmingham World*, 15 May 1963, p. 6.
36. Westin and Mahoney, *The Trial of Martin Luther King*, pp. 49-50.
37. *Birmingham World*, 18 May 1963, p. 8.
38. Interview with Rev. Nelson Henry Smith, Jr. (RR 182); interview with John Drew (RR 446); oral history with Rev. Shuttlesworth, *supra* note 24, chapter 1, at p. 47.
39. King, *My Life with Martin Luther King, Jr.*, p. 218; Nichols, *supra* note 1, chapter 1, at p. 252. In determining the general goals and strategies for Birmingham, Rev. Shuttlesworth conferred closely with Dr. King, Rev. Abernathy, Bayard Rustin, and Clarence Jones. Interview with Rev. Fred L. Shuttlesworth (RR 138).
40. Bishop, *The Days of Martin Luther King, Jr.*, p. 269; Nichols, *supra* note 1, chapter 1, at p. 245; King, *Why We Can't Wait*, p. 54; Holloway, *The Politics of the Southern Negro*, p. 162.
41. Interview with Rev. Nelson Henry Smith, Jr. (RR 025); interview with John Drew (RR 235-245); Bennett, *What Manner of Man—Martin Luther King, Jr.*, pp. 235-45.
42. Interview with Rev. Nelson Henry Smith, Jr. (RR 424); interview with John Drew (RR 248-50); interview with Rev. John Thomas Porter, Jr. (RR 168); interview with Rev. Fred L Shuttlesworth (RR 403-27); "Central Committee Members," (typewritten), Box 10-31-63, KCSC.

43. Rev. John Thomas Porter, Jr., a prominent black preacher in Birmingham, explained the process by which Dr. King convinced many of the local black elite to support the demonstrations:

> In the formation [and planning of the demonstrations], it was agreed upon that the leaders of the [local black] community would have the right to decide from day to day what the actions would be. This is how Dr. King got very conservative leaders, who would not ordinarily touch the demonstrations, to come in and be a part. They were called the Coordinating Committee; the Coordinating Committee had the right to approve or disapprove plans from day to day.

Interview with Rev. John Thomas Porter, Jr. (RR 120).

44. See *Ex Parte National Association for the Advancement of Colored People*, 91 So.2d 214 (Alabama Sup. Ct., 1956)
45. Barbara Deming, "Notes After Birmingham," *Liberation*, Summer 1963, p. 13; "Integration Leaders Examine Lessons of Birmingham," *Liberation*, June 1963, p. 4. James Foreman, the executive secretary of SNCC, met with only limited success when he tried to organize a chapter in Birmingham. Oral history with Rev. Walker, *supra* note 21, chapter 1 (RR 5-420); interview with Rev. Abraham Woods, Jr. (RR 2-462 to 2-472).
46. CORE and SNCC also exerted pressure on national corporations, which had factories in Birmingham, to intervene in the crisis. SNCC, "Big Business Supports Segregation in Birmingham," (mimeographed), Box 10-34-64, KCSC; *West Side News*, 2 May 1963, KCSC.
47. Holloway, *The Politics of the Southern Negro*, p. 167; King, *My Life with Martin Luther King, Jr.*, pp. 232-33.
48. Southern Christian Leadership Conference, *The SCLC Story* (Atlanta: SCLC, 1964), p. 14.
49. Oral history with Rev. Woods, *supra* note 1, chapter 1, at p. 11; interview with Rev. Fred L. Shuttlesworth (RR 133); "A Faith for Difficult and Critical Times," Sermon delivered by Rev. Fred L. Shuttlesworth, Shuttlesworth Papers, Box No. 4, KCSC; interview with James Armstrong, Birmingham, Alabama, 23 August 1976 (RR 520).
50. King, *My LIfe with Martin Luther King, Jr.*, pp. 217-33; White, *the Making of the President—1964*, pp. 167-68; interview with Rev. Nelson Henry Smith, Jr. (RR 246); interview with Rev. Carter Gaston, Jr. (RR 115).
51. King, *Why We Can't Wait*, p. 115; Holloway, *The Politics of the Southern Negro*, p. 163; Southern Christian Leadership Conference, *supra* note 33, chapter 6.
52. King, *Why We Can't Wait*, p. 115; Holloway, *The Politics of the Southern Negro*, p. 163.
53. Holloway, *The Politics of the Southern Negro*, pp. 162-63; oral history with Rev. Shuttlesworth, *supra* note 24, chapter 1, at p. 51; interview with Arthur Hanes (RR 030-035).
54. King, "Letter from Birmingham Jail," p. 119; King, *Why We Can't Wait*, p. 80.

55. Interview with Rev. Fred L. Shuttlesworth (RR 171); interview with Rev. Nelson Henry Smith, Jr. (RR 157); interview with James Armstrong (RR 570); interview with Rev. Carter Gaston, Jr. (RR 523); oral history with Rev. Walker, *supra* note 21, chapter 1 (RR 8-280); Martin Luther King, Jr., "Love and Nonviolence and the Shame of Segregation," *Jubilee*, July 1963, p. 22.

56. King, *Why We Can't Wait*, p. 35; interview with Rev. Fred L. Shuttlesworth (RR 177). In an one analysis, an observer of the 1963 direct action program commented that, "King's movement actually thrived on violence." [Harrison, *supra* note 32, chapter 1, at p. 59.] This analysis misinterprets the civil rights movement, because violence had a counter-productive effect on desegregation efforts.

57. Southern Christian Leadership Conference and Alabama Christian Movement for Human Rights, *supra* note 21, chapter 1, at p. 3; interview with James Armstrong (RR 541-46); interview with Rev. Fred L. Shuttlesworth (RR 106).

58. *SCLC Handbook for Freedom Army Recruits*, Box "Organizations," SRC.

59. Meet The Press, rush transcript, comment by Dr. King. 25 August 1963, p. 12.

60. "An Interview with Congressman Andrew J. Young," in *Martin Luther King, Jr.* ed. Flip Schulke (New York: Norton, 1976), p. 66.

61. *Ibid*.

62. Southern Christian Leadership Conference, *supra* note 48, chapter 6.

63. Andrew Young, "The Day We Went to Jail in Birmingham," *Friends*, 9 February 1964, p. 8; King, *Why We Can't Wait*, pp. 62-63.

64. King, *Why We Can't Wait*, pp. 62-63; interview with Arthur Shores (RR 365); interview with Rev. Abraham Woods, Jr. (RR 510-22); interview with James Armstrong (RR 484). The SCLC staff members who conducted the training sessions in nonviolence included Rev. James Lawson, Rev. James Bevel, Diane Nash Bevel, Rev. Bernard Lee, Rev. Andrew Young and Dorothy Cotton.

65. King, *Why We Can't Wait*, pp. 62-63.

66. Interview with Rev. Abraham Woods, Jr. (RR 545); King, *Why We Can't Wait*, pp. 62-63.

67. Interview with Rev. Abraham Woods, Jr. (RR 2-286); interview with Rev. Carter Gaston, Jr. (RR 512-16); Young, *supra* note 63, Chapter 6, at p. 6.

68. King, *Why We Can't Wait*, p. 35.

69. Southern Christian Leadership Conference, *supra* note 33, chapter 6; oral history with Rev. Walker, *supra* note 21, chapter 1 (RR 13-139); "The Men Behind Martin Luther King," *Ebony*, June 1965, p. 166.

70. Lewis, *King: A Critical Biography*, p. 180.

71. King, *Why We Can't Wait*, pp. 62-63; King, *My Life with Martin Luther King, Jr.*, pp. 218-19.

72. King, *Why We Can't Wait*, p. 71; Westin and Mahoney, *The Trial of Martin Luther King*, p. 49.

73. Oral history with Rev. Walker, *supra* note 21, chapter 1 (RR 13-136).

74. *Ibid*., (RR 1-37 to 1-39); interview with John Drew (RR 055); interview with Rev. Fred L. Shuttlesworth (RR 583).

75. For a discussion of the difference in civil rights militancy between church denominations, see Marx, *Protest and Prejudice*, pp. 98-99.
76. Oral history with Rev. Walker, *supra* note 21, chapter 1 (RR 13-086, 14-293); Sterne, *I Have a Dream*, p. 168.
77. Interview with Rev. John Thomas Porter, Jr. (Rr 541); oral history with Rev. Walker, *supra* note 21, chapter 1 (RR 13-096).
78. King, *Why We Can't Wait*, p. 35.
79. Alabama Christian Movement for Human Rights, *They Challenge Segregation at its Core!*, pamphlet (Birmingham, Alabama: ACMHR), p. 3; Lewis, *King: A Critical Biography*, p. 201.
80. King, *Why We Can't Wait*, p. 29; oral history with Rev. Walker, *supra* note 21, chapter 1 (RR 12-037 to 12-052); interview with Rev. Fred L. Shuttlesworth (RR 312).
81. Oral history with Rev. Walker, *supra* note 21, chapter 1 (RR 12-037 to 12-052); interview with John Drew (RR 293); interview with Rev. John Thomas Porter, Jr. (RR 465); interview with Rev. Nelson Henry Smith, Jr. (RR 226); interview with Rev. Abraham Woods, Jr. (RR 3-286).
82. Nichols, *supra* note 1, chapter 1, at p. 290.
83. Interview with Rev. Abraham Woods, Jr. (RR 3-340).
84. Interview with Rev. Nelson Henry Smith, Jr. (RR 230).
85. Interview with Rev. Fred L. Shuttlesworth (RR 149-54); interview with John Drew (RR 030); interview with Rev. John Thomas Porter, Jr. (RR 385); oral history with Rev. Shuttlesworth, *supra* note 24, chapter 1, at p. 51.
86. White, *The Making of the President—1964*, p. 170; Watters, *Down to Now,* p. 265. In a very frank interview, Rev. Wyatt Tee Walker provided a strikingly different perspective on the confrontation. Rev. Walker commented that:

> The so-called Battle of Ingram Park wasn't any battle. It was a Roman holiday . . . The tempers of the firemen got short . . . the blacks were waiting for something to happen; they started teasing the firemen; they [the firemen] started putting water on them. It was a game . . . They [the blacks] were trying to see who could stand up against the fire hoses . . . It wasn't any damn battle, it was a Roman holiday.

Oral history with Rev. Walker, *supra* note 21, chapter 1 (RR 6-050 to 7-071).

87. Theodore C. Sorenson, *Kennedy* (New York: Harper and Row, 1965), p. 489; Schlesinger, *A Thousand Days,* p. 960; Southern Christian Leadership Conference, *supra* note 48, chapter 6, at p. 31.
88. See chapter 4, pp. 59-60.
89. Dr. Martin Luther King, Jr., quoted in King, *My Life with Martin Luther King, Jr.*, p. 231.
90. Interview with Arthur Shores (RR 407); interview with Rev. John Thomas Porter, Jr. (RR 042-055).
91. Oral history with Rev. Walker, *supra* note 21, chapter 1 (RR 2-292); King, *Why We Can't Wait*, p. 67.

92. Interview with Rev. Fred L. Shuttlesworth (RR 261); interview with John Drew (RR 218-25); "An Interview with Congressman Andrew J. Young," *supra* note 60, chapter 6.

93. Interview with Rev. Abraham Woods, Jr. (RR2-030); interview with Rev. Fred L. Shuttlesworth (RR 625); Bishop, *The Days of Martin Luther King, Jr.*, p. 288; Lewis, *King: A Critical Biography*, p. 179; Miller, *Martin Luther King, Jr.*, p. 135.

94. King, *Why We Can't Wait*, p. 67.

95. *Ibid.*

96. See *supra* notes 42, 43, chapter 6.

97. Interview with Rev. John Thomas Porter, Jr. (RR 115); interview with Rev. Carter Gaston, Jr. (Rr 272); interview with Rev. Abraham Woods, Jr. (RR 2-348 to 2-357); interview with Orzell Billingsley, Jr. (RR 2-141); interview with Arthur Shores (RR 398); oral history with Rev. Abraham Woods, Jr., *supra* note 1, chapter 1, at p. 20. In a survey conducted in Birmingham in 1964, 95% of the blacks questioned felt that Martin Luther King, Jr. had done more than any other civil rights leader to help the black community. Marx, *Protest and Prejudice*, p. 26.

98. Interview with Rev. Fred L. Shuttlesworth (RR 250); interview with Rev. John Thomas Porter, Jr. (RR 058, 231-54); interview with Rev. Nelson Henry Smith, Jr. (RR 510); interview with Rev. Abraham Woods, Jr. (RR 2-052).

99. August Meier, "On the Role of Martin Luther King," *New Politics*, Winter 1965, pp. 52-59.

100. Oral history with Rev. Walker, *supra* note 21, chapter 1 (RR 7-095); Southern Christian Leadership Conference, *supra* note 33, chapter 6.

101. The SCLC staff members involved in the recruitment of school children were Rev. Andy Young, Dorothy Cotton, Rev. James Bevel, and Rev. Bernard Lee. Southern Christian Leadership Conference, *supra* note 33, chapter 6; King, *Why We Can't Wait*, p. 97.

102. Deming, *supra* note 45, chapter 6, at p. 15.

103. Coles, *Children of Crisis: A Study of Courage and Fear*, p. 332; Young, *supra* note 63, chapter 6, at p. 5; interview with Rev. Carter Gaston, Jr. (RR 160).

104. Rev. Don E. Bush, recorded interview by Richard J. Waters, 16 April 1976, Daniel Payne College Oral History Project; oral history with Rev. Shuttlesworth, *supra* note 24, chapter 1, at p. 60; Lewis and *The New York Times*, *Portrait of a Decade*, p. 182. Another factor that contributed to the massive turnout of school children was the normal strong cohesion of peer groups in school. Once some school children participated in the demonstrations, their friends also wanted to demonstrate. K. Lenihan, "Birmingham: A Sociological Perspective," June 1963, Box 10-30-63, KCSC.

105. Interview with Rev. Abraham Woods, Jr. (RR 2-621); interview with J. Mason Davis (RR 164); *The Militant*, 20 May 1963, p. 1, KCSC.

106. Oral history with Rev. Walker, *supra* note 21, chapter 1 (RR 7-120); Nichols, *supra* note 1, chapter 1, at p. 276.

107. Interview with Rev. Nelson Henry Smith, Jr. (RR 277); oral history with Rev. Shuttlesworth, *supra* note 24, chapter 1, at pp. 64-65. Rev. Shuttlesworth

would often say that before the civil rights struggle was over, they were going to make a "steer out of the bull." Oral history with Rev. Woods, *supra* note 1, chapter 1, at p. 13.

108.Oral history with Rev. Walker, *supra* note 21, chapter 1 (RR 7-071); interview with Rev. Nelson Henry Smith, Jr. (RR 281-82).

109.Oral history with Rev. Shuttlesworth, *supra* note 24, chapter 1, at p. 64.

110."Points for Progress, Birmingham, Alabama," Box 10-31-63, KCSC; King, *Why We Can't Wait*, pp. 102-3;interview with Rev. Abraham Woods, Jr. (RR 2-143).

111.O'Dell, *supra* note 45, chapter 5, at p. 79; unrecorded interview with Local Merchant No. 2.

112.Oral history with Rev. Woods, *supra* note 1, chapter 1, at p. 18; interview with Rev. Fred L. Shuttlesworth (RR 086, 194-95); in oral history with Rev. Shuttlesworth, *supra* note 24, chapter 1, at p. 55; Rustin, *supra* note 34, chapter 5, at p. 7.

113.Interview with Rev. Nelson Henry Smith, Jr. (RR 450); Reese Cleghorn, "Martin Luther King, Jr.: Apostle of Crisis," *Saturday Evening Post*, 15 June 1963, p. 17; Southern Christian Leadership conference, *supra* note 33, chapter 6.

114."Don't Buy Segregation," (mimeographed sheet), Box 10-31-63, KCSC.

115.*Wyatt Tee Walker v. City of Birmingham*, petition for writ of certiorari to the circuit court of the tenth judicial circuit of Alabama, attorneys for petitioners-respondents, p. 10, ADS/Crd. 4/2, Talladega College Historical Collections; oral history with Rev. Walker, *supra* note 21, chapter 1 (RR 9-387); Martin Luther King, Jr., *Where Do We Go From Here; Chaos or Community?* (New York: Harper and Row, 1967), p. 143; interview with Rev. Nelson Henry Smith, Jr. (RR 205); King, *Why We Can't Wait*, p. 69.

116.Oral history with Rev. Walker, *supra* note 21, chapter 1 (RR 9-397): see *supra* note 23, chapter 5.

117.See *supra* note 24, chapter 5.

118.King, *Why We Can't Wait*, p. 69. The march by local blacks on the Jefferson County Courthouse to register to vote on April 17, 1963 was attempted in hopes of making the Birmingham dispute a federal matter. Rev. Andy Young, in commenting on the purpose of the march said, "This is the only way we can get the Justice Department in on this. If we get tangled up in this, they can step in." *New York Times*, 18 April 1963, p. 21; see also *supra* note 11, chapter 2.

120.Interview with John Drew (RR 186).

121.See chapter 2, pp. 31-32.

122.Interview with Rev. John Thomas Porter, Jr. (RR 395); interview with John Drew (RR 285).

123.Interview with John Drew (RR 285); interview with Rev. John Thomas Porter, Jr. (RR 395).

124.*Birmingham World*, 18 May 1963, p. 8.

125.Interview with J. Mason Davis (RR 038); oral history with Rev. Walker, *supra* note 21, chapter 1 (RR 5-357).

126. Alabama Christian Movement for Human Rights, "Project 'C' General Format—Mass Meeting," Box 10-31-63, KCSC; interview with Rev. Nelson Henry Smith, Jr. (RR 094); Clarke, *These Rights They Seek*, p. 27.
127. Alabama, Christian Movement for Human Rights, *supra* note 126, chapter 6.
128. King, *Why We Can't Wait*, pp. 61-62; oral history with Rev. Woods, *supra* note 1, chapter 1, at p. 20.
129. King, *Why We Can't Wait*, p. 60.
130. Interview with Rev. Fred L. Shuttlesworth (Rr 335); interview with Dr. Arthur George Gaston, Sr. (RR 135); oral history with Rev. Shuttlesworth, *supra* note 24, chapter 1, at p. 50.
131. Interview with Rev. John Thomas Porter, Jr. (RR 226); Southern Christian Leadership Conference, *supra* note 33, chapter 6; Lenihan, *supra* note 104, chapter 6, at p. 3; B. Richardson, "That's All Right—Birmingham, Alabama," *Freedomways*, Winter 1964, p. 69.
132. Interview with Arthur Shores (RR 371); interview with Rev. John Thomas Porter, Jr. (RR 083); interview with Rev. Abraham Woods, Jr. (RR 2-407); Southern Christian Leadership Conference, *supra* note 33, chapter 6; Lenihan, *supra* note 104, chapter 6, at pp. 2-3.
133. Interview with Rev. Nelson Henry Smith, Jr. (RR 123); interview with Rev. Carter Gaston, Jr. (RR 339); Lenihan, *supra* note 104, chapter 6, at pp. 3-4.
134. Interview with Rev. John Thomas Porter, Jr. (RR 330-65). It can be argued that some of the civil rights demonstrators did not hold deep religious beliefs; instead, they were willing to accept religion as a strategy to achieve the goal of desegregation. Rev. Shuttlesworth supported this argument by stating that some participants in the civil rights movement "were willing to conform to religion as a tactic." Interview with Rev. Fred L. Shuttlesworth (RR 016).
135. See chapter 6, p. 107.
136. Interview with Rev. Fred L. Shuttlesworth (RR 041-060, 235-39); interview with Orzell Billingsley, Jr. (RR 2-135).
137. Rustin, *supra* note 34, chapter 5, at p. 8; interview with Rev. Shuttlesworth (RR 061).
138. Within ten days of the start of Project C, some members of the black elite began to express publicly their support for the direct action program. Twenty-six black doctors and dentists, who were members of the Mineral District Medical Society and the Jefferson County Dental Study Club, published a statement in a local newspaper expressing their support of the demonstrations. Another thirty black leaders published a similar statement on April 12, 1963.
139. Interview with Rev. Fred L. Shuttlesworth (RR 341); interview with John Drew (RR 305). The demonstrations were usually structured so that a few of the city's prominent black leaders, especially clergymen, would participate in each march. Interview with Rev. John Thomas Porter, Jr. (RR 283).
140. Interview with John Drew (RR 082); oral history with Rev. Shuttlesworth, *supra* note 24, chapter 1, at p. 61.
141. It is informative to note the roles played by individuals from various social classes in the direct action program. Dr. King was overstating the case when he wrote that, "doctors marched with window cleaners. Lawyers demonstrated

with laundresses. Ph.D.'s and no-D's were treated with perfect equality by the registrars of the nonviolence movement." [King, *Why We Can't Wait*, p. 39.] Instead, the social structure of the local black community was partially reflected in the direct action program. The local black elite determined strategies and provided funds. Although there were always a few prominent local blacks leading the daily marches, lower-class blacks constituted the vast majority of the demonstrators.

142. Moore, *Behind The Ebony Mask*, p. 115.

143. The business interests of which Dr. Gaston was president included Booker T. Washington Business College, New Grace Hill Cemetery, Finley Park Garden Apartments, A.G. Gaston Motel, Citizen's Federal Savings and Loan Association, Booker T. Washington Insurance Company, Citizen's Drug Store, and Smith and Gaston Funeral Directors, a chain of eight funeral homes throughout Alabama. Moore, *Behind The Ebony Mask*, p. 116.

144. "A.G. Gaston, Sr.," *New York Times*, 8 July 1963, p. 16.

145. Dr. A.G. Gaston, Sr. quoted in Nichols, *supra* note 1, chapter 1, at p. 262.

146. A.G. Gaston, *Green Power* (Birmingham, Alabama: Birmingham Publishing Co., 1968), pp. 125-28; interview with Dr. Arthur George Gaston, Sr. (RR 047).

147. Interview with Dr. Arthur George Gaston, Sr. (RR 144); oral history with Rev. Walker, *supra* note 21, chapter 1 (RR 11-029).

148. Interview with Rev. Abraham Woods, Jr. (RR 2-128).

149. Alabama Christian Movement for Human Rights, "King Aide Terms Gaston Blast Unfair," press release, Box 10-31-63, KCSC.

150. *Ibid.*; oral history with Rev. Walker, *supra* note 21, chapter 1 (RR 2-289, 11-026); interview with Dr. Arthur George Gaston, Sr. (RR 062).

151. Interview with Arthur Shores (RR 620); interview with Dr. Arthur George Gaston, Sr. (RR 054); *Pittsburgh Courier*, 18 May 1963, p. 2 SRC.

152. Oral history with Rev. Walker, *supra* note 21, chapter 1 (RR 11-026.)

153. Interview with Dr. Arthur George Gaston, Sr. (RR 068-073); Alabama Christian Movement for Human Rights, *supra* note 149, chapter 6; "Central Committee Members," *supra* note 42, chapter 6.

154. Rustin, *supra* note 34, chapter 5, at p. 8; interview with Rev. Fred L. Shuttlesworth (RR 061).

155. Interview with Rev. Fred L. Shuttlesworth (RR 500); interview with John Drew (RR 374); interview with Rev. John Thomas Porter, Jr. (RR 375); King, *Why We Can't Wait*, pp. 100-104.

156. Lenihan, *supra* note 104, chapter 6, at pp. 2-8; Lewis, *King: A Critical Biography*, p. 202.

157. Interview with Rev. Abraham Woods, Jr. (RR 2-254); oral history with Rev. Walker, *supra* note 21, chapter 1 (RR 8-285); interview with Rev. Nelson Henry Smith, Jr. (RR 132); interview with John Drew (RR 430)

158. James Weldon Johnson, the noted black author and diplomat, provided a vivid description of this desperate class that was as accurate in 1963 as it was when it was written in the early twentieth century:

> The ex-convicts, the bar-room loafers are in this class. These men conform to the requirements of civilization much as a trained lion with muttered growls goes through his stunts under the crack of the trainer's whip. They cherish a sullen hatred for all white men, and they value life as cheap. I have heard more than one of them say: 'I'll go to hell for the first white man that bothers me.'

Johnson, *supra* note 20, chapter 56, at pp. 76-77.

159. L.D. Reddick, "The Negro as Southerner and American," in *The Southerner as American*, ed. Charles Grier Sellers, Jr. (Chapel Hill, North Carolina: The University of North Carolina Press, 1960), p. 133.
160. Lenihan, *supra* note 104, chapter 6, at pp. 2-3; See also Dollard, *Caste and Class in a Southern Town*, p. 291.
161. Nichols, *supra* note 1, chapter 1, at pp. 259-64.
162. David Danzig, "The Meaning of Negro Strategy," *Commentary*, February 1964, p. 41; *Washington Post*, 12 May 1963, SRC; Dave Dellinger, "The Negroes of Birmingham," *Liberation*, Summer 1963, p. 21; Rustin, *supra* note 34, chapter 5, at p. 8.
163. Bayard Rustin, "From Protest to Politics: The Future of the Civil Rights Movement," *Commentary*, February 1965, p. 25.
164. Interview with Rev. Fred L. Shuttlesworth (RR 206); interview with Rev. John Thomas Porter, Jr. (RR 259); interview with Rev. Carter Gaston, Jr. (RR 170).
165. Interview with Rev. Fred L. Shuttlesworth (RR 2-003); interview with Rev. Carter Gaston, Jr. (RR 170).
166. *Birmingham World*, 10 April 1963, p. 6; *Ibid.*, 8 May 1963, p. 6.
167. Moore, *Behind The Ebony Mask*, pp. 188-90; see also Dollard, *Caste and Class in a Southern Town*, pp. 291-92; see also interview with Charles Zukoski (RR 2-029).
168. See *supra* note 57, chapter 2.
169. Oral history with Rev. Shuttlesworth, *supra* note 24, chapter 1, at p. 61; Alabama Christian Movement for Human Rights, *supra* note 23, chapter 2, at p. 18.
170. Holloway, *The Politics of the Southern Negro*, pp. 175-76.
171. The black population in Birmingham in 1960 was 135,267. U.S. Bureau of the Census, *supra* note 2, preface, at p. 47.
172. Interview with James Armstrong; interview with Rev. Abraham Woods, Jr. (RR 2-069); interview with Rev. John Thomas Porter, Jr. (RR 276); Lenihan, *supra* note 104, chapter 6, at p. 13. Although the participation level within the Birmingham black community was relatively low, the national civil rights leaders felt that it was sufficient. Dr. King felt that, "If a people can produce from its ranks 5% who will go voluntarily to jail for a just cause, surely nothing can thwart its ultimate triumph." [King, *Why We Can't Wait*, p. 44.] Rev. Wyatt Tee Walker basically agreed with Dr. King's assessment by stating

that 2 percent of the population was sufficient to create a revolution. *Wyatt Tee Walker v. City of Birmingham, supra* note 115, chapter 6, at p. 11.

CHAPTER SEVEN

1. A non-violent police strategy had been successfully employed by Police Chief Laurie Pritchett in Albany, Georgia, when civil rights demonstrations had occurred there in 1962.
2. Southern Christian Leadership Conference, "Martin Luther King, Jr. Reports Birmingham 'Living Up to Agreement'," press release, 17 July 1963, Box 10-27-63, KCSC.
3. Holloway, *The Politics of the Southern Negro*, p. 177.
4. Marx, *Protest and Prejudice*, p. 44.
5. *Ibid.*, p. 18.
6. Holloway, *The Politics of the Southern Negro*, p. 177; Danzig, *supra* note 162, chapter 6, at p. 41.
7. LaMonte, *supra* note 14, chapter 1, at pp. 263-64; Nichols, *supra* note 1, chapter 1, at p. 353.
8. LaMonte, *supra* note 14, chapter 1, at pp. 263-64; Nichols, *supra* note 1, chapter 1, at p. 353.
9. *New York Times*, 16 Sept. 1963, p. 1.
10. George C. Wallace to Lawton Ford, 6 January 1964, Official Governor's Papers—George C. Wallace, Drawer 399, ADAH.
11. Holloway, *The Politics of the Southern Negro*, p. 183.
12. *Ibid.*, p. 179.
13. Navasky, *Kennedy Justice*, p. 97.
14. *Ibid.*; Henry Fairlie, *The Kennedy Promise* (Garden City, New York: Doubleday and Company, 1973), p. 231.
15. Navasky, *Kennedy Justice*, p. 243.
16. President Kennedy had 20 federal judgeships to fill in the Fifth Circuit, which encompassed Florida, Texas, Georgia, Alabama, Louisiana, and Mississippi. Five of these 20 appointees have been singled out by students of judicial decision-making in the South as anti-civil rights, racist, segregationist, and/or obstructionist. Navasky, *Kennedy Justice*, p. 244.
17. Among other actions, Judge Cox issued an injunction against CORE, restraining it from encouraging Negroes to use the McComb, Mississippi interstate bus terminals after the Interstate Commerce Commission had declared it desegregated. Navasky, *Kennedy Justice*, p. 245.
18. Oral history with Burke Marshall, *supra* note 12, chapter 4, at p. 102.
19. *New York Times*, 12 June 1963, p. 20.
20. Schlesinger, *A Thousand Days*, p. 968; Theodore C. Sorensen, recorded interview by Carl Kaysen, May 3, 1964, p. 131, John F. Kennedy Library Oral History Program, JFKL.
21. Holloway, *The Politics of the Southern Negro*, p. 181.

22. Sorensen, *Kennedy*, p. 489; Schlesinger, *A Thousand Days*,; p. 971.
23. Oral history with Burke Marshall, *supra* note 12, chapter 4, at p. 102; oral history with Theodore C. Sorensen, *supra* note 20, chapter 4, at pp. 124, 125, 130.
24. *New York Times*, 12 June 1963, p. 20.
25. Lewis and *The New York Times*, *Portrait of a Decade*, p. 124.
26. *Ibid.*, p. 125.
27. Holloway, *The Politics of the Southern Negro*, p. 179.
28. Wyatt Tee Walker, "The Meaning of Birmingham," in *The S.C.L.C. Story*, *supra* note 48, chapter 6, at p. 31.
29. See also Good, *supra* note 45, chapter 5.

Bibliography

This bibliography consists exclusively of material cited in the notes, and does not include a considerable body of additional related material on the civil rights movement examined during the course of research. A number of items cited in the notes are not cited here. These consist of individual items located in the manuscript collections that were used.

A short description of what each individual interviewed was doing in 1963 is included here; the set of actors to which each person belongs is also included in parentheses preceding the description. Similar information is provided for individuals interviewed in the oral history projects that were used.

MANUSCRIPT COLLECTIONS

Atlanta, Georgia. Martin Luther King, Jr. Center for Social Change (abbreviated "KCSC" in the notes). Fred L. Shuttlesworth Papers.

Atlanta, Georgia. KCSC. Southern Christian Leadership Conference Papers.

Atlanta, Georgia. Southern Regional Council (abbreviated "SRC" in the notes). Newspaper and Organization Files.

Montgomery, Alabama. Alabama Department of Archives and History (abbreviated "ADAH" in the notes). Official Governor's Papers—Chauncey Sparks.

Montgomery, Alabama. ADAH. Official Governor's Papers—George C. Wallace

Talladega, Alabama. Talladega College Historical Collections. Arthur Shores Papers.

Waltham, Massachusetts. John F. Kennedy Library (abbreviated "JFKL" in the notes). John F. Kennedy Library Oral History Program.

Waltham, Massachusetts. JFKL. Robert F. Kennedy Papers.

Waltham, Massachusetts. JFKL. Burke Marshall Papers.

INTERVIEWS

Armstrong, James. Birmingham, Alabama. 23 August 1976. (Local black). Armstrong, a barber, was a member of the Alabama Christian Movement for Human Rights (ACMHR) in 1963.

Billingsley, Orzell, Jr. Masonic Temple Building, Birmingham, Alabama. 3 Sept. 1976. (Local black). Billingsley provided legal representation to officials from the ACMHR and the Southern Christian Leadership Conference (SCLC) during the demonstrations.

Black, Don. Hueytown, Alabama. 19 Sept. 1976. (White extremist). Although a child in 1963, Black as Titan of the Knights of the Ku Klux Klan in Alabama still provided background information.

Boutwell, Albert. John A. Hand Building, Birmingham, Alabama. 21 Sept. 1976. (City Council). A former Lt. Governor of Alabama, Boutwell was elected Mayor of Birmingham in 1963.

Davis, J. Mason. Bessemer, Alabama. 16 August 1976. (Local black). A Birmingham attorney, Davis had taken part in civil rights legal action during the late 1950's and early 1960's.

Drennen, Alan T., Jr. Protective Life Insurance Building, Birmingham, Alabama. 20 Sept. 1976. (City Council). Drennen was a general insurance agent when he was elected as a Councilman in 1963.

Drew, John. Alexander and Co., Inc., Birmingham, Alabama. 2 Sept. 1976. (Local black). An insurance broker, Drew was a close friend of Dr. King.

Fields, Edward. National Headquarters—National States Rights Party, Marietta, Georgia. 15 Sept. 1976. (White extremist). Fields was Information Director of the National States Rights Party.

Gaston, Dr. Arthur George, Sr. Citizen's Federal Bank, Birmingham, Alabama. 20 Sept. 1976. (Local black). Gaston was a wealthy businessman.

Hanes, Arthur. Frank Nelson Building, Birmingham, Alabama. 26 August 1976. (City Commission). Hanes was Mayor of Birmingham, under the City Commission form of government, from 1961 to 1963.

Hawkins, Don A. Central Bank Building, Birmingham, Alabama. 10 Sept. 1976. (City Council). Hawkins was an industrial salesman when he was elected as a Councilman in 1963.

Hess, Emil. Parisian, Inc., Birmingham, Alabama. 1 Sept. 1976. (White business leader.) Hess was president of a downtown retail store, Parisian, which was being boycotted.

Holt, Thad. Southern Natural Gas Building, Birmingham, Alabama. 25 August 1976. (White business leader). Holt was a management consultant.

LeGrande, Duard. *Birmingham Post-Herald*, Birmingham, Alabama. 25 August 1976. (White liberal activist). LeGrande was city editor of the *Birmingham Post-Herald.*

Local Merchant No. 1. Bessemer, Alabama to Birmingham, Alabama. Unrecorded telephone interview, 8 Sept. 1976. (White business leader).

Local Merchant No. 2. Birmingham, Alabama. Unrecorded interview, 20 Sept. 1976. (White business leader).

Moore, Jamie. City Federal Building, Birmingham, Alabama. Unrecorded interview, 27 August 1976. (City Commission). Moore was chief of police in Birmingham.

Overton, Dr. E.C. 5 Points West, Birmingham, Alabama. 1 Sept. 1976. (City Council). An optometrist, Overton was elected as a councilman in 1963.

Parsons, James. City Hall, Birmingham, Alabama. 26 August 1976. (City Commission). Currently chief of police in Birmingham, Parsons was a detective on the city's force in 1963.

Porter, Rev. John Thomas, Jr. 6th Avenue Baptist Church, Birmingham, Alabama. 31 August 1976. (Local black). Porter was the pastor of the large 6th Avenue Church.

Shelton, Robert M. Ramada Inn-Downtown, Tuscaloosa, Alabama. 2 Sept. 1976. (White extremist). Shelton was Imperial Wizard of the United Klans of America.

Shores, Arthur. Citizen's Federal Bank, Birmingham, Alabama. 20 Sept. 1976. (Local black). Shores provided legal representation to officials of the ACMHR and the SCLC during the demonstrations.

Shuttlesworth, Rev. Fred L. Cambridge, Massachusetts to Cincinnati, Ohio. Telephone interview, 19 Oct. 1976. (Local black). Although he had become pastor of a church in Cincinnati by 1963, Shuttlesworth retained the presidency of the ACMHR; he was also secretary of the SCLC.

Smith, Rev. Nelson Henry, Jr. New Pilgrim Baptist Church, Birmingham, Alabama. 31 August 1976 (Local black). Smith was secretary of the ACMHR

Smyer, Sidney W., Sr. 2780 Smyer Circle, Birmingham, Alabama. 9 Sept. 1976. (White business leader). A member of the Senior Citizens Committee, Smyer was president of the Birmingham Realty Co.

Spencer, William III. Motion Industries, Birmingham, Alabama. 2 Sept. 1976. (White business leader). A member of the Senior Citizens Committee, Spencer was president of Owen-Richards Co.; he was also serving as president of the Birmingham Chamber of Commerce.

Vann, David J. City Hall, Birmingham, Alabama. 10 Sept. 1976. (White liberal activist). Vann was an attorney in a large law firm.

Wall, George. City Hall, Birmingham, Alabama. 30 August 1976. (City Commission). A captain in the Birmingham Police Department, Wall worked closely with Bull Connor.

Wiggins, M. Edwin. City Hall, Birmingham, Alabama. 30 August 1976. (City Council). Wiggins was retiring as treasurer of Alabama Power Co. when he was elected as a councilman in 1963: he was the president of the City Council.

Woods, Rev. Abraham, Jr. St. Joseph Day Care Center, Birmingham, Alabama. 7 Sept. 1976. (Local black). A faculty member at Miles college, Woods was third vice-president of the ACMHR.

Zukoski, Charles. Jefferson County Planned Parenthood, Birmingham, Alabama. 23 August 1976. (White business leader or white liberal activist). Zukoski had been dismissed from his position as executive vice-president of a large bank in Birmingham prior to the beginning of the demonstrations.

ORAL HISTORIES

Bryan, Dr. John E. Birmingham, Alabama. Recorded interview by George Stewart. March 1972. Birmingham Public Library. (City Council). A former superintendent of Jefferson County Schools, Bryan was elected as a councilman in 1963.

Bush, Rev. Don E. Birmingham, Alabama. Recorded interview by Richard J. Waters. 16 April 1976. Daniel Payne College Oral History Project. (Local black). Bush was a high school student, who participated in the demonstrations.

Fleming, Nettie. Birmingham, Alabama. Recorded interview by Cornelius Brown. 2 May 1976. Daniel Payne College Oral History Project. (Local black). Fleming, an ACMHR member, participated in the demonstrations.

Marshall, Burke. Washington, D.C. Recorded interview by Anthony Lewis. 20 June 1964. John F. Kennedy Library Oral History Program. JFKL.

(Federal Government). Marshall was the Assistant Attorney General in charge of the Civil Rights division.

Shelton, Robert M. Northport, Alabama. Recorded interview by Ben Hendrix. 21 January 1975. Samford University Oral History Program. (White extremist). Shelton was Imperial Wizard of the United Klans of America.

Shuttlesworth, Rev. Fred L. Cincinnati, Ohio. Recorded interview by James Mosley. Sept. 1968. Civil Rights Documentation Project. (Local black). Although he had become pastor of a church in Cincinnati by 1963, Shuttlesworth retained the presidency of the ACMHR; he was also secretary of the SCLC.

Sorensen, Theodore C. N.P. Recorded interview by Carl Kaysen. 3 May 1964. John F. Kennedy Library Oral History Program. JFKL. (Federal Government). Sorensen, a Special Counsel to the President, was also a close, personal friend of President Kennedy.

Walker, Rev. Wyatt Tee. New York, New York. Recorded interview by Mike Nichols. October 1973. (National black leadership). Walker was Executive Director of the SCLC and Executive Assistant to Dr. King.

Woods, Rev. Abraham, Jr. Birmingham, Alabama. Recorded interview by Addie H. Pugh. October 1975. (Local black). A faculty member at Miles College, Woods was third vice-president of the ACMHR.

UNPUBLISHED MATERIAL

Boutwell, Albert. "Speech to the National Conference of Christians and Jews." Birmingham, Alabama., 19 April 1963.

Harrison, Mary Phyllis. "A Change in the Government of the City of Birmingham: 1962-1963." M.A. thesis, University of Montevallo, 1974.

Hintz, Stephen E.C. "Citizenship and Race: Confrontation in Rhodesia and Alabama." Ph.D. dissertation, Yale University, 1971.

Holt, Thad. "Memorandum on the Martin Luther King Demonstrations in Birmingham, Alabama." 10 May 1963.

LaMonte, Edward S. "Politics and Welfare in Birmingham, Alabama: 1900-1975." Ph.D. dissertation, University of Chicago, 1976.

Nichols, Mike. "Cities Are What Men Make Them." Senior thesis, Brown University, 1973.

PUBLIC DOCUMENTS

Alabama. *Code of Alabama*. 1940, recompiled 1958.

_____. *Journal of the House, 1963*. Regular Session.

_____. *Journal of the House, 1965*. Regular Session.

Birmingham, Alabama. *The General Code of the City of Birmingham, Alabama*. 1944.

_____. "Minutes of City Commission 1962-1963."

_____. "Minutes of City Council 1963."

_____. "Recapitulation Sheets of 1963 City Elections."

Birmingham Police Department. *Annual Report 1963*.

Jefferson County, Alabama. Board of Registrants. "Registration Figures by Precinct, 1962 and 1964."

United States Bureau of the Census. *U.S. Census of Population: 1960*. Vol. I, *Characteristics of the Population*, part 1, United States Summary.

_____. *U.S. Census of Population and Housing: 1960. Census Tracts*. Final Report PHC (1)-17.

JUDICIAL DECISIONS

Connor v. State, 153 So. 2d 787 (Alabama. Sup. Ct., 1963).

Ex Parte National Association for the Advancement of Colored People, 91 So. 2d 214 (Alabama. Sup. Ct., 1956).

Wyatt Tee Walker et al. v. City of Birmingham, 181 So. 2d 493 (Alabama. Sup. Ct., 1965).

_____. 18 L. Ed.2d 1210 (1967).

NEWSPAPERS AND PERIODICALS

Birmingham Bulletin
Birmingham News
Birmingham Post-Herald
Crusader
Examiner
Leeds News
New York Times

Race Relations Law Reporter
South: The News Magazine of Dixie
Thunderbolt

PAMPHLETS

Alabama Christian Movement for Human Rights. *People In Motion*. Birmingham, Alabama: Alabama Christian Movement for Human Rights, 1966.

_____. *They Challenge Segregation At Its Core!* Birmingham, Alabama.: Alabama Christian Movement for Human Rights, n.d.

Fields, Edward R. *Jews Behind Race Mixing*. Marietta, Georgia: The Thunderbolt, Inc., n.d.

Forster, Arnold and Epstein, Benjamin R. *Report on the Ku Klux Klan*. New York: Anti-Defamation League of B'nai B'rith, 1965.

Hammer, Greene, Siler Associates. *The Economy of Metropolitan Birmingham*. Atlanta: Hammer, Greene, Siler Associates, 1966.

Martin Luther King's Communist Record. Marietta, Georgia: The Thunderbolt, Inc., n.d.

National States Rights Party Official Platform. Marietta, Georgia: The Thunderbolt, Inc., n.d.

Southern Christian Leadership Conference. *The SCLC Story*. Atlanta: Southern Christian Leadership Conference, 1964.

Taylor, Rev. Fred and Brooks, Tyrone. *The Movement*. Atlanta: Southern Christian Leadership Conference, 1975.

ARTICLES

Brown, Joe David. "Birmingham." *Saturday Evening Post,* 2 March 1963, pp. 12-18.

Cleghorn, Reese. "'Bustling' Birmingham." *New Republic*, 20 April 1963, p. 9.

_____. "Martin Luther King, Jr.: Apostle of Crisis." *Saturday Evening Post*, 15 June 1963, pp. 15-19.

Connor, Eugene (Bull). "Birmingham Wars on Communism." *The Alabama Local Government Journal*, August 1950, pp. 7, 36-38.

Cort, David. "The Voices of Birmingham." *Nation*, 27 July 1963, pp. 46-48.

Danzig, David. "The Meaning of Negro Strategy." *Commentary,* February 1964, pp. 41-46.

Dellinger, Dave. "The Negroes of Birmingham." *Liberation*, Summer 1963, pp. 17-21.

Deming, Barbara. "Notes After Birmingham." *Liberation*, Summer 1963, pp. 13-16.

"Editor Reports Children's Revolution in Alabama." *Liberation*, May 1963, p. 5.

Flynt, Wayne. "The Ethics of Democratic Persuasion and the Birmingham Crisis." *The Southern Speech Journal* 35 (Fall 1969); 40-53.

Good, Paul "Birmingham Two Years Later." *The Reporter*, 2 December 1965, pp. 21-27.

Grindstaff, Carl T. "The Negro, Urbanization, and Relative Deprivation in the Deep South." *Social Problems* 15 (Winter 1968): 342-52.

Harding, Vincent. "A Beginning in Birmingham." *The Reporter*, 6 June 1963, pp. 13-19.

"Integration Leaders Examine Lessons of Birmingham." *Liberation*, June 1963, p. 4.

"Interview with a Former Grand Dragon." *New South,* Summer 1969, pp. 62-79.

King, Martin Luther, Jr. "Love and Nonviolence and the Shame of Segregation." *Jubilee*, July 1963, pp. 22-23.

Lodge, George C. "The Introduction of Change." Harvard Business School Case 9-371-003.

Meier, August. "On the Role of Martin Luther King." *New Politics*, Winter 1965, pp. 52-59.

"The Men Behind Martin Luther King." *Ebony*, June 1965, pp. 165-73.

O'Dell, J.H. "How Powerful is the Southern Power Structure?" *Freedomways*, Winter 1964, pp. 76-83.

Osborne, George R. "Boycott in Birmingham." *Nation*, 5 May 1962, pp. 397-401.

Richardson, B. "That's All Right—Birmingham, Alabama." *Freedomways*, Winter 1964, pp. 63-75.

Rustin, Bayard, "From Protest to Politics: The Future of the Civil Rights Movement." *Commentary*, February 1965, pp. 25-31.

_____. "The Meaning of Birmingham." *Liberation*, June 1963, pp. 7-9, 31.

Shuttlesworth, Fred L. "Birmingham Revisited." *Ebony*, August 1971, pp. 114-18.

_____. "Birmingham Shall Be Free Some Day." *Freedomways*, Winter 1964, pp. 16-19.

Shuttlesworth, F. L. and Smith., N. H. "The Birmingham Manifesto." *Freedomways,* Winter 1964, pp. 20-21.

Young, Andrew. "The Day We Went to Jail in Birmingham." *Friends*, 9 February 1964, pp. 3-11.

Zanden, James W. Vander. "The Citizens' Councils." *Alpha Kappa Deltan*, Spring 1959, pp. 3-9.

_____. "The Klan Revival." *American Journal of Sociology* 65 (March 1960): 456-62.

BOOKS

Barnard, William J. *Dixiecrats and Democrats: Alabama Politics, 1942-1950.* University, Alabama: The University of Alabama Press, 1974.

Bartley, Numan V., and Graham, Hugh D. *Southern Politics and the Second Reconstruction*. Baltimore: The Johns Hopkins University Press, 1975.

Bennett, Lerone, Jr. *What Manner of Man—Martin Luther King, Jr.* Chicago: Johnson Publishing Co., 1968

Bishop, Jim. *The Days of Martin Luther King, Jr.* New York: Putnam, 1971.

Chalmers, David. *Hooded Americanism.* Garden City, New York: Doubleday, 1965.

Clarke, Jacquelyne Johnson. *These Rights They Seek.* Washington, D.C.: Public Affairs Press, 1962.

Cleghorn, Reese., *Radicalism: Southern Style*. Atlanta: The Southern Regional Council, 1968.

Coles, Robert. *Children of Crisis: A Study of Courage and Fear.* Boston: Little, Brown and Co., 1964.

Dollard, John. *Caste and Class in a Southern Town.* Garden City, N.Y.: Doubleday, 1947.

Elovitz, Mark H. *A Century of Jewish Life in Dixie.* University, Alabama: The University of Alabama Press, 1974.

287

Fairlie, Henry. *The Kennedy Promise*. Garden City, New York: Doubleday, 1973.

Frazier, E. Franklin. *Black Bourgeoisie*. London: Collier Books, 1962.

_____. *The Negro Church in America*. New York: Shocken Books, 1974.

Garson, Robert A. *The Democratic Party and the Politics of Sectionalism, 1941-1948*. Baton Rouge, Louisiana: Louisiana State University Press, 1974.

Gaston, A.G. *Green Power*. Birmingham, Alabama: Birmingham Publishing Co., 1968.

Holloway, Harry. *The Politics of the Southern Negro*. New York: Random House, 1969.

Jennings, M. Kent. *Community Influentials*. New York: MacMillan Co., 1964.

Johnson, James Weldon. *The Autobiography of an Ex-Coloured Man*. New York: Alfred A. Knopf, 1927.

King, Coretta Scott. *My Life with Martin Luther King, Jr.* New York: Avon, 1970.

King, Martin Luther, Jr. "Letter From Birmingham Jail." In *What Country Have I?*, pp. 119-31. Edited by Herbert J. Strong. New York: St. Martin's Press, 1970.

_____. *Where Do We Go From Here: Chaos or Community?* New York: Harper and Row, 1967.

_____. *Why We Can't Wait*. New York: The New American Library, 1963.

Lewis, Anthony and *The New York Times*. *Portrait of a Decade*. New York: Random House, 1964.

Lewis, David L. *King: A Critical Biography*. New York: Praeger Publishers, 1970.

McMillen, Neil R. *The Citizens' Council*. Urbana, Illinois: University of Illinois Press, 1971.

Marshall, Burke. *Federalism and Civil Rights*. New York: Columbia University Press, 1964.

Marx, Gary T. *Protest and Prejudice*. New York: Harper and Row, 1969.

Miller, William Robert. *Martin Luther King., Jr.* New York: Weybright and Talley, 1968.

Mills, C. Wright. *The Power Elite*. New York: Oxford University Press, 1956.

Moore, Geraldine. *Behind The Ebony Mask*. Birmingham, Alabama.: Southern University Press, 1961.

Morgan, Charles, Jr. *A Time to Speak*. New York: Harper and Row, 1964.

Navasky, Victor S. *Kennedy Justice*. New York: Atheneum, 1971.

Reddick, L.D. "The Negro as Southerner and American." In *The Southerner As American*, pp. 130-47. Edited by Charles Grier Sellers, Jr. Chapel Hill, North Carolina: The University of North Carolina Press, 1960.

Rowe, Gary Thomas, Jr. *My Undercover Years with the Ku Klux Klan*. New York: Bantam Books, 1976.

Schlesinger, Arthur M., Jr. *A Thousand Days*. Boston: Houghton Mifflin, 1965.

Schulke, Flip, ed. *Martin Luther King, Jr.* New York: Norton, 1976.

Sorensen, Theodore. *Kennedy*. New York: Harper and Row, 1965.

Sterne, Emma Gelders. *I Have A Dream*. New York: Alfred A. Knopf, 1965.

Watters, Pat. *Down To Now*. New York: Pantheon Books, 1971.

Westin, Alan F. and Mahoney, Barry. *The Trial of Martin Luther King*. New York: Thomas Y. Crowell, 1974.

White, Theodore. *The Making of the President—1964*. New York: Atheneum Publishers, 1965.

Authors' Biographies and Bibliographical Information

Lee E. Bains, Jr., was born and raised in Bessemer, Alabama, which is on the outskirts of Birmingham. After receiving his Bachelors degree with honors from Harvard College, he graduated with honors from Harvard Law School. He is presently a shareholder and director in the Birmingham law firm of Maynard, Cooper, Frierson & Gale, P.C. His essay in this volume, *Birmingham, 1963: Confrontation over Civil Rights,* was written as a B.A. Honors Essay at Harvard University in 1977. It is published here for the first time. It has been edited for publication, but otherwise is published as it was originally written.

William D. Barnard is Associate Professor and Chairman of the Department of History at the University of Alabama. His many publications include *Dixiecrats and Democrats: Alabama Politics, 1942-1950* (University of Alabama Press). He received his Ph.D. from the University of Virginia and his B.A. from Birmingham-Southern College. He was born in Birmingham. His *Introduction* was written especially for this volume.

Glenn T. Eskew is presently working on a Ph.D. at the University of Georgia in the Department of History. He attended high school in Birmingham and received his Bachelors degree from Auburn University. His article "Demagoguery in Birmingham and the Building of Vestavia" appeared in *The Alabama Review*. The essay published here, *The Alabama Christian Movement for Human Rights and the Birmingham Struggle for Civil Rights, 1956-1963*, was originally written as an M.A. thesis in the Department of History at the University of Georgia. It is published here for the first time. It has been edited for publication, but otherwise is published as written.

The late *Lewis W. Jones* was for many years Professor of Sociology at Tuskegee Institute and was also associated with the Race Relations Department of Fisk University. His essay in this volume, *Fred L. Shuttlesworth, Indigenous Leader*, based on extensive interviews with Reverend Shuttlesworth, was written in 1961 and is published here for the first time. It has been edited for publication, but is otherwise published as written.

Index

Martin Luther King, Jr.

and the

Civil Rights Movement

DAVID J. GARROW, EDITOR